TECHNICAL AND CONCEPTUAL SKILLS FOR MENTAL HEALTH PROFESSIONALS

LINDA SELIGMAN
George Mason University

D1400991

PEARSON

Merrill
Prentice Hall

Upper Saddle River, New Jersey
Columbus, Ohio

Library of Congress Cataloging in Publication Data

Seligman, Linda.
  Technical and conceptual skills for mental health professionals / Linda Seligman.
    p. cm.
  Includes bibliographical references and index.
  ISBN 0-13-034146-0
    1. Mental health personnel. 2. Mental health personnel—Training of. 3. Occupational
training. 4. Performance standards. I. Title.

RC454.4.S457 2004
616.89'0071'1—dc21

                                        2002044871

Vice President and Executive Publisher: Jeffery W. Johnston
Assistant Vice President and Publisher: Kevin M. Davis
Editorial Assistant: Autumn Crisp
Production Editor: Mary Harlan
Production Coordination: Lea Baranowski, Carlisle Publishers Services
Design Coordinator: Diane C. Lorenzo
Cover Designer: Thomas Borah
Cover Image: Superstock
Text Design and Illustrations: Carlisle Communications
Production Manager: Laura Messerly
Director of Marketing: Ann Castel Davis
Marketing Manager: Amy June
Marketing Coordinator: Tyra Poole

This book was set in Berkeley by Carlisle Communications, Ltd. It was printed and bound by R. R. Donnelley &
Sons Company. The cover was printed by The Lehigh Press, Inc.

Pearson Education Ltd.
Pearson Education Singapore Pte. Ltd.
Pearson Education Canada, Ltd.
Pearson Education–Japan

Pearson Education Australia Pty. Limited
Pearson Education North Asia Ltd.
Pearson Educación de Mexico, S.A. de C.V.
Pearson Education Malaysia Pte. Ltd.

10 9 8 7 6 5 4 3 2 1
ISBN: 0-13-034146-0

For My Husband
Bob Zeskind

PREFACE

As a counselor educator, I have spent many years teaching students to view their clients holistically, to consider their worldviews, to understand them as complete human beings, and to pay attention to their environments. However, when I turn my attention to skill development, the literature tends to undermine the messages I give my students. Rather than focusing on promoting understanding of a person and helping clinicians conceptualize the relationship between individual and environment, the skill development literature emphasizes applied skills such as asking open questions and making reflections of feeling. I have been dismayed by this apparent conflict between a broad and holistic vision of how clinicians should conceptualize their work and the emphasis on applied skills that I perceive in the mental health literature. This book, *Technical and Conceptual Skills for Mental Health Professionals,* grew out of my concern about this conflict.

This book is intended to help mental health professionals develop competence in both technical skills and conceptual skills and successfully integrate the two types of skills in their work. In this way, clinicians can effectively accomplish both the in-depth, comprehensive understanding of their clients that is espoused by nearly all mental health professionals and the use of strong clinical skills that reflects that understanding and is likely to lead to successful treatment outcomes.

ORGANIZING FRAMEWORKS

Several organizing frameworks are used to give a clear and useful structure to this book: BETA framework, technical and conceptual skills, general and specific skills, and explanations, illustrations, and applications.

BETA Framework

The leading theories of counseling and psychotherapy, along with their associated strategies and skills, can be organized into four broad categories that reflect their particular emphasis. This organizational framework, represented by the acronym BETA (standing for Background, Emotions, Thoughts, and Actions) includes the following theories:

- *Background*—Sigmund Freud and psychoanalysis, Alfred Adler and individual psychology, Carl Jung and Jungian analytical psychology, transactional analysis, brief psychodynamic therapy, and other developmental and psychodynamic treatment systems.
- *Emotions*—Carl Rogers and person-centered counseling, existential therapy, Gestalt therapy.
- *Thoughts*—Aaron Beck and cognitive therapy, Albert Ellis and rational emotive behavior therapy.
- *Actions*—behavior therapy, cognitive behavior therapy, reality therapy, brief solution-based therapy.

The BETA framework was used to organize treatment theories in *Systems, Strategies, and Skills of Counseling and Psychotherapy* (Seligman, 2001). This framework has been used in this text as well, but here the emphasis is on skills rather than theories of counseling and psychotherapy.

The use of this organizing framework in both books facilitates understanding of the broad range of treatment approaches available to clinicians. It also paves the way for the use of this text as a companion to *Systems, Strategies, and Skills of Counseling and Psychotherapy*, although each book is separate and is designed to be used by itself.

Most clinical skills can be logically connected to one of the elements of the BETA framework more than to the other three. For example, reflection of feeling is most strongly associated with treatment theories that emphasize emotions; modification of distorted cognitions is most strongly associated with theories emphasizing thoughts; and contracting is most strongly associated with approaches emphasizing actions. However, readers should keep in mind that most clinicians today use a broad range of interventions and do not limit themselves to those most strongly linked to their theoretical orientations. Similarly, as readers develop their own clinical styles, they should feel free to draw on skills presented throughout this book.

Technical and Conceptual Skills

In addition to being organized according to the BETA framework, the chapters of this book are organized according to whether their focus is on technical or conceptual skills. Technical skills are presented first (Part II) because they are viewed as the building blocks of counseling and psychotherapy and also because they are generally easier to learn than conceptual skills. Then the conceptual skills are presented, building on and making use of technical skills and moving readers to a deeper, more meaningful level of thinking about their clients and their work.

General and Specific Skills

Most of the skill development chapters include both general and specific skills. General skills include fundamental interventions that are used by almost every clinician with every client. Examples of general skills include asking questions, conducting intake interviews, establishing goals, and developing treatment plans. Specific skills are those that most clinicians use only occasionally in the treatment of certain clients, problems, and disorders. Examples of these are reframing, guided imagery, and use of lifelines and genograms.

Explanations, Illustrations, and Applications

People learn in different ways, and this text seeks to offer a variety of learning opportunities to maximize learning for everyone. When a skill is first presented in this book, a description of the skill is provided along with available and important research on the value of that skill and the appropriate use of that skill. Examples are then provided to illustrate the use of the skill in practice. Finally, at the end of each chapter, exercises allow readers to apply the learning they have gained. These exercises include:

- written exercises
- discussion questions
- a role-play exercise
- an Assessment of Progress Form, enabling readers to describe and evaluate what they have learned
- personal journal questions that allow readers to apply the material to themselves and their own lives, personalizing and making more meaningful the skills presented in the chapter

Table P-1 presents this book's organization.

TABLE P-1   Organization of Text

Chapter Number/Name	BETA Element	Type of Skill
1 Establishing the Foundation for Skill Development		
2 Using Technical Skills to Understand and Address Background	Background	Technical
3 Using Technical Skills to Elicit, Attend to, Reflect on , Assess, and Change Emotions	Emotions	Technical
4 Using Technical Skills to Identify, Assess, and Modify Thoughts	Thoughts	Technical
5 Using Technical Skills to Identify, Assess, and Change Actions and Behaviors	Actions	Technical
6 Using Conceptual Skills to Understand, Assess, and Address Background	Background	Conceptual
7 Using Conceptual Skills to Make Positive Use of and Modify Emotions	Emotions	Conceptual
8 Using Conceptual Skills as Frameworks for Clinicians' Thoughts	Thoughts	Conceptual
9 Applying Conceptual Skills to Actions for Positive Change	Actions	Conceptual
10 Reviewing, Integrating, and Reinforcing Learning		

OVERVIEW OF CHAPTERS

Organized according to the frameworks described previously, the 10 chapters of this book highlight the following topics and skills.

Chapter 1 provides an introduction. It discusses the process of becoming an effective mental health professional, emphasizes the importance of theory and ethics, and describes the progression from theory to treatment. Also presented is information on the use of feedback from colleagues and supervisors, leading to continuous professional development.

Chapter 2 begins the presentation of technical skills, focusing on those skills that are especially important in obtaining background information. General skills presented include the use of questions, both open and closed, and conducting an intake interview. Specific skills described in this chapter include the use of earliest recollections, the lifeline, and the genogram. Eileen Carter, the client who is featured throughout this book to illustrate many of the skills, is introduced via an intake interview.

Chapter 3 focuses on useful skills to help people express, identify, manage, and change their emotions. General skills focus on attending and following and include encouragers to promote accurate listening (paraphrase, restatement, and summarization), reflection of feeling, and addressing and using nonverbal communication and silence. Specific skills include guided imagery and focusing as well as making use of body language.

Chapter 4 presents skills that clinicians can use to help their clients identify, evaluate, and modify their thoughts. General skills include reflection of meaning, analyzing and modifying cognitions, problem solving and decision making, and information giving. Specific skills introduced in this chapter are positive self-talk and affirmations, anchoring, reframing, thought stopping, journal writing, mind mapping, and meditation.

Chapter 5 introduces skills that are especially helpful when clients want to make changes in their actions and behavior. Important general skills included in this chapter are developing behavioral change plans, contracting, goal setting, using advice and homework, and confrontation. Specific skills include empowerment, systematic desensitization, relaxation, role playing, and modeling.

Chapter 6 begins the presentation of conceptual skills. The conceptual skills in this chapter are linked to eliciting information about and understanding clients' backgrounds, building on what has already been learned about technical skills in chapter 2. Chapter 6 focuses on understanding the context of treatment, using the mental status examination as part of the intake process, identifying and addressing transference and countertransference, and developing multicultural counseling competencies. Attention also is paid to the use of interpretation to promote insight.

Chapter 7 focuses on conceptual skills that promote healthy emotions and reduce negative and self-destructive emotions, building on the technical skills presented in chapter 3. This chapter presents information on the establishment of a positive therapeutic alliance, the importance of the core conditions (genuineness, immediacy, congruence, empathy), helpful ways to provide support and encouragement, the place of values and spirituality in the treatment process, and the use of clinician self-disclosure. Attention also is paid to dealing with strong client emotions, including suicidal ideation, depression, and rage, as well as client reluctance and client crises.

Chapter 8 takes a different perspective, focusing on conceptual skills that can improve the thinking of the clinician rather than that of the client. Included in this chapter is information on assessment and testing, problem definition, case conceptualization, diagnosis using the *Diagnostic and Statistical Manual of Mental Disorders,* and treatment planning.

Chapter 9 continues the focus on the clinician rather than the client and presents action-oriented conceptual skills that can improve clinical effectiveness. This includes referral and collaboration, assessment of client progress, structuring sessions and the treatment process, writing session notes, generating solutions, and terminating both sessions and the overall treatment process.

Finally, chapter 10 affords readers the opportunity to apply much of what they have learned throughout this book and to evaluate the learning they have gained. The first section provides an intake interview, and readers are then given a series of exercises to apply to this case, reflecting their newly honed skills. The second part includes all of the Assessment of Progress Forms that have been presented throughout this book. This offers a comprehensive picture of all the skills that have been learned and gives readers a final opportunity to rate themselves on these skills, increasing awareness of the progress and learning they have achieved.

USES OF THIS BOOK

There are many ways to make productive and effective use of the material in this book.

1. This book is ideally suited to a two-semester skill development course, with the first semester devoted to the development of technical skills and the second semester focused on conceptual skills.
2. The teaching of both technical and conceptual skills can be combined into one semester. If that is the case, some of the specific skills may need to be omitted while the general skills are emphasized.
3. This book can be combined with either my book on theories of counseling and psychotherapy (*Systems, Strategies, and Skills of Counseling and Psychotherapy*) (Seligman, 2001) or with another theories book to integrate the in-depth teaching of both skills and theories.
4. This book can be used as a textbook for students in practicum and internship who have already had basic skill development coursework. This book could provide a review of the fundamental skills they have already learned and serve as a vehicle for helping them develop more advanced skills.
5. Practicing clinicians in mental health, school, or other settings could use this book on their own to review and refine their skills. Almost all clinicians can learn new skills from this book and will deepen their understanding of their clients and the treatment process as they use this text.
6. Units of this book could be selected to teach one or a group of skills in a special seminar or could be incorporated into another type of course. The following are a few examples:
   * The information on diagnosis might be included in a course on abnormal psychology.

- The information on the development of multicultural counseling competencies might be included in a course on multicultural counseling.
- The information on the development of a positive therapeutic alliance and the use of the core conditions might become part of an introductory course in counseling or psychology.

Feel free to innovate and experiment in your use of this book!

ACKNOWLEDGMENTS

I am grateful for all the personal and professional support I received while writing this book. I am especially thankful to Lynn Field, Ph.D., LPC, psychotherapist in private practice in Fairfax, Virginia. As my graduate assistant at George Mason University, she unfailingly provided excellent research and editing skills as well as good judgment, clear feedback, and encouragement.

Thanks also to Diana Gibb, Ph.D., faculty member at George Mason University and associate of The Center for Counseling and Consultation. Dr. Gibb carefully reviewed this manuscript and provided knowledgeable, helpful, and detailed feedback. Her understanding of graduate students and beginning clinicians helped me shape this book.

Loretta Rowe, LPC, psychotherapist in private practice and specialist in anger management, made another important contribution. She provided information on the development, manifestations, and treatment of anger as well as case study material, incorporated into chapter 7.

I also appreciate the contributions of Shannon Peters, Ph.D., LPC, of George Washington University. Dr. Peters wrote the instructor's manual to accompany this book.

Many thanks to the administrators at George Mason University who provided me a study leave during which I wrote this book. In addition, the faculty, administrators, and staff of the Graduate School of Education at George Mason University, particularly Associate Dean Martin Ford, Dr. Gerald Wallace, and Janet Holmes, provided time and support that facilitated my work on this book. I am also grateful to the many students and clients I have met over the years and from whom I have learned so much. I especially thank those who reviewed the manuscript for their many helpful comments: William A. Anderson, Minnesota State University, Mankato; J. Kelly Coker, University of Nevada–Las Vegas; and Robbie J. Steward, Michigan State University.

This book would not have happened without Kevin Davis, Assistant Vice President and Publisher at Merrill/Prentice Hall, who invited me to write this book as well as *Systems, Strategies, and Skills of Counseling and Psychotherapy*. He and his staff facilitated the development of this book in many ways. I am appreciative of all their assistance along the way.

Special thanks are due to my family and friends who have remained supportive through the pressures of this, my ninth book. My husband, Dr. Robert M. Zeskind, and my dear friend Bettie Young have been especially important to me during this time, as always, in ensuring that I have some balance in my life.

ABOUT THE AUTHOR

Linda Seligman has been a professor in the Graduate School of Education at George Mason University in Fairfax, Virginia, for more than 20 years. She served as co-director of the Doctoral Program in Education, coordinator of the Counseling and Development Program, Associate Chair, and head of the Community Agency Counseling Program. She is also an adjunct faculty member at Johns Hopkins University and Walden University.

Dr. Seligman received a Ph.D. in Counseling Psychology from Columbia University. Her research interests include diagnosis and treatment planning, counseling people with cancer and other chronic and life-threatening illnesses, and career counseling. She has written nine books, including *Systems, Strategies, and Skills of Counseling and Psychotherapy; Selecting Effective Treatments; Diagnosis and Treatment Planning in Counseling; Developmental Career Counseling and Assessment;* and *Promoting a Fighting Spirit: Psychotherapy for Cancer Patients, Survivors, and Their Families.* She also has written more than 75 professional articles and book chapters. In addition, she has lectured throughout the United States as well as internationally on diagnosis and treatment planning and is a recognized expert on that subject.

Dr. Seligman has extensive clinical experience in a broad range of mental health settings, including drug and alcohol treatment programs, university counseling settings, psychiatric hospitals, correctional facilities, and counseling programs for children and adolescents. She currently has a private practice in Fairfax, Virginia.

Dr. Seligman has served as editor of the *Journal of Mental Health Counseling* and as president of the Virginia Association of Mental Health Counselors. In 1986, her colleagues at George Mason University selected her as a Distinguished Professor, and in 1990, the American Mental Health Counselors Association designated her as Researcher of the Year.

DISCOVER THE COMPANION WEBSITE ACCOMPANYING THIS BOOK

THE PRENTICE HALL COMPANION WEBSITE: A VIRTUAL LEARNING ENVIRONMENT

Technology is a constantly growing and changing aspect of our field that is creating a need for content and resources. To address this emerging need, Prentice Hall has developed an online learning environment for students and professors alike—Companion Websites—to support our textbooks.

In creating a Companion Website, our goal is to build on and enhance what the textbook already offers. For this reason, the content for each user-friendly website is organized by topic and provides the professor and student with a variety of meaningful resources. Common features of a Companion Website include:

For the Professor—

Every Companion Website integrates **Syllabus Manager**™, an online syllabus creation and management utility.

- **Syllabus Manager**™ provides you, the instructor, with an easy, step-by-step process to create and revise syllabi, with direct links into Companion Website and other online content without having to learn HTML.
- Students may logon to your syllabus during any study session. All they need to know is the web address for the Companion Website and the password you've assigned to your syllabus.
- After you have created a syllabus using **Syllabus Manager**™, students may enter the syllabus for their course section from any point in the Companion Website.

- Clicking on a date, the student is shown the list of activities for the assignment. The activities for each assignment are linked directly to actual content, saving time for students.
- Adding assignments consists of clicking on the desired due date, then filling in the details of the assignment—name of the assignment, instructions, and whether it is a one-time or repeating assignment.
- In addition, links to other activities can be created easily. If the activity is on-line, a URL can be entered in the space provided, and it will be linked automatically in the final syllabus.
- Your completed syllabus is hosted on our servers, allowing convenient updates from any computer on the Internet. Changes you make to your syllabus are immediately available to your students at their next logon.

For the Student—

- **Counseling Topics**—17 core counseling topics represent the diversity and scope of today's counseling field.
- **Annotated Bibliography**—includes seminal foundational works and key current works.
- **Web Destinations**—lists significant and up-to-date practitioner and client sites.
- **Professional Development**—provides helpful information regarding professional organizations and codes of ethics.
- **Electronic Bluebook**—send homework or essays directly to your instructor's email with this paperless form.
- **Message Board**—serves as a virtual bulletin board to post—or respond to—questions or comments to/from a national audience.
- **Chat**—real-time chat with anyone who is using the text anywhere in the country—ideal for discussion and study groups, class projects, etc.

To take advantage of these and other resources, please visit the *Technical and Conceptual Skills for Mental Health Professionals* Companion Website at

www.prenhall.com/seligman

BRIEF CONTENTS

CONTENTS

PART II: TECHNICAL SKILLS FOR MENTAL HEALTH PROFESSIONALS

Chapter 3:
Using Technical Skills to Elicit, Attend to, Reflect on, Assess, and Change Emotions   60

Chapter 4:
Using Technical Skills to Identify, Assess, and Modify Thoughts   98

PART III: CONCEPTUAL SKILLS FOR MENTAL HEALTH PROFESSIONALS

PART IV: SOLIDIFYING TECHNICAL AND CONCEPTUAL SKILLS

CHAPTER 1

Establishing the Foundation for Skill Development

HISTORICAL OVERVIEW

Over the past 60 to 70 years, the fields of counseling and psychotherapy have evolved and deepened. Before the middle of the 20th century, treatment of emotional difficulties focused primarily on disorders involving a loss of contact with reality (psychotic disorders) and disorders characterized by disabling depression or anxiety (neurotic disorders). Psychiatry and psychoanalysis dominated the mental health field, and treatment usually entailed medication and lengthy, intensive psychodynamic treatment. Clinicians paid relatively little attention to problems of adjustment and life circumstance, to relationship difficulties, and even to the treatment of people with drug and alcohol problems. Understanding of problems and disorders such as physical and sexual abuse, attention-deficit/hyperactivity disorder, and borderline personality disorder was almost nonexistent.

Counselors and social workers played a limited role in mental health treatment up to the middle of the last century. Counseling was just beginning to develop as a profession. Counselors, at that time, focused their efforts primarily on what were then called school guidance programs and on vocational counseling. Social workers, too, had a limited role, focusing their efforts on programs to help the poor and disabled and working with the families of people treated by psychiatrists. Psychologists had a relatively broader role but they, like the psychiatrists, largely practiced psychodynamic therapy and treated a limited range of emotional difficulties.

Prior to the 1950s, much of the mental health literature was in the theoretical realm, making the transition to practice and application a difficult one. The writings of Freud, Jung, Adler, and their followers dominated the field. Case studies and their own therapy and supervised practice gave clinicians some ideas about the dynamics of mental disorders and the theoretical underpinnings of their treatment. However, little attention was paid to helping clinicians make sense of a particular client (conceptual skills) and to helping them determine the interventions that were most likely to help (technical skills).

Carl Rogers's writings (1951, 1967) in the 1950s and 1960s were among the first to call attention to the specific words and interventions (technical skills) clinicians used and the great impact those strategies could have on the treatment process. Allen Ivey's (1971) development of microcounseling skills, initially developed in the 1970s, enhanced clinicians' awareness of the importance of choosing their interventions carefully and deliberately. The rapid development of cognitive and behavioral approaches to treatment during the 1980s and 1990s (Beck, 1995) accelerated the movement toward technical competence. As specific treatment approaches and interventions drew increasing attention, clinicians seemed to focus less on conceptual skills, on developing a coherent, holistic, in-depth, and valid understanding of their clients.

RESULTING SHORTCOMINGS IN CLINICAL PREPARATION

By the beginning of the 21st century, many clinicians recognized the shortcomings of a skill- or techniques-driven approach to treatment and substantiated their observations with research. Fong, Borders, Ethington, and Pitts (1997), for example, found that counselor education students manifested only small gains in cognitive development over the course of their training. Therefore, those researchers concluded, "Results suggest a need to emphasize student cognitive development as strongly as skills development in graduate programs (p. 100)." Fong et al. (1997) identified three levels of clinician thinking that needed attention and development as part of clinical training:

1. *Cognitive events or discrete thoughts.* These include clinicians' decisions on use of specific technical skills and interventions (for example, how to reinforce a client's gains or whether to confront a discrepancy between the client's values and actions).

2. *Cognitive processes.* These involve more complex thinking skills such as those involved in clinicians' efforts to help clients solve problems or make decisions. For example, a clinician may plan a series of interventions to help a woman overcome her fear of snakes or to help an adolescent improve his social skills.

3. *Cognitive structures or schemas.* These encompass broad systems of organizing perceptions and are the skills that enable clinicians to understand the dynamics of a client's difficulties, formulate a diagnosis, and develop a treatment plan that is likely to be effective. For example, a clinician may recognize and address the impact of a woman's birth order and upbringing on her current problems in her career and her marriage. She is still trying to win the love of her parents by making choices that meet with their ap-

proval but is not recognizing that those choices do not mesh well with her own abilities and interests.

Whiston and Coker's (2000) findings support the conclusions of Fong et al. Whiston and Coker determined that "research findings suggest a significant link between counselor skillfulness and counseling outcomes" (p. 233). They further concluded that counselor education programs, in general, are not providing students the knowledge and experiences they need to become skilled clinicians. As a result, Whiston and Coker stated, "We also advocate that the reconstruction of clinical training focus more on increasing students' levels of cognitive complexity."

Fong et al., Whiston and Coker, and many other educators, clinicians, and researchers agree that mental health training programs and treatment plans have apparently gone from one extreme to another. The theoretical writing that dominated the professional literature until the mid-20th century yielded its place to technical writing on skills, strategies, and interventions. The treatment process was not solidly grounded in theory and in a clear conceptual model for understanding and helping a person with emotional difficulties. Rather, techniques dominated the literature. To provide an analogy, clinicians were following recipes but lacked a sound understanding of nutrition.

PURPOSE OF THIS BOOK

The purpose of this book, *Technical and Conceptual Skills for Mental Health Professionals,* is to help clinicians improve and refine the full range of skills they need to be effective. Not only is attention paid to promoting clinicians' skillful and purposeful use of specific techniques and interventions, but research, information, examples, and exercises also are provided to teach, improve, and refine higher level conceptual clinical skills. This integration of important technical and conceptual skills should enable clinicians to truly understand their clients and, based on that understanding, to use interventions that are likely to be successful.

ORGANIZATION OF THIS BOOK

Two organizing frameworks provide the structure for this book. The **first organizing framework** is the division of skills into **technical skills and conceptual skills.** Technical skills will be presented first, in chapters 2 through 5 of this book. Whiston and Coker (2000) defined these skills as ". . . those basic interviewing or counselor interpersonal skills that facilitate the general purposes of counseling" (p. 234). These are the building blocks of the counseling process, the tools that clinicians use to accomplish their goals. Knowledge of technical skills provides clinicians with a repertoire of interventions they can use to join with and help their clients. It enables clinicians to make statements and use language that demonstrate sound listening; that help clients become more aware of their emotions, thoughts, and actions; and that help them to acquire the knowledge and skills they need to resolve their issues. Technical skills seem easier for most people to learn than the more complex conceptual skills.

Chapters 6 through 9 are designed to teach readers the conceptual skills they need to become effective counselors and psychotherapists. These conceptual skills provide clinicians with blueprints for making purposeful and competent use of their technical skills. Conceptual skills enable clinicians to develop a positive therapeutic alliance, to assess and understand their clients, to see patterns, to comprehend the links between past and present, and to put together their technical skills into meaningful treatment plans. Chapters 6 through 9 will build on the technical skills that readers have acquired through the earlier chapters of this book and help them to integrate their technical and conceptual skills in effective ways.

The **second organizing framework** for this book entails the grouping of technical and conceptual skills of counseling and psychotherapy into **four broad categories**, represented by the acronym BETA, first described in my book *Systems, Strategies, and Skills of Counseling and Psychotherapy* (Seligman, 2001):

B—Background
E—Emotions
T—Thoughts
A—Actions

This grouping is based on two premises.

1. Treatment approaches are more alike than they are different. All approaches to counseling and psychotherapy pay some attention to all four elements in the BETA model: background, emotions, thoughts, and actions. These are universal ingredients in all treatment processes.

Increasing evidence is accumulating in the literature to demonstrate that all approaches to counseling and psychotherapy have underlying commonalities and that many of these common ingredients in treatment are associated with positive outcomes (Lambert & Bergin, 1994). Individual clinicians and treatment systems differ in terms of how they conceptualize cases, the proportion of time they devote to each of the four elements in the BETA framework, and the way they elaborate on each of these elements during the treatment process. However, whether clinicians adhere strictly to one theoretical approach or use an integrated approach to treatment, whether they work with children or adults, whether they work in schools or mental health agencies, whether they are counselors, psychologists, social workers, or psychiatric nurses, all mental health treatment providers use the basic ingredients or general skills that are presented in this book.

In addition, as integrated and eclectic approaches to treatment increasingly become the norm, clinicians find they can combine strategies from apparently incompatible treatment theories. For example, the clinician who describes her theoretical orientation as primarily person-centered may pay attention to background factors when working with a young woman who was sexually abused in childhood. Similarly, the clinician who emphasizes cognitive strategies in his work may rely on reflection of feeling, paraphrase, and encouragers when working with an angry and skeptical client.

In light of the flexible boundaries between treatment approaches and the underlying commonalities among clinicians, this book uses a variety of terms interchangeably, including *clinician* and *counselor* and *psychotherapy* and *counseling*. Today's clinicians are more alike than they are different, sharing diagnostic systems, conceptions of mental health, treatment theories, and strategies of intervention.

> 2. Treatment theories, strategies, and skills can be categorized and distinguished according to whether their primary emphasis is on understanding and changing the impact of past experiences (background), current feelings and sensations (emotions), thoughts and cognitions, or actions and behaviors.

Although this book is not designed to educate readers about theories of counseling and psychotherapy, the skills presented in this book are drawn from and organized according to the treatment systems represented by the BETA model. Therefore, familiarizing themselves with the following list, reflecting the way treatment systems are grouped in this model, should help readers to better understand the corresponding grouping of technical and conceptual skills.

Treatment Systems Emphasizing Background

- Sigmund Freud and psychoanalysis
- Alfred Adler and individual psychology
- Carl Jung and Jungian analytical psychology
- Developmental/psychodynamic theorists (Helene Deutsch, Karen Horney, Harry Stack Sullivan, Anna Freud, object relations theorists, Heinz Kohut)
- Eric Berne and transactional analysis
- Brief psychodynamic therapy

Treatment Systems Emphasizing Emotions

- Carl Rogers and person-centered counseling
- Existential therapy
- Gestalt therapy
- Emerging approaches emphasizing emotions (narrative therapy, constructivist therapy, feminist therapy, transpersonal therapy, focusing-oriented therapy)

Treatment Systems Emphasizing Thoughts

- Aaron Beck and cognitive therapy
- Albert Ellis and rational emotive behavior therapy
- Emerging approaches emphasizing thoughts (eye movement desensitization and reprocessing, neuro-linguistic programming, thought field therapy, cognitive therapy of evaluation)

Treatment Systems Emphasizing Actions

- Behavior therapy
- Cognitive behavior therapy
- Reality therapy
- Solution-based brief therapies

TABLE 1-1   Technical and Conceptual Skills in BETA Framework

	Background	Emotions	Thoughts	Actions
Technical Skills	• Open questions • Closed questions • Intake interview	• Attending • Encouragers • Reflection of feeling/empathy • Identifying and managing emotions • Nonverbal communication	• Reflection of meaning • Modifying cognitions • Problem solving • Decision making • Information giving	• Contracting • Goal setting • Advice giving • Challenging/ confronting
	Specific Skills • Earliest recollection • Lifeline • Genogram	**Specific skills** • Imagery • Focusing • New perspectives • Reassurance/ support • Distraction • Body language	**Specific skills** • Affirmations • Anchoring • Reframing • Thought stopping • Journaling • Mind mapping	**Specific skills** • Empowerment • Systematic desensitization • Relaxation • Modeling/ role-playing
Conceptual Skills	• Understanding context • Initiating treatment • Organizing background information • Addressing transference and countertransference • Multicultural counseling competencies • Interpretation	• Establishing a therapeutic alliance • Role induction • Core conditions • Providing support • Values and judgments • Crisis intervention • Handling strong emotions • Addressing reluctance • Clinician self-disclosure	• Assessment • Testing • Mental status exam • Defining the problem • Case conceptualization • Diagnosis • Treatment planning	• Referral • Collaboration • Structuring sessions • Critical incidents • Assessment of progress • Session notes • Generating solutions • Termination

Just as treatment systems can be organized according to the BETA framework, so can technical and conceptual skills. Of course, the organization is not as definitive as table 1-1 may imply. The conceptual and technical skills presented here are used by most clinicians. However, each skill is most strongly associated with the element in the BETA format under which it is listed.

BECOMING AN EFFECTIVE HELPER

Learning technical and conceptual skills of counseling and psychotherapy is essential to the development of all mental health professionals. However, at least as important is the clinicians' personal growth. This book is designed to facilitate the personal and professional development of clinicians. Discussion questions, role-play exercises, and especially the personal journal questions at the end of each chapter have been crafted to promote that development. This process will be facilitated if readers take a truthful look at themselves as they move through this book. Particularly important is awareness of their motives for entering a helping profession, the relationship between their own personal characteristics and those of the effective clinician, and an understanding of the transitions clinicians are likely to encounter as they progress in their fields.

Motives for Entering a Helping Profession

People enter the fields of counseling, psychology, psychiatric nursing, and social work for a wide variety of reasons. Of course, most of them want to help others. However, other motives probably also are present. The following are some of the common reasons that people enter these professions:

- They are altruistic; they want to help others and make a contribution to society.
- They are seeking a vehicle for their need to take care of others.
- They want to be needed by others.
- They are following in the footsteps of their own therapists and want to share with others the benefits they derived from therapy.
- They received little help with their own difficulties while they were growing up and don't want others to lack help as they did.
- They had a disappointing experience in counseling and believe they can improve the profession so that others will get more help than they did.
- They believe that becoming a clinician will enable them to resolve their own difficulties.
- They have a need for status, control, and power that they believe will be met by advising others on how to improve their lives.
- They view themselves as good listeners and helpful friends and want to use those skills in their work.
- They are psychologically minded and enjoy learning about and trying to understand others.
- They are concerned with cultural, political, or societal issues and want to address those broad problems through their clinical interventions.
- They view the helping professions as well paying.
- They want to leave teaching or another profession and view counseling as easier, more flexible, and more enjoyable.

Just as people have a variety of motives behind their interest in entering the fields of counseling or psychology, so do they have a broad range of ideas about the nature of the counseling process. The ideas are not always on target. Some people have the misconception that counseling involves telling people what choices or actions would be best for them. Many enter training for a mental health profession with little awareness of the differences between helping a troubled friend and helping a troubled client. Some expect high salaries and flexible hours, not recognizing the limited budgets of most educational and social service agencies and forgetting that people often need evening, weekend, or emergency appointments. Fortunately, many people do have an accurate understanding of the counseling process, gained through reading, conversations with clinicians or people who have received mental health treatment, or through their own experiences.

An important initial step for you as a novice clinician is assessing your own motivation for seeking to become a counselor or psychologist and developing a clear awareness of what you expect those professions to be like. You will probably benefit from thinking about your image of the practicing clinician, including where your image of the profession came from, what you envision to be the work of the clinician, and what sort of relationships you expect to have with your clients. Being aware of your preconceptions can help you to identify discrepancies between your image and the reality of the clinician's role, as presented in this book.

Carefully review again the previous list of common motives for entering a helping profession. Your motives may not resemble any of these but, chances are, one or more of the items on this list reflect your reasons for entering this field. Try to be honest with yourself and identify the two or three motives that led you to seek training as a clinician. Then ask yourself:

- What impact is each of my motives likely to have on my work with my clients?
- Do my motives reflect a realistic understanding of the profession for which I am being trained?

Information on the mental health professions, the roles of client and clinician, the treatment process, and transitions often encountered by clinicians will be presented throughout the rest of this book. That information will help ensure that you have a realistic understanding of your profession. In addition, questions and checklists included in this chapter will help you relate that information to yourself and facilitate your own development as a helping professional.

Characteristics of the Effective Clinician

A key factor in determining the outcome of the treatment process is, of course, the clinician. Clinicians bring with them personal and interpersonal characteristics, attitudes, and behaviors. Their professional training and experience will build on those qualities and shape and enhance their work.

Research, as well as my own professional experience as clinician, professor, and supervisor, suggest that effective clinicians have a cluster of desirable characteristics and attitudes. Careful and honest self-assessment can help clinicians identify and build on their strengths and reduce or eliminate some of their weaknesses. Think about the qualities and skills you currently have as you review this section of the book.

Jennings and Skovholt (1999) conducted a study of peer-nominated outstanding therapists and found that these clinicians were characterized by nine qualities:

1. They are eager learners.
2. They draw heavily on their extensive experience.
3. They value and can deal with ambiguity and complex concepts.
4. They can recognize and accept people's emotions.
5. The are emotionally healthy and nurture their own emotional well-being.
6. They are self-aware and can assess the impact their own emotional health has on their work.

7. They have strong interpersonal skills.
8. They believe in the importance and value of the therapeutic alliance.
9. They can use their good interpersonal skills to develop a positive therapeutic alliance.

Although counseling and friendship are very different processes, many of the same qualities that make someone a good friend and capable of healthy interpersonal relationships can also make that person an effective clinician. Research has shown that personal qualities such as being responsible, ethical, sensitive to and respectful of individual differences, stable, well adjusted, and optimistic are more important in determining a clinician's efficacy than are factors such as age, gender, or cultural background (Sexton & Whiston, 1991).

The following checklist encompasses many of the desirable qualities of clinicians. I suggest you use this checklist to assess yourself. Mark your strengths with a +. Put a − by each item you view as a weakness or a quality you have not yet developed. If you are uncertain whether or not an item describes you, mark it with a ?. You might also ask a trusted friend, colleague, or family member to identify those items on the list that he or she perceives as your strengths.

Checklist of Clinician Strengths

_____ Able to ask for help
_____ Able to deal with ambiguity and complexity
_____ Able to express oneself clearly, both orally and in writing
_____ Able to give credit to others for their accomplishments
_____ Aware of own political, spiritual, interpersonal, and other values
_____ Can see details as well as the big picture
_____ Can draw on and learn from past experience
_____ Caring
_____ Creative
_____ Comfortable with networking and collaboration
_____ Emotionally stable
_____ Empathic and able to identify emotions in self and others
_____ Ethical and respectful of laws, rules, standards, and boundaries but also able to exert efforts to change harmful standards
_____ Flexible and resourceful
_____ Hard working
_____ High frustration tolerance
_____ Insightful and psychologically minded
_____ Intelligent
_____ Interested, curious, an eager learner
_____ Maintains balance in own life
_____ Maintains own physical and emotional health
_____ Manifests good interpersonal skills and has some close relationships
_____ May have own concerns, but is addressing them and does not impose them on others
_____ Respectful and appreciative of others and their differences

_____ Self-aware and honest with oneself
_____ Serves as a role model and inspiration to others
_____ Sound capacity for attention and concentration
_____ Willing to listen to feedback and make changes as needed

Now that you have completed the checklist, think about how this information can help you progress toward becoming an effective clinician. Write down three steps you can take to minimize your weaknesses, build on your strengths, and get to know yourself better:

1.
2.
3.

Making the Transition from Novice to Accomplished Clinician

By now, you have probably realized that becoming an effective clinician is a process that involves hard work, considerable thought, learning, and change. It can be a rewarding process or may be fraught with obstacles and disappointments. Developing clinicians probably will encounter many transitions along the way. The following are some of the common ones:

- the transition from student to independent professional
- the transition from theory to practice
- the transition from focusing on one's own worldview to understanding the worldviews of others
- the transition from having a broad understanding of one's profession to focusing on an area of specialization
- the transition from having an external structure (college, graduate school) to being more self-directed
- the transition from perceiving oneself as all-knowing to recognizing how much there is to learn
- the transition from believing we can "fix" all of our clients to the recognition that we can be powerful facilitators but that only clients can truly control their own lives
- the transition from idealism to the awareness of the demands of managed care and school and agency budgets

These and other transitions in our professional and personal lives can be opportunities for growth even as they present challenges. With the recognition of our own strengths and the realization that transitions such as these are common and predictable aspects of developing professional effectiveness, clinicians can still maintain optimism and turn change and challenge into growth.

How This Book Will Contribute to Your Professional Development

Effective clinicians not only have many personal strengths but also have developed a broad array of technical and conceptual skills that enable them to help their clients meet their goals. As a result of this book, you should be able to acquire the following skills. (The section of the book in which each skill is presented is indicated in parentheses.)

- Gather important information about your clients' life experiences, resources, strengths, and difficulties (Chapter 2—technical skill focused on background).
- Acquire a conceptual understanding of the nature and dynamics of your clients' difficulties (Chapter 6—conceptual skills focused on background).
- Identify and respond in helpful ways to clients' strong feelings (Chapter 3—technical skill focused on emotions).
- Develop a positive therapeutic alliance with your clients (Chapter 7—conceptual skill focused on emotions).
- Promote client learning and change in dysfunctional cognitions (Chapter 4—technical skill focused on thoughts).
- Collaborate with your clients to establish realistic and mutually agreeable treatment goals and develop treatment plans that are likely to succeed (Chapter 8—conceptual skill focused on thoughts).
- Use contracts, suggestions, and challenge to promote positive change (Chapter 5—technical skill focused on actions).
- Know when and how to measure progress and complete treatment (Chapter 9—conceptual skill focused on actions).

Learning these skills should enhance your efforts to become an effective clinician. In addition, exercises throughout this book will continue to enhance and strengthen your self-awareness and other personal characteristics that will contribute to your professional success.

OTHER ESSENTIAL INGREDIENTS OF TREATMENT

Although the effectiveness of the clinician is central to the success of treatment, the therapeutic process actually includes three ingredients: the clinician, the client, and the context of treatment. These combine to create the therapeutic alliance. Each of these elements almost always plays an important role in determining the success or failure of the treatment process.

Context of Treatment

The treatment context is the setting in which the counseling or psychotherapy takes place. The location and size of the office, level of privacy, décor, temperature, parking, support staff, and even the magazines in the waiting room combine with the clinician's initial response to the client's request for help to create that person's first impression of the treatment process. Whether the context is a private practice, a school counseling office, a community mental health center, or a residential treatment program, the treatment context ideally should be

- easily accessible to all, including people with disabilities
- comfortable and welcoming

- able to maintain privacy of both client and confidential records
- responsive to client needs in terms of rapid responses to telephone calls and dealing with billing and third-party payers

Although more attention will be paid in this book to the clinician and the client, the importance of the clinical setting should not be overlooked when mental health services are provided.

The Client

People seeking treatment, of course, are not blank slates; they bring with them:

- *Background*—A history of relationships, experiences, disappointments, successes, and perhaps traumas has shaped who they are. Their families and their spiritual and cultural backgrounds also contribute greatly to their development.
- *Emotions*—Depression and anxiety are people's most common presenting concerns. Many other emotions arise and need attention during counseling, such as low self-esteem, rage, suicidal ideation, and terror. Positive emotions such as pride, love, and self-confidence should receive attention, too, and can serve as the foundation for positive change.
- *Thoughts*—Each person has his or her own views of the world, expectations about people and events, and an individual way of reasoning, thinking, and making decisions. People's inner experiences and their experiences with people and events are filtered through these lenses. Most current approaches to mental health treatment take a phenomenological perspective, seeking to understand how each client sees and makes sense of the world.
- *Actions*—People's actions both reflect and shape their emotions and thoughts. How much they study in school, how they choose a partner, where they decide to live, what jobs they hold, and how they spend their money are only a few of the many important actions that shape people's lives.
- *Problems, goals, and expectations*—People usually seek counseling because they are dissatisfied or in pain and want to make some changes or because another person has encouraged or required them to obtain some help. When people enter treatment, they may be optimistic or pessimistic, enthusiastic or reluctant about the treatment process. They have certain expectations about what will happen in treatment. They may have goals that they hope to accomplish through counseling. These may be realistic, such as improving their mood or changing their eating habits, or they may be unrealistic, such as finding a way to prevent a husband from having affairs or never again feeling shy or fearful.

In general, people who benefit most from treatment are those who have a realistic view of that process, are motivated to make changes, and can take some responsibility for their difficulties. They have reasonably good ego strength, have had some rewarding relationships, and are psychologically minded (Lambert & Cattani-Thompson, 1996).

Of course, many people do not fit this profile of the ideal client. This book will help you to get to know and understand your clients better, to maximize the strengths they bring with them to the treatment process, and to reduce the barriers that can impede their progress.

The Therapeutic Alliance

The therapeutic alliance, the working relationship between the client and the clinician, has been shown in study after study to be the best predictor of treatment outcome (Lambert & Cattani-Thompson, 1996; Sexton, 1995; Walborn, 1996). In addition, when clients identify what they found most helpful about counseling, the item that ranks first is the counselor facilitative interpersonal style (Paulson, Truscott, & Stuart, 1999). This means that having a clinician who is supportive, personable, attentive, and understanding has great importance in the development of a positive therapeutic alliance. In addition, role induction, the process of teaching people to be successful clients, can greatly enhance treatment outcome.

This book will help you to assess the essential ingredients of the treatment process: the context, the client, the clinician, and the therapeutic alliance. In addition, it will provide you strategies to maximize the strengths of these ingredients and address barriers or areas of difficulty that may limit treatment success.

IMPORTANCE OF THEORIES OF COUNSELING AND PSYCHOTHERAPY

Although this book is not designed to teach treatment systems and theories of counseling and psychotherapy, knowledge of the range of treatment systems available to clinicians is another important element in the treatment process. Without that information, it is unlikely that clinicians can develop successful treatment plans and determine interventions that are likely to be effective with a particular person.

More than 75% of today's clinicians describe their theoretical orientation as eclectic or integrated (Walborn, 1996). For these treatment providers, in particular, familiarity with a broad range of clinical theories and interventions is essential. That knowledge gives them the ability to select ingredients from several theoretical approaches and logically develop an integrated treatment plan designed to meet the needs of a given client.

Research suggests that 60% or more of the reasons for clients' progress in treatment can be attributed to the treatment systems and strategies used by the clinician (Seligman, 2001). Not only do treatment systems make a difference through the way the client's difficulties are conceptualized and through the particular interventions and strategies used, but also through the power of the treatment system to promote a positive therapeutic alliance and to engender hope and optimism in clients.

Having a clear and clinically appropriate theoretical framework for any treatment provided is also important in demonstrating accountability. Clinicians are increasingly being asked to justify their work to their clients, their employers, and third-party payers. Knowledge of treatment systems and their use enables clinicians to plan successful treatments and to explain their reasons for selecting particular approaches or interventions. In addition, although malpractice suits against mental health professionals are uncommon, clinicians are sometimes sued by angry or disappointed clients who believe they were harmed by their treatment. Here, too, information on the research supporting a given treatment system and its application is a clinician's best defense in the event of a lawsuit.

Having a solid grounding in treatment systems is expected to become even more important in the next 5 to 10 years in light of the increasing use of manualized treatment programs. The fields of counseling and psychology are witnessing a rapid growth in treatment protocols that have been developed and proven effective in ameliorating the symptoms of a particular mental disorder (Chambless et al., 1998). Manuals have been developed and empirically validated for the treatment of anxiety disorders, behavioral difficulties, mood disorders, and some eating disorders. In order to use these treatment protocols and incorporate them into their work, clinicians once again will need to have their therapeutic efforts solidly grounded in a broad and deep understanding of treatment systems.

MAKING THE TRANSITION FROM THEORY TO TREATMENT

Determining which theoretical framework is most appropriate for a particular client and which interventions are most likely to be helpful involves having a sense of purpose or direction. Only when we know what we want to accomplish and what our desired destination is can we determine the best way to get there. Treatment is likely to be most successful if clinicians have a sense of purpose at each level of treatment: the overall therapeutic process, the individual session, and the specific intervention. If asked, skilled clinicians should be able to:

- explain what they hoped to accomplish with each intervention and each session
- assess whether and how their goals have been met
- modify the treatment process as needed to achieve their desired outcomes

Desired outcomes that frequently arise during treatment can be categorized according to the BETA format and according to whether the desired outcome is a large-scale goal to be accomplished in one or more sessions or a small-scale goal to be accomplished in one or more interventions. Table 1-2 presents typical counseling objectives or purposes.

TABLE 1-2   Typical Treatment Goals for Interventions and Sessions Organized According to the BETA Framework

	Background	Emotions	Thoughts	Actions
Interventions	Obtain information. Make an interpretation.	Reflect feelings. Promote awareness of emotions. Promote expression of emotions. Increase motivation. Provide support and encouragement. Enhance the therapeutic alliance.	Orient to treatment. Promote awareness of meaning. Elicit thoughts. Dispute dysfunctional cognitions. Obtain clarification. Provide information, advice.	Identify target behaviors. Establish a contract. Set limits. Give homework and directives. Change the focus of the session. Reinforce gains. Challenge, confront.
Sessions	Promote insight. Take a history. Conduct an assessment. Make the unconscious conscious. Facilitate working through past issues.	Improve ability to manage emotions. Improve ability to identify and express emotions. Reduce painful emotions. Increase positive emotions.	Modify thinking patterns. Promote sense of responsibility and ownership.	Change dysfunctional behaviors. Prevent relapse. Empower. Develop skills. Promote self-control.

Additional information will be presented later in this text on goal setting and determining interventions that target particular goals.

THE ROLE OF ETHICS IN TREATMENT

Like theories of counseling and psychotherapy, ethical standards are not a primary focus of this book. However, ethics must always be a backdrop to clinical work. Although a detailed and comprehensive discussion of ethical standards is beyond the scope of this book, a brief review of those ethical standards that are most important to the clinician is presented here. This is intended to remind readers to keep these standards in mind as they develop their skills and gain experience in providing treatment. The skill of maintaining an ethical practice is essential for all clinicians.

Each of the major professional associations for mental health treatment providers has a set of ethical standards to guide the practice of its members. The American Counseling Association has its Ethical Standards, the American Psychological Association has the Ethical Principles of Psychologists, the National Association of Social Workers has its Code of Ethics, and the American Association for Marriage and Family Therapists has the Code of Ethical Principles for Marriage and Family Therapists. Both students and practitioners in these fields should obtain copies of the current ethical standards for their profession, should be familiar with these standards, and should be sure the standards are reflected in their work.

The most important ethical standards are reflected by three concepts: beneficence, trustworthiness, and safety.

1. **Beneficence** is the intent to do good, to help clients in any way that is ethical and professionally appropriate. This entails
    *   taking the time to get to know clients well as individuals and as members of a variety of cultural and social groups
    *   developing sound treatment plans, using strategies that will empower and promote positive change
    *   never acting in ways that may lead clients to experience shame or guilt or a worsening of their concerns
2. **Trustworthiness** involves acting responsibly and with integrity and honesty. Trustworthiness affects many dimensions of the treatment process. It entails
    *   following through on commitments and responsibilities by returning telephone calls, starting and ending sessions on time, and handling billing promptly and accurately
    *   being fair, just, and truthful with clients
    *   recognizing your limits and ensuring that the scope of your practice does not extend beyond your areas of competence
    *   focusing on clients' needs and not letting your own bad moods or disappointments intrude on the counseling process
    *   upholding the parameters of the counseling process, remaining in a professional role, and never using the counseling relationship or your clients to fulfill your personal needs

3. Providing for clients' **safety** is another one of the important responsibilities of the clinician. This includes
   - maintaining clients' confidentiality under most circumstances
   - if clients present a danger to themselves or others, taking steps to protect them, even if it entails breaking confidentiality to report an instance of child or elder abuse or to alert a family member of a client's suicidal thinking
   - being aware of your own safety needs and acting in ways that protect you, both emotionally and physically

Over the course of your training, you will probably have coursework on ethics that will deepen your understanding of these principles. You also may learn one of the many models that are available to help you make ethical decisions (Cottone & Claus, 2000). However, remembering these three concepts, **beneficence**, **trustworthiness**, and **safety**, will help you to operate in ethical ways at all times.

USING THIS BOOK EFFECTIVELY

The first part of this chapter provided you with the background you need for making good use of this book. This included information on

- the importance of both technical and conceptual skills
- the BETA (background, emotions, thoughts, actions) framework for organizing treatment systems as well as the skills presented in this book
- characteristics of effective clinicians
- the essential ingredients of the treatment process, including the context, the client, the clinician, and the therapeutic relationship
- the importance of having a solid grounding in treatment systems
- typical treatment objectives and purposes
- the role of ethics in treatment, especially the principles of beneficence, trustworthiness, and safety

The rest of this chapter orients you to the ways in which this book will promote the development of your technical and conceptual skills. Understanding how to participate fully and constructively in the practice exercises presented throughout this book is especially important. Whether you are in the role of client, clinician, or observer and whether you are giving or receiving feedback, your listening and communication skills and your involvement in the exercises determine how much you and the other members of your group will learn from the exercises.

PROMOTING SKILL DEVELOPMENT

This book is designed to promote your learning in a variety of ways. Each chapter introduces a group of skills that have common threads:

- Either all are conceptual skills or all are technical skills.
- All are linked to the same element in the BETA framework (background, emotions, thoughts, actions).

When a skill is initially presented, I generally provide you with a description of that skill, along with information on what research, case studies, and experience have taught us about the appropriate use of that skill. Illustrations of the appropriate use of the skill are then presented.

The Learning Opportunities section at the end of each chapter affords you many opportunities to review and practice the skills presented in that chapter. Discussion questions will help you talk about the skills with your classmates or colleagues. Written exercises are designed to give you practice in that chapter's skills. In addition, a group activity will help you practice the skills via role plays and obtain useful feedback from others. Forms and checklists provided in each chapter can help you keep track of your learning, assess your progress, and refine your goals so that you continue to improve your skills. Finally, topics for you to write about in a personal journal afford you one more opportunity to deepen and consolidate the learning you gained from the chapter.

PRACTICE GROUP EXERCISES

You will probably find that, as a developing clinician, your most valuable learning experiences will come from the practice group exercises suggested throughout this book. These experiences provide you the opportunity to try out new skills, build on skills already learned, give and receive feedback, and demonstrate improvement.

The practice group sessions can be rewarding experiences, involving shared learning and professional growth, facilitated by useful and meaningful feedback. Group members frequently develop strong and supportive relationships and benefit both personally and professionally from the practice group sessions.

On the other hand, the practice sessions can be anxiety-provoking experiences in which people feel attacked and belittled. Our apprehensions and self-doubts may get in the way of our listening carefully to feedback and understanding it fully. We might interrupt to defend or explain ourselves and may become more concerned with being right than with learning from the feedback.

Maximizing Learning from the Practice Groups

In order to maximize the benefit you obtain from the practice group exercises, I suggest the following strategies:

- Participate fully in the group exercises.
- Tape record an entire practice group session and review the tape before the next session, listening for ways in which you might improve both your clinical skills and your participation in the group.
- Adhere to the guidelines that follow for giving and receiving feedback.
- Complete the Assessment of Progress form at the end of each chapter, beginning with the form at the end of this chapter.
- Practice what you are learning between class meetings. Use your daily interactions as an opportunity to observe how you communicate with others and consciously use what you have learned to improve your communication.

Constructing the Practice Groups

I suggest the class be divided into groups of three or four people. The composition of these groups should change no more than once, if at all, over the course of a semester. Continuity allows participants to build rapport and trust, become familiar with each other's styles of interaction, see development and improvement in skills, and foster positive change based on the feedback that has been shared in the group.

During the exercises presented throughout this book, one or two members of the practice group will serve as observers, depending on whether the group has three or four members. Their task is to take careful notes on the role play, using the feedback sheets as guides. One of the observers should also assume the role of timekeeper, reminding the group when only 2 to 3 minutes remain in the role play and then letting the group know when the allotted time has elapsed.

The other two members will engage in a role play, with one assuming the role of client and the other in the role of clinician. The clinician's task, described specifically in each chapter, is to demonstrate the skills highlighted in the exercise, in the context of sound overall counseling.

The group member in the client's seat also has a challenging and potentially growth-promoting role. The client has the choice of either presenting actual concerns or role-playing a hypothetical client. More will be said on this choice and on the client role later in this chapter.

Practice Group Sessions

In order to maximize your learning, I recommend that your practice group sessions adopt the steps that follow. Once this structure becomes familiar to you, your group will be able to move efficiently through the steps:

1. The practice group members review the exercise to be sure they have a clear understanding of the nature and purpose of the experience.

2. Practice group members review the Assessment of Progress forms to remind themselves of their goals.

3. Determine group members' initial roles. Think about the three or four possible roles in terms of a sequence and progress through all roles in the first meeting: clinician, observer 1/timekeeper, client, and, for four-member groups, observer 2. For each subsequent group session, assume the role in the sequence that comes next after the one you first took in the previous session. In other words, if you began the first practice group session in the role of clinician, you should begin the second session as observer 1, then become the client, then observer 2 (for four-member groups), and finally, again, the clinician. For the third practice session, you would initially assume the client role. This rotation ensures that the same person will not repeatedly be the clinician either first or last (both of which have advantages and disadvantages) and that each person will have approximately the same amount of time in each of the three or four roles over the course of the practice group's meetings. This rotation also ensures that, for four-person groups, you will not have to assume client and clinician roles back-to-back, a potentially stressful sequence. Sufficient time should be allowed for each exercise so that group members have the opportunity to assume all four roles.

4. Practice group engages in the first iteration of the skill development exercise.

5. Feedback begins with the person in the clinician role, describing and assessing his or her own performance. That person addresses the following:
- brief overview of the exercise
- strengths of clinician and session
- clinician's ability to demonstrate the skills highlighted in the exercise
- areas needing improvement or causing clinician discomfort or concern
- any questions the clinician might have for the group on his or her skill development

6. The person in the client role should provide feedback next, addressing the following:
- overall reaction to the experience
- helpful parts of the interaction
- clinician's ability to demonstrate the skills highlighted in the exercise
- ways the role play could have been even more helpful

7. The one or two people in the observer roles should provide feedback last, addressing the following:
- overall perceptions of the experience
- parts they perceived as helpful
- clinician's ability to demonstrate the skills highlighted in the exercise
- ways to improve the role play

8. While receiving feedback, the clinician makes sure he or she has a clear understanding of the feedback and takes notes on important points on the Assessment of Progress form.

9. Practice group members then change roles, moving on to the next role in the sequence as described previously, and these steps are repeated.

The Nature and Importance of Helpful Feedback

One of the most important determinants of the nature and value of the practice group sessions is how group members give and receive feedback. Giving feedback is a learning experience, as is receiving feedback. Giving and receiving feedback can be a challenge but also is an art that can be learned.

I find that I have benefited greatly from listening to my students' counseling, reading their papers, and sharing with them my reactions and perceptions. I anticipate that you, too, will enhance your clinical skills by observing the work of your colleagues and finding ways to give them both reinforcement and helpful suggestions.

Consequently, it is important that you play an active part in your group. Avoid dominating the group and allow ample time for others to share their perceptions and ideas. Learning to give and receive feedback effectively can greatly enhance the value of the groups. These skills also can be productively used in many other personal and professional settings.

Giving feedback.   The following are two examples of feedback given to clinicians:

> **Unhelpful Feedback**—I just didn't like the way you interacted with the client. You looked like you would rather be having lunch than talking to the client.
> **Helpful Feedback**—Your eye contact seemed much better this week; you didn't

look down much the way you had in the last session. I did notice that you crossed your arms when Ginger started to cry. It seemed like you were putting a barrier between the two of you. What is your recollection of that part of the session? . . . Perhaps next time you could try to avoid that posture so that you communicate acceptance throughout the session.

The differences between the two examples are probably clear to you. The clinician in the first example speaks in vague and critical terms without offering specific examples or suggestions. The focus is on the clinician rather than the interventions. In addition, the language seems insulting and unprofessional.

On the other hand, the second speaker begins with positive feedback, is specific, focuses on interventions rather than the person, asks for the recipient's reactions to the feedback, and suggests ways to improve. The feedback is respectful and professional, yet it points out areas that might benefit from change.

The following guidelines will help you to provide useful feedback:

- Feedback should be gentle, supportive, respectful, and professional.
- Feedback should focus on strengths first and then address areas that need improvement.
- All feedback should be specific so that the recipient can readily grasp the information.
- Feedback should focus on the behavior, not the person.
- Feedback should focus on a few important areas; the person should not be inundated with information.
- Feedback should include specific but tentative suggestions for improvement.
- Feedback should be linked to goals and previous skill development exercises.
- Impact and understanding of feedback should be checked out with the recipient, and discussion should be invited.

Receiving feedback.   Listening to feedback and making good use of helpful suggestions are at least as difficult as giving sound feedback, especially for novice clinicians who may doubt and devalue their abilities. At the same time, hearing objective and useful feedback is one of the best ways to learn new skills and improve your effectiveness as a clinician. Over the course of your training, you will receive feedback from other students, from your professors, from yourself, and perhaps from colleagues, supervisors, and more advanced graduate students. The following information will help you make good use of the information you receive about your skills from others.

Let's look at some additional examples of feedback and some common types of responses to the feedback.

Feedback 1:   You really heard the client's underlying anger. However, when the client said she wished she could "just disappear," you shifted the topic back to her work conflict. You might have missed some very strong feelings, perhaps even suicidal ideation. Maybe you should have reflected her feelings there. What do you think?

Response 1:   I was going to address her statement as soon as I was clear on the nature of her work conflict.

Response 2:   She always gets melodramatic whenever we discuss substantive issues. I didn't want her to get off the track again.

Response 3: Thank you for pointing that out.

Response 4: That's a good point. Maybe I was scared by what she said. How might I have reflected her feelings?

The feedback here reflects several helpful strategies. It is supportive and respectful, it is specific, it suggests a way to improve the intervention, and it invites a reply from the recipient.

Despite the high quality of the feedback, the four respondents have very different reactions. The first two people seem more concerned with defending their interventions than they are with acquiring new learning. The second respondent even blames and disparages the client. Response 3 is a neutral one; it is hard to determine whether that person really absorbed and thought about the feedback. The fourth respondent seems most likely to benefit from the feedback; that person has clearly heard the feedback, tries to understand what led him to overlook the client's strong statement, and then seeks to learn even more by asking for additional help. Responding to feedback in that way is most likely to promote skill development.

Let's look at another type of feedback, followed again by some responses.

Feedback 2: I can't believe you missed the statement that she wished she could "just disappear!" She's practically telling you that she wants to kill herself and you just keep talking about her work problems!

Response 1: I guess that really was a dumb mistake. I do need to be more careful. I wonder if I really have what it takes to be a good clinician.

Response 2: Maybe so, but we can't pick up on everything. Remember when your client said she'd been throwing up again and you didn't stop to explore that?

Response 3: OK. Anybody have any comments on anything else?

Response 4: You probably have a good point, but the way you're talking to me isn't helpful. It just makes me feel angry and put down. Can we come at this in a different way?

Although the person providing feedback here may have a good point, the delivery is far from growth promoting and is likely to elicit self-blame and defensiveness from the recipient. Response 1 reflects those feelings of self-blame, while response 2 is a defensive and attacking one. Response 3 is probably the most common reaction to the type of feedback illustrated in this example. The person may well have some strong reactions to the attack but pushes those feelings away, at least temporarily, and changes the subject. Making a response like the fourth one is not easy; it calls for courage, honesty, and the ability to take a risk. However, the fourth response is most likely to promote skill development and personal growth for both giver and receiver of feedback.

The following guidelines for responding to feedback will help you maximize the learning you receive from that process:

• *Be aware of and address any discomfort you experience when hearing negative feedback*—Negative feedback can contribute to our own self-doubts and even make us question our career choices. Novice clinicians are particularly susceptible to placing too much weight on criticism of their work and ignoring praise.

• *Avoid being defensive and attacking in response to negative feedback*—If your reactions to feedback are getting in the way of your using the feedback constructively or feeling good about your successes, work on changing the self-talk underlying those re-actions. Discussing your reactions with a faculty member, supervisor, or colleague might be helpful.

• *Write down the feedback you receive*—Sometimes, the pressure of the moment makes it difficult to absorb feedback when it is received. Later, you may not be able to recall the feedback well enough to determine whether or not it provides useful infor-mation, or you may recall the criticism much more clearly than you can remember the praise. Writing down the feedback you receive on the assessment forms presented in each chapter can help you obtain a balanced and accurate picture of the feedback you receive. Having a written record of the feedback affords you the opportunity to think it over, assess its value, and, if necessary, obtain more information later to help you un-derstand and use the feedback in helpful ways.

• Remember that if you believe the delivery of the negative feedback is harsh or at-tacking, be courageous and *state how the delivery or content of the feedback could have been made more helpful.*

• *Be aware of and address any discomfort you experience when hearing positive feedback*—Positive feedback, too, can be hard to hear. Our own self-doubts might lead us to believe that people are just praising our work to avoid hurting our feelings or we might feel like an impostor, concealing our shortcomings from others. We might even feel that we can-not live up to the positive images people have of us and might experience considerable pressure when others are impressed by our skills. These are all common responses to positive feedback, especially for novice clinicians. Making a written record of the feed-back you receive can help you appreciate your strengths and identify areas needing im-provement.

• *Be sure you have a clear understanding of both the positive feedback you receive and the suggestions for improvement*—Restate the feedback you receive to be sure you have heard it correctly. Ask for examples and elaboration of people's reactions to your work so that you know exactly what they mean. If they have not offered specific ways for you to improve your skills, ask them what you might have done differently or how you might improve on your work.

• *Keep track of your goals and the progress you make toward those goals*—The Assess-ment of Progress forms provided in each chapter will help you accomplish that. Seeing yourself moving forward can be empowering and rewarding and can encourage further improvement.

• *Focus on your strengths and improvements, but continue to set realistic goals for yourself*—One of the exciting aspects of becoming a counselor or therapist is that the pos-sibilities for new learning and professional growth are limitless. Our field is stimulating but can also be intimidating and overwhelming. You will probably feel successful and satisfied in this field if challenge and growth seem like exciting prospects to you and if you continue to promote your own learning and development in realistic ways.

Role-playing a Client

Just as there are skills and strategies that help you succeed in the clinician role, so are there skills that will help you enjoy and learn from the client role. These skills also will enable you to help the other students in your practice group when you are in the client role.

As a client, you will be talking about concerns or issues that are likely to benefit from some counseling. When you are in the client role, you can choose whether to present concerns that you are experiencing in your own life or to assume a persona and talk about problems that are not really your own. You might role-play one of your clients, someone you know, or a hypothetical client. Of course, you must change any identifying information to protect the confidentiality and privacy of the person who is the model for your role play. Each of these choices has both benefits and drawbacks.

Role-playing an actual or hypothetical client

Benefits

- There is little risk that the person in the client role will become hurt or upset.
- The person can observe how another clinician might treat a challenging problem or client.

Drawbacks

- The person might not be able to provide a realistic presentation of the client.
- The clinician might not take the problem or person seriously.
- The clinician will not have the opportunity to see the interventions actually make a difference in the client's life.

Presenting one's own actual concerns

Benefits

- This will make the exercise more realistic.
- The person in the client role may experience some personal growth as a result of this process.
- Clinicians can assess the impact of their interventions by looking at changes in the targeted concerns over time.

Drawbacks

- Clinicians might find themselves dealing with issues that are too challenging for them.
- Clinicians might be reluctant to ask personal questions of their colleagues.
- Clients might become upset or hurt during the process.

Instructors might want to recommend whether people in the client role present their own concerns or those of an actual or hypothetical client. If instructors choose to leave this decision up to the individual group members, the decision should be made with care and deliberation. People who choose to present their own concerns in the practice group sessions can minimize the risks of that decision through careful selection of the types of issues they present.

Selecting appropriate concerns to present when you are in the client role is crucial to the success of the process. Select concerns that focus on you rather than on another person, that seem amenable to change, and that are not painful or difficult for you to discuss. Present concerns that are meaningful and important but that are not likely to feel overwhelming, either to you or to the clinician.

The following are categories of concerns that might be suitable for discussion in the practice group sessions. Examples are provided for each category.

- *Professional goals and direction*—deciding whether to pursue doctoral study, whether to change jobs, whether to become a school counselor or a mental health counselor.
- *Finding more balance in your life*—balancing family and professional responsibilities, maintaining a leisure life while being a graduate student.
- *Current relationships*—improving your relationship with your best friend, achieving more closeness in a family relationship, getting to know other students, dealing successfully with supervisors or professors.
- *Changing habits or behaviors*—stopping smoking, developing an exercise routine, getting clutter under control, improving study habits, eating more nutritionally.
- *Developing interpersonal skills*—improving parenting skills, becoming more assertive, managing anger.
- *Coping with current issues*—dealing with a parent's illness, developing new friends and interests after a divorce, deciding whether a romantic relationship should be continued.
- *Dealing with disappointments and fears*—fear of cats, disappointment over your failure to receive a promotion, apprehension about meeting new people.

The following are concerns that probably should not be the focus of your client role plays in the practice group:

- serious drug or alcohol problems
- suicidal ideation
- severe depression or anxiety
- traumatic experiences
- issues that date back to childhood
- dealing with your own life-threatening illness

After reviewing these lists, identify two or three topics that you would feel comfortable discussing in your practice group. Remember that you are in control of yourself; you can reveal as much or as little as you choose. Although I assume you want to be helpful to the other group members, you, like all clients, should collaborate with the clinician in setting the agenda for your sessions, and you have the right to let your clinician know that you choose not to discuss certain areas of your life. Be sure to take care of yourself so that your experience as a client is a rewarding one.

Confidentiality

Maintaining the confidentiality of the practice group is essential. This needs to be clearly stated as a ground rule for the group. Only if group members are confident that information about their lives or their performance in the practice group will not be shared inappropriately can they feel comfortable engaging in the exercises in such a way as to promote personal and professional growth.

Exceptions to the guideline of confidentiality may exist, and these should be stated and explained before the first practice session. Professors or supervisors, responsible for this learning experience, may want group members to provide written or oral feedback on their own performance in the group and on that of their colleagues. This should be presented in such a way as to be a learning experience rather than one that may promote feelings of competition and vulnerability. Emphasis should be placed on people's self-evaluations rather than how others evaluate them.

Although I strongly encourage group members to present concerns that are not highly charged, the direction of counseling is often unpredictable. Unanticipated worrisome issues may arise. As in the real world of counseling and psychology, clinicians are permitted to break confidentiality if clients present a danger to themselves or to others. However, this is not a decision to be made lightly; breaking confidentiality usually should only be done after consultation with a colleague or supervisor. If you believe that someone in your practice group presents a danger or if you believe that the concerns presented by a group member are serious enough to require professional help, you should discuss this matter with the group member and then with your professor or supervisor. This guideline, too, should be clearly stated before the group begins its role plays so that all participants understand the circumstances under which confidentiality may need to be broken.

Multicultural Counseling Competence

One of the essential learning experiences for clinicians at all levels of training is the importance of viewing their clients in context. People's cultural, ethnic, and socioeconomic backgrounds and their gender and life experiences influence their worldview, which affects all their perceptions and interactions. In the practice group exercises presented in this book, participants are strongly encouraged to maintain awareness of and sensitivity to the many influences that have an impact on both themselves and other practice group members.

An in-depth presentation of multicultural counseling and its competencies are beyond the scope of this book, although additional attention will be paid to these competencies in later chapters. However, readers are encouraged to educate themselves about research and theory related to multicultural counseling and to realize that cultural influences provide a backdrop in all clinical experiences.

LEARNING OPPORTUNITIES

Written or Discussion Questions

1. What reactions did you have to the finding that counselor education has neglected the development of students' conceptual skills? What conceptual skills do you think are especially important for clinicians?
2. The BETA model (background, emotions, thoughts, and actions) is used in this book as a framework to organize treatment systems and skills of counseling and psychotherapy. What are your reactions to this framework? What are some ways in which you can use the BETA framework to help you develop your knowledge and skills?
3. Research suggests that theories of counseling and psychotherapy have more commonalities than they do differences. Did you find this surprising? Why or why not? What do you think are the most important commonalities?

4. Ethical guidelines in the helping professions can be summarized as including beneficence, trustworthiness, and safety. Discuss what each of these concepts means and how it will affect your work.

5. This chapter has described the practice groups that you will be using to improve your skills. What are your initial reactions to these groups? What do you see as their advantages? Their drawbacks?

6. Discuss the differences between helpful and unhelpful feedback. Develop three examples of helpful feedback and three examples of unhelpful feedback.

7. What steps can you take to ensure that you are paying enough attention to your client's context and worldview?

Assessment of Progress

An Assessment of Progress form appears at the end of each chapter, with sections included in each form to reflect the salient skills that have been targeted in that chapter. A complete set of Assessment of Progress Forms is included in chapter 10. Complete each chapter's Assessment of Progress Form as you finish the reading, exercises, and practice group experiences associated with that chapter. When you have finished this book, the complete set of Assessment of Progress Forms in chapter 10 will afford you the opportunity to assess the overall progress you have made.

Assessment of Progress Form 1

Name: _____

Date: _____

1. List three clinical skills that you believe are strengths for you:

    a.

    b.

    c.

2. List three clinical skills that you believe you need to develop or improve:

   a.

   b.

   c.

The Personal Journal

One of the learning tools you will be using in conjunction with this book is the personal journal. You should obtain a blank book that will be used for this journal. The primary purpose of the personal journal is to provide you the opportunity to think about some of the issues raised in this book and enable you to become more aware of yourself as a developing clinician.

This book contains a great many exercises and questions. You are not required to respond to all of these but rather to select those that are most meaningful to you and most likely to help you achieve your learning and skill development goals. If you are using this book in conjunction with a course or a training experience, your supervisor or instructor will probably tell you which questions and exercises to address. Of course, feel free to respond to any additional items that seem important to you and your professional growth. The personal journal questions are especially likely to promote your self-awareness and development.

The personal journal, like the rest of this book, is designed to be used flexibly and to be adapted to the needs of a particular learning environment. When I use the journal as part of my teaching, I do not grade the students' journals to encourage them to think and express themselves freely about important personal and professional issues. Rather, I briefly review the journals at the end of the semester to be sure they have been completed as directed. Instructors may follow this format, they may choose to put students on their honor to complete the journal assignments, or they may decide to grade the journals as an assignment. Whatever choice is made, students should be advised at the beginning of the course who will read their personal journals and if and how that material will be evaluated.

Personal Journal Questions

The following are the personal journal questions for this chapter.

1. What were your reasons for entering the field of psychology or counseling?

2. Before you began your training what did you think it would be like to become a counselor or psychotherapist? How have your ideas changed as a result of your training?

3. On pages 9-10, this chapter provides a list of qualities characterizing effective clinicians. If you have not already done so, rate yourself on those qualities as directed in the instructions that precede the list. Then, based on your self-evaluations, include in your journal three ways in which you could build on your strengths, develop your self-awareness, and minimize your weaknesses.

4. Do you currently have a treatment system or theory of counseling and psychotherapy that you prefer to use in your clinical work? What attracts you to that particular approach?

5. The practice groups include three roles: clinician, client, and observer. Describe what you think it will be like for you to take on each of the three roles.

6. List two or three concerns that you have which would be appropriate to discuss in the practice groups. List two or three concerns that you have which would not be appropriate to discuss in the practice groups. What do you see as the differences between the two groups of concerns?

7. On page 6 of this chapter, a list of skills is presented, organized according to the BETA format. In your journal, list up to five of those skills that you view as strengths and up to five of those skills that you want to improve.

CHAPTER 2

Using Technical Skills to Understand and Address Background

OVERVIEW

Part II of this book, encompassing chapters 2–5, is designed to teach you the important technical skills you will need as a counselor or psychotherapist and to give you a variety of opportunities to learn and practice these skills. The technical skills are presented before the conceptual skills (part III, chapters 6–9) because I believe that the technical skills provide the building blocks that facilitate understanding of the conceptual skills. Just as you must learn to walk before you can dance, so must you develop some mastery of the technical skills before you are ready to move on to the more complex conceptual skills and eventually to the multifaceted role of the clinician.

Both part II and part III of this book are organized according to the BETA format discussed in part I. Each of the four chapters in parts II and III focus on one of the four elements of that format (background, emotions, thoughts, and actions). The chapters in part II focus on the technical skills that will help you understand and address each of these four elements, while the chapters in part III focus on the conceptual skills linked to each of the four elements.

Each of the chapters in these two parts will be organized according to the following structure:

1. list of skills to be addressed in the chapter
2. learning goals for the chapter
3. description of skills to be learned
4. examples, clarifying helpful and unhelpful uses of the skills
5. written exercises and discussion questions, to deepen understanding and initiate practice of the skills
6. practice group exercises to provide actual experience using the skills
7. Assessment of Progress Form for development and review of goals, assessment and recording of progress
8. Personal Journal questions

Items 3 and 4 will be repeated for each skill presented in a particular chapter.

Although learning is typically an incremental process, people learn best in different ways. The structure described here is designed to provide experiences that will gradually build and strengthen your skills. This structure will also afford you several different ways to learn the material, to increase the likelihood that you will achieve competence in the skills presented.

IMPORTANCE OF BACKGROUND

Theories and treatment systems of counseling and psychotherapy do not all give the same level of attention to clients' backgrounds and histories. For example, most psychodynamic theorists believe that the origins of people's current difficulties lie in early childhood experiences and that those years must be a prominent focus of treatment. Most person-centered, cognitive and behavioral clinicians, however, de-emphasize the importance of the past and concentrate their work on current experiences.

Despite this difference in emphasis, most treatment approaches in the 21st century take a holistic perspective. They acknowledge the importance of understanding people's contexts and multiple perspectives on the world and recognize that early attachment experiences are likely to have an impact on later relationships. Consequently, some attention to background is an essential ingredient of almost all counseling or psychotherapeutic relationships.

Case Example

The following provides a clear example of the importance of background. Natasha was born in a remote area of Russia more than 50 years ago. Her family was mistreated because of their religious beliefs and her parents could not earn an adequate living in their native country. When Natasha was about 8 years old, her parents took her and her two brothers, ages 5 and 10, and escaped from Russia. The danger and hardship they experienced while fleeing Russia and the death of her younger brother along the way were experiences Natasha would never forget.

After several difficult years, the family immigrated to the United States. They rarely talked about the past but emphasized the importance of looking forward. Natasha graduated from college, became a language teacher, married, and had a son and a daughter. When he was a teenager, her son was severely injured in an automobile accident. For Natasha, this experience felt unbearable, not only because of the injuries to her son, but because it echoed the loss of her brother many years earlier. Those painful memories that had never been discussed or resolved compounded her grief at her son's injuries. This usually composed and capable woman became depressed, inconsolable, almost incapacitated. Therapy, initially focused on fear and worry related to her son's accident, had little impact on Natasha. Only when she and her counselor recognized the link between the present situation and her past loss and addressed both experiences did Natasha become able to mobilize her resources and move out of her depression.

Benefits of Background Discussion

As you can see from Natasha's story, paying some attention to background can lead to a fuller understanding and appreciation of a person's concerns and difficulties. That, in turn, can lead to more successful treatment.

Discussion of background can accomplish the following:

- Enable us to view people in context
- Encourage us to take a holistic and comprehensive view of people
- Facilitate respect for the importance of people's past experiences
- Provide understanding of people's worldviews and multiple perspectives
- Highlight connections between past issues and present symptoms
- Provide historical information on symptoms that contribute to an accurate diagnosis
- Reduce our biases and preconceptions

SKILLS TO BE LEARNED

This chapter focuses on the use of questions and other interventions that are particularly useful in exploring background. Although questioning is the first important skill presented in this book, readers should be cautious about the use of this intervention. Overuse of questions can turn the treatment session into an interrogation and can make clients feel uncomfortable. Questions should be used judiciously and in combination with encouragers, reflection of feeling, and other basic interventions presented in the next three chapters. In addition, clinicians should make particularly careful use of questions until some rapport, as well as the beginning of a collaborative therapeutic alliance, has been developed between client and clinician. This will be discussed further in later chapters.

This chapter presents the following skills:

- General skills
  - open questions

- closed questions
- conducting an intake interview
- Specific skills
  - genogram
  - lifeline
  - earliest recollections

The use of these skills is by no means limited to exploration of background. Open and closed questions are among the most important technical skills used by clinicians to promote dialogue in sessions. However, these skills are especially useful in gaining information on background and in deepening our understanding of our clients.

GOALS OF CHAPTER

By the time you complete the reading, discussion, and exercises in this chapter, you should be able to:

1. Understand the appropriate use of questions in counseling and psychotherapy.
2. Describe the difference between open and closed questions and determine whether a question is open or closed.
3. Determine the appropriate use of open and closed questions.
4. Formulate questions that will help you gather important information and promote communication with your clients.
5. Combine questions with other interventions to promote a smooth flow in the treatment process.
6. Identify the key topics in an intake interview.
7. Conduct a comprehensive intake interview.
8. Describe the nature of genograms, lifelines, and earliest recollections.
9. Use genograms, lifelines, and earliest recollections to obtain background information.
10. Expand your self-awareness through the use of the genogram, lifeline, and earliest recollections.

FORMULATING HELPFUL QUESTIONS

Questions are one of the most frequent and powerful interventions that clinicians use. Questions can accomplish the following purposes:

- encourage dialogue
- yield information on facts, experiences, emotions, thoughts, or actions
- provide clarification
- focus or change the direction of a conversation
- promote thought, introspection, exploration, and elaboration
- encourage consideration of new possibilities, options, and solutions

- promote people's identification and awareness of their strengths
- help them feel empowered
- encourage clients to synthesize their therapeutic work and consolidate their gains

However, used inappropriately, questions can undermine the therapeutic alliance and leave clients feeling shame, anger, and discouragement.

Example

Consider the probable impact of each of the five clinician questions following the client statement below:

           Client: I got so angry with my father-in-law, I punched him.
    Clinician 1: Don't you know you could get arrested for that?
    Clinician 2: What led up to this incident?
    Clinician 3: Why did you do that?
    Clinician 4: How did you feel after you punched him?
    Clinician 5: How did your father-in-law react?

Each of these questions is likely to have a different impact on the quality and direction of the counseling process. Although it may well be important to help the client consider the possible legal consequences of his behavior, question 1, the only closed question of the five (in that it calls for only a minimal and factual response), sounds critical and judgmental. It does not allow the client an opportunity to explain his action and so seems precipitous. Question 2 is a neutral response and an open question, encouraging the client to elaborate and provide information that might help make sense of the action. Question 3 also is an open question and asks for explanation and elaboration but is phrased differently than question 2; like most questions that begin with "why," it sounds harsh and critical. Question 4 suggests concern for the client; unlike question 2, it will probably encourage the client to focus on emotions rather than facts. Finally, question 5 shifts the focus away from the client and onto the father-in-law, a direction that is not likely to help the client process and learn from this experience.

Let's see how the client might have responded to each of the five questions from the clinician:

           Client: I got so angry with my father-in-law, I punched him.

    Clinician 1: Don't you know you could get arrested for that?
           Client: Don't tell me what to do. He deserved it.

    Clinician 2: What led up to this incident?
           Client: He was spanking my three-year-old son really hard, just because he spilled his milk.

    Clinician 3: Why did you do that?
           Client: I don't know. I just lost control.

    Clinician 4: How did you feel after you punched him?
           Client: I was still really mad but I felt awful too; how could I have done that?

    Clinician 5: How did your father-in-law react?
           Client: He just gave me a look of disbelief and walked away.

Evaluating the Responses

Which of these interactions seems to move the counseling process in a positive direction? Both questions 2 and 4 yield important information, the first about the circumstances that prompted the behavior and the second about the person's feelings and his recognition that this behavior was probably not helpful. Usually, there is not a single right question or response but several responses, such as questions 2 and 4, which might be productive.

Question 5 does not contribute to the usual goals of counseling. In general, treatment should focus on the person who is present in the session. Discussion of reactions and behaviors of other people typically is not productive for several reasons. First, the client may or may not report accurately how that person acted. Second, the goal of treatment is not usually to gather the facts but to help the client learn and change in positive ways; this can generally best be accomplished by focusing on the client. However, because this intervention was not harmful, the clinician can quickly recover by shifting the focus back to the client.

Questions 1 and 3 detract from the treatment process. The client reacts defensively and fails to provide useful information. Getting the session back on track after these interventions can be difficult.

These five questions might be rank ordered according to their helpfulness, using the following criteria:

- **Extremely helpful**—reflects accurate and insightful listening; moves counseling in a productive direction; promotes self-awareness, new learning, or positive change
- **Moderately helpful**—reflects generally accurate listening; moves counseling in a productive direction, but does not clearly lead to greater self-awareness, new learning, or positive change
- **Neutral**—neither contributes to the treatment goals nor harms the therapeutic process; may not accurately reflect what client has communicated
- **Moderately harmful**—detracts somewhat from the counseling process or therapeutic alliance; reflects poor listening and perhaps disinterest
- **Extremely harmful**—damaging to the treatment process or therapeutic alliance; sounds ridiculing and critical

The five questions in this example can be evaluated in terms of these categories. They might be rated in the following way:

Extremely helpful—Question 4: How did you feel after you punched him?
Moderately helpful—Question 2: What led up to this incident?
Neutral—Question 5: How did your father-in-law react?
Moderately harmful—Question 3: Why did you do that?
Extremely harmful—Question 1: Don't you know you could get arrested for that?

The Importance of Purpose

Perhaps the most important way to increase your chances of making an intervention that is extremely or moderately helpful is to determine the purpose or intention of your intervention before making the intervention. For example, the purpose of question 4 is primarily to explore the client's emotional reactions to punching his father-in-law while the primary purpose of question 2 is to put the incident in context and to understand what led up to the event.

If you are in the early stages of your training, it may seem impossible to think about the intention of an intervention before making that intervention. It may seem to you that you would have to pause for a few minutes after each client statement to figure out what you should say next. Of course, that would be disruptive to the flow of the session. However, as you gain experience, you probably will find that you can quickly determine what you hope to accomplish with each intervention and formulate an intervention that is likely to accomplish your purposes.

One way to help you develop facility in determining purpose and in formulating interventions that correspond to your purpose is to gain practice by working backwards. This entails thinking about an intervention that has already been made and identifying the probable purpose of that intervention. At the end of this chapter, you will be given an opportunity to identify the purpose of some interventions. Having a clear purpose or intention in mind is an important skill for counselors and psychotherapists. Considerable attention will be paid to this skill throughout this book.

Open and Closed Questions

Clinicians have two types of questions in their repertoire of interventions: open questions and closed questions. Both of these have a place in the client-clinician dialogue, but their purposes are different.

Closed questions.   Closed questions are usually intended to elicit a short, specific piece of information, often facts or figures. They typically begin with *is, are, do, who, when,* and *where.* The following are examples of closed questions:

- Is your mother still alive?
- Are you married?
- Do you have legal custody of your child?
- When did you leave school?
- Who suggested that you seek counseling?

As you can see, these questions are not intended to promote thought or generate learning but rather are usually intended to provide the clinician with some necessary facts. Although some clients will provide lengthy responses to closed questions, most will just respond with the requested information.

Closed questions certainly have a useful role in the treatment process. Closed questions can help to slow down and focus a voluble client and can narrow the scope of a fragmented session. They are especially useful in the first few sessions of treatment to provide clinicians with the details and facts they need to develop a picture of a client's history. Closed questions may also be used productively at other points in the treatment process.

However, excessive use of closed questions can create a negative tone in the session and can give a client an erroneous view of the treatment process. A series of short questions and answers can lead clients to think that the clinician can be relied on to direct the sessions and all they need to do is come up with the right answers. Even worse, clients may feel as if they are being interrogated. This is likely to prevent the establishment of a positive therapeutic alliance and may even lead to premature termination of the treatment process.

Open questions.   Open questions, on the other hand, usually encourage clients to think and explore, to gain awareness and new perspectives, to make connections, and to see patterns. Open questions are relatively unstructured and allow ample room for clients to provide full responses. These questions typically do not have specific right-or-wrong answers but rather welcome whatever response the client makes. Open questions usually begin with such words as *what, how,* and *why.* The following are examples of open questions:

- What led up to your decision to leave high school?
- What sort of relationship had you been hoping for?
- How did you feel when your dog was missing?
- How did you support yourself after you lost your job?
- Why did you decide to refuse the recommended medical treatments?
- What led you to seek counseling at this time?

Clinicians generally make much more use of open questions than they do closed questions. Open questions promote dialogue, give the client control over the direction of the session, and are likely to deepen and enrich the session.

However, open questions, too, have some pitfalls. Questions beginning with *why* tend to sound accusatory and critical. In addition, clients may not know why they thought or acted in a particular way and so may feel uncomfortable when asked a why question. Some people, particularly those who are anxious or fearful or who are coping with strong feelings of guilt and shame, may feel uneasy when any type of open question is asked. They may believe that there is a right answer they are supposed to know and have difficulty with the ambiguous and unstructured nature of open questions. Consequently, clinicians should use open questions, as well as closed questions, with care and sensitivity and should generally avoid why questions.

Implied questions.   In addition to open and closed questions, clinicians also use implied questions. These are a cross between a directive (discussed in a later chapter) and a question, but really function like an open question, keeping the focus on the client and encouraging the client to talk. Many clinicians make extensive use of implied questions. Examples of implied questions include:

- Could you tell me some more about that?
- Why don't you give me some details?
- I wonder how you reacted to that.
- I don't have a clear picture of your feelings at that time.
- Tell me what was happening when you started to cry.
- Perhaps looking at what led up to this would give some clarification.

Implied questions typically seem less confrontational and interrogatory than direct questions. As a result, implied questions can effectively promote dialogue and client self-exploration while maintaining a positive atmosphere in the session.

Pitfalls of Questions

Clearly, questions are one of the most important interventions in the clinician's repertoire. They are invaluable in promoting client exploration and self-awareness and in eliciting important information. However, when they are poorly presented or used without a clear purpose, questions can have a negative impact on the therapeutic alliance and on the treatment process. Clinicians should be aware of the following possible pitfalls inherent in the use of questions, some of which have already been mentioned earlier in this section:

Leading questions.   These closed questions telegraph to the client the expected answer and counteract the value of questions as a tool to promote exploration. Examples of such questions are, "Don't you think you overreacted to his statement?" and "You weren't physically or sexually abused, were you?" Much better would be questions such as, "How do you feel about your reaction to his statement?" and "Could you tell me about any times when you felt that you were being physically or sexually abused?"

Shifting focus off the client.   Sometimes curiosity, inattention, or lack of a clear purpose lead us to ask questions that shift the focus away from the client and onto other people in the client's life. While this sometimes yields useful information, clinicians cannot be certain that clients are presenting reliable information about other people. Their perceptions of others are based on incomplete information and are all filtered through the clients' own phenomenological viewpoints. The result may be distorted and inaccurate information. I have found, for example, that the uncaring or malicious family members described by my clients were sometimes caring and well-meaning people who had weak interpersonal and listening skills.

In phrasing your questions about people in a client's life, generally focus on the client's perceptions of that person. For example, rather than asking "What kind of parent was your mother?", ask "How did you experience your mother as a parent?" Most important to the treatment process are the client's memories and images rather than the actual characteristics of the people in the client's life.

Interrogation.   Inappropriate and excessive use of questions can make clients feel that they are being interrogated rather than participating in a collaborative endeavor. This is most likely to happen in the following situations:

- *Clinicians rely almost exclusively on questions in their interventions*   This pitfall can be counteracted by consciously combining questions with other interventions. The combination of a question with a reflection of feeling or meaning, discussed later in this book, is particularly powerful; it lets clients know you have heard them and also elicits additional information. An example of this would be, "It sounds like you feel very angry at your parents (reflection of feeling). How have you tried to deal with that anger (question)?"
- *Clinicians use double or triple questions in one intervention*, such as, "Do you like school? I mean, what are your favorite subjects? How do you get along with your teachers?" This pattern is particularly common among beginning clinicians who are not sure if their clients understand the first question and so rephrase it and then rephrase it again. Trust that you will usually make yourself clear and that, if clients are confused by what you have said, they will let you know.

- *Clinicians ask why questions* such as, "Why did you drop out of high school?" and "Why were you fired from your job?" These tend to sound critical and blaming and can make people feel uncomfortable. Better questions are, "How did you make the decision to leave school?" and "What was your understanding of your supervisor's decision not to keep you on the job?" How and what questions are less likely to be threatening than why questions. Therefore, they typically elicit a better client reaction and more useful information.

Useful Questions

Just as some questions tend to be countertherapeutic, so are some questions likely to advance the treatment process. Several particularly useful types of questions are available to clinicians. These include empowering questions and scaling questions.

Empowering questions.   Skillful use of questions can help clients to develop self-confidence and hopefulness and to become more aware of their strengths. Questions such as these assume that people will be effective and focus on successes and positive exceptions rather than on problems and disappointments.

A well-known example of such a question is the Miracle Question, developed by Steve de Shazer (1991, p. 113): "Suppose that one night there is a miracle and while you were sleeping the problem that brought you to therapy is solved. How would you know? …What would be different?…What will you notice different the next morning that will tell you that there has been a miracle?…What will your spouse notice?" This series of solution-focused questions implies that the problems can be solved and elicits specific evidence of their resolution that can suggest ways to address the problem.

Other types of empowering questions can also be helpful to clients. Examples include:

- What will your life be like when you have resolved this difficulty? (assumes success and effectiveness)
- Could you tell me about some times when you did enjoy what you were learning in school? (looks for exceptions)
- It sounds like you and your son got along well yesterday. What did you do to make that happen? (strength-promoting)
- Although you are having difficulty coping with your current situation, you have overcome a great deal in your life. For example, how did you deal with your father's suicide? (identifying effective coping skills)

Scaling questions.   Scaling questions are particularly useful in setting goals and assessing whether and how much progress has been made. Although not a precise or scientific measurement, clients usually have little difficulty responding to scaling questions and find them useful to quantify change. Examples of scaling questions are:

- On a 0–10 scale, with 0 representing no fear and 10 representing the highest possible fear, what number would best reflect your current fear of heights? (establishes a baseline)
- When we began counseling, you rated your parenting skills as a 2 on a 0–10 scale, with 0 representing a complete lack of parenting skills and 10 represent-

ing the best possible parenting skills. Now that you have had the opportunity to learn and practice some new parenting skills, how would you rate your parenting skills on that 0–10 scale? (measures progress)

- On a 0–10 scale, with 0 representing the lowest possible self-esteem and 10 representing the highest possible self-esteem, what would be a realistic number for us to target as a goal as we work on improving your self-esteem? (establishes reasonable goals)

Summary

Clearly, questions are an extremely useful type of intervention for all clinicians. They are important in promoting dialogue and eliciting information, whether or not you are exploring background and whether or not you view an in-depth discussion of background as essential to successful treatment. For greatest effectiveness, questions should be combined with other types of interventions that promote self-expression, discussed later in this book. Exercises at the end of this chapter will afford you the opportunity to practice and improve your questioning skills while exercises in later chapters will help you learn to combine questions with other interventions.

USING QUESTIONS EFFECTIVELY IN INTAKE INTERVIEWS

Questions are the most useful intervention when clinicians elicit client information during an intake interview. Conducted either prior to the start of counseling or during the first session or two of the treatment process, the intake interview lays the groundwork for successful treatment. An intake interview is generally intended to accomplish the following purposes:

- clarify the clients' presenting problems and reasons for seeking treatment
- orient clients to the treatment process
- begin to develop a positive and collaborative therapeutic alliance
- obtain relevant information on clients' background, history, and context
- identify concerns that seem amenable to counseling
- clarify the diagnosis, if a mental disorder is present
- determine whether clients present a danger to themselves or others and, if so, facilitate immediate action

Questionnaires and checklists are often incorporated into the intake process. This can streamline that process. In addition, some people find it easier to write down personal information rather than to speak about it to a relative stranger. Clients should be offered several ways to present information and should be reassured that, although the intake interview is an important part of treatment, clients have the right to disclose as much or as little as they choose. Following the guidelines already presented on asking helpful questions will go a long way toward making the intake process a comfortable and productive experience.

A typical intake interview elicits information on the following topics (Seligman, 2001, p. 41):

- Demographic information, including age, marital status, family composition, educational background, occupation, and living situation
- Presenting problems, including reasons for seeking help at the present time, symptoms, onset and duration of difficulties, and the impact of concerns on the person's lifestyle
- Prior psychological and emotional difficulties, treatment history and outcomes
- Current life situation, including important relationships, occupational and educational activities, and social and leisure activities
- Cultural, spiritual, religious, and socioeconomic information
- Family background, including information on composition of current family and family of origin, structure of and relationships within the families, parenting styles, role models, family rules and values
- Developmental history, including important experiences and milestones
- Career and educational history
- Medical history, including significant past and current illnesses, medical treatments, and medication
- Health-related behaviors, including use of drugs and alcohol, exercise, diet, and overall self-care
- Additional information that clients view as important

EXAMPLE OF AN INTAKE INTERVIEW

The following example illustrates a typical intake interview, covering the information categories listed previously. It also will serve to introduce Eileen Carter, a client who is used to illustrate many of the skills presented in this book. Eileen is a 24-year-old African American woman who sought counseling at a university counseling center. Assume that Eileen has already been oriented to the counseling process.

As you review this intake interview, pay particular attention to the flow of the interview and the way questions are used, either alone or in combination with other interventions, to gather information. Also notice the development of the therapeutic alliance during this interview. Topics for discussion at the end of this interview will help you see how the technical skills used here further the goals of the intake process.

Clinician 1: Eileen, when you called for an appointment, you sounded pretty upset. You talked about your life being "one big mess." Could you tell me about that?

Eileen 1: Yes. I'm a student here at the college, taking my first college course. For years, I thought about going to college and becoming a nurse, and I finally saved up some money and enrolled in English 101. And now I might have to drop out of the course…I feel so discouraged.

Clinician 2: So college represents a sort of dream come true for you. What might interfere with that?

Eileen 2: Well, I'm married and I have a 4-year-old son, Charles Junior. At first, my husband said he would stay with Junior while I went to class in the evening, but now he's saying that it's my job to take care of our son, that he's too busy, and what do I need an education for anyhow.

Clinician 3: How did you react when he said that?

Eileen 3: I was blown away. I had told him how much it meant to me to start college and I thought that maybe for once he cared about how I felt. Stupid me! I should have known better.

Clinician 4: Sounds like this was very upsetting to you.

Eileen 4: You got that right. I didn't want my husband to know I was upset so I went in the bathroom, turned on the water so he couldn't hear me, and just cried and cried and cried.

Clinician 5: What kept you from sharing your feelings with your husband?

Eileen 5: He would have just laughed at me, and then later he'd use the situation to prove to me what a hopeless mess I am.

Clinician 6: I'm hearing several issues here, concerns about your relationship with your husband as well as about continuing in college. How do you think I can help you?

Eileen 6: I really want to stay in school. I thought maybe there were some resources here at the college that could help me, like child care or financial aid. And I could certainly use some help with my marriage.

Clinician 7: We can work on all that, but before we start to focus on those issues, I would like to put them in context. It helps me to understand your current concerns if I know something about your background. How would you feel about filling me in on your background?

Eileen 7: Fine. Whatever you think would help.

Clinician 8: All right. Maybe you could start by telling me about the family in which you grew up.

Eileen 8: Well, there were my parents and I had two brothers, one four years older and one four years younger. And I had two dogs and a cat.

Clinician 9: What was it like for you to grow up in that family?

Eileen 9: Until I was about 10 or so, it wasn't particularly good or bad. My parents both worked hard; Dad was an electrician and Mom was a beautician. We had to be pretty self-sufficient, just let ourselves in after school, do our homework, and make dinner. We were like ships passing in the night. I had my pets and that really helped.

Clinician 10: Sounds pretty lonely. And then things changed when you were about 10?

Eileen 10: Yes, my dad died suddenly of a heart attack. I guess he had high cholesterol or something but nobody really knew. My family hardly ever went to doctors. My mom really couldn't handle it, put us all in foster care for awhile, got a second job. Dad had hardly left her any money, and things were really tough. After about six months, she took us back home but things had gone from bad to worse. She was out dating all the time; I guess she thought that if she got married again, things would get better. She had no time for us. I felt like I was invisible.

Clinician 11: It sounds like you lost both parents in a way.

Eileen 11: Yes, it was pretty awful. I didn't know what to do to feel better. Then one day when I was home alone, I went to the liquor cabinet and started drinking. For awhile, I felt better, sort of warm and safe. Of course, by the time my mom got home, I was really sick, but even that wasn't so bad. She didn't know why I was sick, but she put me to bed and fed me toast and tea. That was pretty good, too.

Clinician 12: So you discovered that alcohol made you feel better, at least for a little while.

Eileen 12: Yes, but usually one of my brothers was home with me so I didn't get much opportunity to raid the liquor cabinet. Then I found another solution. Some of the kids at school were sniffing glue, and I started hanging out with them. Sometimes they would have liquor or marijuana and we would cut school, go out to the woods, and party.

Clinician 13: How did you feel about that part of your life?

Eileen 13: Now I feel pretty bad about it, but then I was just numb. And when I met Jay, things got even worse.

Clinician 14: Even worse?

Eileen 14: Yeah, I guess I got the message from my mom that you had to have a man in your life. I was about 12 then and Jay was 16 and had a car. He wanted to have sex right away and I thought, why not. So we did and that was like the alcohol, helped me feel warm and safe. But it sure didn't last. He started to knock me around and I knew he was going out with other girls. I don't know why I didn't break up with him, but I didn't. He finally dumped me.

Clinician 15: So what started out feeling good wound up being another loss for you.

Eileen 15: Yeah, but did I learn anything from that? Of course not. So after Jay, there was Mike and then Tyrone. By then, I had dropped out of school and was working in bars, waitressing or dancing or whatever would pay the bills. I moved in with Tyrone when I was 17 and he sure wasn't paying for anything. I got pregnant twice when I was with Tyrone and I had two abortions. It was a terrible choice for me but I just didn't know what else to do; I couldn't support a child and didn't want my child to have Tyrone as a father.

Clinician 16: It sounds like you went through some very tough years. How did you get from that situation to where you are now?

Eileen 16: Well, after Tyrone, there was Charles. He's my husband. He seemed different from the rest; at least he didn't hit me. And then I got pregnant again. Maybe I thought it would be OK if I got pregnant by Charles. At least he had a decent job, even though we met in a bar and I knew he drank too much. He said we should get married and so we did. That was four years ago.

Clinician 17: And how have those four years been for you?

Eileen 17: My son has been God's gift to me. He makes it all worthwhile. But marriage sure wasn't what I thought it would be. We don't seem to have any love in our marriage and I feel very alone.

Clinician 18: I wonder if these feelings remind you of feelings you had as a child?

Eileen 18: You know, they really do. More ships passing in the night.

Clinician 19: You've gone through a great deal to find that warmth and comfort you crave, but it sounds like you still haven't found what you're looking for.

Eileen 19: Except with my son.

Clinician 20: Except with your son. Are there other parts of your life that give you a sense of gratification?

Eileen 20: School does.

Clinician 21: What makes school so special for you?

Eileen 21: I never had any interest in school before. But it's so different now. I'm there for me, because I really want to be there. And it makes me feel like I have hope in my life. I even tell my son about the books we're reading and I read him an essay I wrote. I want him to have a different kind of life.

Clinician 22: School has really made many important changes in your life. What else helps you feel hopeful?

Eileen 22: I did stop drinking, or at least drinking the way I used to. When I was pregnant, I knew that alcohol could really harm my son and so somehow I managed to stop drinking. I still smoke and I know that's not good, but I really have alcohol under control. Smoking is next on the list.

Clinician 23: You've taken some big steps to improve your health. Have you had any medical problems or health concerns?

Eileen 23: I do have high cholesterol like my father. It must be genetic because you wouldn't expect someone my age to have that problem.

Clinician 24: That must be frightening, to have the same medical problem that might have killed your father. Are you taking any medications for the high cholesterol?

Eileen 24: It did scare me to get that diagnosis, but the doctor just said to watch my diet; I know I need to do that. And I should exercise more too.

Clinician 25: Perhaps that is another goal you have. What leisure or social activities do you have?

Eileen 25: Not much. Cleaning the house, cooking meals, and running after my son, that's my life. I do enjoy talking with the other women with young children whenever I take Charles Junior out. There's a group of us that all take our kids to the park when the weather is decent. That's how I found out about this school, from one of the other women.

Clinician 26: So you do have some people you socialize with. Are you employed now?

Eileen 26: I do some telephone work from home; I call to see if people are interested in having siding put on their houses and then, if they sound interested, I pass on the lead to this siding company. They pay me for every lead they get an appointment with and I get a bonus if they make a sale. Nothing else since I got married. Charles wanted me to stay home. I think I'd like to get a part-time job once Junior is in school next year.

Clinician 27: So working for pay isn't a big part of your life right now. What kinds of jobs have you had?

Eileen 27:   Just working in bars and nightclubs. I did get my G.E.D. but I don't have any special training. I learned to deal with all kinds of people in the bars, though, and I think I could do pretty well in sales. I even do pretty well on the phone and that's tough; people hang up in your face and even curse at you.

Clinician 28:   You see yourself as being pretty good with people, then.

Eileen 28:   Yes, I think so. I really like to talk to people.

Clinician 29:   So that's a strength you have. One area we haven't talked about is your religious beliefs and cultural background. Could you tell me about that?

Eileen 29:   Sure. I was brought up with Christian beliefs, even though we never went to church. I always valued my African American heritage and have a strong faith in God. But sometimes I feel so bad about all the mistakes I made in my life, I wonder if even God can forgive me. And yet he gave me my son so I can't be that bad.

Clinician 30:   Sounds like you're feeling some guilt and regret.

Eileen 30:   That's an understatement. Part of me wants to have a better marriage, to make a good home for my son, to continue my education. But then another part of me thinks that I don't deserve all these good things, that I should be punished for the abortions and the other terrible things I did.

Clinician 31:   I hear lots of mixed emotions. What are you feeling now as you talk about this?

Eileen 31:   So many regrets, so much guilt. I want so much to give Junior the love and family I never had, but I'm not sure I can do it. I can't believe I'm telling you all this. I came in to talk about a college course and look where we wound up!

Clinician 32:   We did cover a great deal of ground. What reactions are you having to our talk today?

Eileen 32:   I'm not sure. It all seems like a big ball of yarn and I don't know where the beginning is.

Clinician 33:   It does seem like many parts of your life are intertwined: your family background, your use of drugs and alcohol, your regrets about some of the choices you made, your marriage, your love for your son, and now your feelings about school. We'll certainly want to look more closely at all of these issues and establish some goals, but I wonder how you feel about our continuing to work together?

Eileen 33:   I think I feel all right about it. You're really the first person I've talked to about all this. I'd be afraid my women friends would think I'm a terrible person if I told them about my past. Charles knows about all this, but he's not much help. Whenever I mention anything to do with another man, he gets really jealous so lots of topics are off limits. He says I should just put the past behind me and move on. Maybe he's right. In a way, I'm afraid I'll feel worse if I keep talking about all this.

Clinician 34:   I can understand that you wouldn't want to keep feeling pain from those past experiences, and I will do my best to help you deal with those feelings. But I think that counseling might be able to help you

not only find a way to continue your education but feel better about
yourself.

Eileen 34: I would certainly like that. Where do we go from here?

Clinician 35: We do have a little more time before the end of our session. How
would it be to look at some of your options for continuing school and
then set up an appointment to meet again?

Eileen 35: Sounds good to me.

Discussion Questions

The following questions will help you to examine this intake interview more closely.
They also should help you to improve your counseling skills, especially your understanding of appropriate and helpful ways to use questions.

Notice the types of interventions that were used in this interview, particularly the
use of questions. Respond to the following questions in terms of your assessment of the
interventions used in the interview.

Quality of Interview Questions

- Were the questions mainly open questions or mainly closed questions? What
  differences, if any, do you notice in the client's responses to the open vs. the
  closed questions?
- Did the interviewer rely too heavily on the use of questions? If so, what might
  the interviewer have done differently? If not, what did the interviewer do to
  keep this interview from sounding like an interrogation?
- Which questions seemed particularly fruitful? What made these good questions?
- Were there questions that did not seem to work very well? If so, how might you
  have improved on these questions?

Goals of the Interview Questions

- Compare this interview with the list on page 40 of those topics that are usually
  covered in an intake interview. What topics, if any, were omitted? Should they
  have been included in this session, or are they better left for a subsequent session?
- Did this interview accomplish the important purposes of an intake interview,
  stated on page 39? To determine that, consider the following questions:
  - Was the clinician successful in initiating a positive therapeutic alliance with
    this client? If so, what made that happen? If not, what might the clinician
    have done differently?
  - Can you explain why Eileen sought treatment at the present time and de-
    scribe the nature of her presenting concerns?
  - Did the clinician obtain enough relevant information about Eileen's back-
    ground, history, and context? What information seems especially important
    to you? What additional information, if any, would have been helpful to the
    treatment process?
  - What concerns does Eileen have that seem amenable to counseling?

- Are you able to determine from this interview whether Eileen might present a danger to herself or others? (This information can be inferred from the overall content of the interview or discovered through specific questions.) Would you have done anything differently to assess for dangerousness?

Overall Assessment of Intake Interview

- Overall, how would you assess the quality of this intake interview? What do you see as its strengths? Its weaknesses? How would you have improved on or changed this interview?
- Now that you have some preliminary information about Eileen and her reasons for seeking help, how do you think treatment of this client will progress? What would you want to keep in mind and be sure to address in your work with Eileen? More information will be provided on Eileen's treatment throughout this book.

SPECIFIC TECHNICAL SKILLS TO OBTAIN BACKGROUND INFORMATION: EARLIEST RECOLLECTIONS, GENOGRAMS, AND LIFELINES

The use of effective questions and the ability to conduct a successful intake interview are two of the fundamental skills used by clinicians seeking to gain understanding of a person's background. However, many additional tools are available to facilitate this process. Three of them will be briefly presented here: earliest recollections, genograms, and lifelines. Applying these tools to yourself, as well as to your clients, will enhance your repertoire of clinical skills and can also contribute to your own professional and personal development.

EARLIEST RECOLLECTIONS

The use of early recollections in treatment stems from the pioneering work of Alfred Adler (1963), a Viennese psychoanalyst who wrote and practiced during the late 19th and early 20th centuries. Adler was originally a follower of Sigmund Freud, but he eventually broke with Freud and went on to develop his own approach to treatment, Individual Psychology. Although Adler's ideas about human development are less deterministic than those of Freud, Adler, too, emphasized the value of understanding people's early childhood years. This is reflected in the importance he placed on eliciting and exploring earliest recollections.

The process of eliciting and processing early memories includes the following four steps (Seligman, 2001, p. 94). Notice that, although the early recollections stem from past experiences, they are useful in shedding light on people's current emotions, thoughts, actions, and relationships.

1. *Eliciting the recollections.* People are asked to describe at least three memories that they believe to be their earliest recollections. These should be memories of incidents in which the person was actually present. Whether or not these events actually occurred as recalled and whether they are really the person's earliest memories are not important;

what matters are the person's perceptions. The clinician should write down the memories as they are presented.

2. *Processing the memories.* Explore each memory with the teller, inquiring about
- emotions, thoughts, and actions related to the memories
- interactions in the recollection between the client and other people
- the most important or vivid parts of the memories
- the meaning each memory has for the client

3. *Analyzing the memories.* Client and clinician together process the memories, looking especially for patterns and commonalities in the situations and in the client's reactions and interactions with others in the memories.

4. *Interpretation and application.* Drawing on that analysis of common themes and responses, the clinician develops a hypothesis as to what these recollections reveal about the client's worldview, goals, and lifestyle. This hypothesis is then presented to the client for discussion and clarification. Information obtained through this process often provides considerable insight into clients and the impact their perceptions of their early years have had on the way they lead their lives in the present.

The following three recollections were provided by Eileen, the client presented earlier in this chapter:

Recollection 1.   This must have been a really long time ago because I'm in my crib in this memory. I remember feeling bad; I guess I was hungry or needed to be changed or something. But I knew I wasn't supposed to cry. I was just supposed to wait until someone got ready to take care of me.

Recollection 2.   I remember when my younger brother was born and my parents brought him home from the hospital. My older brother was there and they were letting him hold the baby. I asked if I could hold him and my parents said, "No, Eileen, he's too delicate, you might hurt him." They were all together and I was left out. I just went out of the room and played with my dog. That helped me feel a little better.

Recollection 3.   I remember being at a playground with my mom and my two brothers. My mom kept my hair real short then so she could manage it easier. A little white girl walked by us and said to her mother, "Why are those boys all so dark?" I knew the girl thought we were different or that there was something wrong with us, and I sure didn't like that. And she didn't even know that I was a girl, like she didn't even really look at me. It made me feel ugly and confused about who I was and what was wrong with me. I looked at my mom but she didn't do or say anything, just kept talking to her friends. I didn't do anything either.

Discussion questions.   Before reading the analysis of these three early recollections, think about your answers to the following questions:

- What patterns of emotions, thoughts, and actions appear in Eileen's three recollections?
- What patterns of interaction appear in the three recollections?
- What shared themes emerge in the three recollections?
- What hunches do you have about what these memories tell us about Eileen?

Analysis. In all three recollections, Eileen feels sad, lonely, and excluded. People around her are talking and interacting but she remains passive, no matter how badly she feels. She seems to long for approval, nurturance, and involvement with others. However, she doesn't have effective ways of helping herself or of asking others for help.

These patterns are reflected in Eileen's adolescence as well as in her adulthood. As a young adolescent, she did not know how to cope directly with the difficulties in her family or how to make good choices for herself. Consequently, she turned to alcohol and destructive relationships in order to have some sense of belonging and importance. As an adult, she continues to feel that she wants more out of her life but, once again, she feels helpless in light of her husband's demands and the needs of her son.

As you can see, earliest recollections provide clinicians a rich tool for gaining understanding of people's backgrounds. Most clients find the process of exploring early memories to be an interesting and rewarding one and have little difficulty providing useful memories. Of course, clinicians need to exercise caution in working with people who may have had very painful or traumatic memories. The exercises later in this chapter offer you an opportunity to gain some experience in working with earliest recollections.

GENOGRAMS

Murray Bowen (1974), one of the leading theoreticians and practitioners of family therapy until his death, deserves most of the credit for establishing the genogram as an important tool for clinicians. Bowen focused his work on family therapy and believed that patterns in a current family or individual stem from patterns in those people's families of origin and even from patterns in their grandparents' families. He believed that behaviors, personality traits, and family roles and relationships are passed on from one generation to another via a process called intergenerational or transgenerational transmission. People learn from their families about how they are supposed to feel, think, and act; what relationships are like; what are appropriate and acceptable male and female gender roles; and how to parent. The genogram is a tool that is designed to help clinicians gather information on a person's family background and identify important family patterns and messages (Kaslow, 1995). This can be used with individuals, couples, or families and is helpful to highlight not only family patterns but also career patterns.

Based on information provided by the client, the clinician constructs a genogram on a large sheet of paper. Usually, the genogram includes the current person or family, their families of origin, and their grandparents' families, reflecting three generations of family patterns. The symbols in figure 2-1 are used to describe family membership, structure, and interactions (McGoldrick & Gerson, 1988).

Once the family members and structure of the family have been mapped on the genogram, the clinician and client can fill out the genogram with descriptive information on both the families and the people who belong to the families. There is no one right way to elaborate on a genogram. A simple approach is to list years of birth and death as

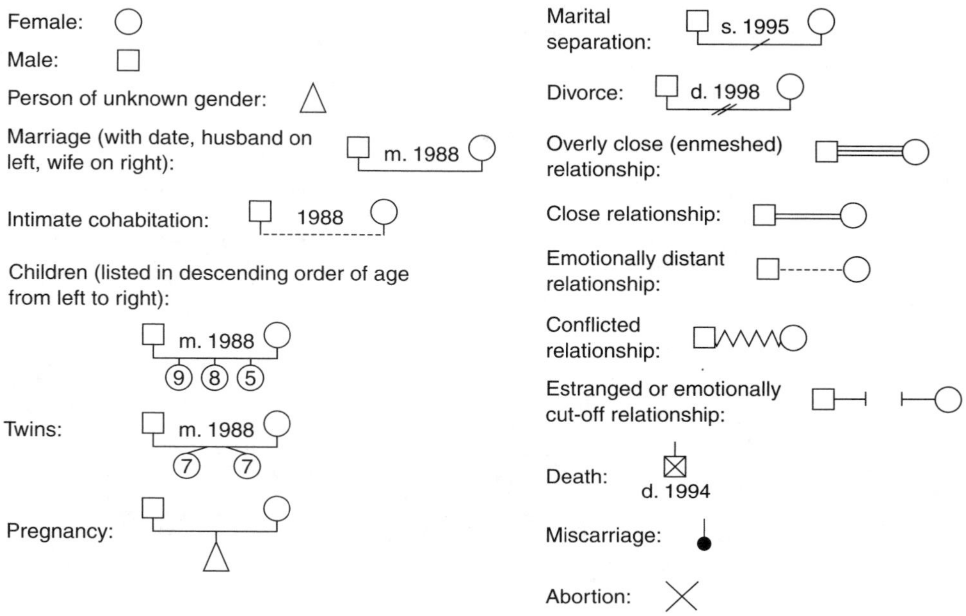

Female: ◯

Male: ☐

Person of unknown gender: △

Marriage (with date, husband on left, wife on right): ☐— m. 1988 ◯

Intimate cohabitation: ☐ 1988 ◯

Children (listed in descending order of age from left to right): ☐ m. 1988 ◯ ⑨ ⑧ ⑤

Twins: ☐ m. 1988 ◯ ⑦ ⑦

Pregnancy: ☐ ◯ △

Marital separation: ☐ s. 1995 ◯

Divorce: ☐ d. 1998 ◯

Overly close (enmeshed) relationship: ☐══◯

Close relationship: ☐═◯

Emotionally distant relationship: ☐----◯

Conflicted relationship: ☐⋁⋁⋁◯

Estranged or emotionally cut-off relationship: ☐—| |—◯

Death: ☒ d. 1994

Miscarriage: ●

Abortion: ✕

FIGURE 2-1 Genogram symbols

well as occupations for each person, along with three adjectives for each one. Mottoes can be developed to reflect parental or family messages. In addition, clinicians can ask questions to clarify family dynamics. Examples of such questions include:

- Who do you think you are most like?
- Did any of these people have problems with drugs or alcohol? Depression or other emotional difficulties?
- How were the children disciplined in this family?
- What differences, if any, were there between the roles of men and women in this family?
- What were the religious, cultural, and spiritual beliefs and practices in each of these families?
- Who was closest to whom in each of these families?
- What conflicts or estrangements were present in these families?
- What were the expectations for the children in each of these families?
- How did the family make decisions?

Clinicians can be creative when they ask questions about the genogram, tailoring the questions to the client or to a particular issue or pattern.

Figure 2-2 presents a three-generational genogram of Eileen Carter's family. Review the genogram, looking for patterns that might help you better understand Eileen and her background. Then compare your thoughts with the analysis following the genogram.

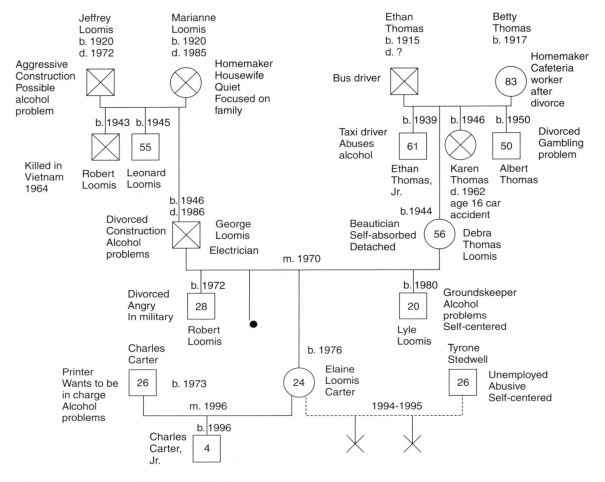

FIGURE 2-2   Genogram of Eileen Carter's family

Analysis of Eileen's Genogram

Several family patterns emerge from this genogram that seem relevant to understanding Eileen's development and her current situation and difficulties. These include:

- Harmful use of alcohol
- Problems with impulse control (aggressiveness, gambling, use of alcohol)
- Relatively low expectations for the children
- An imbalance in gender roles, with men apparently having more power and economic success than women
- Women predominantly in maternal and nurturing roles
- No involvement in higher education
- Relationship difficulties, reflected in divorces and other behaviors
- Losses through early deaths and divorces

From this genogram and analysis, you can see some of the connections between Eileen's family background and both her past and her current concerns. These include the following:

- Eileen, like others in her family, has difficulty problem solving and she used substances, at least temporarily, as a solution.
- Along with others in her family, Eileen has had difficulty with impulse control.
- Eileen's family expected little of her, except to avoid causing trouble and not present a burden to her family. This message may have contributed to Eileen's doubts about her ability to succeed in college and in her roles of wife and mother.
- The lack of positive female role models, the apparent dominance of the men in the families, and the lack of family members' involvement in higher education probably also contributed to the difficulty Eileen is having now in believing she has the right to continue her college education.
- Because relationship problems are apparently common in her family, Eileen may not have any models of good relationships. This may make it particularly difficult for Eileen to successfully balance her own needs and those of her husband and son.
- Losses are prevalent in this family and, of course, Eileen lost her father when she was still a child. Now that she has her own family, the specter of those losses may contribute to her fear that if she does not please her husband or be an exceptional mother, she, too, may experience the loss of her family.

THE LIFELINE OR LIFE CHRONOLOGY

The lifeline or life chronology is another tool available to clinicians seeking useful ways to gather background information. The lifeline or chronology is intended to provide a clear and concise overview of a person's history, facilitating identification of high points, disappointments, milestones, hopes, and patterns. This can be done as a list or as a graph. A list is the simplest way to compile this information. After one or two sessions of counseling, the clinician might ask the client to complete a form such as the one that follows:

Directions.   The purpose of this form is to gather important information about your life so far and your hopes for the future. For each group of ages listed below, provide a description of your life during those years, including the following information:

- Primary activities (e.g., attending elementary school, caring for my family)
- Highlights
- Disappointments
- Any other milestones or important information

For ages older than your current age, indicate what you hope will be your primary activities and highlights during those years.

1. Birth–age 4
2. Ages 5–10

3. Ages 11–18
4. Ages 19–24
5. Ages 25–34
6. Ages 35–44
7. Ages 45–54
8. Ages 55–65
9. Ages 66–74
10. Ages 75 and beyond

Additional information can also be incorporated into the chronology. This might include the person's assessment of his or her negotiation of each group of years, a positive and a negative word associated with each group of years, and an identification of the one most rewarding and one most disappointing point in the person's life. As with the genogram, clinicians can be creative and adapt the exercise to the particular client.

If client and clinician believe that a graphic representation of the person's life is preferable to a list, the chronological life history outlined previously can serve as the basis for developing a lifeline, using peaks and valleys to reflect the high and low points in a person's life. A solid line can reflect the person's life up to the present and a dotted line can reflect expectations for future years. Events that are associated with each peak or valley on the lifeline should be written down to provide clarity.

Eileen's Life Chronology

Eileen prepared the following chronology of her life:

1. Birth–age 5
   - Primary activities—Just being a kid, following my older brother around.
   - Highlights—My younger brother was born, I started kindergarten, and I got my first puppy.
   - Disappointments—Not much attention for me with two noisy brothers.
   - Any other milestones or important information—My mother had an operation. I was scared.
2. Ages 5–10
   - Primary activities—attending elementary school, playing with my pets.
   - Highlights—I did well in school and won a good citizenship award.
   - Disappointments—My father died when I was 10.
   - Any other milestones or important information—I remember wishing for a sister so I would have somebody to play with and talk to.
3. Ages 11–18
   - Primary activities—Attended school and then dropped out and went to work in a bar, serving drinks and dancing.
   - Highlights—I thought having my first boyfriend was a highlight then but it sure didn't turn out that way.
   - Disappointments—My schoolwork went downhill fast, my mom was always out running around, didn't have much time for us. That was also when I moved in with Tyrone and had the abortions.

- Any other milestones or important information—Started using drugs and alcohol; I felt so awful about my life but I didn't know how to change it.
4. Ages 19–24
   - Primary activities—Quite a change over these years. Still working in bars at 19 but then met Charles, got married, had my son, raising my son, starting college.
   - Highlights—My son and college and finally feeling like I have some hope.
   - Disappointments—My marriage hasn't turned out the way I thought it would.
   - Any other milestones or important information—Improving my relationship with my mother and brothers.

Future years
5. Ages 25–34
   - Primary activities—Of course, being a mother. I hope I'll still be married and going to college.
   - Highlights—Seeing Junior grow up. Maybe finishing some courses, maybe even getting an A.A. degree. I guess I might have another child if Charles and I stay together.
   - Disappointments—I'm worried that my marriage might not make it or that I might not be able to continue school.
6. Ages 35–44
   - Primary activities—Being a parent always comes first. I'll probably return to work, hopefully in a decent job, maybe sales or something helping people. I'd also love to work with a vet or a dog breeder.
   - Highlights—I guess by now Junior would be graduating from high school. That would really make me proud. If I have other children, who knows what other wonderful experiences I might have.
   - Disappointments—My mom might not be doing so well by this time, maybe sick or need my help in some other way. I sure hate to think about losing her now that I've just begun to find her again.
7. Ages 45–54
   - Primary activities—The kids will be grown up by now. I'll probably still be working, maybe still married. I'd like to be breeding dogs myself.
   - Highlights—Junior will probably be married. I could even be a grandmother. Maybe Junior will even graduate from college. I'd like to travel, go to Africa and South America.
   - Disappointments—I don't suppose I'll like being middle aged much, but nothing could be as bad as being a teenager. I don't know if my mom will still be around.
8. Ages 55–65
   - Primary activities—I'd like to see myself with my kids and grandkids, still married, still working, maybe even still taking courses.
   - Highlights—Knowing that I made it, that I stayed on track and really reached my goals.
   - Disappointments—The marriage keeps coming up as the big unknown. I don't want to be alone like my mother.

9. Ages 66–74
   • Primary activities—I'm sure I'll be retired by now, maybe doing volunteer work with the Humane Society or an animal rights organization, maybe helping young women who can't get their lives on track.
   • Highlights—You know, I could even be a great-grandmother by this time, one good thing about having Junior when I was young. I hope I'll still be healthy and really able to get involved in the community, have enough money to be comfortable.
   • Disappointments—Losing people I love, my mom, aunts and uncles, and who knows who else.
10. Ages 75 and beyond
   • Primary activities—I just can't imagine that time in my life. My dad died when he was so young. I might be widowed, or that might have even happened earlier. I don't even think I'll be around this long.

Analysis of a Life Chronology

Once a life chronology has been completed, analyzing the chronology with the client can make the experience a powerful learning opportunity for the client. The following questions are some of those that might be explored when analyzing a life chronology. The Learning Opportunities section that follows will afford you an opportunity to analyze Eileen Carter's life chronology.

• What patterns did you notice?
• What sorts of highlights are repeated throughout the life history?
• What worries and disappointments keep reappearing?
• What strengths and resources does the client seem to have?
• How could you use this information to plan your counseling and establish goals with this client?

LEARNING OPPORTUNITIES

Throughout this book, you will be given a variety of learning opportunities that will help you develop the skills presented. This section will include written exercises, discussion questions, practice group exercises, Assessment of Progress Forms, and personal journal questions.

Keep in mind that you are not expected to complete all of the learning opportunities presented throughout this book. Rather, you or your professors or supervisors should select those exercises that seem most likely to enhance your professional learning and development, help you reach your goals, and be meaningful to you.

The following skills, addressed in the exercises in this section, have been presented in chapter 2:

General Technical Skills
• using questions effectively
• conducting an intake interview

Specific Technical Skills
- earliest recollections
- the genogram
- the lifeline

Written Exercises

1. Determine whether the following questions are open or closed questions:
   a. When will you be home for dinner?
   b. How did you do on your exam?
   c. What was your relationship like with your sister?
   d. Could you tell me some more about that relationship?
   e. Have you been in counseling before?
2. Read the following client statements and rate the helpfulness of each of the possible clinician responses according to the scale, ranging from extremely helpful to extremely harmful, presented on page 34:
   a. I asked my daughter whether she minded if I moved next door to her and she said she did. I must have been a terrible mother to her.
      - Where does your daughter live?
      - How did you reach that conclusion?
      - What feelings did you have after your conversation with your daughter?
      - Why did you want to move close to her?
      - Don't you think that parents should give their adult children some space?
   b. My husband and I really had a wonderful day together for a change.
      - What is your time together usually like?
      - What happened to make that day so special?
      - What did you do to make that day so special?
      - Who took care of the children?
      - How did you spend the day?
   c. My sister still hasn't sent me the money she owes me.
      - How does this affect your feelings about your sister?
      - What impact will this have on your budget?
      - Have you thought about taking her to small claims court?
      - How much money does she owe you?
      - What thoughts have you had about how you will handle this?
3. What characterized the helpful responses?
4. What characterized the harmful responses?
5. Write a helpful question in reply to the following client statements:
   a. My mother says that my dog is really sick and it's time to put her down.
   b. How dare my father criticize my marriage! He's been divorced three times.
   c. No matter how hard I try, I just can't get my work done on schedule.
6. Review your responses to item 5. For each response, indicate what your purpose or intention was in the question you formulated.
7. Write an example of a scaling question that you might use with one of the clients in item 5.

8. Write an example of an empowering question that you might use with one of the clients in item 5.

Written or Discussion Questions

Refer to the life chronology of Eileen Carter on pages 40–45 and respond to the following questions, either in writing or via discussion:

1. What patterns did you notice in Eileen's life chronology?
2. What categories of highlights are repeated throughout her life history?
3. What sorts of worries and disappointments keep reappearing?
4. What strengths and resources does Eileen seem to have?
5. How could you use this information to plan your counseling with Eileen and establish goals with her?

Discussion Questions

1. Sometimes beginning clinicians feel intrusive when they ask clients personal questions. Have you felt that way? What can you do to maximize the likelihood that you will ask helpful questions that are not intrusive?
2. The miracle question has become a popular tool for clinicians. How do you explain the popularity of this question? What risks are inherent in using the miracle question? How can you address those risks?
3. An intake interview is typically conducted in your first session or two with a client. What do you see as the most important goals of that interview?
4. Genograms can be helpful in eliciting information and identifying patterns. How would you integrate genograms into the counseling process? With what sorts of clients or problems do genograms seem especially likely to be helpful?
5. Read these three early recollections, presented by Joe, a 43-year-old man. Then answer the questions that follow.
   - I came from a really big family. I remember that when the weather started to get cold, we would all get out our winter clothes and then pass them down to the next youngest child who was the same gender as we were. I was the second youngest of 11 and by the time I got the clothes, they were really in bad shape.
   - I remember once I fell down some steps and cut myself badly. I was bleeding a lot. My older brother went to help me and he got blood all over himself. When my mother came out to see what all the crying was about, she saw blood all over my brother and thought he was the one who had been hurt. She took him inside to get him cleaned up and didn't even notice that I was the one who had been hurt.
   - My dad worked in the mines. One day there was an accident and we didn't know if he was dead or alive. I remember how scared I was. But then he came home and he was all right. My mom was so happy, she gave us all ice cream. That was great until the dog knocked mine out of my hand.

   Questions:
   a. What patterns of emotions, thoughts, and actions appear in the three recollections?

      b. What patterns of interaction appear in the three recollections?

      c. What themes emerge in the three recollections?

      d. What hunches do you have about what these memories tell us about Joe?

6. If you have not yet done the practice group exercises associated with this chapter, discuss your thoughts and feelings about that upcoming experience. How can you allay any apprehensions you might have about that process and prepare yourself to learn from the experience?

7. If you have already done the practice group exercises associated with this chapter, discuss your reactions to that experience. What was the most beneficial aspect of that experience for you? What was the most challenging or uncomfortable aspect of that experience? How can you make future practice group exercises even more rewarding to you?

Practice Groups Exercise—Questions and Intake Interviews

Divide into your practice groups, as described on pages 18-19. You have probably already had one meeting with your practice groups or have discussed the groups in class and so are familiar with the structure and process of the practice group exercises. If you need a review, refer to the section beginning on page 17. The practice group exercise presented here will help you gain experience in the two essential technical skills described in this chapter: asking effective questions and using questions to conduct an intake interview.

    Each member of the group should have a tape recorder and a blank tape available to facilitate learning from this exercise. Be sure that you tape yourself in the clinician role as well as the feedback you receive on your role play. If the group agrees, I encourage you to tape all of the role plays and feedback sessions. We can learn a great deal from others' experiences as well as from our own. If possible, allow at least 2 hours for this exercise.

Role-play Exercise.   The primary goal of this role play is for you to conduct a brief intake interview with your partner, making effective use of questions. As discussed earlier in this chapter, that means that you will rely primarily on open questions, (particularly those beginning with what and how), and on implied questions to promote dialogue and information gathering. You should be sure to integrate your questions with other interventions so that your interview builds rapport, puts the client at ease, and sounds like a productive conversation rather than an interrogation. Before beginning this role play, you might want to review the categories of information usually covered in intake interviews. These can be found on page 40.

Time Schedule and Format

• Allow 15–20 minutes for each role played intake interview. During that time, one person becomes the clinician, one becomes the client, and the other one or two group members become observers and timekeepers.

• As discussed in chapter 1, when you are in the client role, you will decide whether to be yourself and present accurate information about yourself and your life. Of course, you always have the right not to disclose any particular piece of information that you do not want to share with your group. If you would prefer not to be yourself in this or any other exercise in this book, you can assume the role of someone you know well, being sure to disguise the identity of that person, or you can assume the role of a hypothetical person.

• Following the role play, take about 10–15 minutes to provide feedback to the person in the clinician role. Follow the format presented on page 20. Be sure to begin the feedback process with the person in the clinician role giving himself or herself feedback, focus on strengths first, and offer concrete suggestions for improvement. This should be a positive learning experience, not an experience that makes people feel criticized or judged. Feedback should focus on the areas listed in the following Assessment of Progress Form. Complete the Assessment of Progress Form that follows, reflecting on the feedback you received.

• Receiving feedback can be a difficult experience, especially the first time. Try to listen with an open mind to the feedback you are receiving and ask questions if the information is confusing or unclear. Be sure to play an active role in giving feedback when you are in the client or observer role; those roles, too, can be excellent opportunities for learning.

• After the first round of role-played intake interview and feedback, rotate roles. Continue this process until all group members have had the opportunity to be in clinician, client, and observer roles.

Assessment of Progress Form 2

1. Use of questions
   a. Balance of open and closed questions

   b. Nature of questions (implicit; beginning with how, what, why, or another word)

   c. Integration of questions and other interventions

   d. Helpfulness of questions

2. Intake interview
   a. Identification and exploration of presenting concerns

   b. Ability to elicit relevant information on background, history, context

   c. Ability to develop initial rapport

   d. Strengths of intake interview

   e. Omissions or areas needing improvement

3. Summary of feedback

4. Two or three goals that will help you improve your clinical skills

---

Personal Journal Questions

As discussed in the previous chapter, the personal journal questions are designed to promote your self-awareness and personal and professional learning and development. Your responses to these questions should be written in a journal when you have some quiet time and can give thought to your answers to these questions.

1. Write down three of your own earliest recollections. Then process and analyze them according to the guidelines presented on page 47.
2. Prepare a three or four generation genogram of your own family. Then analyze this genogram, looking for patterns such as those presented on page 49.
3. Develop your own life chronology, using the age categories listed on pages 51-52. Then analyze this chronology according to the guidelines presented on page 54.
4. Listen to the tape recording of the role-played intake interview that you conducted. Respond to the following questions about your role play:
   • What was your overall reaction when you heard yourself in the role of clinician?
   • Identify the anxieties and rewards you experienced in that role.
   • On the scale presented on page 34, how would you rate the overall helpfulness of the interview you conducted?
   • List one or two interventions you made that seemed particularly effective.
   • List one or two interventions you made that you think needed improvement. How would you have modified these interventions?
   • Listen to the opening section of the tape and write down the first five interventions that you made. Identify your purpose in using each of these interventions. For each one, note whether you accomplished your purpose.
   • What is the most important thing you learned from this chapter and its exercises?
   • What one improvement will you try to make in your role plays next time?

SUMMARY

This chapter focused on technical skills that are especially useful in eliciting background information, although these skills can be used for many other clinical purposes. Particular emphasis was placed on asking effective questions. The skill of effective questioning was then applied to the process of conducting an intake interview that is both informative and conducive to developing a positive therapeutic alliance. Attention also was paid to empowering questions, scaling questions, the miracle question, and the use of earliest recollections, genograms, and lifelines or chronologies as tools to provide background information and promote the therapeutic process.

The next chapter will focus on technical skills designed to help people express, identify, and make desired changes in their emotions. Particular emphasis will be placed on attending skills and reflections of feeling.

CHAPTER 3

Using Technical Skills to Elicit, Attend to, Reflect on, Assess, and Change Emotions

IMPORTANCE OF EMOTIONS

"I'm feeling depressed." "I'm not happy with my life." "I'm feeling lonely and scared." "I can't control my anger." Statements such as these reflect the most common reasons why people seek counseling or psychotherapy: they are unhappy and are experiencing painful, undesirable, and unhelpful emotions. Although treatment may eventually focus on exploration of background or on modification of thoughts or actions (the other three elements in the BETA format), identifying, understanding, reflecting, and addressing people's emotions are essential ingredients in almost all treatment systems.

Definition of Emotions or Feelings

The word *emotions* probably does not need to be defined for most of us. We are constantly experiencing emotions or feelings. Pause for a moment to identify the feelings you have right now. You might be interested in this chapter, eager to learn more, hungry for lunch, bored by your reading, or experiencing lingering joy or sadness from experiences unrelated to this chapter.

Feelings or emotions (terms that will be used interchangeably in this book) are affective states that are accompanied by physiological changes such as tension, warmth, shortness of breath, and perspiration. Among the most basic and frequently experienced feelings are fear, joy, sadness, disgust, and anger. However, we can experience hundreds of different emotions and thousands of subtle variations on those emotions.

Although we have a common language of emotions, that language fails to capture those subtle differences. For example, you and I might both love our spouse or partner but, if we talked at length about those feelings, the love you experience for your partner is certainly different from the love that I have for my partner. In addition, we may use the same word to describe very different feelings that we have. Our love for our partners is different from our love for our children, which is different from our love for our parents or our closest friends or our pet or our new house. Clearly, understanding and communicating empathy for another person's emotions is a challenging task. Nevertheless, this process is also one of the most important and powerful clinical skills.

Benefits of Attending to and Understanding Emotions

Paying attention to people's emotions can contribute to the treatment process in the following ways:

- *Allow emotional release*—Many people who seek treatment have kept their feelings locked up inside themselves. The process of simply verbalizing those feelings can bring a great sense of emotional release and relief. Paulson, Truscott, and Stuart (1999) found this discharge of emotions to be one of the most helpful experiences in counseling.
- *Foster self-acceptance*—Expressing one's emotions to another person who is attentive and accepting can be reassuring. That process can help people realize that their feelings are normal and understandable and that others are not horrified by or disapproving of their feelings. This can, in turn, help people to be more accepting of themselves.
- *Promote the therapeutic alliance*—Sharing feelings with another person who has empathy for those feelings usually leads to an increased sense of trust, closeness, and caring. Clients who believe that their clinicians hear and understand them are more likely to be optimistic about the success of the treatment process and to participate more fully in that process. Similarly, once clinicians have heard clients express deep and personal feelings, those clinicians almost inevitably have more caring for and motivation to help those people. This helps clinicians to join with their clients and build rapport.
- *Establish direction*—Even experienced clinicians sometimes feel confused by a client and unsure of the most helpful direction or intervention. Attending to and reflecting people's feelings can be the best strategy when a clinician feels stuck. Following the client's lead and tracking feelings, when all else fails, usually brings clarity to the conversation and eventually points to a productive direction for treatment.
- *Relieve symptoms*—The expression of emotions can be a healing process. Sharing painful feelings with another person can reduce the discomfort associated with those feelings; help people label, sort out, and understand their feelings; and move toward changing undesirable feelings into emotions that are more rewarding and helpful.

- *Move treatment forward*—Emotions are often the most accessible route to obtaining a full picture of clients and their strengths and difficulties. Expression and exploration of feelings usually leads easily into exploration of background, thoughts, and actions and paves the way for clinicians to formulate specific treatment goals and interventions.

Guidelines for Understanding and Addressing Emotions

The following guidelines can help you to successfully understand and address people's emotions:

- Focus on present emotions, especially those that are evident in the session. This is usually more powerful and productive than focusing on past and distant emotions.
- Emotions can be expressed both verbally and nonverbally. Be sure to pay attention to both modes of communication. Especially important in treatment are discrepancies between verbal and nonverbal emotions.
- Do not judge, dismiss, or disparage feelings. Clients need to access and verbalize their feelings, whatever they might be. Clinicians can then help clients determine whether their emotions are helping or hurting them and decide whether they want to work on changing some of their emotions. The client makes these choices with the help of the clinician; they are not made by the clinician.

SKILLS TO BE LEARNED IN THIS CHAPTER

Six basic technical skills that help clinicians identify, understand, and address clients' emotions will be presented in this chapter:

1. effective attending
2. tracking
3. encouragers (accents, restatements, paraphrases)
4. accurate empathy and reflections of feeling
5. summarization
6. helpful use of nonverbal communication

In addition, the following specific skills will be reviewed, as they are used to elicit, contain, and change emotions:

- analysis of emotions
- focusing
- using the body as a vehicle of communication
- introducing new perspectives
- reassurance and support
- distraction and thought stopping
- using the imagination
- use of language

- use of logic
- use of rational emotive imagery

GOALS OF CHAPTER

As a result of reading this chapter and completing the exercises at the end of the chapter, you can expect to be able to do the following:

1. Understand the importance of emotions in the treatment process.
2. Understand the importance of attending and following in treatment.
3. Become familiar with the types of verbal encouragers.
4. Develop your ability to accurately identify emotions and communicate empathy.
5. Learn to address and use nonverbal communication and silence.
6. Develop specific skills, including the use of the body as a vehicle of communication, focusing, and imagery, designed to elicit and address emotions in treatment.

EFFECTIVE ATTENDING

Many people enter the helping professions because they view themselves as good listeners. They report that other people confide in them easily, and they seem to have a natural gift for communicating effectively with others. You may sense this about yourself. However, when I ask students what makes them good listeners, they usually have difficulty figuring out exactly what they do that makes them good listeners.

Listening involves more than just hearing words. The counseling literature typically speaks of *attending* rather than listening to communicate the complex task of hearing and understanding what people say and conveying that understanding back to them. Attending is an art that can be learned. Most of the skills presented in this chapter will help you to master effective attending and become a better listener.

Good listeners have the following characteristics:

- They are fully present in the moment and are not distracted or preoccupied.
- They can put their own needs aside temporarily and focus entirely on another person.
- They communicate clearly and concisely.
- They listen intently, not only for the overt content of what is said but also for the underlying messages and meaning.
- They track or follow a person's line of thought and expression of emotions without introducing distracting digressions.
- They convey that they are listening through both verbal and nonverbal means.
- They respond in ways that encourage people to self-disclose and to understand themselves more fully and deeply.

Effective attending is not the same as having a friendly conversation, although effective listening can enhance those conversations as well as client-clinician exchanges. Look at the following examples:

Example 1

Helena: I have surgery scheduled for tomorrow and I'm pretty anxious about it.

Diana: I had surgery last year and I was pretty anxious about it, too, but everything worked out fine. You'll be fine, too. I'm hungry. Are you ready for lunch?

Helena: Yes, I guess so.

This dialogue fails to follow many of the guidelines for attending presented previously. Diana focuses only on the overt message, she allows her own needs to preempt those of her friend, she does not encourage further discussion of Helena's apprehension, and she is distracted by her own interest in having lunch. Compare example 1 with the following example:

Example 2

Helena: I have surgery scheduled for tomorrow and I'm pretty anxious about it.

Sandra: What is making you feel anxious?

Helena: Well, it's supposed to be a minor procedure, but my uncle had a minor operation last year and he wound up with an infection and spent two weeks in the hospital.

Sandra: So you're worried that something will go wrong for you, too?

Helena: Yes, but I know my doctors are very good and so probably everything will be fine.

Sandra: It must help to have confidence in your doctors.

Both examples reflect conversations between friends. However, in example 2, Sandra demonstrates many of the behaviors associated with effective listening. She focuses on Helena and encourages Helena to talk further about her concerns. Sandra concisely rephrases what Helena has said, giving Helena an opportunity to reflect on her own words. In addition, Sandra's own needs do not intrude on the dialogue.

Review the additional examples that follow. For each statement, three alternative responses are given. Consider which of the alternative responses best satisfies the criteria for effective attending:

Example 3

Amanda: I was really relieved that I got a C in math.

Response 1: But you're smart. You could do better than that.

Response 2: Sounds like you were pretty worried about your grade in math.

Response 3: Great!

In example 3, only the second response is consistent with principles of effective attending. In that response, the speaker is listening for underlying messages and is encouraging Amanda to talk further about her math grade. Although both responses 1 and 3 are positive and encouraging, they are not in tune with Amanda's feelings of anxiety and relief and might lead her to feel dismissed or devalued.

Example 4

Vanessa: I'm really worried about my marriage. My husband didn't come home until 2 A.M. last night.
Response 1:   Where was he?
Response 2:   I hope you gave him a piece of your mind.
Response 3:   That must have really upset you.

In example 4, the third response is an example of effective listening. It is concise, it keeps the focus on Vanessa, is in tune with Vanessa's feelings, and encourages further conversation. Both responses 1 and 2 shift the focus away from Vanessa and onto her husband. Respondent 1's curiosity and respondent 2's anger intrude on the dialogue.

Example 5

Paul: I'm angry that I didn't get a bonus this year. I really need the money for my kids.
Response 1:   Sounds like you're upset and worried about finances.
Response 2:   I get some great things for my kids at the Salvation Army Thrift Shops. They don't charge very much.
Response 3:   How come you didn't get a bonus?

The first response to example 5 reflects effective attending. That respondent acknowledges Paul's feelings and encourages him to explore his feelings further. Responses 2 and 3, on the other hand, shift the focus away from what is troubling Paul.

Probably all of the responses in these examples would be acceptable in a conversation between two friends, although some seem better than others. However, only those responses that reflect effective listening should be part of counseling or psychotherapy. The therapeutic relationship is distinct from a friendship, not only in terms of its location but, more importantly, in terms of the goals and focus of the treatment process. Every comment or intervention from the clinician should have the purpose of helping clients meet their treatment goals.

TRACKING

One of the most important ways to communicate listening and attentiveness to clients is by tracking what they are saying. Tracking involves the use of a group of effective listening skills. These include understanding both a person's thoughts and feelings and communicating that understanding to the person. The clinician is listening intently and accurately to the client and is using sound counseling skills to demonstrate that. The clinician's interventions are a direct outgrowth of the client's previous statements. The clinician usually is not redirecting or leading the interview but rather is letting the client set the direction and take charge of the session. At the same time, clinicians contribute to the direction or focus of the session through the nature and wording of their interventions, ensuring that the session is productive.

In tracking, clinicians use techniques such as questions (presented in the previous chapter), encouragers, and reflections of feeling (presented in this chapter) to let clients know that they comprehend what the clients are saying. This process communicates interest and caring and is important in promoting clients' self-expression and self-awareness. It lets clients take the lead in the treatment process, which can be empowering and encouraging. Tracking is generally a safe intervention; it affords clinicians the opportunity to gather information, deepen their understanding of their clients, build a therapeutic alliance and become clear on ways to help their clients before using more active interventions such as challenging the client or providing suggestions. The exercises at the end of this chapter provide you the opportunity to practice your tracking skills.

Notice the tracking demonstrated in the following example. The clinician stays with the client, following the client's lead, while demonstrating the principles of effective listening. By the end of this brief excerpt, Olga is expressing some strong emotions but is also looking at ways to solve the problem she has presented.

Example of Effective Tracking and Attending

Olga: My son really worries me. He'll do fine for awhile and then he'll explode.

Clinician: That must make you feel very uneasy, always waiting for the next outburst.

Olga: That's true. It makes it hard for me to enjoy the good times with him because I feel like I always have to be on guard. I feel like I'm missing all the best parts of our relationship and soon he'll be gone and it will be too late.

Clinician: I hear a real sense of loss.

Olga: Yes, I really wanted to enjoy his last year in high school but I just can't get past this fear that I have.

Clinician: How have you tried to get past the fear?

Olga: I just try to forget about the problem.

Clinician: How has that worked for you?

Olga: Not very well. His outbursts are still so fresh in my mind; I can't forgive him for the damage he's done to our family.

Through tracking and attending, the clinician has helped Olga realize that she cannot push aside her concerns about her son's behavior and that her usual method of coping with his outbursts has not been effective. Now, Olga is probably ready to collaborate with the clinician in developing new and more successful ways of addressing this issue.

Tracking, like the other effective attending skills presented in this chapter, can help you in your personal and business interactions as well as in your clinical work. For the rest of the day today, try to make a conscious effort to use effective listening and tracking skills in your everyday conversations. Note the responses you receive. You might find that people are more open than usual and that your conversations flow more smoothly. This technique can work particularly well in tense and conflicted situations.

VERBAL ENCOURAGERS

Verbal encouragers, also known as minimal encouragers, are one of the most powerful interventions available to clinicians. These basic interventions help people feel heard and understood. Once people know that they have been heard and understood, they are likely to move forward rather than continue to go over the same ground. Verbal encouragers also help people hear themselves and talk about themselves with others. Verbal encouragers promote dialogue, clarification, self-awareness, and exploration. They keep the focus of the session on the client, while the clinician keeps a low profile. They also contribute to the development of a collaborative therapeutic alliance.

Verbal encouragers are typically brief and concise. They underscore an important word or phrase that the client has said and, usually can narrow the focus of the session. Because verbal encouragers are so brief and spare, they appear to be easy to master. However, their simplicity is deceptive; making helpful use of verbal encouragers is a skill that needs to be practiced and developed over time.

The Importance of Purpose

Sound listening and clarity of purpose are the keys to effective use of verbal encouragers. Sound listening and clarity of purpose have been discussed earlier, but, because of their importance, they will be addressed and reviewed many times in this book. When using verbal encouragers, follow the principles of effective listening presented earlier in this chapter on page 63.

In addition, have a clear purpose in mind. That purpose should be reflected by the nature and timing of the encourager you use. For example, look at the following examples. Notice how purpose is reflected in the clinician's responses to Reuben and in the subsequent direction of the discussion.

Examples Illustrating Purpose

Reuben: I'm so overwhelmed by my job that I have no time left for my family or even for myself.

Purpose 1: Explore Reuben's feeling of being overwhelmed.
Clinician: Overwhelmed?
Reuben: Yes, I feel like I can never meet my supervisor's expectations, no matter how hard I try, and I'm afraid I'll lose my job.

Purpose 2: Focus Reuben's attention on his own needs.
Clinician: Even for yourself?
Reuben: Yes, I live on fast food, never get to the gym, and haven't had a chance to relax and read a book in months.

Purpose 3: Explore Reuben's interactions with his family.
Clinician: No time for your family?
Reuben: Yes, my wife and I never have time alone together, and I usually don't even get home until my kids are in bed.

All three of the clinician's verbal encouragers reflect effective attending by keeping the focus on Reuben and prompting him to clarify his statement. However, each one takes the session in a different direction. Even through single words or brief phrases, clinicians can exert considerable influence over the direction of a session. Because of this, you should be deliberate in your use of all your interventions, have a clear and helpful purpose in mind, and be well grounded in the treatment approaches you are using with each client.

Types of Verbal Encouragers

The following four types of verbal encouragers are presented here:

- accents
- restatements
- paraphrases
- summarization

Accents/Restatements

Accents or restatements serve the purpose of underscoring or highlighting a particular aspect of what a client has said. In addition, they encourage further client self-disclosure, particularly about the highlighted topic, and indicate that the clinician is interested and attentive.

Accents or restatements are typically very brief, just a word or phrase repeating part of what the client has said. Sometimes accents are just a supportive murmur of "umm-hmm" accompanied by nonverbal encouragers (discussed later in this chapter). The three interventions in the dialogue between the clinician and Reuben on the previous page are all examples of accents or restatements.

Accents are the simplest of the verbal encouragers. They are not intended to add depth or meaning to what the client has said. Nor are they intended to identify themes or synthesize information like other verbal encouragers discussed later in this chapter. However, the choice of what word or phrase to emphasize and what to ignore can have a powerful impact on the direction of a session. Having a clear purpose in mind when making an intervention helps clinicians determine what accents or restatements are most likely to be productive.

Purpose is reflected by the combination of selective attention and selective inattention to what a client has said. Regardless of what intervention is being used, the clinician's focus will influence the direction and value of the treatment session. That is reflected in the previous dialogue with Reuben. Notice also how, in the following example, the clinician's use of restatement keeps the focus of the session on Petra, the client. This ensures that the session moves in a productive direction and discourages Petra from using the session to complain about others.

Example Illustrating Restatement and Purpose

Petra: I can't believe what just happened. I almost got a ticket because I was parked in a no parking zone. The cop could see I was sitting in the car. Doesn't he have anything better to do than harass me? It really made me mad.

Clinician: Mad?

Petra: Yes, the government seems to be falling apart. I can't get any work done with all this bureaucratic mess around.

Clinician: You're having trouble getting your work done?

Petra: Yes, when I went to law school, I had such high hopes but now I feel like a failure. I just can't accomplish anything worthwhile with all these interferences.

Clinician: You're feeling like a failure?

Although this dialogue became more productive as it went on, you probably became tired of the clinician's use of restatement and accents. Indeed, persistent and repetitive use of any type of intervention can have a negative impact on the treatment process. This is particularly likely when clinicians overuse restatements or accents. Clinicians can sound more like parrots than counselors, and this may lead clients to devalue or ignore the clinicians' input. Sessions may lack energy and fail to hold the interest of both clients and clinicians.

To avoid these pitfalls, clinicians should vary the nature of their interventions. Even if they are relying heavily on encouragers, they can use different types of encouragers, including restatements, paraphrases, and summaries. In addition, interventions sound more natural and spontaneous if clinicians vary the opening of their interventions. For example, consider the following two series of interventions:

Series 1.

Sounds like you were angry with the officer.
Sounds like you are feeling frustrated.
Sounds like you view yourself as a failure.

Series 2.

Sounds like you were angry with the officer.
Could you have been feeling frustrated?
I wonder if you are viewing yourself as a failure.

The first clinician overuses the phrase "sounds like"; as a result, the interventions take on a programmed, almost robotic quality. Although the meaning of the interventions in series 2 is the same as those in the first series, the second clinician varies the beginnings of his sentences and so avoids sounding like he is on automatic pilot.

Paraphrases

The purposes of paraphrases are similar to those of accents and restatements. Paraphrases highlight key words or statements, focus the session, encourage client self-expression, and communicate support, interest, and attentiveness. However, paraphrases also can have the additional purpose of giving clients a new and different perspective on what they have said. This can promote greater self-awareness and give clients an opportunity to reflect on the meaning of their words.

Paraphrases are usually brief, although they are longer than accents and restatements. Generally, they should be limited to one or two sentences and should not be longer than the client's original statement.

In a paraphrase, clinicians are not simply engaging in selective repetition of the client's words. Instead, clinicians use their own words to capture the essence of what the client has said.

To illustrate paraphrases, let's refer to the previous example of Petra. This time the clinician will use paraphrases rather than accents or restatements. Notice how the clinician's use of paraphrase enriches the session and gives Petra more to think about and process than did the earlier interaction, which relied on accents and restatements.

Example of Paraphrase

Petra: I can't believe what just happened. I almost got a ticket because I was parked in a no parking zone. The cop could see I was sitting in the car. Doesn't he have anything better to do than harass me? It really made me mad.

Clinician: You felt that the officer was treating you unfairly.

Petra: Yes, the government seems to be falling apart. I can't get any work done with all this bureaucratic mess around.

Clinician: That must be frustrating to you.

Petra: Yes, when I went to law school, I had such high hopes but now I feel like a failure. I just can't accomplish anything worthwhile with all these interferences.

Clinician: You're sounding pretty hopeless.

Although paraphrases typically add more to a session than do accents and restatements, they also present the clinician with more of a challenge and a risk. What if the clinician misunderstands the client and offers a paraphrase that is not on target? Let's see what happens as the dialogue with Petra continues:

Petra: No, I haven't given up hope yet, but I'm just not sure what else to do to make my efforts meaningful.

Clinician: So you are still hopeful that you can find a way to make your work count. What have you done so far to make that happen?

As you can see, no damage was done by the clinician's inaccurate paraphrase. On the contrary, the clinician's statement offered Petra the opportunity to clarify and expand on her statement and opened up a productive avenue for discussion: finding more successful ways for Petra to make her work meaningful. As long as clinicians remain attentive, continue to track the client's statements, and are open to revising their thinking, a misunderstanding can actually contribute to the session by offering clients the opportunity to think through and clarify their points.

SUMMARIZATION

Summarization can be even more challenging than paraphrasing. In formulating a summary, clinicians synthesize a group of client statements to reflect back to the client the essence of what has been discussed. This can ensure that client and clinician have the same understanding of the dialogue, reinforce learning, and effect a transition or closure. Summarization is most likely to be used when client and clinician have finished discussing a topic or issue or when the session is drawing to a close. However, summarization also can be useful when the session feels fragmented and needs a clearer focus or direction. Like paraphrases, summaries are not intended to be interpretive or analytical but, rather, to provide a clear and concise statement of what may have been a lengthy client/clinician interaction.

The following examples illustrate three common uses of summarization:

Examples of Summarization

- *To establish a focus for the session*—You've talked about quite a few things in the first few minutes of today's session: your dissatisfaction with your job, your recent interview for a new job, your thoughts about returning to graduate school, and your desire to revise your resume. Sounds like you have quite a few concerns related to the direction of your career. Which one of these would you like to focus on first?
- *To bring closure to one issue and effect a transition to another issue*—You seem to be clear that remaining in your present job would not be a good choice for you. Perhaps we could spend some time looking more closely at the other options that you have.
- *To bring closure to a session*—Sounds like you have gained quite a bit of clarity on your career direction today. You've decided to apply to graduate school for the fall and, if you are admitted, to resign from your present job in July. Perhaps next week we can continue our discussion of your choice of graduate schools.

All three of these summaries accomplish two goals: they synthesize all or part of a counseling session, and they move the session forward. In addition, the second and third summaries can reinforce and consolidate gains and decisions. In just a few sentences, these powerful interventions can exert considerable influence on the treatment process. As with paraphrases, however, clinicians should usually check the accuracy of their summaries with the client and be ready to modify the summary if it is not on target. Following a summarization with such questions as, "How do you react to what I said?," "How does that fit with your recollection of what we discussed?," "Any ways in which you want to modify what I said?," "How does that sound to you?," or even "Did I get that right?" are all ways to elicit clients' reactions to summarizations.

COMMUNICATING ACCURATE EMPATHY AND REFLECTING FEELINGS

Like empathy and encouragers, empathy is an essential clinical skill, regardless of the clinician's theoretical orientation. Many definitions of empathy can be found in the literature. Gladstein (1983) described empathy as "responding with the same emotion to another person's emotion" (p. 468). According to Kohut (1984), empathy entails "being attuned to the inner life" of another person (p. 84). Carol Rogers (1959), who perhaps more than anyone else made clinicians aware of the importance of empathy, viewed empathy as a process, not a state. He believed it entailed sensing the private world of another person, feeling and thinking "as if one were the other person" (p. 210).

Barett-Leonard (1981) identified three phases of empathy:

- vicariously experiencing or resonating to the feelings of another person
- expressing accurate empathy to that person
- receiving empathy

For empathy to be meaningful and helpful, all three phases must be on target. The clinician feels deeply connected to and caring toward clients and is in touch with both their verbal and nonverbal expressions of feeling. Further, the clinician communicates that emotional awareness to the clients in such a way that they truly feel heard and understood. This promotes development of a positive therapeutic alliance and creates an atmosphere of safety in the treatment context, enabling clients to take risks and venture into unexplored territory without fear of shame or blame. I have found a strong connection between clinicians' effectiveness in experiencing and communicating empathy and the eventual success of the therapeutic process.

Clinicians sometimes confuse empathy and sympathy. Empathy is feeling *with* a person and has an important role in the treatment process. Sympathy, on the other hand, is feeling sorry *for* a person and rarely enters into the treatment process. Sympathy can lead people to feel like helpless victims, while empathy is designed to empower them. Consider the following examples:

Examples of Empathy and Sympathy

> **Client:** You can't believe how much I had to deal with to get here on time! The baby sitter didn't show up, my car overheated, and then I got stuck in a traffic jam.
> **Empathy:** You have coped with a lot, and yet you got here on time!
> **Sympathy:** I'm so sorry you had to deal with all that.

Reflections of Feeling

Empathy is most often communicated through an intervention called a reflection of feeling. Reflections of feeling or emotion are a type of paraphrase that hones in on a person's emotions. These are powerful interventions because they help people feel heard and understood. They communicate effective listening and caring and contribute to the development of rapport between client and clinician. Simply by naming people's feelings, clinicians help to normalize those feelings and enhance people's efforts to identify, express, and manage their emotions. Reflections of feeling also provide people with another perspective on their emotions. They encourage thought and lead to the development of new options. Reflections of feeling bring a sense of immediacy to the treatment process and can make sessions more meaningful and relevant. Especially powerful are reflections of emotions that are experienced at that very moment in the session.

Dimensions of Emotion

In order to make accurate and helpful reflections of feeling, clinicians must be able not only to identify the emotions that are being expressed but also to identify other important features of clients' emotional experiences. By determining the characteristics of a person's emotional experience and expression, clinicians can understand that person more fully and find more effective ways to help that person recognize, manage, and perhaps change troubling emotions.

The following eight dimensions or characteristics of emotions have been identi-fied (Seligman, 2001, p. 203). Emotions can be:

- emotional, physical, or a combination
- overt, covert, or a combination
- positive, negative, or neutral
- in or out of awareness
- of varying levels of intensity
- appropriate or inappropriate to context and stimulus
- congruent or incongruent
- helpful or harmful

Let's go back to the example of Petra, presented earlier in this chapter, to illustrate the use of these dimensions in deepening understanding of emotions. Petra's initial emo-tion was that of anger at the police officer who threatened to give her a parking ticket. Her emotional reaction can be described as follows:

- Petra experienced her anger in *both emotional and physical* ways (tearfulness, tension in abdomen and shoulders).
- Her anger toward the officer was *overt but was linked to covert emotions,* includ-ing her work-related frustration.
- Her emotion was a *negative* one.
- She was *aware of her anger* but was *not fully aware of her underlying feelings.*
- Her anger was *very intense.*
- Both the nature and the intensity of Petra's anger seemed *inappropriate* and out of proportion to the situation. This is a clue that other, covert emotions proba-bly are present and are even more important to identify than the overt emotions.
- Petra's emotional experience of her *anger and her muscle tension were congruent.* However, her *tearfulness added an incongruent element,* another clue that other emotions were present and needed attention.
- Petra's anger *did not seem helpful* to her.

Analyzing Petra's emotions according to the eight dimensions gives a fuller and richer picture of those emotions. This analysis provides a strong indication that Petra's angry reaction to the police officer is probably misdirected anger stemming from other aspects of her life.

Nature of Emotions

Ivey, Ivey, and Simek-Morgan (1997) identified four basic emotions: sad, mad, glad, and scared. These four basic feelings can provide a starting place for exploration of people's emotions. However, going beyond the basic emotions to an exploration of the subtle, complex, and sometimes conflicting emotions that people typically experience is im-portant in understanding and addressing people's feelings. Clinicians can help clients find the words they need to capture their emotions as fully and accurately as possible. Consider the following examples of reflections of feeling. The feelings expressed by all of these clients might be described as scared. However, the clinician's reflections clarify the distinctions among these scared feelings.

Examples of Reflections of Feeling

Example 1
Client: So there I was on the escalator and all of a sudden I felt scared, my heart started to pound, and I could hardly breathe. I felt so stupid; I knew I wasn't in any danger.
Clinician: It sounds like you were terrified, but also puzzled by your strong reaction to riding on the escalator.

Example 2
Client: When the time came to announce the winner of the math award, I was so scared that I wouldn't get it, but then they called my name. What a relief!
Clinician: You were really worried that you wouldn't be chosen for the award, and that must have made it all the more rewarding when they did call your name.

Example 3
Client: I was scared that I couldn't handle the chemotherapy but afraid that I would die if I didn't undergo the treatments. So I went ahead with the chemo.
Clinician: What a hard decision for you! Both alternatives were frightening, but you made a choice and moved ahead to get the treatments you needed.

Example 4
Client: Then after I got the math award, I started to feel scared again. Could I live up to this award and keep doing good work?
Clinician: Getting recognition for your good work made you apprehensive about whether you could keep it up.

All four clients use the word "scared," and yet their circumstances and feelings are very different. It is the intervention of the clinician, capturing the specific characteristics of each of the scared feelings, which deepens the client's awareness of those feelings and encourages their exploration.

Making an Accurate and Helpful Reflection of Feeling

Typically, a reflection of feeling consists of the following parts:

- an opening
- a feeling word
- a context

Clinicians sometimes add on a fourth part, a phrase to check out the accuracy of their reflection. The parts of a reflection of feeling are illustrated in the following example.

Example

Sounds like (opening) you felt terrified (feeling word) when you were riding on the elevator (context). Does that sound like what you were experiencing?

Including both the emotion and the context helps people reconnect with their feelings. In addition, pairing the stimulus and the reaction encourages clients to consider whether the nature and intensity of their emotional response is in keeping with the stimulus and paves the way for discussion of whether the emotion was helpful to the client.

Just as the effectiveness of questions can be evaluated, so can the effectiveness of reflections of feeling. Robert Carkhuff's (1969) work in this area suggested an approach that has become widely adopted in assessing the communication of empathic understanding. Empathic understanding can be rated on a 1–5 scale ranging from level 1 (the lowest level) to level 5 (the highest and most therapeutic level)

Level 1—Clinician statements demonstrate misunderstanding of the client's feelings or miss important aspects of those feelings.
Level 2—Clinician statements respond to the overt emotions of the client but subtract from the overall feelings.
Level 3—Clinician statements at this level are interchangeable with those of the client. In other words, they are neutral responses, more like restatements than helpful reflections of feeling.
Level 4—These clinician statements add to the client's awareness of his or her feelings, identifying a deeper level of emotion than the client was able to verbalize.
Level 5—Clinician statements greatly enhance the client's expression of emotion. These statements display true attunement to the client's feelings. They enable the client to gain self-awareness and a broader and deeper understanding of the expressed emotions. They also promote exploration and introspection.

The following example illustrates the five levels of empathic attunement.

Example of Levels of Empathic Attunement

Client: I felt such love and closeness, being with Blanca that night, but I was worried that she did not reciprocate my feelings.
Level 1: You found Blanca very attractive and had no thoughts of Marietta. (Misunderstands client's feelings and shifts the focus)
Level 2: You were very concerned that Blanca did not feel about you the way you felt about her. (Misses the strong love the client felt toward Blanca)
Level 3: You felt love and closeness toward Blanca but were worried that she would not reciprocate your feelings. (Interchangeable response)
Level 4: Feeling such deep emotions toward Blanca must have felt risky for you. Would she feel the same way toward you? (Is in tune with the client's emotions and adds the concept of risk to what the client has said)
Level 5: I can imagine you feeling such deep emotions for Blanca and yet struggling with what to do with those feelings. It sounds like you were afraid that she would reject you if you took a risk and expressed your emotions. (This reflection is in tune with the client's emotions and adds significantly to his feelings by mentioning the element of risk and the fear of rejection. This statement is most likely to promote introspection and further discussion.)

Later in this chapter, you will have the opportunity to gain practice in identifying and understanding emotions and making reflections of feeling. In addition, chapters in the second half of this book will afford you additional experience in empathic attunement and reflections of feeling.

NONVERBAL EXPRESSIONS OF EMOTION

Both client and clinician communicate emotions nonverbally as well as verbally. Although verbal messages tend to receive most of our attention, many researchers have concluded that nonverbal messages often are far more powerful than verbal ones. Consequently, in order to be effective listeners and communicators, we need to make sure that both our verbal and our nonverbal messages are clear and that the two are congruent and give the same message.

In addition, we need to be attuned to our clients' nonverbal messages as well as to their verbal ones. We should take particular note of incongruities between verbal and nonverbal messages.

Nonverbal messages can be communicated through the following channels:

- eye contact
- facial expression
- paralanguage (sounds, laughs, tone of voice, volume, intensity, silence)
- posture
- use of space, especially proximity between client and clinician
- body position and movements, especially hand gestures

Eye Contact

Eye contact has long been regarded as one of the most important ways for clinicians to build rapport and join with their clients. Eye contact that is natural, that involves neither avoiding the client's gaze nor staring at the client intently, is likely to create a comfortable treatment environment for most clients and clinicians.

The client's eye contact is, similarly, an important source of information. Especially in the early stages of treatment, some clients have difficulty making eye contact with their clinicians. This can reflect feelings of shame, guilt, shyness, or self-doubt. However, cultural background also may lead people to avoid direct eye contact. When clinicians observe a client, they must be sure they consider the person's cultural background before drawing conclusions about the implications of that person's eye contact.

Changes in eye contact and patterns related to those changes can be particularly informative. For example, whenever Eileen, the client presented in the intake interview earlier in this book, talked about her abortions, she would lean her head back to avoid any possibility of eye contact with her therapist. Over time, she forgave herself for those choices; this was reflected in increased eye contact when she discussed her abortions.

Facial Expression

Facial expression is one of the more easily deciphered sources of nonverbal communication, because of the universal meaning of many facial expressions. Facial expressions, considered in conjunction with verbal statements, often provide good clues to conflicted emotions. For example, while talking about her "nearly perfect" childhood, Sue pursed her lips and clenched her jaw. When this was gently pointed out to her, she acknowledged that she had been repeating family messages but that, in fact, she had often felt ignored and neglected in her large, affluent family.

Clinicians' facial expressions also play an important part in treatment. I had been counseling a couple, both of whom were dealing with diagnoses of cancer. When they told me that the wife's cancer had metastasized, tears came to my eyes as they did to my clients'. Although clinicians rarely evidence such strong emotions in their sessions, my sadness made clear to them the empathy and caring I had for them. At the same time, strong emotions evidenced by the clinician can be distracting and can shift the focus from the client to the clinician. Counselors and therapists need to monitor their own emotions in sessions to ensure that they enhance, rather than detract, from the treatment process.

Paralanguage

Paralanguage is another useful source of information on emotions, particularly when juxtaposed against verbal messages. Take note of when clients' speech speeds up or slows down, becomes louder or softer, and when they sigh or laugh. Changes such as these typically signal changes in feelings and may help pinpoint important emotional responses.

Silences and Omissions

Clinicians sometimes overlook the value of silences in a session and intervene to end the silence and promote dialogue. Instead, try sitting quietly along with a silent client. This may afford the client needed time to process information, sort out some thoughts, or gather the courage to introduce a difficult topic. If a period of silence seems too lengthy, you might simply ask the client, "What has been going through your mind?"

Similarly, keep track of what clients don't talk about as well as what they discuss freely. One of my clients talked frequently about her mother but said little about her father. When I realized this and asked about the omission, the client hesitantly stated that her father had been openly unfaithful to her mother, information her mother had told her never to disclose to other people.

Be sure to use silence effectively yourself. Silence is an intervention, just like an encourager or an open question. Clinicians can use silence to prompt client thought, to underscore an emotional moment, to mark the closure of a topic, and for many other purposes. However, novice clinicians, especially, tend to become uncomfortable with long periods of silence in sessions and often will break the silence prematurely. Just as we need to pause between sets in an exercise routine, so do we often need to pause between emotionally involving segments of a counseling session so that both clinician and client can organize their thoughts, manage their emotions, and shift their focus to a new topic.

Posture

Posture can be a powerful source of information about a person's readiness to connect with another. When we sit with arms and legs crossed, leaning back in our seat, people usually get the message that we are protecting ourselves from too much closeness and intimacy. On the other hand, an open posture in which arms and legs are extended and we are leaning forward is more likely to invite trust and self-disclosure. Be aware of your own posture to be sure that you give others the message you are seeking to transmit. Observing clients' posture can help you determine how best to build rapport and pace the sessions. Of course, cultural background must be kept in mind when assessing posture.

Matching people's posture, body movements, grammar, and language is a way to connect with them. To some extent, we do this naturally and without thinking when we want to build rapport with someone. Although this strategy can be obtrusive and even insulting when overdone, occasional and subtle mirroring of clients' words, posture, and gestures can facilitate the process of joining and advance the therapeutic alliance. Next time you are in a conversation, try mirroring the other person's body language; cross your legs when the other person does, and nod your head at the same time. Notice whether it accelerates the development of rapport.

Personal Space

The posture we assume when interacting with another person is often closely related to the space we prefer to maintain between that person and ourselves. Early in the treatment process, client and clinician both may be more comfortable with some extra distance between them. However, as treatment progresses and as the therapeutic alliance is developed, chairs are often moved closer. Placing your chair closer to a client and leaning forward to minimize distance can add emphasis to what is being said and communicate caring and involvement.

Physical Contact Between Client and Clinician

Much has been written about physical contact between client and clinician. The safest policy, especially for beginning clinicians, is to keep physical contact to a minimum, perhaps a handshake upon meeting. However, with experience, many clinicians learn when a pat on the hand to comfort a distraught client or even an occasional hug can help the therapeutic process. Physical contact must be offered with extreme care and sensitivity, always respecting the needs of the client and that person's cultural background. You might even ask permission before touching a client.

Sometimes, clients initiate physical contact with their clinician. This might represent simply a need for comfort, or it might be the beginning of inappropriate and seductive behavior. Dealing with these overtures can be difficult for clinicians who, of course, do not want their clients to feel shamed or rejected.

In deciding how to respond to client-initiated physical contact, consider both the ethical standards of your profession and your own instincts. Confer with a colleague or supervisor if you are uncertain how to proceed. Remember that dual role relationships (e.g., client and friend or romantic partner) are forbidden by the ethical standards of all mental health professions. Even if the physical contact does not seem unethical, you have the right to set limits on that physical contact if it makes you uncomfortable.

Using empathy, reflection of feelings, and gentleness can make this process successful. For example, you might say to the client, "At the end of our past few sessions, you gave me a hug. I can certainly understand your wanting to show caring for me and appreciation of our work together and maybe seek some support and reassurance. I am concerned, however, that this might detract from our work together, so I'm requesting that we don't hug at the end of our sessions. What reactions do you have to that?"

Body Positions and Movements

Interpreting body movements can be challenging. More will be said about this later in the chapter. However, keep in mind that it is difficult to determine, for example, whether a swinging leg reflects anger, anxiety, or boredom. We should not assume that we can definitively translate body movements into a clear message of feeling. What we can do is be alert to changes or patterns in body movement, take note of the corresponding verbal messages, and consider the relationships between verbal and nonverbal messages. We can also point out the body movements to clients and ask them to speculate on the messages their bodies are sending.

In addition, we should be aware of our own body movements. We want to convey a sense of calm and confidence to our clients that will encourage them to relax and talk openly about themselves. We should be particularly careful to avoid any irritating or distracting movements such as playing with a paper clip, tapping on a table, or clicking a pen. Having an open posture, leaning forward in a natural and comfortable way, and maintaining appropriate eye contact are most likely to facilitate the development of a positive therapeutic alliance.

Nonverbal Communication and Cultural Background

When assessing all of these sources of nonverbal messages, clinicians should bear in mind the ethnic and cultural backgrounds of their clients. Consider also the interaction of client and clinician background and gender. Although facial expressions vary little from one culture to another, gender and culture often considerably influence other nonverbal cues. People from Middle Eastern or Hispanic cultures tend to position themselves relatively close to a person with whom they are interacting and are usually comfortable with quite a bit of physical contact in same-gender interactions. On the other hand, people from the United States or from Great Britain tend to allow more space between people and are less likely to engage in spontaneous physical contact. When I lived in Egypt, I sometimes noticed myself backing away slightly from people from that country, maintaining the distance between us that had become comfortable to me as an American. When counseling people in that country, I had to be very careful to honor the use of space that was comfortable for my clients and to avoid giving inadvertent messages of rejection by my own need for more space.

Clinicians should exercise considerable caution when interpreting nonverbal cues, especially when clinician and client are from different cultures. Doing some reading on their clients' cultures, talking with colleagues from those cultures, and asking clients to verbalize the meaning of their nonverbal messages can help clinicians accurately interpret their clients' nonverbal messages.

ELICITING, CONTAINING, AND CHANGING EMOTIONS

Usually, clinicians view it as therapeutic for clients to be able to identify and express their emotions. That paves the way for them to modify any of those emotions that are unhelpful. Sometimes, however, people become mired in their feelings and cannot move beyond crying or raging and into more constructive forms of self-expression. In such cases, clinicians may actually want to help clients curtail or contain their expression of feelings. This section of the book presents the following strategies to help people express and contain or modify their emotions:

- Facilitate identification and expression of emotions
  - analysis of emotions
  - focusing
  - using body language
  - using the imagination
  - introducing new perspectives
- Encourage containment of emotions
  - reassurance and support
  - distraction and thought stopping
  - using the imagination
- Promote change in emotions
  - use of language
  - use of logic
  - using rational emotive imagery

FACILITATING IDENTIFICATION AND EXPRESSION OF EMOTIONS

This chapter has already described many of the therapeutic benefits that come from helping people express their emotions. To review, these include:

- building caring, trust, and rapport
- promoting hope and optimism in clients
- helping people feel heard
- promoting catharsis and emotional release
- providing reassurance and normalizing feelings
- facilitating problem identification, goal setting, diagnosis, and treatment planning

The most important strategies for enabling people to express and identify their feelings have already been presented in this chapter. These are listed and illustrated in the following examples.

Examples of Basic Interventions to Elicit and Explore Emotions

Client: I told my physician about all the problems with the children and my husband and my mother, and he just said, "Why don't I give you a prescription for some Xanax." I felt so angry.

Accents
Clinician: Angry?

Restatements
Clinician: It made you angry when he suggested you needed medication.

Paraphrase
Clinician: You sound furious that he thought a pill could solve everything.

Reflection of Feeling
Clinician: You must have felt frustrated and devalued when it seemed like the physician hadn't realized that you were asking for some help with the many difficulties in your family.

Summarization
Clinician: You've talked about incidents in which your husband, your best friend, and even your physician seemed to underestimate the seriousness of your concerns. It must be very painful to feel that nobody really understands what you are going through.

Specific Strategies to Elicit and Explore Emotions

In addition to these basic types of interventions, several specific strategies presented here can help you to further enhance clients' ability to express and identify their emotions. These techniques are most powerful when combined with the basic interventions discussed previously. These strategies will be illustrated with examples using Eileen, introduced earlier in this book. Here, Eileen has great difficulty accessing emotions that will be helpful to her.

Example

Eileen: I remember that terrible time when I was living with Tyrone. He would beat me and make me do things . . . things I didn't want to do. And then when I was pregnant, he said he would leave me unless I had an abortion.
Clinician: What feelings come up for you when you think about that?
Eileen: I feel sorry I couldn't make him love me. I tried as hard as I could to please him but nothing worked.

Analysis of Emotions

Regret is the primary feeling that Eileen has identified. This is probably not the only emotion she is experiencing and does not seem likely to be a helpful emotion for Eileen. To clarify the nature of this emotion, the clinician can begin by analyzing the feeling of regret according to the eight dimensions presented earlier in this chapter. The following analysis will help the clinician identify points where additional or different feelings might be accessed.

- *Emotional, physical, or a combination*—Eileen's feelings were experienced both emotionally and physically. She felt the emotion of regret but also felt a tightness in her shoulders and abdomen.
- *Overt, covert, or combination*—Although some of Eileen's feelings were overt, her clinician suspected that other feelings that were more difficult for her to express lay beneath the surface.
- *Positive, negative, or neutral*—Eileen's feelings were negative.
- *In or out of awareness*—Eileen had some awareness of her emotions but the clinician guessed that they were only the tip of the iceberg.
- *Level of intensity*—Eileen's emotions were very intense.
- *Appropriate to context and stimulus*—Eileen's feelings did not seem appropriate to the context and stimulus. She had been treated abusively, yet channeled her negative feelings toward herself rather than her abuser.
- *Congruence*—Eileen's verbalized emotions and her physical experience of her emotions seemed incongruent. Tearfulness, a common correlate of regret, was absent and instead Eileen experienced muscle tension, more likely to be associated with anger.
- *Helpful or harmful*—Eileen's feelings were harmful to her. They led her to blame herself and to feel disappointed that she had not pleased a man who abused her.

A review of the eight-part analysis of Eileen's emotions suggests that points of access to other emotions might be through the following routes:

- appropriateness
- congruence

Questions such as the following, focused on those areas, might help Eileen identify other feelings:

- If your best friend Bettie, whom you admire so much, were involved with a man like Tyrone, how do you think she would feel? (Appropriateness)
- I notice that your words and your physical sensations seem to convey different emotions. What emotions do you sense in your shoulders and abdomen? (Congruence)

Focusing

Focusing is another strategy designed to help people access and express their emotions. Developed by Eugene Gendlin (1996), focusing helps people become more aware of and in contact with their emotions. Focusing is an experiential strategy that uses the body as a source of information on emotions.

Gendlin suggests that people experience, in their body, what he called the *felt sense* that reflects their emotions. Accessing these inner emotions can help people move toward change and growth. Gendlin (1996) recommends training for clinicians who want to use focusing in their work. However, he also suggests that "even therapists who do not know focusing can markedly improve therapy . . . simply by asking how what is being discussed makes them feel *in the middle of the body* and then waiting quietly for the client to sense there" (p. 1). People who have difficulty accessing this felt sense can begin by directing their attention to their right foot and then gradually moving their attention up through the body.

The following is an abbreviated illustration of how focusing might be used with Eileen.

Example of Focusing

Clinician: Eileen, I'd like you to focus your attention in the middle of your body, in your abdomen, and just take some time to see what comes up for you.

Eileen: It feels really tight, like a cramping sensation.

Clinician: Just make some space for whatever comes up and pay attention to your feelings.

Eileen: I'm getting more and more tense, all over my body now. It feels like I want to jump out of my skin.

Clinician: What words or images come up that capture the message of these feelings?

Eileen: I feel ashamed, humiliated. And I feel really angry, more now at Tyrone than at myself. How could I have let him treat me the way he did? I didn't deserve that. And how could I have done the terrible things I did to please him?

Fritz Perls's Use of Body Language

Fritz Perls, who developed Gestalt therapy, pioneered the use of the body as a vehicle for communication of emotions (Fagan & Shepherd, 1970). Like Gendlin, Perls emphasized the importance of clinicians paying close attention to clients' body movements and sensations and then using interventions to help those clients give words to the language of the body. The following examples illustrate the sort of interventions that Perls might have used to help Eileen draw on her body language to access her emotions.

- *Giving a voice to the body*—Become your tense shoulders and give them a voice. What feelings would they share with us?
- *Locating verbalized emotions in the body*—You have told me that you are experiencing regret. Where in your body is that located? Go into that part of your body and try to experience the feelings as fully as possible. Notice what other feelings or experiences come up for you.
- *Exaggerating bodily sensations and movements*—You described a sensation of tension in your abdomen. I'd like you to tighten your abdomen as much as you possibly can, breath in, and pull those muscles together with as much pressure as you can tolerate, and exaggerate the tension you are already feeling. Focus on the tightness, the tension, the discomfort, and tell me what emotions come up for you.

Using the Imagination

The mind as well as the body can promote people's awareness of their emotions. Helping clients recreate an emotionally charged scene in their imagination is another powerful tool for eliciting emotions. Following a relaxation exercise, imagery was used as follows to help Eileen retrieve the feelings associated with a painful memory.

Example of Using the Imagination to Elicit Emotions

Clinician: Eileen, I'd like you to think back to your years with Tyrone and see what images come into your mind.

Eileen: I remember the time right after the abortion. I was in a lot of pain and was trying to take a nap when Tyrone came into the room and said, "You'd better get up and clean this place before the landlord gets here." I had forgotten that the landlord was coming to inspect the apartment before letting us renew our lease. The place was a mess as usual. I dragged myself out of bed and started to empty ashtrays and get the pizza boxes and wine bottles off the floor. Tyrone just sat there, smoking and watching television, even letting the ashes fall on the floor.

Clinician: So there you are, feeling sick, but trying to clean up while Tyrone watches television. You can remember all the details, the messy room, the discomfort you felt, even what you and Tyrone looked like at that time. As you review that scene in your mind, what emotions come up for you?

Eileen: I feel enraged now, at Tyrone and at myself. He treated me like a slave, like a piece of dirt. And I let that happen.

Introducing New Perspectives

One of the fundamental guidelines of ethical and effective counseling or psychotherapy is that clinicians should not devalue clients' emotions, nor should they tell them how they should feel. At the same time, clinicians can sometimes be helpful to their clients by offering them new possibilities in their emotional responses or by giving them permission to experience feelings that may, initially, seem unacceptable to them. This must be done carefully. Possibilities are presented but not forced on clients, and whatever feelings they experience are treated with respect and acceptance. In the following example, the clinician suggests some alternate emotions to Eileen.

Example of Introducing New Perspectives

Clinician: If a man tried to force me to engage in behaviors that felt wrong to me and that man didn't consider my feelings, I would feel pretty angry with him. I wonder if you ever felt angry with Tyrone?

Eileen: Yes, now that I think about it, I did. But I was so afraid that if I told him I felt angry at him, he would hit me or even just walk out and never come back. I didn't think I could survive without him.

CONTAINMENT OF EMOTIONS

A favorite intervention of many clinicians is "How does that make you feel?" Although eliciting emotions is an important component of clinical work, even that can be overdone. Sometimes clients are so overwhelmed by unhelpful emotion that clinicians need to take steps to help them curtail their expression of emotions and contain or diffuse the intensity of those emotions so that they become more manageable. Without this sort of help, people can become almost consumed by their emotions and may be unable to move beyond emotions and onto a more constructive focus on thoughts or actions. In addition, overfocusing on emotions can further entrench those emotions and lead people to feel even worse than they did before seeking treatment. The following are some of the interventions that can be used to facilitate containment of emotions.

Reassurance and Support

Offering reassurance and support is an important aspect of the clinicians' role. More will be said about this in part III. Just as when we suggest new emotions to clients, we need to be careful not to minimize or devalue people's feelings, to tell them how they should feel, or to judge or disapprove of them. If clinicians keep these cautions in mind, they can make some short, simple statements that can help clients feel safe and supported. The following examples illustrate such reassuring statements.

Examples of Reassurance and Support

- You're doing the best you can.
- You have handled this successfully before and you can handle it again.
- Focus on your breathing, and the feelings will gradually lessen.
- You're safe here in this room. You're no longer in danger.
- I'm right here with you.

Distraction and Thought Stopping

Redirecting clients' attention away from overwhelming emotions and onto soothing or distracting stimuli is another strategy to enhance people's efforts to manage their emotions. The following are a few examples of the many ways this can be accomplished.

Examples of Distraction and Thought Stopping

- Remember your affirmation. Keep telling yourself, "I am safe and strong now. I am safe and strong now."
- You can choose to turn your attention away from that painful memory and onto the joys you have in your life now. You can replace that memory of Tyrone with your memory of the day you spent in the park with Junior. Remember his laughter, the way he kicked his feet when you pushed him on the swing, the sunshine warming both of you.

- Bring yourself back into this room and notice all the details, the books on the shelf, the pictures on the wall, the rug on the floor, even the pens on the desk. Focusing your attention on where you are in the present will help you manage those emotions from the past.
- When you are fearful that you will become overwhelmed by your guilt, you can tell yourself to stop the emotion. You may need to do this repeatedly before the feeling starts to recede, but gradually you will probably find that you have more and more control over those feelings of guilt.

Using the Imagination

Just as the imagination can be used to elicit neglected emotions, it can also be used to facilitate containment of overwhelming emotions. The following instructions provide an example. This intervention is designed to give the client a sense of control over her emotions. Using the image of a safe, she can choose to separate herself from her emotions if they threaten to become too painful or overwhelming. On the other hand, if she wants to process and modify those emotions, she can let them out of the safe in small, manageable doses. In this way, she is controlling her emotions rather than allowing her emotions to control her.

Example of Using the Imagination to Contain Emotions

Clinician: Eileen, I'd like you to imagine a very large, very strong safe in front of you, as strong as any bank vault. Only you know the combination to this safe. Imagine yourself turning the dial on the safe and opening the door. Now you can put into the safe all those strong feelings that are making you feel so hopeless and discouraged. You can put into the safe all your anger toward Tyrone, all the guilt you feel about the choices you made while you were with him, all the regrets and disappointments you have about that relationship. Imagine yourself putting any or all of those feelings into the safe. Once you have filled up the safe as much as you choose, you can close the door on the safe. Check it to make sure it is firmly shut. Fasten the combination lock and turn the dial a few times to be sure that no one but you can open the safe. You can leave all those troubling emotions in the safe as long as you want, and you can let some or all of those feelings out whenever you want. It is your choice when and how you want to experience those emotions again.

CHANGING EMOTIONS

The interventions described in this chapter are not only effective in helping people express or contain emotions, they are also useful in promoting positive changes in feelings. The basic strategies of accenting, restating, paraphrasing, summarizing, and reflecting emotions are often enough to enable people to identify, process, and change their feelings. Specific interventions such as exploring incongruities in emotional expression, suggesting alternate emotional reactions, and using imagery can further enable people to modify their emotions. Additional interventions, such as those that follow, also are useful in helping people modify their emotions.

Use of Language

Reality therapy, developed by William Glasser and Robert Wubbolding (1991), emphasizes the importance of people taking responsibility for and recognizing that they can choose their emotions. To encourage clients' belief in their ability to control their emotions, reality therapists use active verbs rather than adjectives to describe emotions. For example, a person would be described as angering rather than angry, depressing rather than depressed, and anxietying rather than anxious. This gives the message that emotions are not fixed states or conditions but actions that can be changed.

Use of Logic

Using logic as part of the process of analyzing emotions can often help people to recognize that their emotions are not warranted and can be replaced with more constructive or appropriate feelings. This is illustrated in the following dialogue.

Example Using Logic to Modify Emotions

Client: I feel so guilty about the kind of father I am. My children don't deserve to have me as a father.

Clinician: What is the worst thing you've ever done to your children?

Client: The worst thing?

Clinician: Yes.

Client: One time I was supposed to pick up my daughter at day care and I got so caught up with my work that I didn't notice it was time to pick her up. The day care director had to call me at work and tell me hurry up and get her before they closed.

Clinician: What happened?

Client: I never moved so fast in my life. I'm lucky I didn't get a speeding ticket. I got to the day care center in record time. It was after their closing time and the director was there waiting with my daughter. I felt so terrible.

Clinician: And how was your daughter?

Client: She was fine. She was enjoying having the playroom all to herself.

Clinician: Have you ever physically or sexually abused your children?

Client: No, of course not. I would never do that.

Clinician: Did you ever send them to bed hungry when you had food for yourself?

Client: No, I would always put my children first.

Clinician: So the worst thing you've ever done to your children is arrive late at day care?

Client: Yes.

Clinician: How many times did that happen?

Client: Only once. I felt so terrible, I never let that happen again.

Clinician: If we think of a 1–10 scale of mistakes parents make, with abusing their children being a 10 on the scale, where on the scale would you put forgetting to pick up your daughter at day care on one occasion?

Client: Well, when you put it that way, I guess it's not so bad. Maybe a 5. But I should have been more responsible.

Clinician: It does sound like you made a mistake. But I wonder if you expect yourself to be a perfect parent?

Client: I don't know . . . maybe.

Clinician: Let's look at this in another way. Can you tell me about some good things you do for your children?

Client: That's easy. I love them, I provide for them, I try to make sure they are safe, I read to them and try to teach them skills as well as values.

Clinician: So you do a great deal to be a good parent.

Client: Yes, I can see that now. I'm not perfect and I've made mistakes but I really try to be a good parent.

Clinician: When we began this discussion, you felt very guilty about your parenting. I wonder how you feel now?

Client: Well, I know there is room for improvement but I'm actually starting to feel some pride in the sort of parent I am.

Using Rational Emotive Imagery

Albert Ellis, founder of rational emotive behavior therapy, developed a strategy called rational emotive imagery (REI), designed to help people change unhealthy and inappropriate emotions into healthy and appropriate ones (Ellis & Dryden, 1997). In REI, people are encouraged to visualize a troubling activating event and then experience the unhealthy emotions associated with that event. For example, Eileen might visualize the time Tyrone insisted that she clean the house even though she was recovering from an abortion and then experience the humiliation and guilt she had felt at that time. Once she had allowed herself to feel those emotions for a few minutes, she would be encouraged to push herself to experience a change in her feelings. Perhaps she would choose to experience some anger toward Tyrone, accompanied by a sense of relief that she was now safe and could no longer be mistreated by him. Practice of REI and repetition of changing the feelings associated with this activating event would probably lead to a genuine and internalized change in Eileen's feelings about the experience.

LEARNING OPPORTUNITIES

This chapter has focused on teaching you the following skills:

Basic Technical Skills:

- effective attending
- tracking
- encouragers (accents, restatements, paraphrases)
- summarization
- communicating accurate empathy and reflections of feeling
- understanding and using nonverbal messages

Specific Technical Skills:

- promoting expression of emotions
  - analysis of emotions
  - focusing
  - using body language
  - using the imagination
  - introducing new perspectives
- facilitating containment and management of emotions
  - reassurance and support
  - distraction and thought stopping
  - using the imagination
- changing emotions
  - use of language
  - use of logic
  - rational emotive imagery
- Your learning goals for this chapter include:
  - developing effective attending skills
  - communicating accurate empathy
  - learning to help clients to express, identify, manage, and change their emotions

The following exercises offer a broad array of learning experiences, designed to help you practice and improve your use of the skills presented in this chapter. As with all of the learning experiences in this book, keep in mind that you are not expected to complete all of these exercises. With the help of your professor or supervisor, select those exercises that are most likely to help you develop and improve your skills.

Written Exercises

1. For each of the following client statements, write:
   - an accent, restatement, or paraphrase
   - a reflection of feeling
   - an open question to build on the skills you developed in the previous chapter

   Client 1: All my life, I've wanted to be a jazz musician. I taught myself to play and I'm really good, but here I am working as a salesman to support my wife and four kids. I feel pretty hopeless about the future.
   - Accent/restatement/paraphrase:
   - Reflection of feeling:
   - Open question:

   Client 2: My mom thinks I have an eating disorder or something. But all the other girls take laxatives and stuff so they won't get fat. That's the only way I can keep from gaining weight.
   - Accent/restatement/paraphrase:
   - Reflection of feeling:
   - Open question:

Client 3: I've had three miscarriages and the doctors just don't think I'll be able to have a child. My husband doesn't seem to care and won't even talk about it, but I feel like there's a big void inside me without a child.
  - Accent/restatement/paraphrase:
  - Reflection of feeling:
  - Open question:

2. Review the reflections of feeling you wrote in response to the three client statements in exercise 1. List your purpose for each of those reflections.
   Client 1 purpose:
   Client 2 purpose:
   Client 3 purpose:

3. Now for each of the three client statements, list another possible purpose that you might have in mind when responding to the client. After each alternate purpose, write a second reflection of feeling that is consistent with that purpose.
   Client 1: Alternate Purpose:
   Reflection of Feeling:
   Client 2: Alternate Purpose:
   Reflection of Feeling:
   Client 3: Alternate Purpose:
   Reflection of Feeling:

4. Review the expanded information provided by 15-year-old Leeza, the second client in exercise 1. Then analyze her emotional responses according to the eight dimensions of emotion in the following list.

   Leeza: My mom thinks I have an eating disorder or something. But all the other girls take laxatives and stuff so they won't get fat. That's the only way I can keep from gaining weight. Last night my parents served this huge dinner; all I ate was salad with no dressing and some carrots, but when I got on the scale this morning, I had gained a pound. I couldn't believe it. I told my mom I was sick and couldn't go to school because I didn't want anyone to see how fat I looked but she said that I didn't seem sick and I had to go to school. So I put on this baggy sweater I have so no one could tell I had gained weight, but I just felt gross, like a fat pig.

Eight Dimensions of Emotions:

- Emotional, physical, or a combination:
- Overt, covert, or a combination:
- Positive, negative, or neutral:
- In or out of awareness:
- Level of intensity:
- Appropriateness to context and stimulus:
- Congruence:
- Helpful or harmful:

5. Consider the following clinician responses to Leeza. Rate each of them according to the 1–5 scale that follows, rating the helpfulness of each intervention. Then indicate what distinguishes the helpful responses from the harmful ones.

Level 1—Clinician statements demonstrate misunderstanding of the client's feelings or miss important aspects of those feelings.

Level 2—Clinician statements respond to the overt emotions of the client but subtract from the overall feelings.

Level 3—Clinician statements at this level are interchangeable with those of the client. In other words, they are neutral responses, more like restatements than helpful reflections of feeling.

Level 4—These clinician statements add to the client's awareness of his or her feelings, identifying a deeper level of emotion than the client was able to verbalize.

Level 5—Clinician statements add significantly to the client's expression of emotion. These statements display true attunement to the client's feelings. They enable the client to gain self-awareness and a broader and deeper understanding of the expressed emotions and also promote exploration and introspection.

Clinician Response 1: I can hear that you are very worried about gaining weight.
Rating:

Clinician Response 2: Even gaining one pound brought up strong feelings of shame and disgust with yourself.
Rating:

Clinician Response 3: You look emaciated to me. You really need to eat more.
Rating:

Clinician Response 4: Your mother is probably right. It does sound like you have an eating disorder.
Rating:

Clinician Response 5: You only ate salad and carrots for dinner?
Rating:

Differences between helpful and harmful responses:

6. Describe one strategy you might use to help Leeza express and explore her emotions.
7. Describe one strategy you might use to help Leeza contain or manage her negative feelings about herself.
8. Describe one strategy you might use to help Leeza change her emotions.

Discussion Questions

1. For many years, helping people express their feelings was considered essential to effective treatment. Many modern approaches to counseling and psychotherapy, however, pay little attention to expression of emotions. How do you explain this shift? Do you believe it is beneficial or harmful to the treatment process?
2. This chapter has reviewed the benefits and drawbacks of focusing a session on emotions. What do you view as the most important benefit and most important drawback to keep in mind? What can you do in a treatment session to maximize the benefits and minimize the drawbacks of exploring emotions?
3. Review the following statement made by Johnny, a 34-year-old man. Next analyze the client's feelings in terms of the eight dimensions of emotion. You may need to make some guesses as to how Johnny might be expressing his emotions. Then

develop an accent or restatement, a paraphrase, a reflection of feeling, and an open question that might serve as helpful responses to Johnny.

> **Johnny:** People don't know what they're talking about when they tell me I'll feel better when I stop drinking. That bottle is my friend, my only friend. It's there whenever I need it. Nobody else is. Nobody else does anything to help me; they just tell me I'm doing everything all wrong. Who needs that!

Eight Dimensions of Emotions:

- Emotional, physical, or a combination:
- Overt, covert, or a combination:
- Positive, negative, or neutral:
- In or out of awareness:
- Level of intensity:
- Appropriateness to context and stimulus:
- Congruence:
- Helpful or harmful:

Interventions:

- Accent or restatement:
- Paraphrase:
- Reflection of feeling:
- Open question:

4. This chapter introduced the idea of providing reassurance and support to clients. This process will be discussed further later in this book. However, based on what you currently know, what guidelines do you think you should keep in mind when providing reassurance? What pitfalls can you identify?

5. Norms for appropriate proximity to another person vary from one culture to another. If you were counseling a client from a culture other than your own, how would you ensure that you did not offend that person with your posture, body movements, or seating arrangement?

6. If you have not yet done the practice group exercise associated with this chapter, discuss your thoughts and feelings about that upcoming experience. How do you feel about sharing your feelings in the role-play session? What did you learn from the first role play that you want to carry with you into the second role play?

7. If you have already done the practice group exercise associated with this chapter, discuss your reactions to that experience. What was the most beneficial aspect of that experience for you? What was the most challenging or uncomfortable aspect of the experience? How did your second role-play experience compare with your first one? How can you make future practice group exercises even more rewarding to you?

Practice Group Exercise—Tracking, Eliciting, and Responding to Emotions and Using Body Language

Divide into your practice groups as described in the previous chapter and beginning on page 17 of this book. The practice group exercise presented here will help you gain experience in the basic technical skills described in this chapter: using accents, restatements, paraphrases, summarization, and reflection of feeling. It also will help you pay attention to body language and refine your skills in tracking.

Preparing for the Role Play.   You should have your tape recorder and a blank tape with you for all practice group exercises. Be sure to tape the session in which you assume the clinician role as well as the group feedback you receive for that role play. Listening to the tape after class will help you to identify your clinical strengths and areas you want to improve. You might also find it helpful to tape the entire role play exercise so that you can learn from the roleplays and feedback of others in your group.

In your last role play, you began to get acquainted with the other members of your group through the process of conducting intake interviews. The current role play will focus on eliciting and understanding emotions, the subject of this chapter. In preparing for this role play, identify an issue or concern in your life or in that of your role-played client that raises some meaningful emotional responses. This issue will be your presenting problem in the current role play.

Think carefully about your choice of an issue. Although your practice group has agreed to maintain each other's confidentiality, you will be sharing this issue with other students in a learning, rather than a therapeutic, environment. The person in the clinician role will probably be a novice clinician. Because of these factors, I suggest you select an issue that brings up only moderately strong emotions and that does not focus on highly charged or long-standing difficulties in your life or in that of your role-played client. Guidelines for choosing issues to present in the practice group exercises are discussed earlier in this book.

Finally, before beginning your role play, review the Assessment of Progress Form that you completed for the previous chapter. Take particular note of the summary of the feedback you received and the goals you established for yourself. Also review the Assessment of Progress Form for this chapter.

Role-Play Exercise.   The goals of this role-play are:
- *To help your client express and explore feelings*—To accomplish this, you should rely primarily on the skills presented in this chapter: accents, restatements, paraphrases, and reflections of feeling. If it would be helpful to you, you may use the eight dimensions of emotions as a structure for helping your client explore his or her feelings. You may also include some questions in your interview, reflecting the technical skills presented in the previous chapter. In addition, you should conclude the interview with a summary of what has been discussed, being sure to check out the summary with your client.
- *To track what your client is saying*—When your client is working productively on exploring emotions related to the presenting concern, you should simply follow or track what the client is saying, using the strategies listed previously. Only if the client seems to go off on apparently unimportant tangents or talks about material that does not seem helpful should you use strategies to help the client refocus the interview.
- *To maintain good body language*—Be aware of your eye contact, your posture, the distance you maintain from the client, your physical gestures and movements, and your

voice quality. Try to communicate interest, effective listening, and concern through your nonverbal and verbal messages.

Time Schedule: As in the previous role play, you will get the most out of this experience if you can devote approximately 90–120 minutes to the exercise. Spend approximately 15 minutes in each role play and another 10–15 minutes sharing reactions and providing feedback to the person who assumed the clinician role during that part of the exercise. Be sure to follow the guidelines for giving, receiving, and recording feedback that were presented earlier in this book.

Assessment of Progress Form 3

1. Promoting expression and understanding of emotions—What use did you make of each of the following interventions? What strengths were evident in your interventions? How might you have been even more successful in promoting the client's expression and understanding of emotions?

    a. Use of accents, restatements

    b. Use of paraphrases

    c. Use of reflections of feeling

    d. Use of questions

    e. Use of summarization

2. Tracking—How well were you able to follow the client? Did you use any strategies to redirect the discussion? How did they work? Should you have made more or less use of redirection?

3. Nonverbal messages—What impact did these have on the counseling process? How might they have been improved?
    a. Eye contact

    b. Posture

    c. Proximity to client

    d. Physical movements and gestures

    e. Tone of voice and rate of speech

4. Summary of feedback:

5. Progress in achieving goals from previous session:

6. One or two additional goals to improve your clinical skills:
    a.

    b.

Personal Journal Questions

1. If you have done the role play exercise for this chapter, listen to the tape recording of that role play. Respond to the following questions about your roleplay:
   - What was your overall reaction when you heard yourself in the role of clinician?
   - What was it like for you to assume the role of client? How did it feel to share your feelings with your partner?
   - On the helpfulness scale on page 75, how would you rate the overall quality of the interview you conducted?
   - List one or two interventions you made that seemed particularly effective.
   - List one or two interventions you made that you think needed improvement. How would you have modified these interventions?
   - What was your overall reaction to a session focused on emotions? Did you find the session interesting and productive, or did you find yourself eager to move on to other areas of focus?
   - What is the most important thing you learned from this chapter and its exercises?
2. How would you describe your typical use of body language? How important a vehicle of communication is your body for you? How has your cultural background influenced your body language?
3. Identify a strong and unpleasant or unhelpful emotion you experienced during the past week. Analyze that emotion according to the eight dimensions of emotions. What did you learn from that process?

   Eight Dimensions of Emotions:

   - Emotional, physical, or a combination
   - Overt, covert, or a combination
   - Positive, negative, or neutral
   - In or out of awareness
   - Level of intensity
   - Appropriateness to context and stimulus
   - Congruence
   - Helpful or harmful
4. Use one of the techniques presented in this book, such as rational emotive imagery, logic, or imagination, to change that unpleasant or unhelpful emotion. What was it like for you to use this strategy on yourself? How successful were you at modifying your emotion?

SUMMARY

This chapter focused on the technical skills associated with helping people express, understand, and manage their emotions. Particular emphasis was placed on using accents, restatements, paraphrases, reflection of feeling, and summarization. The importance of communicating empathy via reflections of feeling was emphasized. A format for analyzing emotions was provided. In addition, this chapter introduced tracking and discussed the importance of nonverbal communication in the treatment process.

Specific strategies also were presented that clinicians might use to help people express and understand their emotions, contain and manage their emotions, and change unhelpful feelings. These strategies included analysis of emotions, focusing, using body language, using the imagination, introducing new perspectives, providing reassurance and support, distraction and thought stopping, using language and logic, and rational emotive imagery.

The next chapter will focus on technical skills designed to help people identify, analyze, and, if appropriate, dispute their thoughts. Particular emphasis will be placed on reflections of meaning, problem solving, and information giving.

CHAPTER 4

Using Technical Skills to Identify, Assess, and Modify Thoughts

IMPORTANCE OF THOUGHTS

The previous two chapters presented technical skills linked to the first two elements of the BETA model. In chapter 2 on background, you learned how to ask helpful questions and to use intake interviews and other specific skills to gather information on your clients. In chapter 3 on emotions, you learned to use accents, restatements, paraphrases, reflections of feeling and other strategies to help people express, analyze, manage, and change feelings.

These skills will continue to be useful to you and will provide the building blocks of this chapter, which focuses on the third element in the BETA model, thoughts. This chapter presents skills that clinicians can use to help people identify, evaluate, and change their thoughts.

Terminology

The term *thoughts* will be used throughout this chapter. Thoughts can also be referred to as *cognitions, ideas, beliefs, values, attitudes, concepts,* and *perceptions.* Some subtle distinctions differentiate these terms.

- The terms **thoughts, cognitions, concepts,** and **ideas** are basically interchange-able. They are notions about ourselves, our lives, and our world. They are often in our awareness but may also reflect an underlying or fundamental viewpoint. Thoughts may be trivial and fleeting, such as "I think I'll have a cup of coffee," or they may be enduring and have a profound impact on our lives, such as "I think of myself as an unattractive and unworthy person."
- **Perceptions** typically reflect an awareness or understanding that developed through use of the senses. Examples are "I can barely perceive the ship way out on the ocean" and "I can perceive the difference between right and wrong."
- **Beliefs** usually are deeply held convictions or opinions, generally not amenable to immediate proof. The statements "I believe that we must protect our envi-ronment for future generations" and "I believe that men and women should have equal right and privileges" exemplify beliefs.
- **Values,** like beliefs, typically involve a judgment, with values emphasizing worth or relative merit. An example is, "Although that doll has little monetary value, it has a great deal of value to me because my parents gave it to me when I was a small child."
- **Attitude** is the last term to be considered here. You have probably heard some-one say, "That person has an attitude." Although this is colloquial speech, it does reflect the nature of an attitude. It is an orientation to the world, perhaps brief and transient or perhaps pervasive and enduring. "She has a negative atti-tude toward her work" and "She has a good attitude, despite all her difficulties" are statements that illustrate the use of the word *attitude*.

Most clinicians probably do not spend much time and effort distinguishing among these concepts. However, when a client expresses an idea, determining whether that idea reflects a thought, perception, belief, value, or attitude can be useful. Making that dis-crimination can help you understand the importance the idea has for the person as well as other dimensions of that idea, to be discussed later in this chapter.

Example of the Power of Thoughts

Most current theories of counseling and psychotherapy are **phenomenological** in na-ture. These treatment approaches recognize that how people perceive and think about their lives and their issues have a significant impact on how they feel about those issues and what actions they take to cope with them. Changing thoughts, therefore, can lead to changes in emotions and actions.

This concept is illustrated by the following example. Hidayah, Selma, and Mona, all women in their 40s, were diagnosed with breast cancer. All three women had mas-tectomies with reconstructive surgery. All three were diagnosed in an early stage of the disease, and all had an excellent prognosis. That is where the similarity ends.

Example 1   Hidayah had immigrated to the United States from Southeast Asia. Although she had been raised in the Muslim religion, she was married to an American man who was Protestant. Hidayah had only been living in the United States for a few years and had not yet developed a support system here; her parents and sisters still lived in Indonesia.

She was devastated by her diagnosis of breast cancer and was certain she would die of the disease. Issues of modesty and privacy, as well as her separation from her family of origin, made it difficult for her to verbalize her concerns and get some help. Because she was deeply depressed, her physician prescribed antidepressants and medication to help her sleep. Hidayah rejected the idea of support groups or counseling to help her.

Example 2   Selma, an African American woman, was also shocked and frightened by her diagnosis. However, her mother and two women in her church had previously been diagnosed with breast cancer and had survived the disease. She talked with them, gathered information, discussed her condition with several oncologists, and became more hopeful about her prognosis. Her diagnosis even helped Selma to make some positive changes in her life. She had been unhappy in her work and, for many years, had thought about returning to college to obtain a teaching certificate. Her diagnosis with a life-threatening illness led her to realize that she could not postpone her dreams indefinitely and that she needed to take action. She enrolled in a special program to prepare college graduates to become teachers and moved forward toward her goals.

Example 3   Mona, a Caucasian woman, described her diagnosis as a "minor inconvenience." Mona's life was a full one; she had three adolescent children, a supportive marriage, and a rewarding job managing a store. She followed the advice of the first physician she consulted, had her surgery, made a rapid recovery, and resumed her previous activities as soon as possible.

Clearly, how these women thought about their diagnoses and prognoses had a profound impact on how they dealt with their disease and the direction of their lives after cancer. This is true of all of us. Our perceptions of our life experiences probably are at least as important as the experiences themselves in determining our responses to those experiences and the impact they have on our lives. Whether you are dealing with a life-threatening illness or a lunch date with a friend, your thoughts about that experience will be a primary determinant of how you negotiate the experience and the impact it has on your life.

This chapter will focus on people's thoughts: how to help people identify their thoughts, assess the validity and helpfulness of those thoughts, and, if appropriate, modify those thoughts so that they are more realistic and helpful to them. Changing dysfunctional thoughts can contribute greatly to improving people's moods, helping them make constructive shifts in their behaviors, and enhancing their self-images and hopefulness (Seligman, 1995).

SKILLS TO BE LEARNED

Two leading clinicians, Albert Ellis (Ellis & Dryden, 1997) and Aaron Beck (Beck, 1995; Beck & Emery, 1985), have been instrumental in providing counselors and psychotherapists with the tools they need to help clients identify, analyze, and modify their thoughts. The workbooks of David Burns (1989) also have enhanced the accessibility of cognitive therapy. The writings and research of these authors provide the foundation for the skills that are presented in this chapter.

Four basic technical skills to help clinicians collaborate with clients in identifying, assessing, and modifying clients' thoughts will be presented in this chapter:

1. eliciting, analyzing, and modifying cognitions
2. reflections of meaning
3. information giving
4. problem solving and decision making

In addition, the following specific skills will be reviewed:

- positive self-talk and affirmations
- anchoring
- reframing
- thought stopping
- meditation
- journal writing
- mind mapping

GOALS OF CHAPTER

As a result of reading this chapter and completing the exercises, you can expect to improve your ability to:

1. Understand the importance of thoughts in the treatment process.
2. Help people identify, assess, and modify their thoughts.
3. Make helpful reflections of meaning.
4. Help people make decisions and solve problems.
5. Provide clients with useful information.
6. Use specific skills to help people change their thoughts, including the use of affirmations, anchoring, mind mapping, reframing, and other techniques that are designed to elicit and address thoughts in treatment.

ELICITING THOUGHTS

Many clinicians, especially those who view themselves as cognitive or cognitive-behavioral in orientation, believe that identifying, assessing, and modifying people's thoughts is the key to helping them make positive changes and cope more successfully with their difficulties. However, even clinicians who do not align themselves primarily with the treatment systems developed by Beck, Ellis, and other cognitive theoreticians typically recognize the therapeutic value of helping people modify their unhelpful thoughts. Often, once thoughts have been modified, emotions and actions improve spontaneously.

Before thoughts can be assessed and modified, clinicians must help clients identify their thoughts. Once the thoughts have been clearly stated, clinician and client can work together to determine whether the client's thoughts are helpful or harmful and whether the thoughts are valid.

Linking Thoughts to Emotions and Actions

When most people come in for an appointment with a clinician, they bring with them an incident, issue, or concern in their lives that they want to address. That typically is a good place to start, because the client is likely to be motivated to deal with that situation. If clients do not bring in such a situation, clinicians might review the past week with them, looking for an upsetting event or experience. Identification of a specific situation facilitates the process of eliciting thoughts.

Reactions to an experience include not only thoughts, but also emotions and actions. Usually, the three are intertwined. Often, they are congruent or compatible. However, sometimes they are incongruent, leading a person to feel conflicted or fragmented.

To understand a person's thoughts fully, clinicians should obtain information about all three areas of response: thoughts, emotions, and actions. Where you begin eliciting information depends on which of the three areas of response is most accessible. In other words, notice which one a client discusses most easily; that will usually be the best starting point for your exploration with that client. The following example of Carrie will be used to illustrate the steps in eliciting, assessing, and modifying thoughts and associated emotions and actions.

Example: Carrie's Thoughts, Emotions, and Actions

Carrie is a 54-year-old woman who is divorced and has no children. She is a music teacher and accompanist who earns a good income from her work and has retirement pay from her earlier career in the military. However, because she is self-employed and single, she worries a great deal about her finances. Carrie has one sibling, a sister, who is married and has three children. Carrie recently learned that her mother has made a new will, leaving only one fifth of her estate to Carrie and the remainder to her sister and the sister's three children. Review the three ways that Carrie might react to this situation and notice, for each example, whether thoughts, actions, or emotions are most accessible in each response.

Client Response 1:   When my mother first told me what she was going to do, I felt really angry at the way she was treating me. Then after I got off the phone with her, I just cried and cried. I felt like I had lost my best friend.

Client Response 2:   What she said just didn't seem fair to me. My mother has two children, so she should divide the estate equally between us. She must think very little of me to have made this decision.

Client Response 3:   As soon as my mother told me what she had done, I said to her, "You've just lost a daughter." I slammed the phone down, and I haven't spoken to her since then.

The first response presents Carrie's strong emotions, the second focuses on her thoughts, and the third emphasizes her actions. As a clinician working with Carrie, you could begin helping her deal with her mother's decision by focusing on thoughts, emotions, or actions. You will probably be most successful in joining with Carrie and helping her move forward if you begin with what is emphasized in her initial response (thoughts, emotions, or actions) and then move onto the other two types of response.

Let's begin with the second example, focused on thoughts, and see how a clinician working with Carrie might begin with those thoughts and then proceed to gather information on emotions and actions. Notice the clinician's use of many of the skills you have already learned: questions, restatement, and reflection of feeling.

Example: Eliciting Carrie's Thoughts, Emotions, and Actions

Carrie: My mother called me last week and told me that she was going to leave one fifth of her estate to me and four fifths to my sister and her three children. What she said just didn't seem fair to me. She has two children so she should divide the estate equally between us. She must think very little of me to have made this decision.

Clinician: When you had the thoughts that your mother was being unfair and must think very little of you, how did you feel?

Carrie: When my mother first told me what she was going to do, I felt really angry at the way she was treating me. Then after I got off the phone with her, I just cried and cried. I felt like I had lost my best friend.

Clinician: I'm hearing a real mix of emotions—anger, sorrow, and rejection.

Carrie: Yes, that pretty much sums it up.

Clinician: And what did you do after your mother told you about the division of her estate?

Carrie: As soon as she told me what she had done, I said to her, "You've just lost a daughter." I slammed the phone down, and I haven't spoken to her since then.

At this point, the clinician has the information she needs to collaborate with Carrie in further exploring her emotions, thoughts, and actions. They can assess the helpfulness to the client of those thoughts, emotions, and actions and, if appropriate, work together to develop more helpful responses.

Identifying and Rating Thoughts, Emotions, and Actions

The first step, begun in the previous example, is to clearly identify a client's thoughts, emotions, and actions. Usually, people have more than one thought and emotion and may have taken several actions. Clinicians should explore clients' reactions enough so that they have a clear picture of the range of important thoughts, emotions, and actions that the clients had in response to the presenting concern. Carrie's thoughts, emotions, and actions are listed in table 4-1.

Once the thoughts, emotions, and actions have been identified and written down, the clinician can help clients rate the intensity of their emotions and the degree of belief they have in their thoughts on 0–100 scales. Carrie's ratings of her thoughts and emotions also are reflected in table 4-1.

ASSESSING THE VALIDITY OF THE THOUGHTS

Once the thoughts have been clearly identified and rated, along with their accompanying emotions and actions, clinician and client can work together to determine whether the client's thoughts are helpful or harmful and whether the thoughts are valid. The following are frequent hallmarks of unhelpful thoughts:

- They make us feel bad.
- They do not encourage constructive change.

TABLE 4-1

Identification of Emotions	Rating of Intensity on 0–100 Scale
Anger	95
Sorrow	90
Rejection	97

Identification of Actions

Slammed down telephone, no further contact with mother

Identification of Thoughts	Rating of Belief in Thoughts on 0–100 Scale
My mother is treating me unfairly.	100
My mother doesn't love me as much as she loves my sister.	98
I am not lovable.	95
Now I will have serious financial problems.	90

- They blame other people or the unfairness of the world for our difficulties.
- They are stated in extreme and absolute terms.
- They contain words such as *should* and *must.*
- They reflect an underlying negative self-evaluation.
- They are illogical and irrational.

Although these hallmarks can help you identify thoughts that need modification, they should be used with caution because many exceptions exist. For example, Carrie may have thought, "I am very disappointed that I did not receive a larger inheritance" and "I should treat my mother with respect, even if I feel angry at her decision." The first of these thoughts would probably make Carrie feel bad. However, this is a rational and understandable thought that does not reflect any of the other hallmarks of unhelpful thoughts; it probably does not need to be changed. Her second thought contains the word "should"; however, that thought, too, is rational and does not reflect any of the other hallmarks of unhelpful thoughts. Be sure not to leap to hasty conclusions when hearing these hallmarks in your client's words. Both client and clinician should reflect on and assess any thoughts that contain these hallmarks before concluding that the thought is unhelpful, dysfunctional, and in need of modification.

Carrie's actual thoughts reflect not one, but many, of these hallmarks. They all make her feel bad and do not promote constructive change. They blame another person (her mother) and reflect an underlying negative self-evaluation (I am unlovable). They include the word "should" and are stated in extreme terms (end my relationship with my mother). Consequently, Carrie's thoughts about her mother's decision probably are unhelpful, distorted, and dysfunctional.

Once the clinician and client have determined that the client has some unhelpful thoughts, the next step in the treatment process is to determine whether those thoughts are valid and accurate. This certainly does not mean that clinicians argue with their clients or tell them that they should think differently. Rather, evaluating thoughts is a collaborative process of exploring the reasoning behind the thoughts, gathering information to support or refute the thoughts, and using other strategies to determine whether the thoughts are grounded in reality or reflect unwarranted assumptions and faulty logic.

Cognitive therapists have developed many ways to assess the validity of cognitions (Beck, 1995; Ellis, 1995; Moorey & Greer, 1989). Some of the most powerful of these include:

- *Reality testing*—This entails assessing the accuracy of the thought using the client's previous experiences, logic, research, and other sources of information. Carrie might look at the history of her relationship with her mother to determine whether there is evidence that her mother does not love her, or Carrie might ask her mother directly about her feelings.
- *Seeking alternative explanations*—Sometimes we can see only one explanation for an event or action. However, when client and clinician look for other possible explanations for an event or a person's behavior, alternative and more acceptable possibilities may emerge. For example, Carrie's mother may have decided to leave less money to Carrie because the mother has so much confidence in Carrie's ability to take care of herself.
- *Redefining or reconceptualizing a situation*—When people are not thinking clearly, they tend to overemphasize some pieces of information and overlook others. Obtaining a more balanced picture can help them modify their cognitions. For example, Carrie's parents had paid for her college education. Her sister had not attended college and so had, thus far, received far less money from her parents than had Carrie. Perhaps Carrie's mother was trying to balance out her financial contributions to Carrie and her sister.
- *Decatastrophizing*—When people experience failures or disappointments, they sometimes exaggerate the implications of these experiences and anticipate disaster. Looking at possible outcomes in a reasonable way can be reassuring. When Carrie learned that she would receive only a small inheritance from her mother, her doubts about her competence surfaced and she imagined herself homeless and penniless. In fact, Carrie had always supported herself without difficulty, had adequate savings, and had a sizable pension.
- *Viewing a situation through another person's eyes*—This strategy can help counteract extreme or polarized thinking and provide alternate perspectives. Although Carrie initially felt enraged at her mother's decision, she was eventually able to understand that her mother might have felt a strong responsibility to her grandchildren as well as to her children. Carrie was still disappointed, but her rage toward her mother and her feelings of rejection dissipated.

Example: Disputing Carrie's Unhelpful Thoughts

The following dialogue with Carrie illustrates one way that her clinician might collaborate with Carrie to dispute her unhelpful thoughts. Again, notice the clinician's use of interventions, especially reflection of feeling and open questions.

Carrie: I always suspected that my mother loved my sister more than she did me. Now this proves it to me.

Clinician: It must be very painful to you to believe that your mother doesn't love you as much as you want. What other evidence of that have you had over the years?

Carrie: Until now, she's always been pretty fair about money. She and my father paid for my college education, which really helped me out. But she always spends much more time with my sister than she does with me.

Clinician: And that means to you that she loves your sister more?

Carrie: Well, yes.

Clinician: Are there other possible explanations for that?

Carrie: Like what?

Clinician: Maybe where you both lived or who needed her help more.

Carrie: My sister has always lived close to my mother. I traveled so much when I was in the military that she didn't get to see me much. But she did come to Japan to visit me. And I guess my sister did need more help; she had three children in the first five years of her marriage, and it seemed like she had at least one sick kid for years. She really did need my mother's help.

Clinician: So it's hard to find any clear evidence that your mother doesn't love you as much as she does your sister.

Carrie: I suppose so, but shouldn't your children come first? I don't want to wind up homeless and penniless.

Clinician: You sound very worried about that. What makes that a worry for you?

Carrie: Well, I'm single and I don't have a husband or children to take care of me.

Clinician: How do you do at taking care of yourself?

Carrie: Actually, pretty well. I've saved quite a bit of money, and I get a pension from the military. I never have trouble getting music students. I've been very careful with my money and work closely with a financial planner.

Clinician: So you have really been able to take care of yourself very well financially. Let's look at the worst case scenario for a moment. Suppose you did not inherit any money from your mother and became disabled so that you could no longer teach music. How would you manage?

Carrie: I do have disability insurance, health insurance, and pretty good savings. My townhouse is paid off, and I also own a rental unit. I guess I could still manage.

Clinician: It must be reassuring to know that you can take care of yourself, no matter what happens.

Carrie: Yes, it is. I just always counted on a sizable inheritance from my mother, and it was such a shock when I learned that wasn't going to happen.

Clinician: So it's more the shock and what it might mean about your relationship with your mother that are troubling you than the actual loss of the money.

Carrie: Yes, that's true. But I just can't imagine what was in my mother's mind if it's not that she doesn't love me.

Clinician: You're really puzzled by her decision. Could you ask her how she arrived at her decision to leave you one fifth of her estate?

Carrie: Ask her? After I slammed the phone down on her and told her I wasn't her daughter any more?

Clinician: You were certainly very shocked and angry when you did that. I wonder how you feel now about your actions.

Carrie: Actually, not too good. You know, my mother is very sick, and that's why she's dealing with her will. It feels like she's expecting to die soon. I've already lost my father, and I don't want to lose her too.

Clinician: I can hear how upset you feel when you think about losing contact with your mother. Have there been other times in your life when you acted out of anger and then regretted what you had done?

Carrie: Of course, hasn't everybody done that at least once?

Clinician: Most everybody I know. What did you do, in the past, when you regretted an action you had taken in anger?

Carrie: Usually I swallowed my pride and apologized. When I didn't do that, I wound up feeling even worse.

Clinician: So apologizing seemed the best strategy in the past. How would it feel to apologize again?

Carrie: Kind of mixed. I really don't want to abandon my mother at this point in her life, but I just can't agree with the way she decided to divide her estate.

Clinician: You don't want her to think that contacting her means that you agree with her estate plans.

Carrie: Yes, that's it.

Clinician: Sometimes we love someone, but we don't like a specific behavior or choice they made. How would it feel to let your mother know that you love and care about her but still don't like her decision?

Carrie: I guess that would be all right. And this way I could explain my thinking to her. She probably doesn't even understand why I got so angry.

Clinician: So I'm hearing quite a few benefits to contacting your mother again.

LABELING THE DISTORTED THOUGHTS

Labeling the types of distorted thoughts that a person has is another helpful step in the process of changing those thoughts. Labeling the thoughts promotes understanding and awareness of those thoughts. In addition, it enables people to realize that it is not unusual to have thoughts that are confused or self-damaging and that other people have had similar thoughts. Becoming aware of common varieties of distorted cognitions can facilitate people's efforts to recognize and change their own unhelpful thoughts. Good sources of information on common types of distorted cognitions include Judith Beck's (1995) book *Cognitive Therapy* and David Burns' (1999) book *The Feeling Good Handbook*.

Example: Labeling Carrie's Distorted Thoughts

Let's look at Carrie's distorted thoughts and label or categorize them:

• *My mother is treating me unfairly*—This thought reflects *selective abstraction* and *emotional reasoning*. Carrie is overlooking the many ways in which her mother has helped her and is drawing a conclusion based on her feelings of hurt and rejection rather than on logic.

• *My mother doesn't love me as much as she loves my sister*—With this thought, Carrie is *jumping to conclusions* and *engaging in mind reading*. Here, too, emotional reasoning leads her to unwarranted assumptions.

- *I am not lovable*—This thought reflects *all-or-nothing thinking* or viewing a situation in terms of extremes as well as *overgeneralization*.
- *Now I will have serious financial problems*—*Catastrophizing* characterizes this thought.

MODIFYING DISTORTED THOUGHTS

Once the distorted cognitions have been disputed and labeled, clients are probably ready to modify their thoughts. Clinician and client work together to develop replacement thoughts that are both acceptable and more helpful to the client. Thoughts that are acceptable to the client may not always be as positive as the clinician would like them to be; however, imposing the clinician's thoughts on the client is, of course, not helpful. The client's acceptance of the new thoughts is essential to their effectiveness.

Example: Carrie's Modified Thoughts

Carrie felt comfortable with the following modified thoughts:

- I don't like the decision my mother made about the distribution of her estate, but I can see that she has made many other decisions that were helpful to me.
- My mother has said and done many things that show that she really does love me.
- I have some close friends, and even my ex-husband did love me, so I believe I am a lovable person.
- Although I will not be as financially comfortable as I would have been if my mother divided her estate equally, I will be able to take care of my financial needs.

CHANGING EMOTIONS AND ACTIONS

Changing distorted thoughts to more helpful ones usually enables people to change the unhelpful emotions and actions that accompany those thoughts. Again, although clinicians may offer possibilities or suggestions, clients determine which helpful emotions and actions feel acceptable and comfortable to them.

Example: Carrie's Modified Thoughts and Actions

Carrie came up with the following modified emotions and actions:

Modified Emotions

- Disappointment in her mother's decision
- Pride in being able to take care of herself without her mother's help

Modified Actions

- Contact mother and reestablish relationship
- Let mother know Carrie's feelings of disappointment with mother's decision
- Schedule an appointment with her financial planner to review her financial situation and make changes as needed

RERATING THOUGHTS AND EMOTIONS

Rating the new thoughts and emotions and rerating the earlier unhelpful ones can help assess progress and solidify gains. This clear measurement of change also can be reinforcing to clients.

Example: Carrie's Revised Ratings

Carrie came up with the revised ratings of her emotions in table 4-2. Revised ratings of thoughts are in table 4-3.

The intensity of Carrie's initial emotions, especially her feelings of anger and rejection, declined considerably. To a large extent, pride, a much more positive feeling, and disappointment, a more manageable and realistic emotion, replaced these emotions.

TABLE 4-2   Revised Emotions

Unhelpful Emotions	Rating of Intensity on 0–100 Scale
Anger	60 (formerly 95)
Sorrow	85 (formerly 90)
Rejection	52 (formerly 97)
Revised Emotions	**Rating of Intensity on 0–100 Scale**
Disappointment	90
Pride	87

TABLE 4-3   Revised Thoughts

Unhelpful Thoughts	Rating of Belief in Thoughts
My mother is treating me unfairly.	65 (formerly 100)
My mother doesn't love me as much as she loves my sister.	45 (formerly 98)
I am not lovable.	20 (formerly 95)
Now I will have serious financial problems.	35 (formerly 90)
Revised Thoughts	**Ratings of Belief in Thoughts**
I don't like the decision my mother made about the distribution of her estate, but I can see that she has made many other decisions that were helpful to me.	95
My mother has said and done many things that show that she really does love me.	99
I believe I am a lovable person.	82
I will be able to take care of my financial needs.	80

A comparison of Carrie's ratings of her initial and revised thoughts indicates that here, too, she has made considerable progress. The degree of her belief in her initial unhelpful thoughts has declined, although the issue of unfairness still troubles her. In contrast, her belief in her revised thoughts is quite strong although indications are that Carrie is not yet fully convinced of her lovableness and her ability to take care of her financial needs. Continued counseling can address these concerns further.

OVERVIEW OF PROCESS OF MODIFYING THOUGHTS

The process of modifying thoughts has been illustrated by the example of Carrie and her concerns about her inheritance. The steps in the process include the following:

1. Identify key issue or event.
2. Elicit related thoughts, emotions, and actions.
3. Rate intensity of emotions and extent of belief in thoughts.
4. Assess the validity of the thoughts.
5. Categorize any unhelpful and distorted thoughts.
6. Dispute the thoughts.
7. Replace the distorted thoughts with more helpful thoughts.
8. Identify new emotions and actions.
9. Rate intensity of both initial and new emotions.
10. Rate extent of belief in both initial and revised thoughts.

The rest of this chapter will provide additional strategies that will help you elicit and modify people's distorted thoughts. These include the basic skills of reflection of meaning, problem solving and decision making, and information giving. This chapter also includes the specific skills of positive self-talk, affirmations, thought stopping, reframing, meditation, journal writing, and mind mapping. The exercises at the end of this chapter will give you the opportunity to practice the skills you have learned to modify unhelpful cognitions.

REFLECTIONS OF MEANING

The previous chapter presented the skill of reflection of feeling, which is very useful in helping people identify, express, manage, and modify their emotions. A similar skill, reflection of meaning, is useful in enabling people to deepen their awareness and understanding of their thoughts and in subsequently assessing and changing those thoughts.

Even the smallest happening in our lives has a personal meaning associated with it. Often, the personal meaning of the event determines its impact on our lives, rather than the event itself. That was illustrated in the example of Hidayah, Selma, and Mona, the three women diagnosed with breast cancer, presented on pages 99–100. Helping people understand the personal meaning of events and interactions in their lives promotes self-awareness and enables people to better understand their own values, beliefs, and goals. This, in turn, can help them to resolve their difficulties and develop thoughts, emotions, and actions that are more helpful to them.

To understand the concept of personal meaning, assume that you receive a grade of *B* in a course. If this is a course that has been very difficult for you and if you anticipated receiving a *C*, the meaning of the *B* will be a positive one for you. On the other hand, if you have received *A*s in all your other courses, the *B* will probably be a disappointment to you because it has marred your excellent academic record.

Examples of Reflection of Feeling and Reflection of Meaning

Both reflections of feeling and reflections of meaning are extremely useful interventions. To help you distinguish between the two, consider the following examples:

Experience 1—You have given birth to your first child.
Reflection of Feeling—You are filled with joy and love.
Reflection of Meaning—Now you finally have your own family.
Experience 2—Your parents discovered illegal drugs in your backpack.
Reflection of Feeling—You feel shame and guilt.
Reflection of Meaning—You have let your parents down and lost their trust.
Experience 3—A close friend was killed in a car accident.
Reflection of Feeling—You feel grief and anger.
Reflection of Meaning—You have lost a wonderful friend.

Most clinicians use both reflection of feeling and reflection of meaning with their clients. However, keep in mind that reflections of feeling focus the session on a person's emotions while reflections of meaning focus the session on the person's thoughts. Think about your purpose in making a reflection and whether you want to focus on emotions or thoughts.

Reflections of feeling can be particularly useful when people have trouble identifying or managing their emotions. They also may make emotions more vivid.

Reflections of meaning are useful in helping people move beyond their immediate and automatic responses to situations and become aware of the deeper underlying significance that those events have for them. Reflections of meaning can also facilitate the identification, assessment, and modification of distorted thoughts. Modification of unhelpful thoughts often is a more direct and effective route to positive change than is a focus on background or emotions, especially in people who do not have good coping skills or who are apprehensive about the treatment process. Exercises at the end of this chapter will afford you the opportunity to practice using reflections of meaning and to distinguish them from reflections of feeling.

PROBLEM SOLVING

People often seek help because they do not know how to think through a particular problem or because they are having difficulty making a decision. Perhaps they are unsure how to go about building friendships, whether to make a career change, how to improve their grades, or whether to end a marriage. These are only a few of the many problems and choices that can benefit from counseling. The interventions that clinicians use to help people solve problems can make a great difference in whether or not the clients actually benefit from treatment.

Most clinicians are understandably eager to help their clients achieve their goals. However, that very enthusiasm can lead clinicians to treat clients as though they were helpless and incapable of solving their own problems. Beginning clinicians are particularly likely to rush in to resolve people's problems for them. Clients are likely to learn and benefit more if, instead, clinicians teach them the skills they need to resolve their own difficulties and take the time to help them arrive at choices that are right for them. Consider the following dialogue and, while you read it, think about the weaknesses in the clinician's interventions:

Example of Ineffective Problem Solving

Aja 1:   I'm thinking about retiring from the university next year but I'm not sure whether that's the best decision for me. I'm tired of the bureaucracy and all the meetings, but I love teaching and dealing with the students.

Clinician 1:   Maybe it's too early for you to retire.

Aja 2:   I'll only be 62, but my health hasn't been good and there are other things I want to do with my life.

Clinician 2:   Could you cut back to half time?

Aja 3:   I've looked into that, but my university won't allow me to do that.

Clinician 3:   Maybe you could retire from your present university and work half time at another institution.

Aja 4:   That would feel like starting all over. I don't want to do that at my age.

Clinician 4:   Could you teach as an adjunct professor?

Aja 5:   Maybe, but the pay is really low for adjunct faculty.

Although the clinician means well, the session becomes a "yes but" sort of interaction in which Aja presents reasons why each of the clinician's suggestions will not work for her. A session like this would probably be very frustrating for both client and clinician; the clinician feels blocked at every turn, and Aja fails to get the help she needs. Even if the clinician had succeeded in finding a viable alternative for Aja, she would still not have had the opportunity to learn effective ways to solve problems and make decisions on her own. The immediate problem might be solved, but the treatment process would not lead to growth in Aja's skills and self-confidence.

Now let's examine another sort of interaction with Aja. Notice the differences between this dialogue and the first one, and try to identify what makes this one more successful.

Example of Effective Problem Solving

Aja 1:   I'm thinking about retiring from the university next year, but I'm not sure whether that's the best decision for me. I'm tired of the bureaucracy and all the meetings, but I love teaching and dealing with the students.

Clinician 1:   Sounds like you have some conflicted feelings about leaving the university.

Aja 2:   Yes, I wish I could just teach and advise students and forget about all the rest of my job.

Clinician 2:   The student interaction is the most rewarding part of your job for you.

Aja 3:   It sure is. I especially like teaching the introductory psychology courses. It's like opening up a new world for the students, giving them a new way to think. And many of them make some important personal changes as a result of learning about psychology.

Clinician 3:   So helping people learn, both personally and professionally, is very important to you. I wonder if you have thought about some ways to help people grow and develop other than through full-time teaching?

Aja 4:   No, I guess I just thought of my job as an all-or-nothing proposition.

Clinician 4:   How about if we try to brainstorm some options, just make a list of possibilities, and then we can go back and evaluate them?

Aja 5:   That sounds like a good place to start. Let's see . . . I guess I could teach as an adjunct professor. I'd like to work half time but my university doesn't have any half-time employees. I don't think I want to do this, but maybe I could go to another university.

Clinician 5:   I've jotted down three possibilities so far: adjunct teaching, going half time, or moving to another university. What others might there be?

Aja 6:   That's about all I can think of.

Clinician 6:   Could there be some ways to have an impact on people's lives through teaching that doesn't involve a university?

Aja 7:   I never thought about that. I guess I could teach adult education or even do volunteer tutoring or mentoring.

Clinician 7:   I'll add those to the list. Any other possibilities?

Aja 8:   I always thought I'd like to be a visiting professor at a college overseas. That would be a real adventure for me! That's about all the options I can think of.

Clinician 8:   How would you feel about our taking a close look at each of the options on our list and figuring out their benefits and drawbacks?

Aja 9:   That makes sense to me.

What differences did you see between the first and second interviews? Did you notice the following in the second dialogue?

- The second clinician used a wider variety of interventions, including reflections of feeling and meaning and open questions.
- That clinician takes the time to understand what it is that Aja finds meaningful about teaching; this facilitates development of new possibilities.
- The clinician encourages Aja to come up with most of the options rather than suggesting them.
- In intervention 6, the clinician encourages Aja to think more creatively but does not actually offer suggestions.
- The strategy of brainstorming is used to expand possibilities before evaluation is begun.
- Aja and the clinician operate as a team; the clinician does not direct or take charge but rather guides Aja through the process.

Problem solving can offer important learning experiences for clients, teaching them thinking skills they can apply to future problems and decisions. Clinicians who use the strategies illustrated and identified previously are more likely both to help people find satisfactory solutions to their concerns and to enable them to develop important new skills than are clinicians who try to solve clients' problems for them.

INFORMATION GIVING

Clients are more likely to feel empowered and to take ownership of ways to resolve their difficulties if they generate their own possible solutions. However, sometimes the clinician has useful knowledge, information, or ideas that the client does not yet have. Sharing that information can be a helpful part of the treatment process, as long as the information is presented in a way that broadens the client's thinking and helps the client to make better decisions rather than specifying what the client should do or making the client feel inadequate. Positive use of information giving is illustrated in this continued dialogue with Aja:

Example of Information Giving

Clinician: I wonder if you have considered the option of job sharing?

Aja: No, I never thought about that.

Clinician: I understand that many businesses and institutions nowadays are encouraging job sharing; it seems beneficial to both employers and employees.

Aja: It certainly sounds interesting, and I'd like to add that to our list.

Clinician: What interests you about the idea of job sharing?

Aja: It would be a way to work half time and yet collaborate with a colleague to fill a full-time job slot. That could work well, but I don't know if the university is progressive enough to consider that.

Clinician: How could you find that out?

Although the idea of job sharing comes from the clinician, the clinician assesses whether Aja might have some interest in this option. When she seems amenable to considering this idea, the clinician shifts ownership of the idea to Aja by asking how she can obtain more information about the viability of this idea. In this way, the information becomes something that Aja can explore, accept, or reject rather than something that the clinician is persuading Aja to do.

Giving Information on the Treatment Process

One of the most common topics about which clinicians provide information to clients is the treatment process itself. At the beginning of treatment, clinicians typically orient clients to that process. This may be done both in a written format (consent to treatment form) and through discussion. Helping people understand the process of counseling or psychotherapy and how it operates, the anticipated roles of the client and the clinician, and the clinician's usual treatment approach help clients to make the best use of counseling. In addition, new clients should be informed about the ethical aspects of the clinical relationship and such practical matters as fees, scheduling, and contacting the clinician in the event of an emergency.

Acosta, Yamamoto, Evans, and Skilbeck (1983) found that this orientation process, called *role induction,* is associated with greater motivation and optimism in clients and a greater willingness to present and explore their concerns. Transmission of this preliminary information and all information provided throughout the treatment process should be done in a way that empowers clients and enables them to understand, ask questions about, discuss, and assume ownership of the information.

Guidelines for Information Giving

Providing information to clients will usually be most helpful if the clinician follows these guidelines:

- Introduce the information in general terms; provide details only if the client shows interest.
- Remain neutral; don't advocate for your ideas or suggestions. No one can predict what will be best for another person.
- Ask about the client's reactions to the information; use reflections of feeling and meaning and open questions to promote exploration.
- Transfer ownership of the information to the client as soon as possible by encouraging the client to gather additional information and explore the option further.
- Monitor your own reactions; if you feel hurt, angry, or annoyed because a client is not interested in what seems like a good idea to you, explore your own feelings so they do not undermine the treatment process. Supervision or a conversation with a colleague can help, as can an understanding of countertransference (discussed later in this book).

DECISION MAKING

Once people have delineated their options, gathered information, and evaluated the possibilities, they may still have difficulty with decision making. One strategy to facilitate decision making is illustrated in the following dialogue with Aja. She has gathered information on job sharing and has learned that it would take two years to set up such an arrangement; she had planned to retire in one year. She is having difficulty deciding whether to retire as soon as she had planned or to spend an extra year in her full-time position at the university in order to set up a job sharing arrangement with a colleague.

> **Clinician:** Aja, it sounds like you are really struggling with the question of whether to retire in a year or work full time for two more years so that you can share your job.
>
> **Aja:** Yes, that is a real dilemma for me. I had anticipated retiring in a year and had already taken steps to move into a less expensive apartment. But the job sharing idea really appeals to me.
>
> **Clinician:** Let's make up a list of the pros and cons for staying at the university an additional year. Once we have developed the list, we can go back through each item and assign a weight to it, using a 0 to 10 scale to assess the importance that each item has for you. (See table 4-4.)

A table such as this can be an extremely useful tool, not only to facilitate decision making, but also to promote exploration and to help people generate plans that will contribute to the successful implementation of their decisions. Aja's ratings of the drawbacks to remaining at the university added up to 19, while the ratings on her list of

TABLE 4-4   Staying at the University an Extra Year

Pros		Cons	
Opportunity to continue teaching	10	Delay of additional leisure time	4
Continued contact with colleagues	6	Bureaucracy, meetings	8
Financial benefits	5	Potential health consequences	7
Total	21	Total	19

benefits totaled 21. The closeness of the numbers clearly reflected what a difficult decision this was for Aja. A comparison of the totals gave a slight edge to the decision to remain at the university an extra year in order to arrange for job sharing the following year. However, the closeness of the numbers suggested that Aja and her clinician had some more work to do before Aja could make a clear decision.

The next step was for them to take a close look at the ratings to determine their relative strengths and gain a deeper understanding of the meaning the ratings had for Aja. Clearly, the opportunity to continue her teaching and advising was paramount for Aja and seemed to overshadow the other benefits and drawbacks. Further conversation enabled Aja to become even clearer about the great sense of accomplishment and fulfillment she derived from her teaching.

Following an exploration of the ratings, Aja and her counselor sought to determine whether any of the ratings could be modified to increase the weight of the benefits and decrease the weight of the drawbacks. One important drawback was Aja's concern about her health; she was being treated for osteoporosis, high blood pressure, and high cholesterol. Another drawback was her dislike for the bureaucratic aspects of her job. Through discussion, Aja realized that she could reduce some of the less appealing aspects of her job by resigning from several time-consuming committees. This would afford her some additional free time that she could use to begin an exercise program, which might, in turn, ameliorate some of her medical problems. She also decided to have a consultation with her physician about the impact of continued work-related stress on her health. These decisions enabled Aja to make changes in her ratings depicted in table 4-5, leading to a clearer decision to remain at the university for an extra year.

People who are struggling with complicated and important decisions often have difficulty clarifying their thoughts and articulating their concerns. Tools such as the decision-making grid in tables 4-4 and 4-5 can help both client and clinician understand the client's dilemma more clearly, assess the benefits and drawbacks of each choice, identify the decision that seems preferable, and find ways to increase the likelihood that the decision will be a rewarding one.

Not all clinicians are comfortable with the structured paper-and-pencil process illustrated in Aja's example. Clinicians can easily modify this procedure, simply using a less structured discussion of benefits and drawbacks to a particular choice, if that approach is more compatible with the clinician's concept of the treatment process.

TABLE 4-5 Staying at the University an Extra Year (rerating)

Pros		Cons	
Opportunity to continue teaching	10	Delay of additional leisure time	4
Continued contact with colleagues	6	Bureaucracy, meetings	5
Financial benefits	5	Potential health consequences	3
Total	21	Total	12

SPECIFIC TECHNICAL SKILLS RELATED TO THOUGHTS

Cognitive approaches to counseling and psychotherapy are rich sources of intervention strategies that can help people clarify, assess, and modify their thoughts and make changes in emotions and actions as well. The following strategies are reviewed and illustrated with examples of Eileen, the client who has been presented throughout this book, along with examples of other clients:

- positive self-talk and affirmations
- anchoring
- reframing
- thought stopping
- meditation
- journal writing
- mind mapping

POSITIVE SELF-TALK AND AFFIRMATIONS

Most of us keep up a running commentary of thoughts in our minds, although we are not usually focused on that inner monologue. However, that internal commentary has a powerful impact on how we view and cope with our lives. When we make a mistake at work, for example, we may think, "What a mess I've made. I'm really in big trouble. How could I have been so stupid! I hope my supervisor doesn't find out." Or we might think, "I did make a mistake, but I think I can figure out some ways to make it right with some help from my supervisor. I'll have to be more thorough next time." If we can help our clients tune into their inner monologues, assess whether or not those monologues are helpful, and deliberately change the unhelpful messages people are giving themselves, they may well develop improved self-confidence and coping skills. The development of meaningful affirmations can enhance and reinforce this process.

Because she perceived herself as having made some bad choices as an adolescent and young adult, Eileen, introduced in chapter 1, had difficulty recognizing her strengths. When anything reminded her of her past, especially her abortions and her misuse of alcohol, she lost sight of all she had accomplished and viewed herself as both helpless and unworthy of happiness.

For example, on a recent visit to the park with her son Junior, Eileen became absorbed in a conversation with a neighbor. While they were talking, Junior fell down and cut his head, requiring a trip to the hospital for stitches. Eileen's internal monologue went something like this: "Junior was injured because of my selfishness. I should have been watching him every second and not talking to my friend. I'm a terrible mother. I just can't seem to do anything right, no matter how hard I try. I can't forgive myself for all the terrible mistakes I made, and it feels like God is punishing me, too, for all that I did." Clearly, a relatively minor incident sent Eileen into a downward spiral in which she devalued everything about herself.

With her therapist's help, Eileen grew more aware of her inner monologue and was amazed at the way she constantly devalued herself. She learned to interrupt this negative monologue and deliberately replace it with more positive self-talk. Eileen and her clinician worked together to develop some self-talk and an affirmation she could substitute for her negative inner dialogue.

Clients may have difficulty believing unrealistic or extremely positive messages and so may dismiss them or fail to use them in consistent and helpful ways. Clinicians should be sure that any self-talk has language and content that feels right to the client.

Example of Positive Self-Talk and an Affirmation

For Eileen, these included:

> **Positive Self-talk:**   I have made many mistakes but I have learned from them. God loves me and will help me to lead a better life.
> **Affirmation:**   I don't have to be perfect to be a good mother and wife.

The positive self-talk acknowledged Eileen's problem-filled background but emphasized the importance of her strong spiritual beliefs and her own determination to change her life. The affirmation reminded Eileen of her most important roles and strengths and her tendency to devalue herself without justification.

Eileen wrote down both the positive self-talk and the affirmation. She agreed to repeat the positive statement to herself many times during the day, especially when she found herself thinking negative and self-deprecating thoughts. She wrote the affirmation on purple note cards and placed them throughout her house so that she would have frequent and eye-catching reminders of her revised cognitions.

ANCHORING

An anchor is a trigger or stimulus that evokes a specific and consistent response pattern from us. Anchors can be visual (sight), auditory (hearing), kinesthetic (touch), olfactory (smell), or gustatory (taste). Think about some of the anchors you have in your own life such as a special food that reminds you of family dinners, a piece of music that leads you to reminisce about a long-ago romance, or an intersection where you had an automobile accident. These are all anchors that arose spontaneously. However, anchors can also be created to further the treatment process.

Examples of Anchoring

For Eileen, the purple note cards became a visual anchor, reminding her of the affirmation she had created. As often happens, stimulus generalization occurred, and Eileen found that the color purple, her favorite color, became a reminder in itself because of its association with her affirmation.

In addition, Eileen and her therapist created a kinesthetic anchor to reinforce her use and internalization of her affirmation. Eileen paired the repetition of her positive self-talk and her affirmation with the act of clasping her hands in prayer. Not only did this remind her of her faith in God and the strength she derived from her religious beliefs, but it quickly brought back the positive thoughts she had developed. All Eileen had to do to remind herself of those thoughts was to clasp her hands. When she felt discouraged or angry, clasping her hands generally calmed her down and helped her modify her upsetting thoughts.

REFRAMING

Relabeling or reframing is a strategy in which clinicians help people change the language they use to describe experiences or perceptions. The goal of this process is to modify thoughts, emotions, and actions associated with the experiences or perceptions. This can enable people to view their circumstances in a more positive light and as capable of improvement.

Examples of Reframing

The following are some examples of reframing:

- A young child who had been labeled hyperactive is described as having a great deal of energy.
- A therapist suggested to a man who felt hopeless and discouraged that this was his depression speaking and not his usual voice.
- A newly married couple, concerned about their occasional arguments, was encouraged to view the arguments as part of the process of really getting to know each other. This not only put the arguments in a more favorable light but externalized the disagreements, making them part of a useful process rather than an expression of negative feelings.
- Concerned about her mother's safety, a woman had arranged for her mother to move into a nursing home. When the mother refused to make the move, the woman felt like a failure. She was helped to reconceptualize this as presenting her mother with options and honoring her mother's right to make her own decisions.
- Eileen viewed Junior's fall as evidence that she was a terrible and neglectful mother. Instead, her counselor described it as one of the difficult learning experiences of being the parent of a young child.

THOUGHT STOPPING

People who are anxious and depressed, have few positive feelings about themselves and their lives, and feel powerless often are troubled by recurrent negative thoughts. The same word, phrase, or sentence may keep running through their minds, entrenching their feelings of being immobilized, powerless, and hopeless. Affirmations are one way to interrupt these repetitive thoughts and ruminations. Thought stopping is another strategy.

The first step in using thought stopping successfully is identifying the unwanted recurrent thought. Once that has been accomplished, each time people find themselves thinking the upsetting or demoralizing thought, they say to themselves, either aloud or subvocally, "STOP IT!" Like most bad habits, the thought will probably recur before too long but, by teaching clients this simple strategy, the frequency of the thought is likely to diminish over time.

MEDITATION

Entire books have been written about the benefits of meditation (Smith, 1986). Only a very brief overview of that process will be provided here. However, with some additional training and experience, clinicians can teach their clients some simple approaches to meditation that can promote feelings of calm and self-confidence, increase awareness and insight, and help people let go of troubling thoughts and worries. As Borysenko (1988, p. 47) stated, "The final goal of meditation is to be constantly conscious of experience so that relaxation and peace of mind become the norm rather than the exception."

Typically, meditation begins with some brief relaxation exercises, perhaps progressive muscle relaxation or deep, diaphragmatic breathing. Then, according to Smith (1986, p. 67), "The instructions for meditation can be put very simply: Calmly attend to a simple stimulus. After every distraction, calmly return your attention—again and again and again." When people first begin to meditate, they commonly find that their mind drifts off in many directions and they become concerned that they do not have an aptitude for meditation. However, this process of losing and then regaining focus is part of the meditation process; over time, maintaining a clear focus and an open, receptive mind during meditation usually becomes easier and more fulfilling.

When transcendental meditation first became popular in the United States in the 1970s, students of that process were given a special word or phrase to serve as the focus of their meditation. They were sometimes instructed to keep that word secret. Over the years, meditation has lost much of its mystique, and most practitioners recognize that successful meditation does not require a special word or an elaborate process. Rather, any of the following can serve as an appropriate focus for meditation:

- a meaningful word such as peace, hope, or love
- transcendent images such as a spiritual figure or symbol, the sunrise, or the universe
- relaxing images such as a pastoral scene or a sleeping child

- contemplative images such as questions, memories, experiences, or inner guides that can lead to discovery of meaning and direction

Special objects or burning candles can also serve as meditative images, helping people to concentrate their attention and tune out distractions. Some people prefer not to focus their attention when meditating but, rather, to approach the process with an open and receptive mind, waiting to see what thoughts, images, and feelings arise for them. Meditation can also be productively combined with action; some types of yoga and even-paced walking can be conducive to the development of a meditative state.

Ideally, meditation should be practiced on a regular basis. One or two 10- to 20-minute meditation sessions per day seem to yield the greatest benefit. However, even shorter and less frequent meditation can be relaxing and can help people to clarify and modify their thoughts and feelings.

JOURNAL WRITING

Journal writing is another tool that can assist people in identifying and clarifying their thoughts. Many people enjoy keeping journals and find writing in them to be rewarding and meaningful experiences. Other people, however, are reminded of unpleasant and disappointing experiences they had in school and would rather do almost anything than write about their thoughts. Be cautious in suggesting this activity to your clients, and be sure to discuss their reactions to your suggestion. Writing will only be productive and worthwhile if people are motivated to make good use of this experience.

Many books are available to help you encourage and guide people's use of writing. Some that I have found helpful include *Writing From the Inside Out* (Palumbo, 2000), *Inversing Your Life* (Gustavson, 1995), and, for adolescents, *Discovery Journal* (Oshinsky, 1994). However, such books are not necessary as long as you use some thought and creativity in suggesting writing topics to your clients. Particularly useful are topics that are germane to clients' concerns and offer them the opportunity to generate some possible solutions to their difficulties. Subjects that are surprising and thought provoking are also appealing to most people. For example, this chapter has already introduced you to Carrie, concerned about the distribution of her mother's estate; Aja, considering retirement; and Selma, diagnosed with breast cancer. This and earlier chapters have discussed Eileen Carter's counseling. The following might be useful writing topics for these four people:

Carrie

- Why I am a lovable person
- Good memories of my relationship with my mother
- What money means to me

Aja

- What I want my life to be like in 5 years
- Life beyond teaching
- Milestones of my career

Selma

- Two losses and one gain from breast cancer
- What I think caused my cancer
- Cancer as a wake-up call

Eileen

- How my spiritual beliefs can help me
- The transformation of Eileen
- My ideas about good mothering

MIND MAPPING

Mind mapping is another creative tool to promote people's awareness of their thoughts and prompt fruitful exploration. In this exercise, the person begins the map with a central issue or concept that he or she has brought to treatment. A circle in the center of the map represents this central issue. People, experiences, or other thoughts related to the central thought are represented as branching out from that thought. The branches may then have branches of their own, reflecting the complexity of a person's thoughts.

The map in figure 4-1 represents Eileen Carter's mind map of the issue that brought her to counseling, her wish to continue her college education. This issue is written in the circle at the center of the map. Discussion of this central issue led Eileen to create five secondary branches, reflecting the major factors that affect whether or not she would continue her education: Husband, My Past, Resources, Dreams, and Junior. Branches extending from each of these reflect the many complex and often conflicted thoughts Eileen has about continuing her education. For example, extending from the circle representing My Past is the positive thought "behind me" as well as the negative thoughts "shame" and "deserve punishment" that present barriers to Eileen's pursuing her dreams. This rich mind map can help Eileen think through the many factors involved in her decision whether to continue her education and to make a sound and realistic decision. The exercises in the next section afford you the opportunity to create your own mind map and to experiment with some of the other technical skills presented in this chapter that can help people identify, assess, and change their thoughts.

LEARNING OPPORTUNITIES

This chapter has focused on teaching the following technical skills relevant to eliciting, assessing, and modifying thoughts:

Basic Technical Skills

- eliciting thoughts, emotions, and actions
- analyzing and assessing the validity of thoughts
- modifying distorted thoughts
- using reflections of meaning
- facilitating problem solving

FIGURE 4-1   Mind Map by Eileen Carter

- information giving
- facilitating decision making

Specific Technical Skills

- positive self-talk and affirmations
- anchoring
- reframing
- thought stopping
- meditation
- journal writing
- mind mapping

Written Exercises

1. For each of the following client statements, list the dysfunctional thought, the emotion, and the action.

Client 1: I told my wife that I would like us to drive downtown and look at the holiday decorations. So she says, "I'm tired. Would you take me home first?" Well, I wasn't going to let her ruin another holiday for me, so I just ignored her, gunned the engine, and headed downtown.

- The dysfunctional thought:
- The emotion:
- The action:

Client 2: I was really overloaded with work last week, but I didn't want to ask my supervisor for some extra help. If she finds out how snowed under I am, she'll think I can't handle the job and start looking for my replacement. So I worked all weekend and most of the night to get the job done. Even then, I felt pretty bad about what I had produced. I think it's time to hit the Want Ads.

- The dysfunctional thought:
- The emotion:
- The action:

Client 3. All the other girls I know have already had a date. I don't know what's wrong with me. Maybe I'm too tall, or maybe the boys all think I'm weird because I get good grades. They call me the Jolly Green Giant. I'm never going to have dates like the other girls. I might as well just give up.

- The dysfunctional thought:
- The emotion:
- The action:

2. Identify two approaches you might use to help each of the clients in item 1 assess, dispute, and modify the dysfunctional thoughts you have identified.

   Client 1:
       Approach A.
       Approach B.
   Client 2:
       Approach A.
       Approach B.
   Client 3:
       Approach A.
       Approach B.

3. Write a reflection of meaning and a reflection of feeling you might use to respond to each of the client statements in item 1:

   Client 1:
       Reflection of meaning:
       Reflection of feeling:
   Client 2:
       Reflection of meaning:
       Reflection of feeling:
   Client 3:
       Reflection of meaning:
       Reflection of feeling:

4. Write a revised, more helpful thought that might replace each of the harmful and distorted thoughts you listed in item 1.
   Client 1:
   Client 2:
   Client 3:

5. The third client in item 1, a 14-year-old girl, might benefit from some information on adolescent development. Write a brief client/clinician dialogue, including some helpful information that you might give her.

6. You are already familiar with the dilemma presented by Eileen Carter who wants to continue her college education but is discouraged from doing so by her husband's disapproval. Develop a hypothetical decision-making grid similar to the one on page 116, complete with ratings, that Eileen might create to help her determine whether to continue school.

7. Develop a helpful affirmation for one of the three clients in item 1.

8. Describe how you might use reframing with one of the clients in item 1.

9. Identify a journal writing topic that might be helpful to one of the clients in item 1.

Discussion Questions

1. Discuss the relative advantages and disadvantages of focusing on emotions and of focusing on thoughts during the treatment process. Which focus felt more comfortable for you and why? Which focus do you believe will lead to a more productive session and why?

2. Consider the following statement made by Isaac, a 46-year-old man. Assume that you are going to follow the 10-step process of eliciting, assessing, and modifying his thoughts. Discuss how each of the 10 steps listed on page 110 and on page 127 might proceed with this client.
   Isaac: For the past month, I have been communicating with a fascinating woman named Jeannie who I met in an Internet chat room. She really seems to listen to me and care about me. This is what I have been looking for all my life. I have finally found happiness. I'm planning to ask my wife for a divorce and move out west to be with Jeannie. My wife and children will be better off without me. They don't really seem to love me the way Jeannie does.

3. When you have completed a hypothetical description of how, following those steps, treatment might progress with Isaac, identify at least two specific technical interventions you might use to solidify your work with him. How would you present these to him? Which do you think would be most likely to be helpful to him and why?

4. Problem solving and information giving are interventions that clinicians must use with great care. Discuss the possible pitfalls of these interventions. What steps can you take, when using these interventions, to avoid those pitfalls?

5. Develop helpful cognitions that might replace the following unhelpful or distorted thoughts:
   - I left a message at my physician's office, asking him to call me back with my test results. He never returned my call. I guess he doesn't want to give me the bad news.

- I told my parents that I really wanted a dog and that I would take very good care of it. But they said, "No, you're not old enough." I know I could do it, but they still think I'm a baby.
- My job at the library is being phased out and my supervisor gave me a month's notice. I'm almost 60 years old. Who would hire me? What am I going to do? Go on welfare or move in with my children? All my years of hard work have amounted to nothing.
- I told my friend that I liked this boy who rode the school bus with us. She told him what I said! I couldn't believe she would do that to me. I can't face either one of them now.
- My son has had behavioral problems all his life. We started getting extra help for him when he was four years old, but I guess that wasn't early enough. I've really failed him.

6. If you have not yet done the practice group exercise associated with this chapter, discuss your thoughts and feelings about that upcoming experience. What obstacles do you expect to encounter? What can you do to try to avoid them? What did you learn from the previous role-play sessions that you want to carry with you into the role play focused on thoughts?

7. If you have already done the practice group exercise associated with this chapter, discuss your reactions to that experience. What was the most beneficial aspect of that experience for you? What was the most challenging or uncomfortable aspect of the experience? How did this role play compare with your earlier ones? How can you learn even more from future practice group exercises?

Practice Group Exercises—Eliciting, Assessing, and Modifying Thoughts

Divide into your practice groups as described in the previous chapters and beginning on page 17. The practice group exercise presented here will help you gain experience in the basic technical skills described in this chapter: eliciting, assessing, and modifying thoughts; using reflections of meaning; and supplementing these interventions with some of the specific strategies designed to help people modify their distorted thoughts.

Preparing for the Role Play.   Once again, you should have a tape recorder and a blank tape with you. Ideally, you have already reviewed one or more tapes from your previous role-play sessions and have some ideas about ways you might improve your counseling. You have probably realized what a powerful learning experience it is to hear yourself and others on tape and also to review the feedback you received.

You may also have found reviewing the tape recorded sessions to be a painful experience and cringed as you listened to the sound of your voice and some of the weaker interventions you made. This is a common reaction, for both novice and experienced clinicians. Try to view the process as a learning experience, and be sure to focus on your strengths and on areas needing improvement. With that perspective, you will probably see that you have already learned a great deal from these sessions. However, one of the exciting aspects of counseling and psychotherapy is that you can always learn more and refine your skills further. These can be rewarding professions for people who thrive on learning and growth.

As you approach this next role-played session, keep in mind the strengths you have already demonstrated in previous sessions and improvements you want to make in your work. Reviewing both the tape of your previous session and the Assessment of Progress Forms you have already completed will help you identify one or two areas in your work that would benefit from some change. List those here so that they are fresh in your mind:

1.
2.

Once again, you need to select an issue that you will address when you are in the client role. You may build or expand on issues you presented in previous sessions or you may choose to introduce a new topic.

Role-Play Exercise.   The goals of this role play are:

• *To build on the skills you have already learned.* Keep in mind what you have already learned about the use of open and closed questions and reflection of feelings and continue to incorporate those skills into your session. Use accents, restatements, and paraphrases to track what your client is saying and to encourage self-expression. Monitor your body language to be sure that your posture, eye contact, and tone of voice all reflect effective listening.

• *To help your client express, assess, and perhaps modify thoughts.* To accomplish this, the central goal of the role play, you should follow the 10 steps in the process of modifying cognitions discussed earlier in this chapter and presented as follows:

1. Identify key issue or event.
2. Elicit related thoughts, emotions, and actions.
3. Rate intensity of emotions and belief in thoughts.
4. Assess the validity of the thoughts.
5. Dispute the thoughts.
6. Categorize any unhelpful and distorted thoughts.
7. Replace the distorted thoughts with more helpful thoughts.
8. Identify new emotions and actions.
9. Rate intensity of both initial and new emotions.
10. Rate extent of belief in both initial and revised thoughts.

During your session, complete the following tables with your client:

Identification of Emotions	Rating of Intensity on 0–100 Scale

Identification of Actions

Identification of Thoughts	Rating of Belief on 0–100 Scale

Rerating

Unhelpful Emotions	Rating of Intensity on 0–100 Scale
Revised Emotions	**Rating of Intensity on 0–100 Scale**

Revised Actions

Unhelpful Thoughts	Rating of Belief on 0–100 Scale
Revised Thoughts	**Rating of Belief on 0–100 Scale**

- *Using reflections of meaning.* As we discussed earlier in this chapter, helping people grasp the meaning experiences and interactions have for them is important in enabling them to assess the validity of their thoughts and modify any distorted thoughts. Be sure to make use of reflections of meaning during this session, especially during steps 1 (elicit key issue or event), 2 (elicit related thoughts, emotions, and actions), and 4 (assess the validity of the thoughts). Open questions, reviewed in chapter 2, also are important interventions in the process of exploring thoughts.
- *Using a specific technical intervention to reinforce helpful thoughts.* Once you have completed the 10-step process of eliciting, assessing, and modifying thoughts, you have an opportunity to solidify gains that have been made. Using one of the specific interventions presented in this chapter is likely to accomplish that. Conclude your role-played session by helping your client to develop an affirmation or an anchor to reinforce the progress that has been made in the session.
- *Summarizing the session.* Wrap up the session with a brief summary, no more than two or three sentences in length. Be sure to check out the accuracy of your summary with the client.

Time Schedule.   The role-play session presented in this chapter is a complicated and challenging one that probably will require more time than the previous sessions. If possible, allow at least 20 minutes for the role play; 30 minutes would be preferable. In addition, be sure that at least 10 minutes is allocated for feedback to each person in the clinician role.

Assessment of Progress Form 4

1. *Building on the skills you have already learned*—What use did you make of the following skills, learned in previous chapters?
   - Open and closed questions:

- Accents, restatement, and paraphrase:

- Reflection of feelings:

- Attentive body language:

- Summarization:

2. *Helping your client express, assess, and modify thoughts*—As you review your session, both with your practice group and later when you listen to your tape, note whether and how you helped your client progress through each of the 10 steps listed on page 127. Which steps felt most comfortable for you? Which were most productive? Which presented you with the greatest challenge? How might you have improved upon this process?

3. *Using reflection of meaning*—If possible, identify two examples of your use of reflection of meaning. How successful were these interventions in helping the client clarify the meaning or importance of an experience? What contributed to, or limited, the success of these interventions?

4. *Using a specific technical intervention to reinforce helpful thoughts*—Were you able to use one of the specific interventions presented in this chapter to solidify the gains your client made? If not, what got in the way of your using such an intervention? If yes, how effective was the intervention? Do you think another type of specific intervention would have been even more helpful? Use the following rating scale to assess the success of the specific intervention you made.

- **Extremely helpful**—moves counseling in a productive direction; promotes self-awareness, new learning, or positive changes.
- **Moderately helpful**—moves counseling in a productive direction, but does not clearly lead to greater self-awareness, new learning, or positive changes.
- **Neutral**—neither contributes to the treatment goals nor harms the therapeutic process.
- **Moderately harmful**—detracts somewhat from the counseling process or alliance.
- **Extremely harmful**—damaging to the treatment process or therapeutic alliance.

5. *Using summarization to wrap up the session*—How successful was your summarization? How might it have been improved? Did you remember to check out its accuracy with the client?

Personal Journal Questions

1. Listen to the tape recording of your role play. Respond to the following questions about your role play:
   - What did you perceive to be the strengths of your role play?

   - Did you notice any improvement over your previous role-play sessions? If so, what did you do to effect that improvement?

   - What areas needing improvement did you notice? What can you do differently in your next session to effect that improvement?

   - Did you prefer to use interventions that focused on thoughts or on emotions? How do you explain your preference?

2. Identify an experience you had over the past week that bothered you. Be your own counselor and take yourself through the 10-step process of identifying, assessing, and modifying your thoughts. While you are doing that, complete the following table with reference to your own experience.

Identification of Emotions	Rating of Intensity on 0–100 Scale

Identification of Actions

Identification of Thoughts	Rating of Belief on 0–100 Scale

Rerating

Unhelpful Emotions	Rating of Intensity on 0–100 Scale
Revised Emotions	**Rating of Intensity on 0–100 Scale**

Revised Actions

Unhelpful Thoughts	Rating of Belief on 0–100 Scale
Revised Thoughts	**Rating of Belief on 0–100 Scale**

3. Reflect back on the past few days. List the first three events you experienced during that time that come into your mind. Then write a reflection of meaning for each of those events.
4. Identify a decision you need to make. Prepare a decision-making grid similar to the one presented on page 116 to help you determine the best decision.
5. Prepare a mind map, focused on a concern in your life. Once you have completed the map, write briefly about the information that the map provided and how you might use that information in your life.
6. Write down an example of an affirmation or self-talk that might contribute to your own personal and professional growth.

SUMMARY

This chapter focused on the technical skills associated with helping people identify, assess, and modify their thoughts. The chapter presented a 10-step process that could be used in treatment to facilitate those goals. Reflection of meaning was presented as an important strategy to promote awareness of thoughts. Information giving, problem solving, and decision making also were presented as additional tools that help clinicians encourage people to clarify their thoughts.

In addition, specific strategies were presented that clinicians use to help people identify, assess, and modify their thoughts and reinforce gains made in treatment. These specific skills include positive self-talk, affirmations, anchoring, reframing, thought stopping, meditation, journal writing, and mind mapping.

The next chapter will focus on technical skills designed to help people assess and change their actions. Emphasis will be placed on strategies to encourage behavior change, including establishing a baseline; making contracts; using suggestions, directives, and homework to promote progress; and confronting or challenging.

CHAPTER 5

Using Technical Skills to Identify, Assess, and Change Actions and Behaviors

IMPORTANCE OF ACTIONS AND BEHAVIORS

The previous three chapters presented technical skills designed to address the first three components of the BETA model: background, emotions, and thoughts. In this chapter, we focus on the fourth component, actions or behaviors.

Although we can often conceal our backgrounds, our emotions, and our thoughts, our actions are more difficult to hide. They are often overt and observable to others and give a message about who we are. We probably respond more to people's actions than we do to their backgrounds, emotions, and thoughts, although all of those elements influence our choice of actions.

On the day I began to write this chapter, I made a point to take note of actions that caught my attention en route to and during time I spent in a restaurant. I saw many actions and behaviors; some seemed positive while others appeared negative to me (although I had no knowledge of the determinants of any of these behaviors). Those that seemed negative included:

- a woman who was driving too fast in a residential area
- two people loudly arguing in a restaurant

- a woman dining alone who consumed an entire bottle of wine, in addition to several mixed drinks
- a man who spanked his child who had crawled under the restaurant table

I also saw examples of what I interpreted as positive behaviors:

- a woman helping her parents, one in a wheelchair and one in a walker, have dinner in the restaurant
- the waiter who tried to cheer up a crying child
- a large group of people celebrating the birthday of their friend
- a man engrossed in a book I had enjoyed

As I watched these people and took note of their behaviors, I began to form impressions of them. Of course, my first impressions may have been inaccurate, but nevertheless it is people's actions that usually have the greatest impact on our initial perceptions of them. In addition, the actions themselves usually are the primary determinants of how people lead their lives. How well we perform at work, how we communicate love and disapproval to our families, what food and drink we ingest, and how we spend our leisure time all shape who we are, our relationships, and the direction of our lives. Actions, then, are an important focus of our lives and of counseling and psychotherapy.

Focusing on actions in treatment has many advantages (Seligman, 2001):

- Clients' presenting concerns often focus on problematic actions such as procrastination, overeating, harmful use of drugs or alcohol, family arguments, or withdrawal.
- Because changing actions is often people's primary goal in seeking treatment, they are usually willing to discuss their behaviors. In contrast, clients sometimes view discussion of background, emotions, or thoughts as intrusive and irrelevant to their immediate issues.
- Most actions can readily be described, evaluated, counted, and measured.
- As a result, people rarely have difficulty establishing goals that focus on behavior change.
- Learning skills to effect improvement in one behavior often generalizes and facilitates people's efforts to modify other unwanted behaviors.
- In addition, considerable research supports the effectiveness of treatment emphasizing behavior change strategies (Division 12 Task Force, 1996).

OVERVIEW OF DEVELOPMENT OF BEHAVIOR THERAPY

Important research on effective ways to modify actions has been going on for more than 100 years. Many of the early and leading researchers in psychology, such as B. F. Skinner (1969), Ivan Pavlov (1927), John Watson (1925), and Joseph Wolpe (1969), focused their work on behavior change strategies. Prominent modern theoreticians and clinicians who have contributed to our understanding of how to promote behavior change include William Glasser (1998) and Robert Wubbolding (1995) (reality therapy),

Donald Meichenbaum (1985) (cognitive behavior therapy), and Steve de Shazer (1991) and Bill O'Hanlon and Michele Weiner-Davis (1989) (solution-based therapy).

Solution-based and solution-focused therapy, in fact, is currently one of the most dynamic and efficient treatment approaches available to clinicians. Focusing on a solvable, usually behavioral complaint, solution-based clinicians establish measurable goals, design an intervention, suggest strategic tasks, and anticipate rapid improvement. Although these clinicians draw on a broad range of treatment approaches in formulating their interventions and tasks, they are fundamentally behavioral in orientation. The hallmarks of brief solution-based or solution-focused therapy can be seen in the behavioral skills presented in this chapter.

In addition, theoreticians and practitioners who emphasize cognitive therapy such as Aaron Beck (1995), Albert Ellis (Ellis & Dryden, 1997), and Arnold Lazarus (1989) (multimodal therapy) also have added greatly to our knowledge of ways to effect change in actions. The combination of cognitive and behavioral treatment interventions is often used in counseling and psychotherapy and can make a powerful treatment package.

SKILLS TO BE LEARNED

Five basic technical skills designed to help clinicians and clients identify, assess, and change actions will be presented in this chapter:

1. Describing and determining a baseline for undesirable behaviors
2. Goal setting
3. Contracting
4. Giving directives and suggesting tasks
5. Challenging and confronting

In addition, the following specific technical skills will be reviewed:

- empowerment
- visualization
- behavioral rehearsal
- modeling and role-playing
- skill development
- breaking down an action into small steps
- possibility language
- relaxation
- systematic desensitization

GOALS OF CHAPTER

As a result of reading this chapter and completing the exercises, you can expect to accomplish the following goals:

1. Understand the importance of actions in the treatment process.
2. Become able to help people identify their harmful behaviors and establish a baseline reflecting the current frequency or severity of those behaviors.

3. Learn to develop a contract for behavior change that includes establishment of clear, specific, meaningful, and realistic goals.
4. Know helpful ways to give advice and suggest tasks that are likely to promote behavior change.
5. Know when and how to use confrontation or challenge.
6. Learn specific skills, including empowerment, systematic desensitization, relaxation, and modeling, that are designed to facilitate behavior change.

DESCRIBING AND MEASURING PROBLEMATIC ACTIONS AND BEHAVIORS

Even when people present for treatment in order to change behaviors that are harmful to them, they commonly do not have a clear picture of either the undesirable actions or what they need to do differently to meet their goals. The following are typical examples of how people describe self-destructive behaviors when they seek treatment:

- I watch too much television. I need to get out and be with people more.
- I weigh 260 pounds and my doctor has told me to lose weight.
- I drink too much and my wife says it is hurting our marriage.
- I don't get any exercise.
- I don't have any friends at school and don't know how to make friends.
- I procrastinate too much.

These are all good starting points and will help the clinician and client describe and measure the unwanted actions. However, these presenting problems, in their current form, are too vague to allow client and clinician to establish specific goals and develop procedures that are likely to effect positive change. In order to lay the groundwork for changing these behaviors, the actions must be described in concrete, detailed, and measurable ways.

Consider the following revisions of the presenting problems previously listed:

- I watch at least four hours of television each day. I see friends no more than once a week. This has gone on since I got divorced 6 years ago.
- I consume approximately 3,000 calories per day.
- I drink at least 12 beers almost every evening. I have done this since I was in college. I spend no more than 2 hours a week in enjoyable activities with my wife and children.
- I walk to and from the parking lot at work and I take the stairs whenever I can. However, I don't get any formal exercise and would like to establish an exercise program.
- I usually play alone during recess. When another kid tries to talk to me at school, I get embarrassed and just walk away. I have never had a best friend.
- I rarely make deadlines at work, often handing in assignments 2 or 3 days late. I usually pay my bills late, too, and wind up paying late charges.

What changes do you see between the first statement of each problem behavior and the second statement? Notice that in the second series of statements, the behaviors are described in specific terms, with numbers used whenever possible to indicate the duration, frequency, or severity of the unwanted actions.

Establishing a Baseline

Helping clients describe and assess their unwanted behaviors as specifically as possible is an essential first step in establishing a baseline. However, few people know how many calories they consume, how many hours they spend watching television, or perhaps even how much alcohol they consume. Some data gathering is usually needed to establish an accurate baseline, the current frequency, duration, and intensity at which the behavior is manifested.

Discrepancies between clinician and client viewpoints.   Establishing a mutually agreed-upon description of the problematic behavior can be difficult. Clinician and client do not always concur on what actions need to be changed. Consider the following examples:

Examples of Differing Client and Clinician Viewpoints

- Katie is a gifted student who has a D average in her high school courses because she has been cutting classes and doing no homework. Her clinician would like to see her achieve As and Bs, grades that are commensurate with her intelligence. Katie, on the other hand, would be satisfied with Cs; she does recognize that she must attend classes regularly and is willing to do the homework she absolutely must do to pass her courses.
- Lavinia sought counseling for career-related problems. Over the course of her sessions, she disclosed to her counselor that she frequently spanks and slaps her children to control their behavior. Her clinician views this as harmful and possibly even illegal behavior and wants Lavinia to learn other ways of disciplining her children. However, Lavinia states that she was slapped and spanked as a child, with no adverse effects, and sees no reason to change the way she treats her children.
- Curt has been drinking heavily for at least 5 years. He has received several DWI (driving while intoxicated) citations and had his driver's license revoked for long periods of time. He entered treatment at the urging of his wife and does not want his marriage to end but is unwilling to change his consumption of alcohol.

These situations are challenging for the clinician. Each one presents a somewhat different dilemma. Katie is the only one who is willing to make some change in what the clinician views as her problematic behaviors. If her clinician insists on imposing his standards on her, Katie will probably leave treatment and may make no positive changes. The best approach in working with Katie, then, is probably to begin treatment by establishing those goals that seem reasonable to Katie. Perhaps, with some success at school, her motivation will increase and she will subsequently be willing to revise her goals and aim toward As and Bs. Even if that does not happen, Katie has agreed to improve her school attendance and achievement in an effort to graduate from high school, and that is progress.

Lavinia and Curt, on the other hand, are not willing to work on the problems identified by their clinician. Although it may be a matter of opinion whether a bright student has the responsibility to fulfill her academic potential, the laws, as well as public opinion, have determined that Lavinia and Curt's behaviors are harmful and in need of change. Their clinicians, then, cannot simply ignore their problematic behaviors and focus on other goals and issues.

If, indeed, Lavinia's behavior constitutes child abuse, her therapist should inform her of this and may need to report her behavior to the authorities. The clinician should exert great effort to engage Lavinia in changing her treatment of her children, even if her motivation is extrinsic (avoiding legal consequences) rather than intrinsic.

Although Curt's behavior is not immediately reportable to the legal authorities, the clinician cannot ethically agree to Curt's goals in treatment to improve his marriage while continuing his misuse of alcohol. That seems like an impossible goal to achieve. Probably the best approach for the clinician is to inform Curt of this, to help him understand the impact his alcohol use has on his family relationships, and to encourage him to set some goals that address his drinking. Even if Curt is only willing to avoid drinking and driving, that might provide a starting point to treatment, hopefully leading to eventual abstinence. But if Curt is completely unwilling to discuss his alcohol use, extensive treatment focused only on Curt's marriage does not seem like a viable approach.

Drawbacks to the data-gathering process.   Establishing a baseline can be difficult, even if clinician and client have a meeting of the minds on desirable goals. Data gathering may seem to be a tedious and time-consuming process, and it may raise some resistance and negative feelings as people take a hard look at the severity of their unwanted behaviors. They may have underestimated the seriousness of the problem and may feel overwhelmed and discouraged as they tally their actions.

Clinicians can facilitate the process of data gathering if they take steps to reduce these barriers. The following strategies can facilitate the process of data gathering to establish a baseline:

- **Help people anticipate any negative feelings that can arise.** Although it may seem counterproductive to introduce negative emotions that people are not yet experiencing, in reality it is usually helpful to prepare people to address troubling feelings that are likely to arise. Then, if they do experience those feelings, they are not caught off guard and can cope with the feelings more effectively. If they do not experience those negative feelings, they can feel especially proud of themselves.
- **Formulate a plan with the client on exactly how the action will be measured.** This entails determining the following three pieces of information:
  1. *Unit of measure*—Generally, behaviors can be measured in terms of duration, frequency, or intensity. Behaviors such as time per day watching television, time spent completing homework, minutes of exercise per week, and hours of sleep per day can be described in terms of duration. Actions such as the number of beers consumed per day, the number of conversations with another person per day, and the number of times per week someone becomes angry can be measured in terms of frequency. Level of depression or anxiety, degree of rage, and self-esteem are variables that can be measured in terms of intensity.
  2. *Duration of the measurement process*—Determining how many beers or conversations a person has in one day may not be very revealing. However, if a record of those behaviors is kept over a week or two, the data is likely to be more

meaningful and reflective of the person's typical behavior. Client and clinician should decide for how long the client will keep track of the target behavior.

3. *Method of recording information*—Two aspects of the process are important here: accuracy and ease of recording. Suggesting that a person keep a record of how many sentences he exchanges with a spouse may yield interesting information; however, the most likely outcome is that the person will quickly abandon the recording process because it is so cumbersome. On the other hand, suggesting that, at the end of the week, a person list all food consumed during that week may entail a relatively brief recording process but memory lapses will probably result in inaccurate information. Collaborate with your client to find a balance between the need for accuracy and the need for an easy system of recording. If the client does not provide the information needed to establish an accurate baseline, goal setting and behavior change strategies are less likely to succeed.

ESTABLISHING GOALS

Establishing appropriate goals or objectives is an important step in the treatment process, whether the treatment focus is on background, emotions, thoughts, or actions. (The terms *goals* and *objectives* will be used interchangeably here, although some schools or agencies view goals as overarching targets and objectives as specific elements of a goal.) Goals that are too ambitious can be discouraging and can sabotage the treatment process. On the other hand, goals that are too easy can limit progress. Given the choice, goals that are too easy are preferable to those that are too difficult; the process of achieving even small, simple objectives can be empowering and can increase people's optimism and motivation to tackle more challenging goals. Goals reflect the destination of treatment and, as with any journey, the treatment process will be difficult if not impossible if the destination is unknown or unreachable.

Sound goals represent a collaboration between client and clinician and have the following eight characteristics (de Shazer, 1991):

- Important and relevant to the client
- Stated in positive terms
- Clear, concrete, and specific
- Small and incremental
- Measurable
- Realistic and within client's control
- Involving application and effort on the part of the client
- Leading to new learning, skills, or actions

Let's use the case of Yoram to illustrate the process of formulating sound goals. Yoram immigrated to the United States from Israel about a year ago. He had strong technical skills and had little difficulty finding employment as a web page designer. However, although his command of English was relatively good, he felt uncomfortable in his new environment, had difficulty initiating conversations, and had not made any friends since his arrival in the United States. Baseline information indicated that, after work, he spent approximately 4 hours a day watching television and "surfing the net." He had little contact with people outside of work and spent most of his time, both at work and away from work, looking at images on a screen.

Yoram was very unhappy with this situation and sought counseling to help him make a change. Yoram and his therapist collaborated in the development of the following initial goal statement:

> By one week from today, I will initiate conversations with two people and will write in my date book the time, place, and person with whom I conversed for each of these interactions. I also will obtain information on one leisure activity of interest to me.

This goal statement met all eight criteria listed previously. It addressed Yoram's need for more rewarding social and leisure activities and was, therefore, **important and meaningful** to him. The statement was **positive**, indicating what Yoram would do rather than what he would not do. It was **clear, concise, and specific**, indicating how many people he would talk to, how many leisure activities he would investigate, and by when these goals would be accomplished. The statement reflected **small and incremental** goals; certainly, this initial step would not resolve all of Yoram's difficulties, but it would hopefully help him start moving in his desired direction. Future goals would build on this initial goal statement, enabling Yoram to create a more rewarding lifestyle. The goals were **measurable**; the record-keeping process and the information on a leisure activity provided evidence of whether Yoram achieved his goals. Yoram agreed that the activities specified in his goal statement were **within his control** and that he was **capable of reaching the goals**. Finally, **new learning and skills** would emerge from this process. Yoram would identify a potential leisure activity and gather information about that pastime. Discussion with his therapist about his efforts to initiate conversations would help him acquire effective skills for beginning conversations.

Yoram also established the following long-term goal statement, in addition to his short-term goals:

> By one year from now, I would like to have two people I view as good friends who I see or talk to at least every other week. I would like to have two enjoyable leisure activities in which I participate at least twice a month. I would like to watch no more than 10 hours of television per week.

Yoram's long-term goals also met the previous criteria, except that they present an ultimate objective rather than small and incremental steps.

Having both short-term and long-term goals is helpful in facilitating behavioral change. The long-term goals keep people focused on future possibilities and give them a vision of a different and more rewarding life. However, if they only had long-term goals, months or even years might pass before those goals were achieved, perhaps leading to discouragement and hopelessness. The short-term goals counteract this by offering an opportunity for some rapid success and reinforcement. This can be instrumental in maintaining people's motivation and encouraging them to sustain their efforts to make positive changes.

Although goals receive particular attention in treatment systems emphasizing behavioral change, establishing sound goals is important regardless of the clinician's theoretical orientation or the nature of the desired change. Only when clinician and client have clearly identified desirable treatment outcomes can they readily determine whether progress is being made, whether interventions are successful, and when treatment has been completed. Goals have become an essential component of most current approaches to treatment.

CREATING A CONTRACT

Once goals have been formulated, they should be written down. They can then be compared to the eight criteria for sound goals and reviewed with the client. Modifications can be made at that time, if needed. This paves the way for creating a behavior change contract. Developing a contract that specifies when and how people will accomplish their goals is the next important step in effecting behavior change.

Planning and Addressing Obstacles

When preparing a behavior change contract, potential obstacles to goal attainment should be identified and explored and strategies developed to prevent those obstacles from getting in the way of a successful outcome. For example, although Yoram could identify several leisure activities he had enjoyed in Israel, he did not know how to obtain information about those activities in his new community. Following guidelines for information giving discussed in the previous chapter, the clinician provided Yoram with the names of a hiking club and a community recreation center that might offer the leisure activities he had in mind. Yoram and his therapist also identified several people with whom he might initiate conversations and planned some opening comments he could use to begin conversations with them.

Obstacles for goal attainment can seem particularly insurmountable for people who have experienced long-standing oppression and victimization. Examples might include people who are gay or lesbian, people from ethnic minority groups, and people living in abusive or impoverished situations. Clients like these people may be highly motivated to change their behaviors and improve their lives but may not know how or may not feel able to circumvent the barriers facing them. Clinicians need to collaborate with such clients to make a careful and realistic assessment of the obstacles they face. The use of community resources, along with the establishment of extremely small goals that take account of the obstacles, can help to break down barriers for these clients, provide them with resources and needed tools, and help them feel more empowered. (Clinicians may also want to address these obstacles on another level via involvement in governmental or social action programs to reduce some of these obstacles.)

Rewards and Consequences

When people make some progress toward their goals, that progress will be even more meaningful to them if it is reinforced or rewarded in some way. Ideally, the chosen reward should be something that will promote progress. For example, rewarding Yoram's success in achieving his goals with an extra hour of watching television would be counterproductive; on the other hand, treating himself to a new pair of hiking shoes would not only reinforce his accomplishments but would continue to build on those accomplishments.

Rewards should be items or experiences that are personally meaningful to the client. In addition, rewards must be realistic. Yoram might be able to afford a new pair of shoes to celebrate successful achievement of his first short-term goal, but it would not make sense for him to buy a new pair of shoes every week that he reaches his goals. More modest rewards that contributed to his overall goals would need to be established— perhaps a dinner at a special restaurant that would separate him from his television and offer him some interaction with other people.

In general, rewards serve as better motivators than negative consequences or punishments. Rewards are more likely to enhance mood, promote optimism and feelings of empowerment, and strengthen the therapeutic alliance. However, consequences do sometimes have a place in the goal setting and contracting process.

Particularly useful is identification of natural or logical consequences. For example, Yoram recognized that if he rarely went outdoors, obtained little exercise, and had few leisure activities, he would probably become less attractive and interesting to others. On the other hand, if he resumed the regular hiking he had enjoyed in Israel and developed additional leisure activities, he would naturally become more physically fit and attractive and have more to talk about with others. Helping people consider the logical consequences of both their current and their desired behaviors can be helpful in encouraging their effort and progress.

Punishments are rarely used in the clinical setting, primarily because they can impair clients' self-esteem and create a negative therapeutic environment. However, occasionally, rewards are not powerful enough to change behavior and the addition of some planned negative consequences can be beneficial. For example, Mimi had tried many different strategies to stop smoking with little success. What mattered most to her was the welfare of animals; she was horrified by thoughts of hunting animals for their fur. To motivate herself to stop smoking, she decided that every time she smoked a cigarette, she would put 25 cents into a jar. Each time $5 was accumulated in the jar, she would send a donation to an organization designed to protect the rights of hunters. After painfully sending off a few checks, Mimi finally got control of her smoking because of her love for animals. Although there is a place for negative consequences in treatment, these should be carefully determined so that they are not shaming or forced on the client but rather have been chosen by client and clinician working in collaboration to enhance the treatment process.

Commitment

The likelihood that people will achieve their goals is increased if they make a public commitment to put forth the effort they need to reach their goals. The first step toward such a commitment occurs when client and clinician write down the mutually determined goals and agree that the client will work on achieving those goals. Sharing the goals with people outside of the therapeutic relationship can further enhance the likelihood that people will achieve their goals.

For example, one of Helen's goals was to prepare more meals and, correspondingly, to spend less time and money in restaurants. She decided that she would cook dinner for herself and her husband at least twice a week. To facilitate this, she shared her goal with her husband and asked him to support her efforts by helping her clean up after dinner and by suggesting some dishes he would like her to prepare for him. His assistance and enthusiasm for her cooking, as well as the money they were saving, reinforced Helen's efforts to reach her goal.

Putting It in Writing

Just as we "put it in writing" when we buy a house or enter into a business partnership, so is it valuable to put in writing the goals and rewards we have established for ourselves. A written contract with ourselves has the following advantages:

- The terms of the agreement are clear.
- We can refer back to the contract as a reminder or as reinforcement.
- A written contract facilitates making a public commitment.

A comprehensive written contract can include all of the elements already discussed in this chapter: a baseline, specific and concrete initial and long-term goal statements, and rewards or consequences. It might also include suggested strategies for accomplishing the goal; this will be discussed further in the next section.

Example of a Behavioral Change Contract

Such a contract might resemble the following format, illustrated by a contract made between Katie, the 15-year-old girl presented on page 138 and her counselor. Although she was a gifted student who hoped to graduate from high school and maybe attend college, Katie had not been completing her homework on schedule. As a result her grades had dropped from As and Bs to Ds in her 2 years of high school.

- *Baseline*—clear and specific statement of the current severity of the behavior as reflected in frequency, duration, and/or intensity.

  At present, I am spending no more than 1 hour per week in studying at home. Although I have a study period, I am using that time to read magazines or write notes to my friends.
- *Short-term goal*—positive, important and meaningful, realistic, clear and specific, measurable, small and incremental, within the person's control, involving new skills and learning.
  - I will sign up for a course in study skills by the end of next week.
  - I will spend the first 20 minutes of my study period on my homework for at least 3 of the next 5 school days.
  - I will spend at least 30 minutes per day completing my schoolwork at home, for at least 4 of the next 7 days.
- *Record-keeping*—what information and how information will be kept on goal-directed behaviors.

  At the end of each day, I will write down in my planner how much time I spent on schoolwork in study period and at home.

- *Helpful strategies*—skills, tools, and ideas generated by client and clinician that will help the client overcome obstacles and achieve the short-term goals.
  - I will learn more about study skills by taking a class and talking to my school counselor.
  - I will plan in advance those days when I will study at home.
  - I will turn off my cell phone when I am studying at home.
  - I will set a timer for 30 minutes when I am studying at home and will focus on my schoolwork at least until the timer rings.
- *Commitment*—public disclosure of goals.
    I will share my goals and strategies with my parents.
- *Rewards or consequences*—a statement of reinforcements or penalties for achieving or failing to achieve one's goals; stating these in "if/then" terms clarifies the relationship between behavior and response.
  - Each day, if I meet my goals for studying either at home or at school, then my mom will let me spend 45 minutes accessing e-mail on her computer.
  - If I meet all of my goals at the end of the week, then my parents will give me the money to buy a new CD.
- *Long-term goals*—a statement of the eventual desired outcome that is realistic, clear, specific, and measurable.

I will have established a study schedule that allows me to spend at least 6 hours per week on my homework. I will improve my grades by the last marking period of this school year so that I have no grades below a C and have at least two grades of A or B.

GIVING DIRECTIVES AND SUGGESTING TASKS

For many novice clinicians (and unfortunately also for some experienced clinicians), counseling is synonymous with giving advice or telling people what the clinician thinks they should do. I have interviewed many aspiring clinicians seeking admission to graduate programs who explain their interest in counseling or psychology by saying something like, "I didn't get much help when I was growing up, and I want to tell people how to avoid the mistakes that I made" or "I learned so much from my own counseling; I want to pass on what I learned to other people." Although well meaning, statements such as these reflect the misconception of too many clinicians that their role is to tell people how they should lead their lives. One of the most important goals of graduate programs designed to train clinicians is helping them understand how to help people make good choices for themselves. Such programs typically discourage clinicians from giving advice or telling people what to do.

At the same time, carefully and thoughtfully giving certain types of advice or suggestions definitely does have a place in the clinical relationship. Such advice has been referred to as directives, prescriptions, recommendations, suggestions, between-session tasks, or homework assignments. Hill and O'Grady (1985) found that directives, including advice and information giving, constituted one of the main categories of clinician interventions. Scheel et al. (1999) found that many of the suggestions made by clinicians referred to homework or "out-of-session activities suggested during therapy to be performed by the client" (p. 308). The research of Scheel and colleagues concluded that clinicians made an average of 1.85 of these recommendations per session. According to Hay and Kinnier (1998), "Using homework as an adjunct to the work that occurs within the counseling session has been shown to be an effective way to promote therapeutic change in a brief period of time" (p. 122).

Benefits of Between-Session Tasks

Between-session tasks have the following therapeutic benefits:

- They provide clients a sense of direction.
- They continue the therapeutic process between sessions.
- They can enhance and further the work of the sessions.
- They encourage generalization and transfer of new learning and behaviors into a real-life setting.
- They can promote clients' feelings of self-control, responsibility, self-efficacy, and motivation.

Guidelines for Suggesting Homework or Between-Session Tasks

Although between-session tasks or suggested homework clearly have the potential to advance the treatment process, they also can be harmful to clients' motivation and to the therapeutic alliance. If poorly planned and presented, such tasks can make people feel misunderstood, discouraged, and overwhelmed. Failure to perform tasks successfully can lead them to view themselves as "bad students" and even lead them to terminate treatment prematurely.

Following these guidelines can maximize the likelihood that between-session tasks will be beneficial:

- Between-session tasks should be initiated at the first session and made a routine and integral part of treatment.
- Although an activity might be introduced by the clinician, client and clinician should collaborate in determining whether or not it is likely to be helpful and in spelling out the details of the task. The client's perception of the activity seems to be the primary determinant of whether it will be performed and whether it will be useful to that client.
- The task should be relevant and clearly linked to the work that has gone on in the session. Presenting a rationale for the task can help the client understand how it might be beneficial.
- Accomplishment of the task should make use of and build on client strengths, abilities, and interests.
- The level of difficulty of the task should be appropriate to the client. Easily accomplished activities, creating feelings of success, are usually preferable to demanding challenges that are likely to lead to failure.
- Any possible obstacles to completion of the task such as time required by the task, client discomfort with the task, or complexity of the task should be addressed. This will increase the likelihood that the task will be done.
- The suggested task should be written down and reviewed with the client to ensure understanding.

- The results of the task should be discussed in the next session. Of course, avoid blaming or shaming clients who have not completed the task as specified. Instead, emphasize client choices, self-monitoring, and self-assessment. View any outcome to the process as a learning experience and an opportunity to formulate another, perhaps more appropriate task.

Categories of Between-Session Tasks

Scheel et al. (1999) identified eight categories of clinician recommendations. The following list, in descending order of occurrence, includes examples to illustrate each of those categories. Notice that each suggestion is phrased tentatively, inviting discussion and reactions from the client. The clinicians present themselves as helpers and guides, not all-knowing experts. They are careful not to give orders or to exaggerate the power differential between themselves and their clients.

1. *Validation of internal experience*—It sounds like your intuitions are working well for you. Perhaps this week you could write down two intuitions you have and then list the thoughts associated with those intuitions.
2. *Social interactions*—How would you feel about introducing yourself to two people you don't know at church this week?
3. *Reframing meaning*—I wonder if your staying home so that you are always available to your children might be a way to protect yourself. Perhaps it would be useful to write in your journal this week about ways that you protect yourself.
4. *Decision making*—What about making a list of the pros and cons of adopting another child for our next session?
5. *Request for action*—It might help you in your efforts to stop drinking if you were to join Alcoholics Anonymous. I can give you a telephone number to call to obtain information on meetings in your area.
6. *Promotion of self-esteem*—Sounds like you are focusing on a few negatives and overlooking many positives in your work. When you make a list of your billable hours for each day, how about also listing your successes for that day?
7. *Referral*—Perhaps some medication might help you with your difficulty focusing and paying attention. Here are the names of three psychiatrists who specialize in treating attention-deficit/hyperactivity disorder. How would you feel about scheduling an appointment with one of them this week?
8. *Stress management*—We have reviewed some deep breathing and relaxation exercises in our session today. I wonder if you would be able to find the time to practice them for about 15 minutes every day.

Formats for Between-Session Tasks

Regardless of the purpose of the task, suggested activities can take many forms. The following are some of the many formats that between-session tasks can take:

- reading about a topic of interest, either to oneself or aloud to a friend or family member

- writing about a topic of interest or about one's background experiences, emotions, thoughts, or actions
- making lists, perhaps of strengths, successes, or pros and cons
- thinking in a new way or about a particular topic
- obtaining information, either through the Internet, the library, or a knowledgeable person
- joining a support group such as a 12-step program or a group for people coping with a difficult illness or life experience
- taking a course, such as one on assertiveness skills or parent effectiveness
- taking carefully planned and gradual risks
- identifying and engaging in leisure activities and exercise programs
- communicating with other people in new and better ways
- observing interactions or experiences
- planning and scheduling
- taking a break or establishing a relaxation routine

Although the general guidelines I have presented here emphasize the importance of planning task assignments that are nonthreatening, clear, and easily accomplished, several approaches to formulating between-session tasks deliberately violate those guidelines. They can be powerful forces for client change. However, they also have the potential to do harm and so must be used with considerable caution. Although I will describe these strategies here so that you are aware of what they are, they should be reserved for experienced clinicians who have received training or supervision in these strategies.

Shame-attacking exercises stem primarily from the work of Albert Ellis (1995). The idea behind these experiences is that if we inundate ourselves with the very experiences that we most fear we are likely to get over that fear. For example, as a young man, Ellis was apparently apprehensive about asking women out for a date. To overcome this, he assigned himself the task of asking out 100 women. Although none accepted his invitation, the exercise did serve the purpose of reducing Ellis's fear.

In *paradoxical interventions,* derived from the writings of Viktor Frankl (1963), clinicians typically suggest to clients a way of thinking or acting that is the opposite of what they have been trying to do. People might be encouraged to schedule arguments with their partners, to assume that the worst will happen, to do less rather than more, and to schedule a relapse. Doing something radically different from what they have been doing unsuccessfully can often be beneficial to people. In addition, the surprising nature of these interventions can be intriguing to clients, increasing the likelihood that they will complete the task. Of course, suggestions such as these pose a risk and can be discouraging to clients and harmful to the treatment process. Again, these strategies should be used with care and reserved for experienced clinicians.

CHALLENGE AND CONFRONTATION

This book has stressed the importance of empowering people and helping them make choices that seem best for them. Clinicians should not assume a "Counselor Knows Best" stance and tell clients what is best for them. On the other hand, clinicians sometimes have good reason to believe that clients are making choices that are clearly harmful to them or are behaving in ways that are inconsistent with their goals and values. This was illustrated by the cases of Katie, Lavinia, and Curt presented earlier in this chapter. At times like these, clinicians do need to take steps to help clients look at and evaluate the choices they are making and perhaps help them see that other options would be more helpful to them.

This process has been described by many terms. *Confrontation* is probably the best known of these terms. However, in recent years, this term has fallen out of favor because of its negative connotations. Instead, clinicians are more likely to speak of challenging the client or using caring confrontations. Just as the name has changed, so has the nature of this process. Challenges, just like the other interventions in the clinician's repertoire, should be delivered with caring and sensitivity to ensure that they are helpful and enlightening rather than critical and shaming. An effective challenge can promote insight and awareness, reduce resistance, increase congruence between clients' goals and their behaviors, promote open communication, and lead to positive changes in people's emotions, thoughts, and actions.

Ten Types of Client Discrepancies

Generally, the best way to present a challenge is to calmly and gently point out a discrepancy to the client. Ten types of discrepancies that people may present follow, with accompanying examples (Hill & O'Brien, 1999).

1. *Discrepancy between two verbal statements*—Sometimes you tell me how much you love and value your parents, but at other times you tell me that you can't stand being around them and refer to them as "nerds."
2. *Discrepancy between words and actions* (probably the most common type of discrepancy)—Although you have made a commitment to sobriety, you went to a party where you knew there would be a great deal of drugs and alcohol.
3. *Discrepancy between two actions*—You teach courses on ways to promote children's self-esteem, and yet you tell your own children they are stupid and clumsy.
4. *Discrepancy between two emotions*—You long for some close friends, yet your fears and shyness keep you from taking steps to make friends.
5. *Discrepancy between reported emotion and implicit emotion*—You have told me that it doesn't bother you that your girlfriend ended your relationship, and yet I see tears in your eyes when you talk about it.
6. *Discrepancy between values and behaviors*—One of your important values is to maintain the financial security of your family and yet you have lost so much money through high-risk investments that you might lose your home.
7. *Discrepancy between perceptions and experience*—Although you perceive Sheryl to be a loyal and trustworthy friend, you know that she has repeatedly spread false rumors about you and tried to prevent you from getting a promotion.
8. *Discrepancy between ideal and real self*—I know that you have a dream of going to Harvard like both of your parents, but your school records suggest that it would be hard for you to gain admission to that institution.
9. *Discrepancy between viewpoints of client and clinician*—You tell me that you view cancer as a "minor inconvenience" and yet I perceive a life-threatening illness like cancer as an experience that has a profound impact on most people.

10. *Discrepancy between client and outside world*—You have told me that you are not planning to pay your taxes on schedule. I wonder if you are aware of the financial penalties that the Internal Revenue Service can levy against people who don't meet their tax deadlines?

Guidelines for Effective Challenges

Just like advice giving, the use of challenges in treatment poses risks. They may lead clients to feel hurt, attacked, angry, ashamed, confused, scared, insulted, or defensive. However, careful delivery of challenges in the context of a sound therapeutic alliance can increase the likelihood that the challenges will be well received by clients and will lead them to new ways of feeling, thinking, and acting. The following guidelines can improve the delivery of challenges:

- Use careful listening to be sure of the accuracy of your challenge.
- Use empathy and support to demonstrate that you understand and care about the dilemma that clients are facing.
- Time your delivery carefully; challenges are most likely to be effective after you have built a positive therapeutic alliance with the client and have earned the client's trust.
- Use challenges infrequently, generally when no other interventions seem likely to be helpful.
- Be clear and specific when presenting a challenge, citing meaningful examples or statements.
- Be cautious, gentle, and tentative when presenting a challenge. Your goal is to promote dialogue and exploration, not to prove the client wrong.
- After making a challenging statement, process the challenge. Elicit the client's involvement and reactions by asking such questions as, "What do you make of that?" "What is your reaction to that?" "How does that sound to you?" "Help me understand this," and "Had you noticed that?"
- Take into account the cultural background of your clients. Challenges may be so hurtful and offensive to people from some cultural backgrounds that they should not be used at all.

REVIEW OF STEPS TO EFFECT BEHAVIORAL CHANGE

This chapter has presented the basic technical skills that clinicians need to effect behavioral change, although more will be said in the next section on strategies to promote behavioral change. Let's review the steps in the behavioral change process:

1. Describe the undesirable actions as specifically as possible.
2. Establish a baseline, reflecting the current frequency, intensity, or duration of the actions.
3. Determine realistic goals, beginning with short-term goals.
4. Develop a clear contract, specifying goals and rewards or consequences.
5. Put contract in writing and elicit client's commitment to the contract.

6. Address potential obstacles to goal achievement.
7. Provide skills and tasks that will promote goal achievement.
8. Facilitate client's efforts to track and record progress.
9. Assess progress toward goals.
10. Implement plans for rewards or consequences or, if indicated, revise contract.

SPECIFIC STRATEGIES TO PROMOTE CHANGE IN ACTIONS

This section will present the following specific strategies to promote changes in unhelpful actions:

- empowerment strategies
- visualization
- behavioral rehearsal
- modeling and role playing
- skill development
- breaking down an action into small steps
- possibility language
- relaxation
- systematic desensitization

These skills are useful not only in mental health settings but in a wide variety of other settings. They can be helpful in schools and colleges, in businesses, and even at home.

Empowerment

Clinicians sometimes encounter clients who are willing to explore their emotions and analyze their thoughts but are reluctant to take actions that are likely to help them. Many factors can contribute to this lack of movement, including (Burns, 1993; Carlock, 1999):

- *Low self-esteem*—People may view themselves as incapable of even the smallest positive change and are certain they will fail at any undertaking.
- *Anxiety and apprehension*—People become comfortable with the known, even if it is replete with problems, and fear venturing into new areas.
- *Perfectionism*—People are afraid that if they take on new challenges, they may not have immediate success and are reluctant to risk looking bad in their own eyes and in those of others.
- *Procrastination*—People may have difficulty getting started and following through on their plans. They put things off and miss deadlines in many areas of their lives, and that pattern carries over to their treatment.
- *Depression and inertia*—Taking a small step forward and trying something new may appear impossible to people who are depressed. They typically feel as though they are in a dark hole from which there is no escape. Hopelessness and lack of energy keeps them trapped.
- *Cultural messages and disenfranchising experiences*—These can lead people to underestimate themselves and to believe that they have few options.

People often present with a combination of these factors, such as depression and low self-esteem, posing a particular challenge in treatment.

Empowering clients, helping them to view themselves as competent and likely to succeed, and giving them ways to overcome obstacles are important in enabling them to move past the many factors that prevent people from taking effective action. Although the clinicians' support, encouragement, and optimism can contribute to clients' feelings of empowerment, they are not enough. Feelings of worth, power, and competence need to stem primarily from the insights and actions of the client rather than from judgments of the clinician.

As tempted as we might be to say to a client, "I know you can do it if you just give it a try," this can do more harm than good. Statements like this can contribute to the tendency of many clients to base their self-evaluation on the views that others have of them. Instead, we want to promote intrinsic feelings of worth and competence in our clients. In addition, if we assure people that they will succeed and that does not happen, they may lose faith in the treatment process and the therapeutic alliance. Some clients will even deliberately fail at tasks that are initiated by clinicians in order to sabotage treatment and demonstrate that it will not help them. Clinicians should keep in mind, then, the importance of empowering people from within rather than telling them what they should feel, think, or do differently.

Fortunately, many strategies are available to facilitate people's efforts to empower themselves so that they can take constructive action to improve their lives. The following list includes some of the most useful ones, but feel free to develop your own approaches to helping your clients build up their feelings of worth and competence.

Lists of strengths and accomplishments.   Asking people who feel powerless and discouraged to identify their strengths or list their admirable qualities is not likely to be successful. Inherent in most people with low self-esteem is the tendency to exaggerate their flaws and ignore their strengths. However, with some coaching, even these clients can develop a list of strengths and accomplishments. Questions such as the following can facilitate this process:

- If your child (or partner or best friend or employer) were telling someone about you, what would you like them to say about you?
- Tell me about one or two of your accomplishments in your work? Your relationships? Your home management activities? Your leisure activities? Your fund of knowledge? Your contributions to society?
- What qualities about you do you think led your employer to hire you? Your partner to be with you? Your friends to spend time with you? Your customers to seek you out again and again?

Once clients have made a start in developing a list of accomplishments and strengths, clinicians can suggest additions to the list, based on what they have learned about the clients. Clinicians should keep in mind that they are not assessing the worth of the person but rather simply identifying that person's positive qualities and achievements. Clinicians should try to be specific and give examples to promote the clients' awareness of their assets, emphasizing what the clients have said about themselves. In other words, rather than saying, "I think you are a very intelligent person," the clinician might say, "You have two masters degrees and a doctorate in philosophy. What does that say about your abilities?" Of course, clients always have the right to reject or rephrase any suggested additions; clients must believe in the list and view it as an accurate reflection of them if it is to be meaningful.

Drawing one's strengths.   For children or early adolescents, drawing and other creative means can be used to elicit strengths and accomplishments. For example, clinicians might suggest that the children pretend to be medieval knights, creating a shield to represent their power and scare off enemies. The shield might include words, symbols, or pictures that represent the person's strengths and accomplishments. Similarly, a collage with drawings and pictures cut from magazines can be used to create an image of a person's strengths and accomplishments. Even some adults might enjoy these activities and find them less constricting than using only words to describe themselves. Affirmations, discussed in the previous chapter, can be developed to go along with the positive images in order to solidify and reinforce clients' recognition of their strengths.

Visualization

Many successful athletes and performers use visualization to enhance their success. This strategy can be used to increase the likelihood of success in almost any endeavor, including counseling and psychotherapy.

With the guidance of the clinician, clients imagine themselves effectively coping with obstacles and performing desired actions. This might be inviting a friend for lunch, cleaning out a closet, beginning an exercise class, spending a day without consuming alcohol, or almost any other action.

The visualization process typically begins with a brief relaxation exercise (discussed later in this chapter). Then the client imagines a scenario, presented by the clinician, which includes the desired behaviors. The clinician should present a rich and detailed picture, vividly describing the client effectively performing the targeted behaviors and concluding with an image of the client feeling pride and satisfaction. The image should be a fairly realistic one, including descriptions of difficulties that are likely to arise and negative emotions such as fear and anger that the client might experience. However, the visualization should also present the client addressing those difficulties and feelings and overcoming them. Anchoring, discussed in chapter 4, can be used to install a positive image of the client achieving success, allowing ready access to that image in the future.

Behavioral Rehearsal

The old cliché, practice makes perfect, has a great deal of truth to it. When we practice a new or challenging behavior, we can try out a variety of approaches to the behavior, assess and refine our performance, develop new skills and strategies if necessary, and gain confidence through experience and success.

Helping clients find a way to practice desired behaviors can increase the likelihood that the actions will be performed effectively. Practice can happen in a variety of ways:

- Behaviors that involve a transaction between two people can be practiced in a session via a role play involving the client and the clinician. Such transactions could include discussing work-related issues with a supervisor, inviting a friend to an activity, expressing dissatisfaction with someone's behavior, and even proposing marriage. In the role play, clients would be themselves while clinicians assume the role of the other person in the interaction. Here, too, some realism is desirable; when clinicians engage in the role play, they should present clients with some issues or challenges that are likely to arise so that they have the opportunity to try out ways to handle them. The role play can be tape recorded to facilitate discussion and feedback and then reviewed to identify strengths and strategies for improvement.

- Trying out a behavior in a safe setting can afford practice and learning. For example, assume that Jamie typically has difficulty expressing his needs; he wants to practice some new assertiveness skills he has learned. Rather than practicing with his supervisor or even with his partner, which might be too risky, he might be wiser to begin practicing his new skills in a situation where he has no personal investment, such as at the supermarket or auto repair shop. In that way, he will have few repercussions if the practice is not successful; rather, weak application of his new behaviors can provide an opportunity for learning and skill development.

- Using a video or audio tape recorder and practicing in front of a mirror can help people to take a relatively objective look at their performance and identify ways to make improvements. Asking a trusted friend or family member to review and comment on the performance can provide another source of useful feedback.

- Practice can also be internal or covert. Similar to the visualization exercise discussed earlier, people can review in their minds the details of a desired behavior. They can also try out, in their minds, various ways of performing the behavior to determine which feels most comfortable and is most likely to succeed.

Modeling

The purpose of modeling is to provide clients with examples of desirable behaviors to facilitate their learning of these behaviors. Seeing helpful actions performed by others can be encouraging to clients; at least someone can accomplish what they are trying to do! The use of an admired model is particularly likely to be inspiring to clients.

Like behavioral rehearsal, modeling can take a variety of forms. Clinicians themselves can serve as models, demonstrating to their clients new and useful types of behaviors such as initiating a conversation, making a request, and expressing anger. Alternatively, clients might be able to identify people they know who manifest the desired behaviors; clients can then observe these people and learn from them.

Using the **self as a model** is a strategy that can be particularly useful and empowering. Clients practice a new behavior until they are satisfied with their performance. Then they make a tape recording of themselves exhibiting the desired behavior, and watch or listen to it again and again until they believe they have mastered the skill.

Acting as if is another variation on modeling, one that is particularly useful for young people. In this approach, clients select someone they admire who they believe could successfully perform the desired behavior. They might select a superhero, a well-known athlete, or a famous singer or actor. They might even select an admired friend or family member. Then, when they are performing the desired behavior, they act as if they are the admired person. The process of identifying with someone who represents competence, power, and success to clients can enable them to take on some of those feelings vicariously and enhance their self-confidence and success.

Similarly, clients can act as if they have a particular trait or ability such as good social skills, assertiveness, or extroversion. This seems to facilitate people's acquisition of the desired trait or skill and helps them manifest it with greater comfort than they otherwise would have.

Skill Development

Often the biggest barrier to people using new skills is that they have not really learned the skills they need and so continue to use unhelpful behaviors. An appropriate part of the clinician's role is helping people acquire the skills they need. Skills can be taught directly by the clinician or by suggesting reading, films, or workshops that might be useful to clients. These training experiences might focus on such skills as effective communication, anger management, successful parenting, time management, and organization. As you have probably discovered for yourself, having the skills you need to deal with the people and experiences you encounter contributes greatly to your feelings of empowerment and self-confidence.

Breaking Down Behaviors into Small Steps

Often the enormity of a task can be daunting and can discourage people from even starting to move toward accomplishment of the task. Think about yourself as a junior in high school. Assume that your career goal is to become a licensed counselor or psychologist. Consider how many years and how much effort you have spent in achieving that goal. Had you known, when you were 16 or 17, how demanding it would be to achieve your career goal, you might have been discouraged from even considering that goal. However, the process of becoming a clinician can be broken down into many steps that, in themselves, do not seem overwhelming.

For the high school student aspiring to a field in human services, initial steps might include: achieving good grades in high school, taking a course or doing some independent reading in the social sciences, identifying colleges that have a strong undergraduate program in psychology or social work, and applying to college. Even these actions may seem overwhelming but they, too, can be broken into small steps. For example, the process of applying to college usually entails obtaining and completing applications, writing essays, requesting letters of recommendation, scheduling interviews, visiting the colleges, and making final decisions.

Although keeping their final goal in mind can be useful to people, the process of identifying the steps to attaining that goal and taking them one at a time can be far more empowering and more likely to motivate them toward continued action. Keep this strategy in mind when working with clients who seem overwhelmed by how much they will need to do to achieve their goals.

Possibility or Presuppositional Language

Derived primarily from solution-based therapy (O'Hanlon & Weiner-Davis, 1989), possibility language used by clinicians can help people to develop confidence that they can behave more effectively and that positive change can actually happen. In talking with clients, clinicians assume that the desired changes will certainly happen and that difficulties are only temporary. They use language that reflects those assumptions. This creates optimism and helps people feel more confident and more capable of making positive changes.

Clinicians using possibility language might make statements or ask questions such as the following:

- You have not *yet* been able to take the steps you need to resolve this.
- When you take those steps, what do you think it will feel like?
- What will your life be like when you have achieved your goals?
- You can be fearful, *and* you can move forward to change your actions.
- What differences will your family notice when you have made those changes?
- You can clearly see the possibility that you can improve your life.

Relaxation

Relaxation strategies help lessen people's apprehensions about attempting new behaviors and can enable them to perform those behaviors more confidently and effectively. In addition, acquiring relaxation strategies can be empowering, increasing people's conviction that they can learn and use other helpful new behaviors.

Many strategies are available to clinicians who are helping their clients to reduce stress and increase relaxation. These include meditation (discussed in chapter 4), deep diaphragmatic breathing, biofeedback, exercise, yoga, and progressive muscle relaxation. Combinations of strategies (e.g., diaphragmatic breathing, progressive muscle relaxation, and visualization) can be particularly powerful. Describing all of these strategies is beyond the scope of this book, but many resources such as *The Relaxation & Stress Reduction Workbook* (Davis, Eshelman, McKay, & Eshelman, 2001) are available to provide this information to both clients and clinicians. Clinicians also can make tape recordings during sessions in which they teach clients techniques such as deep breathing and progressive relaxation. Then the recordings can be given to clients with the suggestion that they listen to the tapes and practice the exercises daily.

Systematic Desensitization

Systematic desensitization is a powerful strategy to help people reduce fears that might block them from trying new behaviors. This strategy gradually exposes people to their fears while they are in a state of relaxation. Exposure may occur in the imagination (*imaginal desensitization*) or in reality (*in vivo* desensitization).

Careful planning is needed to ensure that the client is ready for each exposure and that the exposure is maintained until the fear has diminished and been brought under control. Stopping the exposure prematurely can lead to an increase, rather than a decrease, in fears. Because the use of systematic desensitization poses some risk for clients, clinicians should acquire training and supervision in this strategy before using it with their clients.

The use of systematic desensitization will be illustrated via its use with Eileen Carter, discussed throughout this book. Eileen had a fear of taking exams. Although she was enthusiastic about her course work and eager to continue her education, her self-doubts and inconsistent academic history led her to become tense and anxious whenever she had an in-class exam. As a result, despite lengthy preparation for the exams, she did not always do her best on the tests. Systematic desensitization was used as follows to help Eileen overcome this fear.

1. *Teach client an effective relaxation strategy.*   An array of relaxation strategies was discussed with Eileen, and she was encouraged to do some reading on that subject. She decided that diaphragmatic breathing would be the best strategy for her; because of its simplicity, she was not likely to forget how to use this technique.

2. *Describe the feared experience or behavior as clearly as possible.*   Eileen explained that her fear began when she sat down to study for the exam. It gradually worsened, becoming acute when she entered the classroom and almost debilitating when the exams were distributed. Her greatest fear was that, when she read the exam, she would discover that she was unable to answer any of the questions.

3. *Establish an anxiety hierarchy.*   Eileen's clear description of her fear facilitated the development of an anxiety hierarchy, a list of fears presented in order from the mildest fear to the most severe. Rating each element in the anxiety hierarchy according to the amount of distress it raised on a 0–100 Subjective Units of Distress Scale (SUDS) ensured that the items were in the proper order. Eileen's anxiety hierarchy is presented in table 5-1.

4. *Provide controlled exposure to the anxiety hierarchy.*   Because the actual test-taking process could not be recreated in the treatment room, Eileen's clinician used imaginal desensitization with her. Her clinician had Eileen use deep breathing to relax and then began with the first item on the anxiety hierarchy. While Eileen relaxed, the clinician described Eileen gathering her study materials and putting her books and notes out on her desk so that she could begin studying. Eileen imagined the scene until she began to get used to it and her SUDS score began to decline. This experience was repeated until Eileen and her clinician believed that she had reduced her fear of the first item to a low and manageable level. They then progressed through the list, repeating this process with each item.

TABLE 5-1   Eileen's Test Anxiety Hierarchy

Stimulus	SUDS Rating
Putting my books and notes out on the desk so I can begin to study	45
Thinking about the exam while I study	55
Running out of time to study	65
Packing up my book bag to go to the exam	70
Driving to school	73
Walking into the room where the exam will be held	80
Waiting for the exam to be distributed	85
Reviewing the exam	92
Taking the exam	95
Turning in the exam	99
Listening to the other students talk about their answers	100

5. *Practice to solidify and reinforce gains.*   Eileen practiced her relaxation between sessions, imagining some of the first few items on the list that no longer raised much anxiety for her. When she began to study for her next exam, she once again used deep breathing to overcome her apprehension about test taking. Affirmations and progressive muscle relaxation further enhanced her efforts to relax. Gradually, Eileen's fear of taking tests lessened enough so that it did not impair her performance on the examinations.

Clearly, clinicians have many strategies they can use to facilitate clients' efforts to change unrewarding and self-destructive behavior. Thoughtful integration of one or more of these strategies into the steps to promote behavioral change, presented earlier in this chapter, can make a powerful treatment package.

The learning opportunities that follow will afford you experience in using some of these strategies. As with all the chapters in this book, you are not expected to complete all the learning opportunities presented here. Select those that seem most likely to enhance the development of your clinical skills.

LEARNING OPPORTUNITIES

This chapter has focused on teaching you the following skills relevant to helping people change undesirable actions and behaviors:

Basic Technical Skills

- describing undesirable behaviors and determining the baseline for those behaviors
- goal setting
- contracting
- giving directives and suggesting between-session tasks
- challenge/confrontation

Specific Technical Skills
- empowerment
- visualization
- behavioral rehearsal
- modeling
- skill development
- breaking down actions into small steps
- possibility language
- relaxation
- systematic desensitization

Written Exercises

1. For each of the clients described here, identify the following:
   - a strategy for measuring the undesirable behaviors or actions
   - a specific and realistic short-term goal
   - a useful between-session task

> **Client 1:** My parents say now that I am in high school, I have to take responsibility for getting my own homework done, but I just don't seem able to do it. I come home from school, sit down with my video games, and before I know it, it's time for dinner. Then my friends start to call. If I spend 20 minutes on homework before I go to bed, it's a lot.

- A strategy for measuring the undesirable behaviors or actions:
- A specific and realistic short-term goal:
- A useful between-session task:

> **Client 2:** I know it's not good for either me or them, but I always seem to be nagging my kids. "Pick up your room, wash your hands, do your homework, shut off the television," and on and on. And half the time they don't even listen to me. I think my nagging has just become like background noise. I need to find another way to interact with them.

- A strategy for measuring the undesirable behaviors or actions:
- A specific and realistic short-term goal:
- A useful between-session task:

> **Client 3:** I think I should cut back on my drinking but that's really difficult. It's so much a part of my life. It's two or three drinks over a business lunch, then more drinking after work, then there's usually a party or reception and that means more drinking. It's just an accepted part of my work. But I find I can't drink the way I used to. I'm putting on weight, I feel wiped out at the end of the day, and even my thinking on the job is being affected.

- A strategy for measuring the undesirable behaviors or actions:
- A specific and realistic short-term goal:
- A useful between-session task:

2. Identify an obstacle to positive change that you think might arise for each of the clients in the item 1 examples and determine a strategy you might use to help them overcome or prevent that obstacle:

   Client 1:
   Obstacle:
   Strategy:
   Client 2:
   Obstacle:
   Strategy:
   Client 3:
   Obstacle:
   Strategy:

3. Like many people, the three clients described in item 1 manifest reluctance to engage in the hard work needed to change their unwanted behaviors. Challenging them may help to overcome their reluctance. Consider each of their statements that follow in relation to the clients' statements in item 1. Identify the type of discrepancy that is presented (see pages 149–150) and then write a challenging statement you might use to help each client become aware of the discrepancy and move forward.

   > **Client 1:** I have a new girlfriend and she really seems to like me. She must call me six or seven times a day. We just talk for hours every day; it really makes me feel special. So I haven't had a chance to follow up on our homework plan.

Type of discrepancy:
Challenging statement:
>   **Client 2:** I really wanted kids so much and I was so happy when they were born. I love them more than anything in the world and want them to know how wonderful they are. I would never do anything to make them feel badly about themselves, like my mother did to me.

Type of discrepancy:
Challenging statement:
>   **Client 3:** (Client smells of alcohol and appears unsteady.) I did just what we agreed. I haven't had a drink all week. No problem!

Type of discrepancy:
Challenging statement:

4. How might you use rewards or consequences to facilitate the behavioral change efforts of these three clients?
    Client 1:
    Client 2:
    Client 3:
5. How might you strengthen feelings of empowerment in each of the three clients?
    Client 1:
    Client 2:
    Client 3:
6. Identify a between-session task that you might suggest to one of the clients in these examples. How would you present that task to maximize the likelihood that the client will actually complete it?
7. How might you use modeling or acting as if to help one of the clients presented in item 1?
8. Identify one of the clients in item 1 who seems likely to benefit from skill development. Identify the skills that seem likely to be useful to that person. Briefly describe how you would go about teaching him or her the desired skills.
9. Write a statement using possibility language that you might use to help one of the clients presented in item 1.
10. Develop a series of small steps that one of the clients presented in item 1 might take to change his or her behavior. Remember to break the process down into incremental steps that are likely to lead to success and feelings of empowerment.

Discussion Questions

1. You have now participated in sessions focusing on background, on emotions, and on thoughts (and perhaps you have already completed the role play focused on actions). Which focus felt most comfortable for you and why? Which led to the most productive session and why?
2. Some clinicians believe that sessions focused on actions tend to be superficial and do not result in important or meaningful changes. What is your reaction to that statement?
3. Juanita is an 11-year-old girl who has been diagnosed with attention-deficit/hyperactivity disorder. She is taking medication that is somewhat helpful, but she

continues to manifest many behavioral difficulties, including impulsive talking, forgetting to raise her hand before responding to the teacher's questions, getting out of her seat at inappropriate times, and being distracted from her school work. Develop a plan to help Juanita change one of her behaviors. Describe your plan according to the following 10 steps:

1. Describe the undesirable actions as specifically as possible.
2. Establish a baseline, reflecting the current severity or frequency of the actions.
3. Determine realistic goals, beginning with short-term goals.
4. Develop a specific contract, specifying goals and rewards or consequences.
5. Put contract in writing and elicit client's commitment to the contract.
6. Address potential obstacles to goal achievement.
7. Provide skills and tasks that will promote goal achievement.
8. Facilitate client's efforts to track and record progress.
9. Assess progress toward goals.
10. Implement plans for rewards or consequences or, if indicated, revise contract.

4. When you have completed a hypothetical description of how treatment, following these steps, might proceed with Juanita, identify at least two specific technical interventions that you might use to advance your work with Juanita. How would you present these to her? Which do you think would be most likely to be helpful to her and why?
5. Clinicians are sometimes uncomfortable with the need to confront or challenge clients. Discuss your thoughts and feelings about this process. Under what circumstances do you think it is particularly important to challenge clients? What steps can you take to maximize the likelihood that this will be a helpful process for both client and clinician?
6. Consider the following clients' behavioral goals. For each one, identify a possible first step, a specific technical intervention that might promote change, and a suggested between-session task:
    Client 1: My goal is to lose 50 pounds in one year.
    - First step:
    - Specific intervention:
    - Task:
    Client 2: I'm 33 years old and I've always been afraid of the water. My goal is to learn to swim so that I can take my children to the beach.
    - First step:
    - Specific intervention:
    - Task:
    Client 3: All my savings are in a bank account, earning about 3% interest. I want to learn about investing and make better decisions about my money.
    - First step:
    - Specific intervention:
    - Task:

> **Client 4**: I have an impulse to cut myself and have done so more than half a dozen times. I have had multiple infections and am very ashamed of my behavior, but I don't seem able to stop. Can you help me?

- First step:
- Specific intervention:
- Task:

> **Client 5**: I recently had a leg amputated after an accident and have been fitted with a prosthesis. The doctors tell me that I can learn to walk again, but I am afraid I will fall. And yet I don't want to have to spend the rest of my life in a wheelchair.

- First step:
- Specific intervention:
- Task:

7. If you have not yet done the practice group exercises associated with this chapter, discuss your thoughts and feelings about that upcoming experience. What obstacles do you expect to encounter? What can you do to try to avoid them? What did you learn from the previous role play sessions that you want to carry with you into the role play focused on changing actions?

8. If you have already done the practice group exercises associated with this chapter, discuss your reactions to that experience. What was the most beneficial aspect of that experience for you? What was the most challenging or uncomfortable aspect of the experience? How did this role play compare with your earlier ones? How can you make future practice group exercises even more rewarding?

Practice Group Exercises—Assessing and Modifying Behaviors

Divide into your practice groups as described in the previous chapters and beginning on page 17 of this book. The practice group exercise presented here will help you to gain experience in some of the basic technical skills presented in this chapter: describing and measuring undesirable actions, goal setting, contracting, and giving suggestions. You may also have an opportunity to draw on one or more of the specific skills presented in this chapter to enhance the effectiveness of your counseling.

Preparing for the Roleplay: As with all the practice group exercises in this book, you will probably be more successful and learn more from the role play if you do some advance preparation. Most important are:

- **Reviewing the tape of your previous role play**, along with the feedback you received from your practice group.
- **Reviewing your previous Assessment of Progress Forms**. By now, you can probably identify some patterns in your counseling. Do you see yourself improving from session to session and adding new skills to your repertoire? Or does it seem like you are stuck and continue to receive the same feedback in one practice session after another? Try to identify the recurrent weaknesses in your counseling as well as your areas of strength. Don't be surprised if, like many novice clinicians, you tend to talk too much, overlook nonverbal messages, or pay more attention to emotions than thoughts. I have

never encountered a beginning clinician who did not have some of these weaknesses. What is important is that you are open to feedback, can identify skills that need improvement, and are willing to take steps to better your skills.

   • **Focusing your efforts.** To avoid feeling overwhelmed by all that you are learning, select one or two skill areas that you want to work on in this session, jot them down, and think about ways you can strengthen those skills. Perhaps you want to review relevant sections of this book or do some extra role playing with a trusted colleague. Taking these steps will help you prepare for the next practice group session. List below those skills that you intend to target this week and how you plan to improve them.

   1.

   2.

   In addition to reviewing your progress and determining ways to improve your skills, you should select an issue that you will address when you are in the client role. In previous practice group exercises, you talked about background, emotions, and thoughts. In this roleplay, you will focus on actions and behaviors.

   Think carefully about your choice so that the session is both beneficial to you and a good learning experience for the other group members. I suggest that you do not present problematic behaviors that you have struggled with unsuccessfully for a long time or that have a significant negative impact on your life. Behaviors of this type might include a long-standing problem with drug abuse or a serious eating disorder in which you binge and purge. Instead, select a less challenging or volatile behavior that might lead to a more comfortable and productive session for you and your partner. Examples of such actions include the following:

   • drinking less coffee
   • establishing more regular sleeping habits
   • getting more exercise
   • eating more fruits and vegetables
   • spending more time (or less time) on your school work
   • improving your ability to initiate or maintain conversations
   • cleaning out your closets

Role-playing Exercise: The goals of this role play are:

   • *To build on the skills you have already learned.* Again, remember to review your Assessment of Progress Forms to remind yourself of the skills that have already been introduced and what you need to focus on to improve those skills. The use of reflection of meaning and both open and closed questions will be especially important to you as you work with your client to assess and change actions. Attending to nonverbal behaviors can also be very helpful in alerting you to signs of reluctance and obstacles to change.

   • *To help your client identify, assess, and change undesirable behaviors and actions.* To accomplish this, you should follow the steps in changing behavior that have been presented in this chapter on page 161.

   • *To afford you the opportunity to use at least one specific technical intervention to facilitate behavior change.* Use one or more of the specific strategies presented in this chapter to promote change, such as empowerment, modeling, behavioral rehearsal, or possibility language.

• *To gain experience in concluding the session with a summarization and suggested between-session task.* As you have done in your other sessions, use a summarization to concisely conclude and describe the nature of the session. Be sure to reiterate the contract you made with your client, whether it entails gathering baseline information or making some small behavioral changes. Be sure to use language that will reinforce gains and empower and encourage the client. Suggest a task for the client to complete by the next session; this may be part of the contract that has already been established. Be sure the client understands and agrees to the task, perhaps modifying it as you discuss it.

Time Schedule.   This role play will probably be most rewarding if it is extended over two or three sessions, separated by 3 to 7 days. The first session should be used to elicit a specific description of the behavior and determine ways for the client to keep a record of the nature of the behavior as well as its baseline frequency or severity. The second session can then be used to review the baseline that has been determined and establish goals and a written contract. If the schedule allows a third session, that session can be used to follow up on the client's efforts to make some positive changes. If it is not possible for you and your partner to spend more than one session on this exercise, complete only the steps suggested for the first session.

During your session, use the following format for taking notes as you and your client complete the steps in the behavioral change process:

Session 1

1. Describe the undesirable actions as specifically as possible.
2. Establish a baseline, reflecting the current severity or frequency of the actions.

Session 2

1. Determine realistic goals, beginning with short-term goals.
2. Develop a specific contract, specifying goals and rewards or consequences.
3. Put contract in writing and elicit client's commitment to the contract.
4. Address potential obstacles to goal achievement.
5. Provide skills and tasks that will promote goal achievement.
6. Facilitate client's efforts to track and record progress.

Session 3

1. Assess progress toward goals.
2. Implement plans for rewards or consequences or, if indicated, revise contract.

Allow 20–30 minutes for each session. It is especially important that the session in which goals and contracts are determined be 30 minutes long, if possible. As usual, be sure that at least 10 minutes are allocated for feedback to each person in the clinician role.

Assessment of Progress Form 5

1. *Improving targeted skills*—Review the skills you had targeted for improvement in this session. List them here and briefly describe what you did to improve those skills. How successful were your efforts? What do you need to continue to do or do differently?
   Skill 1:

   Skill 2:

2. *Building on the skills you have already learned*—What use did you make of the following skills, learned in previous chapters?
   • open and closed questions

   • accents, restatement, and paraphrase

   • reflection of feelings

   • nonverbal communication

   • summarization

   • reflection of meaning

3. *Helping your client describe, assess, and modify actions*—As you review your session, both with your practice group and later when you listen to your tape, note whether and how you helped your client progress through each of the steps listed on page 164. Which steps felt most comfortable for you? Which were most productive? Which presented you with the greatest challenge? How might you have improved upon the behavioral change process?

4. *Using a specific technical intervention to promote behavior change*—Were you able to use one of the specific interventions presented in this chapter to facilitate your client's efforts to change behavior? If not, what got in the way of your using such an intervention? If yes, what was the intervention you used and how effective was it? Do you think that another type of specific intervention would have been even more helpful?

5. *Concluding the session*—How successful were you at coming up with a between-session task that was acceptable to your client? How successful was your summarization? Did you remember to check out both the suggested task and the summarization with the client? How might you have improved on the conclusion of your session?

6. How would you describe your overall effectiveness in this session, using the following rating scale?

- **Extremely helpful**—reflects accurate and insightful listening; moves counseling in a very productive direction; promotes self-awareness, new learning, or positive changes.
- **Moderately helpful**—reflects generally accurate listening; moves counseling in a productive direction, but does not clearly lead to greater self-awareness, new learning, or positive changes.
- **Neutral**—neither contributes to the treatment goals nor harms the therapeutic process; may not accurately reflect what the client has communicated.
- **Moderately harmful**—detracts somewhat from the counseling process or alliance; reflects poor listening and perhaps disinterest.
- **Extremely harmful**—damaging to the treatment process or therapeutic alliance; sounds ridiculing and critical.

What might you have done differently to improve your self-ratings?

Personal Journal Questions

1. Identify a behavior you would like to change. Choose a different behavior than the one you discussed in your practice group. Be your own clinician and take yourself through the 10-step process of describing and assessing your actions, establishing goals, and moving forward to make desired changes. Complete the following list with reference to your actions.

1. Describe the undesirable actions as specifically as possible.
2. Establish a baseline, reflecting the current severity or frequency of the actions.
3. Determine realistic goals, beginning with short-term goals.
4. Develop a specific contract, specifying goals and rewards or consequences.
5. Put contract in writing and make a commitment to the contract.
6. Address potential obstacles to goal achievement.
7. Identify skills and tasks that will promote achievement of your goal.
8. Track and record your progress.
9. Assess your progress toward your goals.
10. Implement plans for rewards or consequences or, if indicated, revise contract.

2. Identify a current situation that provokes anxiety in your life. Then identify some-one you admire who you believe could handle that situation well. When the sit-uation arises, act as if you are that person. Monitor your reactions, including your emotions, thoughts, and actions. What changes, if any, did you notice in your usual reactions to the anxiety-provoking experience? Write briefly about using the acting-as-if strategy to help yourself.

3. Using that same situation or another challenging situation in your life, engage in a behavioral rehearsal to help yourself handle the situation. You can either tape record what you might say in the situation or mentally rehearse the process of suc-cessfully dealing with the situation. Write briefly about using the strategy of be-havioral rehearsal to help yourself.

4. List three strategies that you might use to empower yourself. Then implement at least one of the three strategies and write briefly about that experience.

5. Identify a fear you have or have had. Develop an anxiety hierarchy that reflects the levels of that fear.

SUMMARY

This chapter focused on the technical skills associated with helping people identify, de-scribe, assess, and modify undesirable actions and behaviors. The chapter also presented a 10-step process that could be used in treatment to help people effect behavioral change. Particular attention was paid to describing the behavior in specific terms, es-tablishing a baseline, setting realistic and viable goals, and developing contracts. In ad-dition, information was provided on how to use between-session tasks and challenge to help people overcome obstacles to change and move forward.

Specific technical strategies also were presented that might be incorporated into treatment focused on behavioral change. These included promoting feelings of empow-erment; using relaxation, systematic desensitization, modeling, role play, behavioral re-hearsal, and possibility language; and teaching clients skills that might help them change behaviors.

Now that you have achieved some facility with important technical skills, our fo-cus will shift to the more complex conceptual skills. Part III, like Part II, will be orga-nized according to the BETA format. Part III includes chapters focused on conceptual skills associated with background, emotions, thoughts, and actions. The technical skills might be thought of as the building blocks of counseling and psychotherapy. However, it is the conceptual skills that provide the blueprint, that enable you to conceptualize the dynamics of a case and develop a treatment plan that is likely to be effective.

CHAPTER 6

Using Conceptual Skills to Understand, Assess, and Address Background

INTRODUCTION

Part II of this book presented technical skills designed to help people address and resolve issues related to the four components of the BETA model: background, emotions, thoughts, and actions. Part III presents conceptual skills that will help address those same four components. The two parts are organized so that they parallel each other as follows:

- Chapter 2—technical skills that help clinicians address background
- Chapter 6—conceptual skills that help clinicians address background
- Chapter 3—technical skills that help clinicians address emotions
- Chapter 7—conceptual skills that help clinicians address emotions
- Chapter 4—technical skills that help clinicians address thoughts
- Chapter 8—conceptual skills that help clinicians address thoughts
- Chapter 5—technical skills that help clinicians address actions
- Chapter 9—conceptual skills that help clinicians address actions

Skills that Help Clinicians Address:	Technical Skills:	Conceptual Skills:
Background	Chapter 2	Chapter 6
Emotions	Chapter 3	Chapter 7
Thoughts	Chapter 4	Chapter 8
Actions	Chapter 5	Chapter 9

OVERVIEW

This chapter will focus primarily on conceptual skills related to assessing and addressing background. When people come into counseling or psychotherapy, they are not blank slates; their lives do not begin anew when they start treatment. Rather, they bring with them a lifetime of experiences, emotions, and ideas. Even if you are a preschool or elementary school counselor working with 4-, 5-, and 6-year-olds, the children you are counseling already have formed attachments to their caregivers that will affect the relationships they will have throughout their lives. They have already learned ways to get attention, to meet their needs, and to control their bodies and their emotions. They already have self-images and can talk about what they want to be when they grow up.

Current thinking in counseling and psychotherapy has increasingly recognized the importance of the work of John Bowlby (1978, 1988). Bowlby, an object relations theorist, believed that a strong correlation exists between people's early attachments to their caregivers and their later emotional development and relationships.

These findings and many others suggest that, to understand their clients well and to determine the best ways to help them, clinicians should take a holistic view of their clients that encompasses their development and experiences. The many important aspects of people's lives and the precipitants of their seeking help provide a context that informs and improves the treatment process. Particularly important is understanding people's cultural contexts and worldviews. In addition, an appreciation of clients' important relationships is useful in enabling clinicians to identify and address transference reactions and to understand any countertransference reactions that clinicians have toward their clients. All of these topics and more will be explored in this chapter.

This chapter will present the following conceptual skills relevant to understanding and helping people deal with background issues:

- *Understanding the context of treatment*—person, source of referral, place, time, purpose, presenting concerns
- *Understanding the person seeking treatment*—using intake interviews to gather background information
- *Using interpretation to promote insight*
- *Identifying and making therapeutic use of transference and countertransference*
- *Developing multicultural counseling competencies*

IMPORTANCE OF MASTERING BOTH TECHNICAL AND CONCEPTUAL SKILLS

Until recently, the training of clinicians, especially at the master's level, emphasized technical rather than conceptual skills. However, clinicians can be fully effective only if they have competence in both conceptual and technical skills and can successfully integrate those skills in their work.

Although this may seem obvious, only recently has the professional literature acknowledged the considerable importance of conceptual skills. As Duys and Hedstrom (2000, p. 8) stated, "Counselors encounter conceptually complex variables when working with clients. Case conceptualization skills, understanding the flow and process of the counseling relationship, attending to multicultural dynamics, and the use of counseling theory call for increasingly complex cognitive processes." This point of view was echoed by Granello (2000) who suggested that high-level cognitive functioning allows clinicians to perform multiple functions, comprehend and organize a range of facts and dimensions, integrate and synthesize information, and determine similarities and differences.

Imagine that you would like to have a home built for yourself. You interview three building firms to find the one that best meets your needs. The first organization is well known for its excellent carpenters and electricians, but it lacks architects and designers. The second firm prepares fine blueprints and scale models of your dream home but lacks the applied skills to execute the project. The third firm offers you the combination of skills you need; they have outstanding construction skills *and* experts who can visualize and plan the construction of your home, providing the blueprints and guidelines that the workers need to build the home you want.

The parallel of this analogy to the clinical situation is obvious. Certainly, clinicians need to have facility in such skills as asking open questions, making reflections of feeling and meaning, and using summarization and encouragers. These are the building blocks of effective change strategies. However, unless these skills are combined in coherent and clinically sound ways, they are unlikely to effect significant and lasting change. The combination of technical and conceptual skills characterizes successful treatment and an outstanding clinician.

Conceptual skills enable clinicians to develop a comprehensive and meaningful picture of their clients and their concerns, to organize that information in logical ways, to determine what technical skills to use, and to decide how to combine them into a treatment plan that is likely to be effective. The technical skills are essential ingredients of treatment, but the conceptual skills are the frameworks that guide their appropriate use.

CLARIFYING CONCEPTUAL SKILLS USING BLOOM'S TAXONOMY

Conceptual skills can be broken down into a series of steps. This framework is derived from a taxonomy of educational objectives, developed by Bloom, Engelhart, Furst, Hill, and Krathwohl (1956) and applied to counselors by Granello (2000). I have made some further modifications and adaptations in this taxonomy so that it better meets the needs of developing clinicians.

TABLE 6-1   Modified Version of Bloom's Taxonomy

Content	What Are the Facts?
Process	
• Comprehension	What do I know and understand about the facts?
• Organization	What principles, categories, and generalizations help me to understand this information?
• Analysis/Synthesis	How are these facts related, and what inferences can I draw about their connections?
• Interpretation	What does all of this mean (underlying significance), and what sense does all of this make?
• Application	What approaches seem most likely to be effective in building a sound therapeutic relationship with this client and helping this person achieve his or her treatment goals?
• Evaluation	How effective has my treatment been, how could I make it even more effective, and what can I learn from this experience?

The modified version of Bloom's taxonomy includes two key elements, content and process, with process subdivided into six conceptual skills or steps. This taxonomy is listed in table 6-1, with each step reflected by a question that represents the conceptual processes undertaken at that point. Further explanation of each step, accompanied by an illustrative example, follows.

A. Content

The content is the answer to the question, "What are the facts?" Using the skills developed in earlier chapters (e.g., open and closed questions, reflections of feeling and meaning, minimal encouragers), clinicians can elicit important information about their clients. Clinicians in search of content are almost like reporters, gathering and clarifying information so that they are familiar with the important people and experiences in a client's life, the chronology of that person's life, and the salient thoughts, emotions, and actions that characterize the client. In seeking content, clinicians also seek knowledge of relevant terms and classifications (Miller, Sadler, Mohl, & Melchiode, 1991).

Example: A young woman named Shana presents with symptoms of very low weight and purging. The clinician gathers such information as the duration and severity of the symptoms, the family history of eating and other problems, and the diagnostic criteria and classifications for eating disorders.

B. Process

Once clinicians have obtained the content or information they need, they can process the information so that it becomes useful to them, guiding and informing the direction of treatment. Processing is divided into the following six steps.

1. Comprehend.   In this step, clinicians answer the question, "What do I know and understand about these facts?" This is the lowest level of understanding, making use of information without necessarily relating it to other information or realizing its implications. Clinicians check out their understanding of the information they have received to be sure they correctly heard and grasped the content clients provided. Summarization and paraphrase are particularly useful in ensuring this accurate comprehension.

Example: In early sessions with Shana, clinicians might identify the important underlying aspects of the case, such as the woman's history of self-destructive relationships and her strong bond with her father, and determine what additional information they need. An intake interview is a powerful way to obtain this information. Clinicians also might refer the client for a physical examination or administer a mood inventory to deepen their knowledge and understanding of this person.

2. Organize.   Next, clinicians answer the question, "What principles, categories, and generalizations help me to understand this information?" To make sense of the information they have obtained, clinicians need to organize that information into meaningful categories. Such categories might include developmental milestones, family background, physical health, social relationships, and career history. Eliciting information in a systematic way during initial sessions or intake interviews facilitates the process of organizing client information.

Example: The clinician might draw the following generalizations about the client. She has a history of sabotaging and avoiding relationships, especially with men. She has been in a series of disappointing jobs that have made little use of her abilities or education. She evades questions about her physical health and has not had a physical examination in three years. Her family background reflects a dysfunctional structure; the client reports that her father doted on her and paid little attention to her mother. The client was often drawn into the middle of her parents' conflicted relationship and asked to mediate between them.

3. Analyze and synthesize.   The clinician is now seeking to answer the question, "How are these facts related, and what inferences can I draw about their connections?" Analysis entails identifying patterns: repetitive experiences, behaviors, or ways of feeling and acting in response to life events. The skill of comparing and contrasting client responses and life experiences can facilitate the process of analysis and lead to clarification of organizing principles (Granello, 2000). Synthesis entails integrating information from disparate sources such as interviews, client records, clinician observation, inventories, and discussions with others who are familiar with the client. This step will further contribute to the clinician's efforts to develop a holistic picture of clients, draw generalizations, and develop hypotheses to promote understanding of clients and ways to help them successfully.

The processes of analysis and synthesis enable clinicians to make a multiaxial diagnosis, reflecting the clinician's understanding of both the client and the *Diagnostic and Statistical Manual of Mental Disorders* (*DSM-IV-TR*) (American Psychiatric Association, 2000a). These processes also enable clinicians to develop a preliminary case formulation, an understanding of the dynamics of the case, and possible reasons why clients are having the difficulties they are experiencing.

Example: The clinician makes the connection between the client's family structure and dynamics and her difficulties in interpersonal relationships and self-esteem. Her unhappy role in her family, combined with her enmeshed relationship with her father, has led her to avoid intimate relationships with her peers. Family messages influenced her to view herself as immature and incapable of functioning at a high level, leading to her unhealthy eating, underemployment, and self-doubts. Her diagnoses include both an eating disorder (Anorexia Nervosa) and long-standing depression (Dysthymic Disorder).

4. Interpret.   In this fourth step, clinicians are answering the question, "What does all of this mean, and what sense does all of this make?" Interpretation involves giving a deeper meaning to the information that has been provided, looking at the underlying significance and impact of the client's experiences and reactions. Interpretations should not be viewed as facts but rather as hypotheses or hunches that might explain the client's difficulties. These hypotheses or hunches can then be explored with the client and confirmed, revised, or discarded.

Example: Shana's eating disorder seems to reflect an effort to maintain the safety of her little girl role in her family and her enmeshed relationship with her father. She fears intimate relationships, both because of their sexual aspects and the fact that they remind her of her parents' unhappy marriage. Her emaciated appearance helps her avoid appearing mature and sexual and becoming involved with her peers. In addition, her purging gives her a sense of control that she lacks in other areas of her life.

5. Apply.   In the previous step, the clinician developed an in-depth understanding of a client and the dynamics of that person's difficulties. Now, the clinician is ready to answer the question, "What approaches seem most likely to be effective in building a sound therapeutic relationship with this client and helping this person achieve his or her treatment goals?" Drawing on all they have learned about a client, as well as their academic and experiential learning, clinicians apply this knowledge to the development of sound treatment plans and interventions. Essential to the success of this step is a solid grounding in clinical skills such as diagnosis and treatment planning and familiarity with a broad range of treatment approaches. In addition, clinicians should have developed sound hypotheses about the dynamics of their clients' difficulties and a clear formulation of the case.

Example: The clinician recognizes that development of a sound therapeutic relationship with Shana needs to be a gentle and gradual process, helping her to reduce her fears of closeness and self-disclosure. Treatment should combine psychodynamic, cognitive, and behavioral strategies. This should enable the client to gain insight into the background factors that contributed to her disorder, change her distorted cognitions about her self and her relationships, and modify her unhealthy eating.

6. Evaluate.   In this final step, the clinician answers the questions, "How effective has my counseling been, how could I make it even more effective, and what can I learn from this experience?" Once the treatment plan has been implemented, clinicians should constantly monitor its effectiveness. If the client seems to be responding to treatment, participating in the treatment process, making gains, and completing suggested tasks, the treatment plan is probably an effective one. On the other hand, if client resistance is growing, the client does not seem committed to or engaged in the treatment process, or the client is deteriorating rather than progressing, changing the treatment plan probably is indicated. This typically necessitates a return to earlier stages of this taxonomy, perhaps gathering more background information, seeking alternate interpretations for the client's actions, or revising the hypotheses and case formulation.

Example: The clinician observed that, although Shana gained insight into the connections between her family background and her current difficulties, she was still reluctant to make behavioral changes. Additional attention needed to be paid to the client's fear of becoming an adult and having people expect more from her. Further work on skill development, and more time spent on modifying her cognitive distortions, seemed likely to accelerate the process of behavioral change.

This chapter, like all of those in part III, draws heavily on this taxonomy to facilitate the development of clinical conceptualizing skills.

APPLYING CONCEPTUAL SKILLS TO CONTEXT

Have you ever wondered what leads a person to pick a particular day and time to make a call for help? Have you discussed with clients how they decided to call your particular agency, how they heard about your services, and what expectations they have for the treatment process? Finding answers to questions such as these should enable you to understand a client's frame of reference when beginning treatment. This information is important in helping clinicians initiate treatment in positive ways, quickly identify interventions that are likely to be helpful, and begin development of a sound therapeutic alliance.

Consider the following client responses when the clinician asks four 12-year-old girls, "What led you to seek treatment from me now?" Based only on these brief replies, you will probably begin to form some impressions of these young women. Ask yourself the following questions as you read the four client replies.

- Which one would you be most interested in seeing for counseling? Why?
- Are there any of these young women you would not want to have as a client? Why?
- What differences are there likely to be in the ways you would begin to work which each of these clients?

Client 1:   My parents said that if I didn't stop talking back to them, I would need to see a counselor. Our pastor recommended you, but you can't stop me from telling my parents what's on my mind.

Client 2:   We moved here last month and I haven't really made any friends yet. I've been feeling pretty lonely and keeping to myself a lot. My parents thought it might help me to talk to someone. My school counselor suggested I see you. Can you help me?

Client 3:   Something happened last week, but it's too hard to talk about.

Client 4:   I don't know. Is that clock on your desk really a tape recorder, and are you taping everything I say?

The presenting problems, the apparent motivation toward treatment, the source of referral, the goals, and the openness and emotional health of each client is different. Those differences reflect the initial context for treatment. They are likely to have a great impact on the development of the therapeutic relationship and the nature and effectiveness of treatment.

Ingredients in Context of Treatment

The context of treatment generally includes the following ingredients:

- *Demographic characteristics of the client*—When client and clinician first meet, they typically know little about each other. The clinician's information about the client may be limited to demographic information and a first impression that provides some knowledge of gender, age, ethnic/cultural background, and appearance. Paperwork completed by the client may provide additional information on such items as family composition, place of residence, and medical history. Of course, the clinician will acquire a much better understanding of the client and much more information on the client's background as treatment progresses.
- *Source of referral*—How did the client learn of the clinician and/or the agency? Was it through the telephone directory? A friend or colleague? A lawyer or psychiatrist? A member of the clergy? A managed care organization? The Internet? How and what a client is told about a clinician or agency when given a referral is likely to affect the client's expectations, motivation, and attitude toward treatment.
- *Choice of clinician*—Did the client take time to learn about the clinician's credentials or to talk to several clinicians before making an appointment? Or did the client make a choice based on limited information, perhaps driven by participation in a managed care program, the need for a reduced fee, or a great faith in the referral source?
- *Treatment facility*—Sometimes, the client's choice of a counseling center or clinician provides information about that client's treatment preferences. For example, the woman who seeks help from a program focused on women's issues may be struggling with concerns related to her role as a woman and may feel more comfortable in a setting where most clients and clinicians are female. The African American man who drives many miles from his suburban home to an urban counseling program focused on the needs of African Americans may feel a strong bond with others of his ethnic and cultural background, or he may be seeking to reconnect with his cultural origins. Client's choice of both clinician and treatment facility typically provide useful information about that client.
- *Precipitant for seeking services*—What led the client to seek treatment at this particular time? Had considerable thought and planning preceded the contact, or was it made impulsively or under pressure, perhaps in response to a heated argument, a disappointing experience, or a threatened failure?
- *Motivation*—What is the source of the client's motivation to seek treatment at the present time? Is the motivation intrinsic, reflecting the client's genuine wish for help and change? Or is the motivation extrinsic, coming from a concerned parent, a dissatisfied partner, a critical supervisor, or even a court order?
- *Presenting problem(s)*—The reasons that people initially give for seeking treatment are referred to as their *presenting problems*. These may reflect their own

interest in self-improvement (e.g., I feel sad and tired much of the time) or a concern someone else has about them (e.g., My wife says I should drink less and spend more time with the family). The presenting problem may turn out to be the client's most important concern, or it may be only the first step toward identifying more urgent or fundamental difficulties. Some people are initially reluctant to discuss personal concerns with a stranger, so they present with a more acceptable but less compelling problem. Others are unaware of the real nature of their difficulties. For example, the man who is profoundly depressed and having suicidal thoughts may focus on his problems falling asleep, while the young woman who was sexually abused as a child may initially focus on her disappointing peer relationships.

Seven Elements in the Context of Seeking Treatment

To summarize, seven elements have been identified as important in providing understanding of the context of someone's initial request for clinical services:

- demographic characteristics of the client
- source of referral
- choice of clinician
- treatment facility
- precipitant for seeking services
- motivation
- presenting problem(s)

Case examples.   Contextual information will be presented on a case to develop your understanding of these variables. This information will be organized and discussed according to the seven steps in Bloom's modified taxonomy to help you continue to understand the importance of this framework in facilitating sound use of conceptual skills. Following this illustration, you will have the opportunity to process a second case on your own. Both cases are drawn from the examples of the 12-year-old girls presented on page 174.

> **Client 1/Jolie:**   My parents said that if I didn't stop talking back to them, I would need to see a counselor. Our pastor recommended you, but you can't stop me from telling my parents what's on my mind.

Content (What are the facts?)

- *Demographic characteristics*—Jolie is a 12-year-old white female. She is an only child, living with both parents in a suburb of a large metropolitan area. She is tall and quite slender. She is dressed entirely in black and her hair is very dark. Jolie has multiple piercings in each ear and a stud in her nose.
- *Source of referral*—Jolie's parents brought her for treatment at the suggestion of her school counselor.
- *Choice of clinician/treatment facility*—Jolie's parents sought help from a counselor at a community mental health center in their town. The family's pastor recommended the particular mental health counselor.

- *Precipitant for seeking treatment*—Counseling was sought after several unexcused absences from school led to an argument between Jolie and her parents. Jolie reportedly threatened to run away with her boyfriend if her parents "kept trying to control my life."
- *Motivation*—As Jolie stated, "My parents said that if I didn't stop talking back to them, I would need to see a counselor. Our pastor recommended you, but you can't stop me from saying what's on my mind." Although Jolie's parents sought counseling for her, they stated that they hoped she would not need to come to counseling too many times because their work schedule made it difficult to drive her to the nearby mental health center.
- *Presenting problems*—Jolie's parents expressed concern about her declining grades, her unexcused absences from school, and her threats and verbal arguments with them. They reported a sudden decline in Jolie's behavior about 7 months ago. Jolie, herself, saw no need for counseling.

Process

1. *Comprehension (What do I know and understand about these facts?)*—Both the school counselor and Jolie's parents are concerned about the negative changes they have observed in Jolie, beginning rather suddenly about 7 months ago. These changes are worrisome and suggest she needs help. However, at least at this point, Jolie denies a need for help.
2. *Organization (What principles, categories, and generalizations help me understand this information?)*—Changes in Jolie show up in all aspects of her life. This becomes clear when the initial facts are viewed in terms of the BETA framework. A review of background suggests that the current symptoms are uncharacteristic of Jolie and reflect a sudden change. The parents seem confused by this and are not using effective strategies to address the negative changes in Jolie. They seem reluctant to invest much time and effort in helping her. Family dynamics and relationships may well be a contributing factor in this situation. Emotionally, Jolie expresses anger and resentment. Her thoughts reflect a rejection of family and school and a focus on herself and her peer relationships. Behavioral changes are reflected in a change in appearance (piercings, dressing in black), unexcused absences from school, a decline in school performance, and argumentativeness.
3. *Analysis/Synthesis (How are these facts related, and what inferences can I draw about their connections?)*—The contrast between Jolie's usual attitudes and behaviors and her current patterns are telling. Parents, teachers, and school counselor all agree that Jolie changed about 7 months ago. Other young people with a similar history, adopting dress and behaviors like Jolie's, are often involved in harmful use of drugs and alcohol. Sexual activity may be another factor and is not unusual in young people who manifest sudden negative changes. Jolie's symptoms reflect a diagnosis of Oppositional Defiant Disorder as well as a possible Substance-Use Disorder. Underlying depression also is often present in young people who manifest symptoms such as those that Jolie evidences.
4. *Interpretation (What does all of this mean, and what sense does this make?)*—Jolie is rejecting the guidance and directives of parents and school personnel. Instead, she is strongly affiliating herself with a peer culture that is prone to unwise

choices in relationships and behaviors. She may be motivated by a poor sense of self and a strong desire for peer approval. Intense involvement with a boyfriend at her young age suggests both a need for affirmation and an other-directedness. These negative attitudes and behaviors may, at least in part, have resulted from Jolie's failure to find adequate role models, closeness, and affirmation in her family. The following hypotheses need further investigation:

- Jolie has a poor sense of self and low-self esteem, leading her to seek external validation.
- Difficulties in Jolie's family relationships are contributing to her withdrawal from her family and her negative behavior.
- Jolie is involved in use of drugs and/or alcohol.
- Jolie is engaging in a harmful sexual relationship.
- Other factors, such as depression and academic problems, may be further compounding Jolie's difficulties.

Interviews with Jolie, her parents, and her teachers will be the primary source of information. A drug/alcohol screening and mood disorders inventory can provide further information.

5. *Application (What approaches seem most likely to be effective in building a sound therapeutic relationship with Jolie and helping her make positive changes in her emotions, thoughts, and actions?)*—The clinician must take account of Jolie's reluctance to engage in treatment and her apparent resentment of authority figures. Time must be taken to develop a rapport with Jolie and earn her trust so that she comes to believe that the clinician can help her evaluate her life and make positive changes.

   At this early point in treatment, reality therapy seems likely to be an effective treatment system; that approach emphasizes the development of rapport and typically works well with young people who are acting in self-destructive ways. It emphasizes assessment and modification of thoughts and actions, both problem areas for Jolie. If Jolie does become more motivated over the course of treatment, some exploration of background might help her understand the factors that contributed to her current difficulties. In addition, family counseling is likely to be helpful.

6. *Evaluation (How effective has my counseling been, how could I make it even more effective, and what can I learn from this experience?)*—In this initial stage of treatment with Jolie, evaluation should focus primarily on the development of a collaborative client-clinician relationship. An essential ingredient in successful treatment with Jolie is promoting her engagement in treatment as well as her understanding of the client and clinician roles. As treatment progresses, evaluation will focus on the effectiveness of reality therapy and other interventions used with Jolie.

Client 2/Henye: We moved here last month and I haven't really made any friends yet. I've been feeling pretty lonely and keeping to myself a lot. My parents thought it might help me to talk to someone. My school counselor suggested I see you. Can you help me?

For this second client, you will be provided with the content. Your task is to complete the subsequent six steps in the modified version of Bloom's taxonomy, guiding your processing of that content. In developing your analysis, don't worry if you do not yet have training in diagnosis and in theories of counseling and psychotherapy. Base your processing on whatever coursework you have already completed in your field and on your own understanding of human development and the treatment process.

Content

- *Demographic description*—Henye, like Jolie, is a 12-year-old girl. She and her parents and 17-year-old brother have lived in France for the past 7 years. Her mother, a faculty member at a university in France, is currently spending a year at a university in the southeastern part of the United States. The family arrived in the United States about a month ago, 3 months after the school year began. Henye is somewhat shorter than average for her age but appears well nourished and athletic. She is casually and appropriately dressed in jeans and a white blouse.
- *Source of referral*—Henye and her parents both agreed that some counseling might help her to feel more comfortable with the family's relocation. Her parents requested referrals from Henye's counselor as well as from two staff members at the university counseling center where her mother is working.
- *Choosing a clinician*—Henye's parents conducted brief telephone interviews with three clinicians who had been recommended and selected the one who had the most experience with young adolescents.
- *Treatment facility*—They chose a psychologist in private practice, believing that Henye would be more comfortable in a setting that was relatively small and quiet, compared to a community mental health center. Henye's parents let the clinician know that they would like to be kept informed about Henye's treatment and made some specific suggestions of ways in which they thought the clinician might help Henye.
- *Precipitants for seeking treatment*—Both before and after their move, Henye and her parents talked about the challenges the family might face when they came to the United States. Her parents had not been particularly concerned about Henye's adjustment until the family watched a television program together about France. Henye became tearful and told her parents that she wished they had not come to the United States.
- *Motivation*—Although therapy was a new experience for Henye, her parents explained the process to her and helped her see how it might be beneficial to her. Her parents had been helped by marital counseling in the past and were hopeful that treatment would ease Henye's adjustment to the United States.
- *Presenting problem(s)*—Henye, and her parents, were concerned about Henye's adjustment to the United States, particularly her ability to form peer relationships. Her parents described her as a "quiet girl" whose primary interest was in sports, especially running and swimming. Henye had also been very attached to her pets, now being cared for by relatives in France.

Process.   You now have information on the context of Henye's treatment and are ready to process that information. Using the modified version of Bloom's taxonomy, illustrated with the earlier case of Jolie, complete the following steps, either in writing or via class discussion:

1. *Comprehension*   (What do I know and understand about these facts?)
2. *Organization*   (What principles, categories, and generalizations help me understand this information?)
3. *Analysis/Synthesis*   (How are these facts related, and what inferences can I draw about their connections?)
4. *Interpretation*   (What does all of this mean, and what sense does this make?)
5. *Application*   (What approaches seem most likely to be effective in building a sound therapeutic relationship with Henye and helping her make positive changes in her emotions, thoughts, and actions?)
6. *Evaluation*   (How effective has my counseling been, how could I make it even more effective, and what can I learn from this experience?)

COLLECTING BACKGROUND INFORMATION/INTAKE INTERVIEWS

Once you have some understanding of the context in which a client sought treatment, you can focus your attention on the client's background. Obtaining some background information early in the treatment process is another essential ingredient of effective treatment. It can facilitate understanding of clients' self-image, the reasons for the development of their symptoms, the impact those symptoms have had on their lives, and the clients' strengths and coping skills, along with many other important pieces of information. The intake interview, presented in chapter 2, is an ideal vehicle for beginning to gather background information. Regardless of clinician's theoretical orientation, knowing how to plan, conduct, and process an intake interview is an important clinical skill.

Goals of the Intake Interview

During the intake interview, both client and clinician form their first impressions of each other. Those initial impressions typically exert a powerful impact on the therapeutic process. Often, treatment does not last more than a single session, either because the client leaves treatment prematurely or because client and/or clinician think that only one session is indicated. In a meta-analysis, Bloom (1981) found that 30–35% of people treated at family counseling agencies, 25–30% of those seen at community mental health centers, and 15% of people seen at university counseling centers received only one counseling session. These findings emphasize how important it is for clinicians to rapidly progress toward helping clients accomplish their goals.

Treatment goals can be divided into two categories, those that enhance the therapeutic relationship and those that help the client gain self-awareness and make positive changes. Of course, both are important to the success of treatment. Although the intake interview is designed primarily to facilitate understanding of the client, it also promotes development of a sound client/clinician alliance. The following list includes the typical goals of an intake interview:

Promote the therapeutic alliance

- Introduce the client to the treatment facility and establish the ground rules for the treatment process.

- Begin the development of rapport, trust, and openness between client and clinician.
- Help the client to understand the roles and responsibilities of the client and the clinician and the need to participate actively in the treatment process.
- Initiate collaboration between client and clinician.
- Assess and begin to increase client motivation and reduce resistance.
- Enable client to appreciate the help that treatment can provide.

Increase understanding of the client

- Determine suitability of client and concerns for the agency's and clinician's services.
- Conduct a preliminary inventory of the client's presenting concerns and symptoms.
- Determine any urgent issues, particularly whether the client is in any danger or presents any danger to others.
- Obtain sufficient information for a mental status examination (discussed in chapter 8).
- Obtain sufficient relevant background information to enable the clinician to understand multicultural issues, conceptualize the case, make a preliminary diagnosis, and develop an initial treatment plan.

This chapter will focus primarily on those objectives that increase understanding of the client, including conducting a preliminary inventory of presenting concerns and symptoms; obtaining, processing, and interpreting relevant background information; identifying and addressing transference and countertransference; and demonstrating multicultural awareness and competence. It will also illustrate the application of Bloom's taxonomy to the intake interview. Later chapters will teach the skills that are needed to accomplish the other goals of the intake process.

Procedures for Conducting Intake Interviews

Procedures for conducting intake interviews vary, depending on the nature and purpose of the mental health facility, the theoretical orientation of the clinician, and the nature of the client. The following are three common models, used to gather background information:

1. The intake process is separate from the treatment process and is overseen by a clinician who may or may not also provide the client's treatment. A group of treatment providers may interview the client during this process, perhaps including a mental health counselor or psychologist, a psychiatrist, a social worker, and a vocational rehabilitation specialist. The intake process is designed primarily to assess the client's suitability for the agency's services and to develop an initial diagnosis and treatment plan. This model is especially common at community mental health centers and specialized mental health agencies such as vocational rehabilitation programs and drug or alcohol treatment programs.
2. The first few sessions of the treatment process are devoted to a formal intake procedure. Once enough information has been obtained from that process to develop a diagnosis and treatment plan, treatment will continue with the same clinician

who conducted the initial interview. This model is often used in private practice settings as well as other clinical settings.

3. Treatment begins immediately, with little attention paid to a systematic gathering of background information. Such information will be elicited as needed to further the treatment process. This model is particularly common in settings that emphasize brief, present-oriented treatment such as counseling programs in schools and colleges, crisis intervention centers, and career counseling centers.

Steps in the Intake Process

The intake process typically includes the following steps, regardless of which of the three approaches to intake interviews is being used:

- *Decide what information is needed*—Just as interview procedures vary, so does the information elicited during that process. Discussion of presenting concerns and symptoms will almost always be a part of the process. However, what other topics are included in the interview depends on such factors as the nature of the treatment facility, the clinician's theoretical orientation, and the client's symptoms and concerns. A list of potential intake topics (e.g., work history, family background, medical history) will be presented later in this section to help you select those topics that are important for you to cover in a given interview. Clinicians should have in mind the categories of information they want to obtain from an intake interview to facilitate the process.
- *Decide how to gather information*—A dialogue between client and clinician is usually the primary approach to gathering intake information. However, clinicians might also rely on questionnaires, inventories, client records, and other informants such as a parent or spouse to provide information.
- *Decide how to record the information*—Few clinicians can retain all the detailed information that clients provide in an initial interview. Consequently, note taking or tape recording is generally used to facilitate the clinicians' later review and processing of the information. Most clinicians seem to prefer note taking because subsequent review is less time consuming than listening to a tape recording. In addition, a small percentage of clients are uncomfortable with the process of tape recording while it is extremely rare for clients to object to notes being taken during the session. Of course, clients' informed consent should be obtained before any record of client information is made. The likelihood that clients will agree to note taking or recording procedures is maximized by the clinician explaining that these procedures aid efforts to identify and understand experiences and issues that are important to the clients and are likely to make the treatment process more effective and efficient.
- *Obtain the information*—The technical skills you learned earlier in this book are essential to conducting a successful intake interview. Open questions are usually the most important technique in the intake process, with some use being made of closed questions to gather specific factual information. Paraphrase and summarization also are important to ensure accurate listening and understanding of what the client is communicating. Accents and restatements are useful in maintaining the flow of the interview. Even reflection of feeling and meaning

have important roles in the intake process; those techniques can contribute greatly to the establishment of a positive therapeutic alliance.

- *Review the information for gaps*—Sometimes, omissions are as telling as the information people do provide. When you review the intake information provided by a client, compare that information to the categories of information you wanted to explore. Take note of any omissions or imbalances. For example, the client may talk at length about his mother but say little about his father, or he may say a great deal about his leisure activities but neglect to provide much information about his work. Subsequent discussion of these gaps may prove fruitful.
- *Process the information*—Bloom's modified taxonomy (Bloom et al., 1956) will once again be used to illustrate the processing of information gleaned from an intake interview. However, your school or agency may prefer another approach to processing intake data. Any systematic approach to making sense of the information can be used as long as it enables the clinician to obtain a clear understanding of clients and their concerns and to formulate accurate diagnoses and sound treatment plans.

Processing the Intake Interview

Chapter 2 presented the intake interview of Eileen Carter. Review this intake interview, beginning on page 40, so that the content (the facts) is fresh in your mind. Then read the following analysis of that interview according to Bloom's modified taxonomy. The first part of this analysis, the Comprehension section, lists important categories that often are explored during the course of an intake interview.

Comprehension (What do I know and understand about these facts?)

- *Demographics*—Eileen Carter is a 24-year-old married African American woman. She has a 4-year-old son. She and her family live in a two-bedroom apartment they rent. Eileen has been a full-time homemaker for the past four years but has recently begun taking college courses.
- *Presenting concerns*—Eileen's presenting concerns focused on marital difficulties and her wish to continue her college education. According to Eileen, her husband is opposed to her continuing her education and has refused to provide child care and financial support as well as emotional support.
- *Prior psychological difficulties*—As a teenager, Eileen developed a problem with drugs and alcohol. Her abuse of alcohol continued until she became pregnant with her son. She reports several prior relationships with men in which she was emotionally and physically abused. She had two abortions.
- *Current life situation*—Eileen's only current relationships of importance to her are those with her husband and son. She reports no leisure activities other than playing with her son. She works part-time in telephone sales from her home.
- *Cultural, religious, and socioeconomic background*—Eileen is African American and was brought up to have Christian beliefs. She states that she has a strong faith in God and very much values her cultural heritage.
- *Family of origin*—Eileen is the second of three children in her family of origin. She has two brothers, one four years older than she and one four years younger.

She reports little closeness in her family of origin. She perceives her father, an electrician, as "alcoholic" and her mother, a beautician, as "detached." Her father died suddenly when Eileen was 10 years old. After that, Eileen spent about 6 months in foster care before being reunited with her family. The family is described as "ships passing in the night," with little closeness or intimacy. Especially after the father's death, financial difficulties and the mother's efforts to earn money and meet her own emotional needs led to feelings of estrangement in the family. Family messages encouraged the children not to "cause problems" and to minimize their dependence on the family.

- *Current family*—Eileen reports taking great pleasure in her son. She reports wanting her marriage to improve and is troubled by the conflicts between her husband and herself.
- *Developmental history*—Eileen reports an unremarkable development. Her parents rarely discussed Eileen's early years, and she has little recollection of her childhood.
- *Social and leisure activities*—Eileen has no close friends and, other than her husband and son, is fairly isolated. She expresses an interest in making friends but has taken few steps to make that happen. Similarly, although she expresses an interest in such leisure activities as dancing, listening to music, and visiting museums, she engages in few leisure activities.
- *Career and educational history*—As a child and adolescent, Eileen had little interest in school. She was a satisfactory student in elementary school, but her performance declined after the death of her father. She left school at 16 and received a GED 2 years later. Her feelings about college are quite different, and she is enthusiastic about continuing her education. Eileen's work history has been sporadic. Prior to her marriage, she worked in bars and nightclubs, either as a waitress or a dancer. She has been primarily a homemaker since her marriage, doing some telephone work from her home.
- *Medical history*—Eileen reports high cholesterol that is being treated with medication (Lipitor). She has had two abortions and gave birth to one child.
- *Health-related behaviors*—Eileen has greatly reduced her consumption of alcohol and no longer uses drugs in a dysfunctional way. She smokes 1–2 packs of cigarettes a day but plans to reduce her consumption of cigarettes. She gets little exercise. Her high cholesterol has prompted her to pay some attention to her diet, but she states that her diet needs some improvement.

Organization   (What principles, categories, and generalizations help me to understand this information?)

Eileen's concerns can be organized in the following way:

- *Problems with impulse control*—Early and continuing use of drugs and alcohol, unwise choices in relationships, three unplanned pregnancies.
- *Relationship difficulties*—All of Eileen's important relationships, except her relationship with her son, have been either abusive or distant. She lacks role models for healthy relationships.
- *Issues related to goals and direction*—Until recently, Eileen had little sense of direction. She sought comfort in relationships that did not meet her needs. However,

the birth of her son and her brief time in college have provided her a positive sense of direction for the first time in her life. Her faith in God and her valuing of her cultural heritage also are positive elements that might further enhance her sense of direction.

- *Low self-esteem*—Eileen has little sense of self; she has only limited awareness of her development, her strengths, and her values.

Analysis and synthesis (How are these facts related, and what inferences can I draw about their connections?)   Eileen's family background seems to have been devoid of closeness, warmth, affirmation, and support. Particularly after the death of her father, she received little positive parenting. Emulating the behavior of her mother and seeking to reduce her own loneliness, Eileen placed great importance on having a man in her life. Her desperate need for love led her to involve herself in unhealthy and abusive relationships. She numbed her feelings with drugs and alcohol, at least in part because of the family history of alcohol abuse. She had no image of healthy relationships and had no female role models to help her make use of her potential and develop in positive ways.

By the time Eileen met Charles, she was beginning to realize the self-destructive nature of her choices. Because he was not physically abusive and offered her marriage, she viewed him as a better choice than her earlier relationships. However, Charles' apparent need to be in charge and to have Eileen in a subservient role ultimately led to conflicts between them.

Interpretation (What does all this mean, and what sense does all this make?)   Eileen's lack of nurturing and positive role models throughout her childhood seem strongly related to her subsequent difficulties. She lacked a sense of self-worth, leading her to seek value vicariously through her relationships with men who may have initially appeared powerful but who, in fact, were abusive. Nevertheless, Eileen's strong dependency needs led her to move from one unhealthy relationship to another, seeking a fantasized relationship that might compensate for the loneliness and lack of attachment she had experienced throughout her childhood. Her father's early death probably contributed to her efforts to replace him in her life with a romantic relationship.

Although Eileen does not recognize symptoms of depression in herself, she has probably been experiencing a long-standing underlying depression, characterized by hopelessness, helplessness, and guilt. Sexual relationships, as well as drugs and alcohol, probably served to mask that depression, but it must be kept in mind and addressed in her treatment.

Eileen's marriage to Charles does seem to represent a move toward health as she matured. Although her marriage has difficulties, they are not of the magnitude of those in her earlier relationships. Her pregnancy and the subsequent birth of Charles Jr. were turning points for Eileen. Actually giving birth to a child may have helped to assuage some of Eileen's guilt for her two abortions. Her decision to greatly reduce her consumption of alcohol while pregnant seems to reflect a sincere effort to "do things differently this time." For the first time, when Charles was born, Eileen perceived herself as having an important role and being fully loved and accepted by another human being. This has enabled Eileen to value herself more, leading to her enrollment in college. Her initial success in college further contributed to her sense of empowerment, and Eileen began to envision a different and more rewarding life for herself, one in which she was valued both by herself and by others.

Unfortunately, as Eileen became less dependent on her husband and developed a greater sense of self-efficacy, conflicts emerged in her marriage. According to Eileen, Charles sought to curtail her involvement in college. Despite Charles' objections, Eileen has persisted in her efforts to continue her college education and is trying to pass on her newfound love of learning to her son.

From a diagnostic point of view, Eileen probably has a dysthymic disorder (longstanding underlying depression) along with a prior history of substance abuse and both physical and emotional abuse. She probably also has dependent personality traits.

Application (What approaches seem most likely to be effective in building a sound therapeutic relationship with Eileen and helping her achieve her treatment goals?) Counseling with Eileen might focus on the following areas:

- *Emotional*—The clinician should further assess for the presence of depression and employ interventions that are designed to reduce depression and promote self-confidence and self-efficacy. Eileen is likely to have a strong need for acceptance and support in treatment and needs help in learning to form healthy, close, and caring relationships with other adults. Her strong religious faith and the value she places on her cultural heritage might be used to further enhance her self-esteem. Finding positive female role models in the African American community might be particularly useful to her.
- *Thoughts*—Despite her recent progress, Eileen is still struggling with many of the dysfunctional thoughts that contributed to her difficulties throughout her life. These thoughts might include "I must have a man to take care of me and make me feel important," "I am unlovable," "I have little to offer in a relationship," and "I should put others' needs ahead of my own."
- *Actions*—Particularly important is helping Eileen find a way to continue her education and succeed in her coursework. In addition, she would probably benefit from help with communication skills, enabling her to dialogue more successfully with her husband and develop some friendships. Eileen's health habits also need some attention; she wants to reduce or eliminate her use of cigarettes, she needs to incorporate exercise into her life, and she needs to improve her diet. If conflict increases between her and Charles or if she has difficulty finding a way to continue her education, Eileen might once again turn to alcohol to numb her feelings; preventive interventions are needed to ensure her sobriety. Parenting skills might be helpful to her as well, in light of her own lack of good parental role models.
- *Treatment*—Eileen is likely to benefit from counseling that has a practical and present-oriented focus, but also pays attention to her painful history, especially her attachment and developmental difficulties. Cognitive and behavioral approaches should be emphasized. Cognitive therapy would focus on modifying the dysfunctional thoughts that have led Eileen to make so many self-destructive choices. Behavioral interventions would emphasize finding ways for Eileen to continue in college, develop better communication and parenting skills, and

build a fuller life for herself, including friends and leisure activities as well as better health habits. A detailed multiaxial diagnosis and treatment plan for Eileen are provided in chapter 8.

Evaluation (How effective has my counseling been, how could I make it even more effective, and what can I learn from this experience?)   Once treatment with Eileen has been implemented, monitoring her progress is essential. Eileen has a long history of emotional difficulties and, although she currently seems to be moving in a positive direction, regression clearly is a possibility. Mutually agreed-upon goals that are clear and measurable will facilitate frequent assessment of progress and help ensure that Eileen continues to move forward.

TRANSFERENCE AND COUNTERTRANSFERENCE

Although chapter 7 will provide further information about the development and importance of a sound therapeutic alliance, particular attention will be paid in this chapter to transference and countertransference. These processes are discussed here because they are intricately connected to the backgrounds of both client and clinician. The understanding of those backgrounds and of the signs of transference and countertransference enable clinicians to determine when transference reactions are having an impact on treatment. With that knowledge, they can either reduce the blocking and resistance that can result from transference or understand the transference reactions in a way that enhances the treatment process.

Understanding of transference and countertransference stems from the work of Freud and other early psychodynamic and psychoanalytic therapists. Among today's clinicians, as well, the psychodynamic and psychoanalytic therapists, with their great emphasis on the importance of background, are the clinicians who probably pay the most attention to transference and countertransference. However, most clinicians, regardless of their theoretical orientation, are aware of these factors and may need to address their impact on treatment.

Transference and countertransference can be defined as perceptions of or reactions to another person that are determined primarily by a projection onto that person of past relationships and experiences rather than by the actual characteristics or actions of that person. The term *transference* is used to describe the process of clients projecting onto their clinicians experiences and interpretations that stem largely from the clients' early relationships. *Countertransference* reactions describe the process of clinicians projecting onto their clients experiences and interpretations that stem largely from the clinicians' early relationships.

For example, a man who had a seductive and abusive mother manifested transference; he mistrusted nearly all women, including his therapist, and viewed them as seeking to exploit or take advantage of him. This prevented him from collaborating successfully with his therapist.

Countertransference was evidenced by a counselor whose father viewed any disregard of the rules, particularly lateness, as a personal insult to him; the clinician became annoyed when one of his clients was late for appointments, not recognizing that an attention deficit disorder made it difficult for the client to meet her commitments.

Although some clinicians believe that transference and countertransference reactions are uncommon, many clinicians and theoreticians believe that they are widespread. According to Strean (1994),

> All patients—regardless of the setting in which they are being treated, of the therapeutic modality, or the therapist's skill and years of experience—will respond to interventions in terms of transference. It is important for clinicians of all persuasions to recognize that the most brilliant statement in the world will be refuted by a patient who is in a negative transference. It is equally important for clinicians to recognize that the most inaccurate statement in the world will be positively accepted if the patient is in a positive transference. (p. 110)

Understanding and Addressing Countertransference

Freud and other early psychodynamic clinicians described countertransference as the interference of the unconscious in the therapist's ability to understand a client. This definition has now been broadened to include any emotional reactions that clinicians have to their clients, especially those that are not directly related to the reality of the client's presentation.

Teyber (1997) provided a useful list of common signs of countertransference or clinician reactions that impede the therapeutic process:

- becoming anxious and changing the subject
- withdrawing and becoming silent
- becoming directive and authoritative
- providing clients with unrealistic reassurance
- creating excessive distance between clinician and client
- rescuing clients when they are capable of helping themselves
- engaging in excessive self-disclosure
- having strong emotional reactions to the client
- overidentifying with the client
- demanding that a client make a particular decision or behavioral change

Taken to an extreme, countertransference reactions can lead clinicians to ignore appropriate professional boundaries and establish friendships or even sexual relationships with their clients. Clearly, clinicians must be alert to the development of countertransference reactions and prevent them from damaging their therapeutic relationships.

Does this mean that clinicians should not have any emotional reactions to their clients or that they should not engage with their clients? Of course not! That would certainly be countertherapeutic. As we discuss further in the next chapter, communicating caring, support, hopefulness, and interest to our clients can greatly enhance the treatment process. In addition, clinicians' reactions to clients' demeanor and behaviors can be used to provide clients with feedback on how other people might perceive them. For example, clients who are chronically late for appointments, who behave in angry and aggressive ways both in and out of sessions, and whose poor physical self-care is evident would probably benefit from a clear but gentle statement of the clinician's reaction to those behaviors. The clinician might also provide some information on the reactions those behaviors are likely to elicit from others.

Distinguishing between countertransference reactions and appropriate and helpful responses to clients can be challenging. The following can help clinicians differentiate these:

- Keep Teyber's signs of countertransference in mind.
- Be on the alert for extremely strong emotional responses to clients, especially feelings that stay with you long after the session is over or that lead you to become emotional in the session.
- Know yourself. Be aware of common patterns of reaction that you have toward people. For example, do you typically feel competitive with people about your age who seem more successful than you are? Do you feel judged by people who remind you of one of your parents? Awareness of patterns can help you anticipate and curtail countertransference reactions.
- Monitor yourself whenever you are tempted to engage in a possible boundary violation, such as buying a gift for a client, calling the client for no particular reason, giving the client extra time in sessions, reducing the client's fee, or meeting the client away from the office. These behaviors may be professional and appropriate, but they may also be clues to the presence of a countertransference reaction.
- Seek supervision or consultation with a colleague whenever you find yourself having a strong or puzzling response to a client. Another person with more objectivity can help you sort out your reactions, determine whether countertransference is indeed present, and take steps to ensure that treatment continues in a productive direction.

Additional information on identifying and addressing countertransference reactions can be obtained from the discussion of transference that follows.

Understanding and Addressing Transference

Transference is probably easier to identify than countertransference, if only because we typically have more objectivity in assessing someone else's behavior than our own. In addition, most clinicians try to understand patterns in their clients' lives and may focus particularly on the connection between early relationships and current relationships. That understanding can facilitate the identification of transference reactions.

Clues to the presence of transference are similar to those that signal the presence of countertransference. Especially telling are strong emotional responses to the clinician, particularly those that seem unwarranted or that repeat ways in which the client characteristically responds to other people.

Clinicians differ greatly in their thinking about the appropriate response to transference. Clinicians who have a traditional psychoanalytic orientation, for example, typically believe that transference should be encouraged and that its analysis and working through is an essential ingredient in successful treatment. Clinicians practicing transactional analysis and brief psychodynamic psychotherapy acknowledge the importance of transference but pay only limited attention to that process during treatment. On the other hand, clinicians whose theoretical orientation is cognitive behavioral or person-centered may agree that transference exists but pay little or no attention to that process during treatment unless transference presents a block to progress. Regardless of your own theoretical orientation, the identification and amelioration of both transference and countertransference reactions are important therapeutic skills.

Application of Bloom's Taxonomy to Transference

The modified version of Bloom's taxonomy, presented earlier in this chapter, can be used to help clinicians understand and address transference and countertransference reactions. The reactions of Eileen Carter can be used to illustrate this.

- *Content (What are the facts?)*—Eileen's counselor began to feel uncomfortable with some of Eileen's reactions to her and wondered whether transference might be present. Her processing of Eileen's reactions follows.
- *Comprehend (What do I know and understand about the facts?)*—Eileen manifested both positive and negative reactions to her counselor, a woman about 20 years older than Eileen. Her positive reactions included hugging the counselor at the end of each session, sending her e-mails with profuse expressions of appreciation for the counselor's help, and bringing the counselor flowers that Eileen had grown. Negative reactions included coming late for one session, appearing annoyed and distant in that same session, and becoming angry when the counselor had to cancel a session due to a family emergency.
- *Organize (What principles, categories, and generalizations help me to understand this information?)*—The counselor sought patterns in the timing of Eileen's positive and negative responses. The positive reactions occurred during and after sessions in which the counselor had been especially supportive of Eileen's efforts to continue her education. She had helped Eileen complete an application for financial aid, had seemed impressed by Eileen's efforts to study and complete her assignments while still fulfilling her family commitments, and had shared briefly with Eileen her own efforts to complete her graduate coursework while raising two young children. On the other hand, Eileen's negative behavior followed a session in which the counselor suggested that it might be beneficial for Eileen's husband to join them for a session or two and asked whether Eileen had considered how difficult it might be for her husband to understand her recent changes in goals and behavior.
- *Analyze/synthesize (How are these facts related, and what inferences can I draw about their connections?)*—Eileen had never had a close, supportive relationship with either a man or a woman. As a result, she had little sense of how to form such a relationship and tended to be mistrustful of relationships. Her own mother had been distant and overwhelmed by her life and did not give Eileen the consistent love and approval she craved. Although Eileen longed for closeness, she expected other people, especially women, to be unpredictable and unsupportive like her mother. Initially, Eileen viewed the counselor as a friend and role model, perhaps even a surrogate mother, and hoped that the counselor would help her find a way to continue her education. However, the slightest hint that the counselor was not fully supportive and might even have some empathy for Eileen's husband led Eileen to react with anger and mistrust. Eileen's failure to discuss her concerns with her counselor was also characteristic of Eileen; rather than addressing relationship issues directly, she typically withdrew and often even ended relationships abruptly.

• *Interpret (What does all of this mean, and what sense does all of this make?)*—Eileen's perception that women are unpredictable and untrustworthy, coupled with her deep longing for approval and support, led her to react strongly to some of the counselor's statements. Anything that seemed encouraging of Eileen's efforts to continue her education elicited positive reactions while anything that seemed to question Eileen's resentment of her husband elicited a negative reaction. Eileen seemed to want her counselor to affirm and praise everything that Eileen was doing and thinking. This probably reflected the lack of secure attachment she had in her relationship with her mother as well as her self-doubts and need for external validation.

• *Application (What approaches seem most likely to be effective in addressing this issue?)*— Gentle exploration of Eileen's transference reactions could be very helpful to both the therapeutic alliance and to Eileen's efforts to form healthy relationships. Working collaboratively, Eileen and her counselor could identify times when Eileen had strong emotional reactions to the treatment process and then link these to Eileen's self-doubts, her need for unconditional approval, and her expectation that people will be unpredictable and untrustworthy. Exploration of other relationships Eileen has had would probably indicate that her transference reactions affected those relationships as well. Treatment could then focus on helping Eileen anticipate and curtail transference reactions, build up her inner sense of self, develop the communication skills she needs to address disappointments in relationships more effectively, and become more successful at building rewarding relationships.

• *Evaluation (How effective has counseling been, how could it be even more effective, and what can be learned from this experience?)*—Monitoring Eileen's reactions to the discussion of transference is essential. If not done with great care and considerable support, discussion of this topic may prove threatening and painful to Eileen, who might perceive her counselor as criticizing her. This, in turn, may lead Eileen to terminate treatment prematurely. Engaging Eileen in the evaluation process may help her to feel empowered and less vulnerable, thereby facilitating discussion of the highly charged topic of transference.

The modified version of Bloom's taxonomy also can be used to help clinicians better understand and address their countertransference reactions. You will have an opportunity to apply the taxonomy to a clinician's countertransference reactions in the Learning Opportunities section of this chapter.

MULTICULTURAL COUNSELING COMPETENCIES

The cultural, ethnic, spiritual, and socioeconomic backgrounds of both clients and clinicians are other important variables in the treatment process. Over the past 20 years, attention to the importance of multicultural counseling competencies and sensitivity has had a powerful impact on the professions of counseling and psychotherapy. Several factors have contributed to this. First is the growing numbers of people in minority or underrepresented groups. According to Sue, Arredondo, and McDavis (1992), well-known researchers in multicultural counseling, by 2010 "racial and ethnic minorities will become a numerical majority" (p. 278). Accompanying this numerical growth has been a growth in power; Derald Wing Sue, Patricia Arredondo, Courtland Lee, and others from underrepresented groups have become increasingly vocal and persuasive about the importance of multicultural counseling competencies. Their position has been strengthened by the writings of Allen Ivey, Paul Pedersen, and others who recognize that effective counseling and psychotherapy requires all clinicians to understand and make positive use of diversity in their work.

The Evolution of Multiculturalism

How clinicians view multicultural counseling has changed and evolved over the past 50 years. The counseling literature from the 1950s and 1960s presents a picture of clinicians as being color-blind. Diversity and cultural differences were largely ignored as was clients' context; the treatment focus was primarily on people's inner experiences rather than their context. This color-blindness was viewed as desirable and as reflecting open-mindedness and lack of prejudice.

This perspective changed in the 1970s when clinicians began to realize they were doing people a disservice by ignoring their cultural backgrounds. Although some writers like Derald Wing Sue took a broad perspective and discussed the importance of understanding people's worldviews, most focused on the special needs of each ethnic group. Articles and book chapters addressed such topics as counseling African Americans and counseling women.

Although certainly some attention to the particular characteristics and special counseling needs of such groups is necessary, many clinicians have come to view literature that is narrowly focused on a particular group as contributing to feelings of differentness and separateness, perpetuating an us-and-them perspective. Consequently, during the 1980s and early 1990s, attention shifted away from specific groups to the importance of taking a broader perspective of diversity, emphasizing the understanding and appreciation of cultural context and of individual differences. Multicultural competencies emphasized the importance not only of cultural, ethnic, and religious differences but also differences in gender, sexual orientation, abilities, and socioeconomic status.

Multicultural counseling in the late 1990s and early part of the 21st century has continued to move forward. Now, multiculturalism and multicultural competencies are broadly defined. According to Constantine and Ladany (2000), multicultural counseling competency "has been defined as the aggregate of counselors' attitudes/beliefs, knowledge, and skills in working with individuals from a variety of cultural (e.g., racial, ethnic, gender, social class, and sexual orientation) groups" (p. 155). Constantine and Ladany go on to state that those with high levels of multicultural counseling abilities and sensitivity "recognize the importance of considering cultural issues in the context of therapeutic tasks such as case conceptualization" (p. 162). For this reason this text emphasizes the importance of multicultural counseling competence.

Multicultural counseling in this century has not only taken a broad perspective but has also sought to strengthen and empower people who may have been disenfranchised because of their religious beliefs, cultural background, or sexual orientation. As Robinson (1997) stated,

> Multiculturalism means willingly sharing power with those who have less power. . . . Multiculturalism uses unearned privilege to empower others. . . . Within a multicultural framework, differences are honored and celebrated through the conscious process of unlearning learned prejudices. . . . With multiculturalism, differences are valued and are viewed as indispensable to a healthy society. (p.6)

In addition to these changes, the focus of multicultural counseling has shifted away from a close scrutiny of the client. It now takes a perspective that encompasses not only the context and characteristics of the client but also the characteristics, attitudes, and skills of the clinician and the relationship between the client and the clinician. It also views multicultural counseling competence as an evolving and ongoing process.

The Multiculturally Skilled Clinician

In line with these shifts, Sue, Arredondo, and McDavis (1992) identify three important dimensions of a culturally skilled counselor: (1) beliefs, (2) attitudes, and (3) knowledge and skills. They describe a culturally skilled counselor as:

- one who is "actively in the process of becoming aware of his or her own assumptions about human behavior, values, biases, preconceived notions, personal limitations, and so forth" (p. 481). Such clinicians have knowledge of their own assumptions as well as of their own racial and cultural heritage; they understand how it affects them, both personally and professionally (Arredondo, 1999, p. 107); in addition, they understand how "oppression, racism, discrimination, and stereotyping" affect people in all aspects of their lives.
- one who "actively attempts to understand the worldview of his or her culturally different client without negative judgments" (p. 481). Culturally skilled clinicians are aware of their own culturally based perceptions and can nonjudgmentally compare their worldviews with those of their clients. In addition, they understand the impact that sociopolitical constructs can have on people (e.g., poverty, powerlessness, stereotyping) and their self-images (Arredondo, 1999).
- "in the process of actively developing and practicing appropriate, relevant, and sensitive intervention strategies and skills in working with his or her culturally different clients" (p. 481). Culturally skilled counselors take steps to eliminate stereotyping and discrimination in the way clients and others are evaluated, tested, described, and treated by clinicians, organizations, and society as a whole.

The Process of Becoming a Culturally Skilled Clinician

Clearly, becoming a culturally skilled clinician involves attending not only to the individual client but also to yourself and to the social, political, and cultural contexts that affect both you and your clients. It entails careful treatment planning that matches treatment approaches and interventions to the clinician's understanding of the client's cultural context and worldview.

Use of the following questions, organized according to the modified version of Bloom's taxonomy, can help you improve your multicultural understanding of your clients. Similar questions, applied to the clinician's multicultural counseling competence, are also provided.

Multicultural counseling competencies related to clients. The example of Eileen Carter will illustrate the process of using the taxonomy to better understand a client's multicultural context. Review the following questions and responses, which integrate the previously discussed multicultural counseling competencies with the modified version of Bloom's taxonomy.

Content—What multicultural variables characterize the client?   Eileen is an African American woman who grew up in a lower middle-class neighborhood in a mid-Atlantic state in the United States. Her father died when she was a child. Despite her mother's efforts to earn enough money to support the family, it was a struggle to provide for the family's basic needs, and they had to apply for public assistance. Because she was so overburdened, Eileen's mother was able to maintain little involvement with her community and her church.

Eileen is currently married to an African American man and has one child. They live in a middle class suburb of a large city.

Eileen was raised in the Protestant religion. Although religious observances were not a big part of her family life, her parents communicated a strong belief in God. Eileen has been more strongly drawn to her religion as an adult but has not been attending church.

Process

- *Comprehension. What implications have these variables had for the client?*   Most of the families in Eileen's neighborhood and most of the children who lived nearby and attended elementary school with Eileen were African American. Consequently, Eileen felt comfortable in her elementary school. However, her middle and high schools were dominated by children from Jewish and Italian backgrounds, many of whom seemed to have a stronger educational foundation than did Eileen. Shortly before Eileen entered middle school, the death of her father caused a precipitous decline in family finances and led her mother to return to work. The family was now clearly poorer than others in the neighborhood and, as far as they knew, they were the only family receiving public assistance. Many of the mothers in Eileen's neighborhood were employed outside of the home and some were single parents; however, this was unusual in her middle and high schools, and teachers seemed to assume that all students came from financially comfortable two-parent families with mothers who stayed at home. This pattern was reflected in the literature that was read in school.

Eileen's gender further contributed to her difficulties. Her mother had different expectations for Eileen than she did for Eileen's brothers; Eileen was expected to do the housework that her mother no longer had time to do while her brothers were encouraged to play with their friends and complete their homework. Throughout her childhood years, her parents had paid more attention to her brothers' academic and athletic successes, a common attitude for parents at that time. In addition, Eileen had few role models of achieving women; other than her teachers who reportedly paid little attention to Eileen, she only saw women who stayed at home with children or worked in low paying, unrewarding jobs.

Eileen increasingly felt out of place and different from her peers. She became less and less involved and interested in school; her use of drugs and alcohol and her early sexual involvement began. As an attractive young woman, she found that she could obtain the attention and sense of importance she craved via her relationships with men.

On the surface, Eileen seems to fit in well in her current environment. She and her husband live in a townhouse in a neighborhood that includes people from a wide range of ethnic and cultural backgrounds. Most are families with young children. Some of the mothers are employed outside of the home while others are at home with their children. However, Eileen feels like she doesn't really belong in this setting.

- *Organization. What are the central themes or topics that characterize the impact the client's social, political, economic, and cultural background has had on him or her?*   The

following central themes and topics characterize the impact that Eileen's background
has had on her:
- feelings of differentness and not belonging
- lack of close ties with her neighborhood, her culture, and her church
- low self-esteem

- *Analysis and synthesis. What meaning do these central themes have for the client now? What is her or his worldview?* As a girl, Eileen's cultural, ethnic, and socioeconomic background combined to lead her to feel different and inferior to her peers. Her self-esteem suffered greatly, and she came to believe that her sexuality and her relationships with men were the only way she could find a place for herself and gain some affection and prestige.

Being a child of the 1970s and 1980s also contributed to Eileen's difficulties. The women's movement was gaining momentum, and Eileen got some messages that women could aspire to educational and professional success. However, few of the women around her reflected this image of women. In addition, her male peers who meant so much to her tended to disparage the women's movement and advocated a secondary and subservient role for women.

In terms of her worldview, Eileen believes that the appropriate role for an African American woman is to become a wife and mother and put her own needs after those of her family. She believes that success for women is measured by the views of others, especially those of the men in their lives. She perceives life as difficult and joyless, especially for people with less money than those around them, and she thinks nothing can be done to change that.

- *Interpretation. How have the dynamics and development of the client's difficulties been shaped by multicultural factors in his or her background and present life?* Although Eileen is currently leading a comfortable middle-class life, the impact of her social, cultural, ethnic, and economic background has stayed with her. In fact, the contrast between the context of her life during her adolescent years and her current context has contributed greatly to her confusion regarding her appropriate role.

Eileen's family and multicultural background led her to have experiences and attitudes that had a profound negative impact on her. Her feelings of not belonging, her low self-esteem, her devaluing of her racial and gender identity, and her lack of role models all influenced her decisions to neglect her studies in middle and high school, to drop out of school as soon as possible, and to become other-directed, deriving her tenuous sense of self from her sexual relationships.

Now that Eileen has matured, she has achieved a somewhat greater sense of belonging and importance. Much of that stems from her role as mother of a son. Eileen's current context, including her marriage to an African American man, her middle-class lifestyle, and her contacts with other women with whom she seems to have much in common, has somewhat enhanced her self-esteem and given her the courage to begin college. This step is particularly important for Eileen because it represents such a departure from the worldview she has held for many years and from the worldview of her family and childhood neighbors. For the first time, she is making independent choices that are enhancing her self-esteem.

However, Eileen's feelings about this choice are conflicted. Part of her perceives herself as a fraud and doubts her ability to succeed in college. That perspective is strengthened by her husband's objections to Eileen continuing her education and Eileen's own belief that she owes her primary loyalty to her husband and son rather than to herself. Her guilt about her past is another limiting factor, leading her to feel ashamed and out-of-place when she ventures into school or church or even socializes with others whom she perceives as better than she.

The healthy, growing part of Eileen longs to continue her education, to find in college a place where she can achieve in a way that is right for her and where she has a sense of accomplishment and belonging. She wants to make friends, affirm her cultural and religious heritage by joining a church, and have personal goals that include, but go beyond, creating a loving home environment for her family.

• *Application. What are the treatment implications of this analysis and interpretation?* Clearly, consideration of multicultural factors in Eileen's background is important not only in understanding her but also in the choice of clinician and the development of a treatment plan. Eileen seems most likely to benefit from a clinician who provides her with a role model and contributes to her feelings of competence and power. Consequently, a woman, perhaps an African American woman, seems especially well suited to serve as Eileen's clinician. Also important is the establishment of a collaborative therapeutic relationship that encourages Eileen to take charge of her own life, make wise and thoughtful decisions, and appreciate her many strengths. The clinician's communication of caring, support, and acceptance will contribute further to empowering Eileen.

Eileen seems likely to benefit from a treatment approach that helps her understand the impact that multicultural factors have had on her. At present, she blames herself for the unrewarding choices she made in her relationships, her limited education, and even her treatment of her body. Although taking responsibility for one's choices is an important part of healthy development, Eileen's self-blame is not promoting healthy development. Rather, it is holding her back and making her feel like she cannot do anything right and will never find a sense of accomplishment and joy in her life. Perhaps by understanding how ethnic, social, political, cultural, and economic factors in her background all contributed to the poor choices she made, Eileen could reduce her feelings of self-blame and low self-esteem. Perhaps she can come to believe that, now that she has matured and has sought out some help, she can make far more rewarding choices.

At the same time, extensive analysis of her past does not seem likely to be helpful to Eileen. She has some decisions she must make fairly rapidly. While she is interested in understanding herself better, she sought counseling primarily because she wanted to improve her present life. Although some exploration of her background is likely to help Eileen, that should not be the primary focus of her treatment. Instead, she needs help in using her increased knowledge of the impact multicultural factors have had on her development as well as her understanding of her worldview to make positive changes in the present.

• *Evaluation. To what extent and in what ways has treatment helped the client to understand the impact of multicultural factors on her or his worldview and development? How has that understanding been reflected in changes in the person's emotions, thoughts, and actions?* Although a final evaluation cannot be done because Eileen's treatment has not yet been completed, a clinician working with Eileen might look for the following signs of positive change (Arredondo, 1999):

- Eileen can describe important multicultural factors, both in her background and her present.
- She has knowledge of ways in which those factors shaped her development.
- She can identify societal factors such as stereotyping and discrimination that contributed to her difficulties. She is alert to the presence of those factors in

her current life and has ways of successfully addressing their negative impact, both for herself and for others.

- She reports feeling greater self-esteem and enhanced empowerment.
- She can articulate both her past and present worldviews and can identify positive and helpful changes in her worldview.
- She reports greater feelings of well-being and a greater sense of joy in her life; feelings of shame and differentness have been reduced and replaced with an awareness of herself as a capable person.
- She has made thoughtful and positive choices that will enable her to move forward with both her family goals and her personal goals.
- She has improved relationships with family, friends, and associates.

Improving the Clinician's Multicultural Competence

The questions that were used to enable you to understand and address the impact of multicultural factors on Eileen can be rephrased so that they promote awareness of your own multicultural dimensions and competence. Respond to the following questions as they pertain to you:

Content—What multicultural variables characterize your background as well as your present life?

Process

- *Comprehension*—What implications have these had for you?
- *Organization*—What are the central themes or topics that characterize the impact that these multicultural variables have had on your life?
- *Analysis and synthesis*—What meaning do these central themes have for you now? What is your worldview?
- *Interpretation*—How have the dynamics and development of your joys and difficulties been shaped by multicultural factors in your background and in your present life?
- *Application*—What are the treatment implications of this analysis and interpretation? In other words, what could you do, either on your own or through therapy, to make positive changes in your emotions, thoughts, and actions via increased understanding of your own multicultural characteristics and worldview? Also, what does this information suggest about the types of treatment approaches and interventions that are most likely to appeal to you, both as a client and as a clinician?
- *Evaluation*—To what extent and in what ways would treatment be likely to help you to understand the impact of multicultural factors on your worldview and development?

Implications for Practice

The process of looking at both yourself and Eileen through a multicultural lens has probably increased your awareness of the importance of multicultural factors and of multicultural counselor competencies. Like many of us, you may have realized that this is a neglected area of learning for you. You may also have realized that you have characteristics of what Srebalus and Brown (2001, p. 48) called "unintentional racists," people who believe that they are not racists but who continue to practice or tolerate racism, usually without understanding that they are engaging in stereotyping or discrimination themselves.

Ferreting out and moving toward the elimination of those attitudes in ourselves and in others is a challenging process. However, we are likely to have success in improving our multicultural counseling competencies if we can:

- Be aware of our own heritage and background.
- Be open to learning about and participating in cultures that differ from our own.
- Be honest and realistic about our own reactions and experiences.
- Be aware of issues of power and privilege.
- Recognize our limitations.
- Notice ways in which we are both similar to and different from others.
- Remain curious, interested, and surprised.

INTERPRETATION AND INSIGHT

Interpretation is a process that is intended to give people a new frame of reference, a different and usually deeper understanding of themselves and their lives. Interpretation often links past and present, drawing on past experiences to shed light on present responses. Interpretation goes beyond what people have stated or perceived and gives them new perspectives and explanations. In other words, they gain greater insight into themselves and their lives. This can enable them to reconceptualize their lives and to present a revised and more helpful narrative of their experiences. Equally important are the changes in emotions, thoughts, and behaviors that insight can facilitate.

On the other hand, interpretation can undermine the treatment process and detract from the therapeutic alliance. A poorly timed or intrusive interpretation can make people feel misunderstood and shamed, can lead them to mistrust and doubt their clinicians, and can leave people feeling unsafe and vulnerable. Consider the following example that reflects the use of effective and ineffective interpretations and also facilitates comparison of interpretations with other types of interventions presented earlier in this book.

Example: *Client statement:*   It didn't bother me at all when my fiancee broke our engagement. I always expected it to happen anyway so it was no surprise.

Clinician response

- *Restatement:* It didn't bother you at all when your fiancee broke your engagement.
- *Paraphrase:* You weren't upset when your fiancee broke your engagement because you had anticipated she would do that.
- *Encourager:* No surprise?
- *Open question:* What led you to expect her to break the engagement?
- *Reflection of feeling:* Perhaps you even felt a sense of relief when what you anticipated finally happened.

- *Helpful interpretation:* I wonder if your mother's abandonment of you has led you to expect that all women will leave you?
- *Helpful interpretation:* And yet I know you had hopes that this relationship would work out for you. Could it be that you are protecting yourself from feeling pain by convincing yourself that the end of the relationship was inevitable?
- *Unhelpful interpretation:* You are clearly in denial of your true feelings, perhaps because you have never fully dealt with the pain of losing your mother.

As you can see, unlike the other types of interventions, the three interpretations offer a new perspective on the client's experience. They are designed to encourage him to take a closer and deeper look at his feelings and perhaps gain greater insight and self-awareness. The first two interpretations, while strong statements, are phrased as gentle questions and allow the client the opportunity to reject these ideas. The third interpretation, however, sounds accusatory and is likely to make the client feel uncomfortable and perhaps even angry. Interpretations are powerful tools but must be used with great care and sensitivity.

Differing Viewpoints on Interpretation

Clinicians differ in terms of the importance they ascribe to interpretation and insight and the place they believe those processes have in treatment. Freud and his followers were the first and most vocal proponents of the importance of interpretation and insight. They viewed insight as the ultimate goal of psychotherapy and directed many of their interventions toward its achievement. Modern clinicians who practice from a psychoanalytic or psychodynamic framework continue to place great importance on interpretation and insight.

However, many clinicians do not share that perspective. Cognitive, behavioral, person-centered, and solution-focused therapists, for example, tend to minimize the role of interpretation in their work and, instead, emphasize present thoughts and actions.

Despite this variation, nearly all clinicians recognize that, at least occasionally, interpretation can be a helpful addition to any treatment process. Current clinical thinking seems to be that, even if interpretation is viewed as a necessary part of treatment, it is not sufficient to accomplish the changes in emotions, thoughts, and actions that are generally the goals of modern counseling and psychotherapy.

Effective Use of Interpretation

Many types of interpretations are available to clinicians. Clinicians' personal style and theoretical orientation, the specific client, the presenting concerns, the nature of the therapeutic alliance, and the goals of treatment all influence the type of interpretation that is used. Interpretations may be especially helpful under several specific circumstances.

Times when interpretations may be especially useful

- When treatment has reached an impasse
- When clients keep repeating the same harmful patterns and behaviors
- When present emotions, thoughts, or actions don't seem to make sense

- When the client seems to be overreacting to an event or interaction
- When the client has strong emotional reactions to the clinician that do not seem based in reality
- When the present is a clear repetition of the past

Interpretations can stem from a variety of perspectives. Some of these follow, with accompanying examples.

Interpretive frameworks

- *Feminist/gender based interpretation*—It sounds like your role as a woman is very different from that of your mother. I wonder if that is creating some conflict for you?
- *Developmental*—You seem to be saying that when most of your friends were asserting their independence and establishing strong connections with their peers, you and your father continued to be each other's primary sources of support. I wonder if that has a lot to do with your being a sort of late bloomer, just beginning to establish your independence as you approach 30.
- *Multicultural*—I wonder if at least part of the reason for the conflict you are having with your daughter has to do with cultural issues. You came to the United States in your late 20s and still view yourself as Vietnamese while she was born in the United States and ascribes little importance to the traditional Asian values that are so important to you.
- *Psychodynamic*—Some clinicians view depression as anger turned inwards. Could it be that your depression reflects anger you have toward yourself?

Formats for interpretation.   Language is an important factor in the effectiveness of interpretations. Consider the following examples that reflect helpful formats for the delivery of interpretations.

- *Hunches*—I have a hunch that you enjoy all the attention you receive when you are sick and can't go to school. Maybe that makes it hard for you to get well. What do you think about that?
- *Noting themes*—I've noticed a theme of men mistreating you that keeps coming up in our conversations. You've talked about your father's verbal abuse, your math teacher's criticism of your work, your physician's lack of caring when you are in pain, your supervisor's failure to praise your work, and several of your boyfriends who seemed neglectful. What do you make of that?
- *Noting connections*—Your strong reaction to your teacher's inability to be present at your recital reminds me of the feelings you had as a child when your parents separated and your father stopped coming to your soccer games. I wonder if you see any connection there.
- *Noting discrepancies*—You've had many disappointing relationships with family and friends. It strikes me that this relationship seems to be different for you, perhaps because you have more control in this relationship. What is your reaction to that?
- *Reframing*—You've described yourself as a "hopeless workaholic" but you also derive great satisfaction from your ability to immerse yourself in your work.

Illustration of an Interpretation

Let's take a simple example to illustrate how interpretation, leading to greater insight, can enrich clients' lives and facilitate positive change. Flo had been raised in a spiritual family; a bedtime prayer was an important ritual in her family. As she moved into her teenage years, one of the ways she asserted her independence was by refusing to participate in the family prayers. She felt comfortable with her decision and rarely gave it a second thought.

However, 15 years later, Flo sought counseling for depression following the birth of her first child. Despite considerable evidence to the contrary, Flo persisted in believing that she was not doing a good job as a mother. Exploration of Flo's feelings for her child and her role as a mother shed no light on her self-doubts as a parent. The clinician then shifted to the past, looking for patterns and connections, and asked Flo about her family of origin, especially the mothering she had received. Now that she had an adult perspective, Flo was able to recognize the importance of the nightly prayer in unifying her family and providing a sense of security and belonging. Because Flo had not been providing her daughter the same spiritual foundation she had gained from her family, she had a sense that something was missing and that she was an inadequate parent. Through discussion with her husband, Flo was able to create a personal prayer that was compatible with the beliefs that she and her husband shared. Establishing a nightly ritual of saying this prayer with her current family enhanced Flo's perception of herself as a mother and helped her create in her new family the sense of closeness and security she had in her family of origin.

This example reflects many of the characteristics of the positive use of interpretation in counseling and psychotherapy. These and other important characteristics of helpful interpretations follow.

Characteristics of Effective Interpretations

Purpose.   Interpretations should

- be designed to help people resolve their presenting concerns.
- help people make sense of their emotions, thoughts, and actions.
- promote awareness of patterns and connections.
- encourage a greater sense of self-control and direction.
- facilitate change, not just promote insight.

Delivery.   Interpretations should

- focus on the present and possible current explanations before moving to the past.
- be combined with empathic interventions to provide support and encouragement and reduce any threat presented by the interpretations.
- be delivered with a clear purpose in mind.
- be used sparingly.
- be carefully timed so that the client is receptive rather than resistant.
- be elicited from the client as much as possible.
- be gently suggested, not forced; insights should not be rushed.

- always be checked out with clients; give them the opportunity to react to, modify, or reject the interpretation.
- be revisited as appropriate to ensure that they are meaningful and useful to clients.

The Learning Opportunities that follow will afford you the opportunity to practice making some interpretations. In addition, you will have the opportunity to critique and improve on interpretations made by others.

LEARNING OPPORTUNITIES

This chapter has reviewed the importance of mastering conceptual skills as well as technical skills and introduced you to an array of conceptual skills related to understanding and making therapeutic use of a client's background information. These include the following:

- using the modified version of Bloom's taxonomy to facilitate case conceptualization and analysis
- understanding and making good use of information on the context of treatment
- understanding the person seeking treatment by collecting and processing background information/intake interviews
- understanding and making good use of transference and countertransference
- developing multicultural counseling competencies
- making interpretations

The following exercises, like those in previous chapters, afford you the opportunity to apply the skills that have been presented in this chapter. This section includes written exercises, discussion questions, practice group exercises, an assessment tool to use in your practice groups, and questions and activities to address in your personal journal.

Written Exercises/Discussion Questions

1. Describe the differences between the analysis/synthesis and interpretation parts of Bloom's taxonomy.
2. Your client is an 18-year-old woman known as Nati, a high school junior, who sought treatment at a community mental health center at the suggestion of her school counselor. When counseling was suggested to Nati, her initial reaction was negative and she seemed hurt by the suggestion that she might need help. However, after the purpose of counseling was clarified for her, Nati cautiously agreed to some counseling.

   About a year ago, Nati's family immigrated to the United States from their home in Africa to seek medical treatment for Nati's younger sister who had developed cancer. The family had been relatively affluent in Africa, but Nati's parents had difficulty finding professional jobs in the United States. Consequently, they worked long hours at low-paying jobs. Nati became the primary caregiver for her sister, age 8, and her twin brothers, age 10. Nati has been performing poorly at school, appears fatigued and depressed, and has not made friends with other students.

Analyze the contextual information provided previously, using the modified version of Bloom's taxonomy. Be sure to include information on all of the following elements in Bloom's model:

- Content
- Process
  - Comprehension
  - Organization
  - Analysis/synthesis
  - Interpretation
  - Application

3. Multicultural counseling competencies are very important in finding effective ways to help Nati. In her native land, women's primary role is that of wife and mother; domestic skills, especially the ability to bear and care for children, are highly valued. When Nati's parents gave her responsibility for her younger siblings, they told her that this experience would improve her prospects for making a good marriage. Address the following questions in relation to Nati, using the information provided in both this question and question 2:

   - What multicultural variables are relevant to this client?
   - What implications do these variables have for understanding Nati?
   - What are the central themes or topics that characterize the impact Nati's social, political, economic, and cultural background is likely to have had on her?
   - What meaning are these central themes likely to have for her now? What conflicts or issues are likely to arise for Nati in the United States in light of these themes?
   - What do you think that Nati's worldview is like? How do you think that might have changed since her immigration to the United States?
   - How have the dynamics and development of Nati's difficulties probably been shaped by multicultural factors in her background as well as in her present life?
   - What are the treatment implications of this analysis and interpretation?

4. Nati's clinician is an African American woman in her mid-30s who was born in the United States. She has always been a strong supporter of women's rights. She and her husband value an egalitarian marriage and, at present, he is the primary caretaker of their two young children.

   - What transference issues seem most likely to arise here?
   - What countertransference issues seem most likely to arise here?
   - How would you suggest that Nati and her therapist address both transference and countertransference issues?
   - In what ways, if any, do you think that transference and countertransference reactions can be used positively in Nati's treatment?

5. Clinicians vary greatly in terms of the importance they place on identifying and analyzing transference reactions in treatment. Discuss your ideas on the most helpful ways to address transference in treatment. In what ways will your treatment of transference be affected by the client's presenting concerns, that person's motivation toward treatment, the severity and urgency of the client's difficulties, and the setting in which treatment is taking place?

6. Either write out a hypothetical intake interview with Nati or, if the questions in this section are being discussed in class, have two of the students (or the teacher and one student) role-play an intake interview with Nati. Feel free to add information, as long as that information is consistent with what you already know about Nati. Then respond to the following questions:

   - What do you know about the following aspects of Nati's life?
     - Demographics?
     - Presenting concerns?
     - Prior psychological difficulties?
     - Current life situation?
     - Cultural, religious, and socioeconomic background?
     - Family of origin?
     - Developmental history?
     - Career and educational history?
     - Medical history?
     - Health-related behaviors?
     - Relationships?
     - Leisure activities?
   - Process the content of the interview, according to the following steps in the modified version of Bloom's taxonomy:
     - Comprehension
     - Organization
     - Analysis and synthesis
     - Interpretation
     - Application

7. Develop an effective interpretation you might make to Nati, focused on the conflict she is experiencing between the values inherent in her family and background and those reflected in her current social environment.

Practice Group Exercises—Conceptual and Technical Skills, Focused on Background

Divide into your practice groups, as described starting on on page 17. By this time, you probably have had several meetings with your practice groups and so are familiar with the structure and process of the practice group exercises focused on the development of technical skills. In addition, the earlier chapters of this book should also have provided you with an awareness of the important technical skills of the clinician and at least a rudimentary ability to use those skills.

The practice group exercises in this and the following chapters will use your knowledge of technical skills as a foundation and will build on that foundation through the addition of conceptual skills. While learning and practicing your conceptual skills, you will have an opportunity to further refine your technical skills. Continue to tape-record your practice sessions, both for the group's review and for your own review of your session. I recommend that you tape not only the practice session but also the subsequent discussion. This will enhance your efforts to improve your technical skills and develop your conceptual skills.

Purpose of Exercise.   In chapter 2 of this book, you conducted an intake interview that emphasized the use of open and closed questions. In this chapter, you will build on what you learned in chapter 2. Integrating your technical and conceptual skills will make the intake interview more meaningful and will help you understand why an intake interview is essential to giving you the information and insight you need to provide effective treatment to your clients.

This exercise will encompass the following skills:

Technical Skills—
- appropriate use of open and closed questions
- ability to conduct an intake interview
- ability to use a range of interventions
- ability to elicit essential information

Conceptual Skills—
- ability to process intake information
- ability to understand and apply Bloom's taxonomy
- demonstration of multicultural counseling competencies

Role-play Exercise.   In each dyad, one person will assume the role of clinician and the other will assume the role of a client. For purposes of this exercise, the person in the client role should pre-sent as a person with multicultural dimensions that are important in both understanding that person and making sense of that person's presenting concerns. Examples of such people might include:

- a man who had been hospitalized for schizophrenia, now stabilized on medication, who must seek employment
- a child from a biracial family background who is confused about her sense of self
- a Jewish woman whose parents strongly disapprove of her relationship with a man from Saudi Arabia
- a gay man who is uncertain whether to tell his conservative father about his sexual orientation

If multicultural dimensions in your own life have an impact on your current concerns, you can choose to be yourself when you are in the client role. However, be sure that you are comfortable talking about the issues you present and that those issues are not too complex for you to discuss briefly with other learners. If you choose to assume a role for this exercise, you can act as if you are one of the people described previously, present the concerns and issues of someone you know (of course, being sure to conceal that person's identity), or be creative and make up a client who interests you.

The person in the clinician role will conduct an intake interview, seeking to cover the important topics in such an interview, discussed in this chapter and in chapter 2. The interviewer should try to make good use of technical skills, especially open and closed questions, and should pay particular attention to multicultural dimensions and their relationship to the client's presenting concerns. In addition, the clinician should try to demonstrate the multicultural counseling competencies discussed earlier in this chapter. This includes maintaining awareness of your own assumptions, actively seeking to understand the worldview of your client, and making sure that your interview is free of stereotyping and discrimination.

Time Schedule.   If possible, allow approximately 3 hours for this exercise, with each of the four role plays and their discussion taking 45 minutes. If you do not have this much time, do only two role plays, one for each dyad. The drawback of this is that each person will have the opportunity to be either client or clinician but will not be able to try out both roles.

- Allow 20–25 minutes for each role-played intake interview.
- Take about 15 minutes to provide feedback to the person in the clinician role. Be sure to begin the feedback process with the person in the clinician role, focus on strengths first, and offer concrete suggestions for improvement. Like all the practice exercises suggested in this book, this should be a positive learning experience, not one that makes people feel criticized or judged. Feedback should focus on the areas listed in the following Assessment of Progress Form.

In addition, during the feedback process, spend a few minutes responding to the following questions, related to the impact of the client's multicultural characteristics on the treatment process:

- What multicultural variables are relevant to this client?
- What implications do these variables have for understanding the client?
- What impact is this client's social, political, economic, and cultural background likely to have had on him/her?
- In light of this, what central themes, conflicts, or issues are likely to arise in the course of this person's treatment?
- What do you think this client's worldview is like?

Assessment of Progress Form 6

1. Describe the types of interventions you used during the intake interview.

   a. Should a particular type of intervention have been used more or used less?

   b. How effective was the balance of open and closed questions?

    c. How well were other interventions integrated with the questions?

2. What was the flow of the interview like? What made it flow well? What would have made it flow more smoothly?

3. What interventions contributed to the development of rapport? What might you have done to enhance the therapeutic relationship even more?

4. How well did you succeed at conducting a comprehensive intake interview? What topics were omitted or discussed too briefly? What issues received too much emphasis?

5. What interventions or clinician attitudes demonstrated multicultural counseling competencies? Should you have done anything differently in dealing with multicultural issues?

6. Summary of feedback:

Personal Journal Questions

1. Many students, and even many practicing clinicians, are uncomfortable when dealing with transference and countertransference in treatment. However, these are common processes that appear in treatment as well as in our daily lives. Write briefly about a time in your life when your reactions to a person stemmed more from your early experiences than from your actual interactions with that person. What can you learn from that experience to help you to become a more effective clinician?

2. Identify at least two multicultural variables that have been important in your own development. Write about the ways that these dimensions made you who you are.

3. Have you ever felt that people were discriminating against you or seeing you in stereotyped ways? Write about how that felt and how you handled that situation.

4. Do you believe that the fields of counseling and psychology pay too much, too little, or appropriate attention to multicultural issues? Write briefly about your response to this question.

5. Listen to the tape recording of the role-played intake interview in which you participated. Respond to the following questions about that role play.

   • What improvement, if any, did you notice in your clinical skills if you had the opportunity to assume the role of clinician? If you did not have that opportunity, what improvement, if any, did you notice in your group?

   • List one or two interventions you made or heard another person make that seemed particularly effective:

      a.

      b.

   • List one or two interventions you made or heard that you think should have been changed. How might you have improved upon these interventions?

   • What do you view as your greatest clinical strengths at the present time?

   • List two or three goals you currently have to improve your clinical skills:

      a.

      b.

      c.

6. What is the most important thing you learned from this chapter and its exercises?

SUMMARY

This first chapter focusing on conceptual skills emphasized those skills associated with clients' backgrounds. A modified version of Bloom's taxonomy was introduced to provide a framework for understanding and making therapeutic use of background information. This chapter paid particular attention to understanding and processing information gathered via intake interviews; to understanding and making good use of transference and countertransference; to developing multicultural awareness and competencies; and to the effective clinical use of interpretation.

Chapter 7 will focus on conceptual skills associated with emotions. Included in that chapter is information on developing a positive therapeutic alliance and dealing with suicide, rage, and other strong emotions that clients might present during the course of treatment.

CHAPTER 7

Using Conceptual Skills to Make Positive Use of and Modify Emotions

INTRODUCTION

When she was three years old, my granddaughter began asking me what I do when I "go to work." Seeking to synthesize what I do as a counselor and psychologist into one sentence that she could readily understand, I told her that "I help sad people to feel better." I believe that is the essence of our work. Whether treatment addresses the consequences of early attachment problems (background), dysfunctional and self-destructive cognitions (thoughts), or harmful habits and behaviors (actions), psychologists and counselors help people feel better about themselves and their lives.

Chapter 3 presented the technical skills that are important in helping people express and identify their emotions and in helping clinicians attend to those emotions: encouragers, restatement, paraphrase, summarization, and reflection of verbal and nonverbal feelings. That chapter also described specific technical skills designed to increase people's awareness of their feelings: guided imagery, use of nonverbal communication, and focusing. This chapter builds on these technical skills and helps you develop the ability to identify complex and challenging emotions and enable people to modify troubling emotions.

Emotions that are present in the treatment setting can be divided into three groups:

- *Emotions that clients bring into treatment*—These may include positive feelings such as love, joy, and fulfillment but, at least in the early stages of treatment, are more likely to include negative emotions such as despair, anxiety, and rage. Clinicians who are skilled at helping clients identify, express appropriately, and modify their emotions are likely to make a great difference in people's lives.
- *Emotions that clinicians bring into treatment*—Although our emotions are rarely the focus of our sessions, clinicians, too, bring emotions into the sessions. Those emotions can have a powerful impact on the direction and success of treatment. Emotions such as caring, optimism, and commitment to our clients can greatly enhance treatment if expressed in helpful ways. On the other hand, we may also have negative feelings toward our clients such as disapproval, disappointment, dislike, fear, and annoyance; those emotions can undermine the best treatment plans. We also bring into our sessions emotions from our own lives; we may be tired and overworked, excited about an upcoming celebration, or angry about an argument we just had. These emotions, too, have the potential to affect the treatment process. Consequently, our ability to be aware of our own feelings and deal with them constructively is an important clinical skill.
- *Emotions that arise in response to the treatment process*—Finally, we must consider the emotional interaction of the client and the clinician. Having a shared vision of better possibilities, working together to make those possibilities a reality, trusting each other, and sharing the struggles and rewards of treatment can engender positive emotions in both client and clinician, and serve as powerful ingredients in effective treatment. On the other hand, if client and clinician fail to develop a sound therapeutic alliance and are not collaborating effectively to achieve shared goals, both may feel discouraged. Their effort and motivation may diminish, and treatment may be ineffective.

Considering emotions in treatment from all three of these perspectives, this chapter will present the following conceptual skills:

- Developing a positive therapeutic alliance
- Initiating effective treatment, setting the stage via role induction and other approaches
- Dealing with strong client emotions (suicidal ideation, responses to crisis, rage)
- Making positive use of clinician self-disclosure
- Addressing client reluctance

Moving beyond technical skills, this chapter helps clinicians to understand the impact of emotions on the treatment process, to facilitate the appropriate expression of emotions, and, if indicated, to modify those emotions. As in the previous chapter, the modified version of Bloom's taxonomy will be used to facilitate an in-depth understanding of the emotional dimensions to be addressed in this chapter.

DIMENSIONS AND IMPORTANCE OF THE THERAPEUTIC ALLIANCE

The nature and quality of the therapeutic alliance has a profound impact on the success of the treatment process. Research study after research study has found that the therapeutic relationship is the best predictor of therapeutic outcome (Orlinsky, Grawe, & Parks, 1994). Horvath and Symonds (1991), for example, conducted a meta-analysis of 24 studies "relating the quality of the working alliance to therapy outcome" (p. 139). They found a "moderate but reliable association" between outcome and therapeutic alliance that was not a function of the length or type of treatment. These researchers found that collaboration and negotiation of mutually agreeable goals and plans were particularly important ingredients in the therapeutic alliance.

You may find this surprising. Most graduate programs training counselors and psychologists devote much less time to helping clinicians learn to develop a positive therapeutic alliance than they do to helping them learn the important theories and strategies of treatment. Of course, the nature of the treatment plan does have a significant effect on outcome. Yet, without a collaborative alliance that promotes client motivation and hopefulness, the most appropriate and detailed treatment plan is unlikely to succeed.

In this way, the connection between client and clinician resembles many other relationships. You will probably make a return visit to a restaurant that feels warm and welcoming and that pays attention to your needs, as long as the food is also satisfactory. Of the many people you might meet at a party, you will probably remember and perhaps contact the ones who seemed interested in you and with whom you felt some rapport. In counseling and psychotherapy as well, the initial contact and the relationship that evolves usually are the primary determinants of the success of treatment and even of whether the client returns for subsequent appointments.

Nature of the Therapeutic Alliance

Therapeutic alliances vary in terms of their nature and pattern of development. Bachelor (1995) surveyed clients on their perceptions of the therapeutic relationship and found three types of alliances:

- *Nurturant*—46% of those surveyed described their clinicians as respectful, nonjudgmental, empathic, and having good listening skills. Support and reinforcement were emphasized. The clients had a trusting relationship with their clinicians and felt comfortable and at ease during the treatment process.
- *Insight-oriented*—39% described their treatment as focusing on improving self-understanding. Clinicians emphasized underlying causes and dynamics and used interpretation, exploration, and clarification to increase self-awareness.
- *Collaborative alliance*—Only 15% of clients surveyed reported that they were actively involved in the treatment process and described an alliance that emphasized mutuality as well as client commitment and responsibility.

Development of the Therapeutic Alliance

Kivlighan and Shaughnessy (2000) looked at the development of the therapeutic alliance from a temporal perspective. They confirmed that the working alliance was a strong predictor of therapeutic outcome. Their research identified three patterns of development of the therapeutic alliance:

- *stable alliance*—in which the initial level of strength of the alliance is maintained throughout the treatment process
- *linear growth*—characterizing a working alliance that improves with time
- *quadratic growth*—in which a strong alliance develops initially, then declines or is damaged during the middle phase of treatment, followed by a rebuilding in the concluding phase of treatment

Regardless of the specific pattern of development of the therapeutic alliance, the literature suggests the importance of rapidly establishing a positive therapeutic alliance. Walborn (1996) concluded that a positive therapeutic alliance must be in place by the fifth session if treatment is to have a successful outcome. Kivlighan and Shaughnessy (2000) found that clinicians and clients could even develop a strong working alliance by the end of the first session!

Characteristics of a Positive Therapeutic Alliance

The therapeutic alliance is a synthesis of many elements. The most important of these are the characteristics of the clinician and the characteristics of the client, to be discussed later in this chapter. In addition, factors such as the treatment setting, the nature of the referral, the attitudes that significant people in the client's life have toward the treatment process, and even the weather and traffic at the time of the client's first appointment all contribute to the development of the therapeutic alliance. Clearly, clinicians can control only some of these factors but should keep the others in mind as potentially important variables. Having a vision of what a positive therapeutic alliance is like can help clinicians build such an alliance with their clients.

A review of the literature suggests that a positive therapeutic alliance has the following characteristics:

- It provides a safe and protective environment for clients.
- It encourages collaboration, with both clients and clinicians playing an active role in the treatment process.
- It has mutuality or a feeling of shared warmth, caring, affirmation, and respect.
- Clients can identify with their clinicians, perhaps using them as role models.
- Client and clinician have an agreement on goals and procedures; sessions are structured in such a way as to clearly move toward accomplishment of those goals.
- Client and clinician view themselves as engaged in a shared endeavor that seems likely to succeed.

INITIATING AND DEVELOPING A POSITIVE THERAPEUTIC ALLIANCE

Clinicians can maximize the likelihood of developing a positive therapeutic alliance if they take steps to understand the essential ingredients of such a relationship and strive to include those ingredients in the treatment process. The research studies cited previously conducted by Bachelor and by Kivlighan and Shaughnessy demonstrate that sound therapeutic alliances can take many forms and develop in a variety of ways. However, strong and positive therapeutic alliances, and the clinicians who facilitate their development, typically share some key characteristics.

A review of the literature suggests that the following 10 characteristics reflect the work of clinicians who are skilled at developing positive therapeutic alliances with their clients (Seligman, 2001). Review the following descriptions of these qualities and their associated strategies.

1. Empathy

Description.   "Empathy is the clinician's ability to see the world through the client's eyes and to communicate that understanding so that the client feels heard and validated" (Seligman, 2001, p. 18). This does not mean that we participate in clients' feelings or that we feel pity for them; rather, we let them know that their emotions make sense in light of what we know about them and their lives and are neither bizarre nor reprehensible. According to Rogers (1980),

> It [empathy] means entering the private perceptual world of the other and becoming thoroughly at home in it. It involves being sensitive, moment by moment, to the changing felt meanings which flow in this other person, to the fear or rage or tenderness or confusion or whatever that he or she is experiencing. It means temporarily living in the other's life, moving about in it delicately without making judgments. (p. 142)

Empathy is an orientation toward people, a way of being with them, not just a technical skill.

Communicating empathy.   Reflection of feeling, discussed in chapter 3, is the most powerful tool for communicating empathy. This technique is most effective when it not only reflects people's verbalized emotions but also acknowledges both covert and nonverbal emotions. Identifying core emotions or persistent feelings can be especially powerful and helpful. By letting clients know we are attuned to their deepest emotions, many of which may even be out of their own awareness, we truly let them know we understand them. Use your own emotional reactions to help you tune into the client's affective world; if you are feeling confused and overwhelmed by the client's story, that may well be how the client is feeling, too. Remember to communicate empathy frequently, even when your focus is on background, thoughts, or actions. Use your own words, rather than restating what the client has said, to deepen client self-awareness and demonstrate your understanding. Be tentative and allow the client ample opportunity to react to or revise your empathic statements so that you really understand what that other person is feeling.

2. Good listening skills

Description.   Most of us do not take the time to listen to ourselves and to hear the important messages we are giving. Clinicians who listen carefully and deeply to their clients and communicate that listening are serving as a sort of mirror for their clients, helping them to hear and understand themselves. Communicating empathy and demonstrating good listening skills are closely related. To succeed in both, you must focus intently on the client and not allow yourself to be distracted by your own needs unless they are relevant to the therapeutic situation. Listen for and acknowledge both overt and covert messages and recognize that silence and the absence of a response or an action are often important messages. If you are listening closely but are not understanding, ask questions; you may have identified an area that is conflicted or confusing to the client as well.

Demonstrating good listening.   All of the technical skills described in chapters 2 through 5 of this book are important in demonstrating that you are listening well. Paraphrase lets clients know you have grasped the point of what they are saying. Open questions are important in clarifying confusing information. Reflections of feeling and meaning and summarization synthesize what has been said, pull together themes, and recognize indirect communications. Remember that listening is an active, rather than a passive, process; clients only know that we are listening well if we demonstrate that to them in helpful ways.

3. Trustworthiness, reliability, and ethical behavior

Description.   Many of our clients enter treatment with a history of impoverished and unstable relationships. They may expect all their relationships to follow that pattern and may feel leery and mistrustful of the therapeutic relationship. Consequently, we must facilitate our clients' trust in us to counteract their negative expectations. According to Kottler and Brown (2000, p. 93), trust is crucial to productive treatment and includes "respect for the client's right to be his or her own person, warm regard for the client as a unique being, and genuineness, which means being honest and real." When clients trust their clinicians, they believe that the clinicians are on their side, that the clinicians will never hurt or shame them, that the clinicians will follow through on their commitments, and will always behave in ethical and professional ways.

Demonstrating trustworthiness, reliability, and ethical behavior.   We must demonstrate to clients, both through words and actions, that we are not interested in exerting power over them or forcing them to change to meet our needs. Rather, we want to help them to be the best they can be and to meet their own needs in healthy ways. We must demonstrate and model reliability for our clients. For example, we should be on time for appointments, remember important information about our clients, and return telephone calls in a timely way. If we make a mistake, and we all do that sometimes, we acknowledge that to the client and make amends as needed. For example, a clinician who inadvertently scheduled two clients at the same time did not charge the client who was forced to return the next day for an appointment. We are aware of the ethical standards of our profession and always behave ethically, never crossing boundaries inappropriately and always considering what will promote our clients' healthy development.

4. Caring and concern

Description.   An angry adolescent once said to my colleague, "If you weren't paid to see me, you wouldn't bother to talk to me. I'm just a 45-minute slot in your week." The role of the clinician is a complicated and often confusing one. Nearly all of us are paid for our work and that is essential to our well-being, but finances are unlikely to be the primary reason we chose our professions. We are mental health professionals because we deeply care about the welfare of others and believe that we can contribute to making their lives better. Caring entails empowering our clients, helping them in proactive ways, being interested in what is important to them, and consistently communicating support, empathy, and good listening.

Demonstrating caring and concern.   We communicate caring when we teach our clients the tools they need to feel more powerful and take charge of their lives, when we inquire about important milestones in their lives, when we do something out of the ordinary that demonstrates our concern about a client, and when we let clients know that we are there to help them. We also demonstrate caring when we point out to our clients the negative as well as the positive consequences of their actions, when we think about them in context and offer help to their communities and families, and when we accept and understand both their joys and their disappointments. Caring usually is expressed in the context of the treatment sessions. However, moving slightly, but always ethically, away from the standard role of the clinician can be especially powerful in communicating caring and concern. Examples of this include calling a client who has just returned home after surgery, contacting a client's teacher to discuss his progress (of course, with the client's permission), sending a client an encouraging e-mail before a big event, and asking clients to bring in photos of their wedding or new baby.

5. Genuineness, sincerity, and congruence

Description.   Another way to build trust and counteract the exploitative and hurtful relationships experienced by so many clients is for clinicians to be genuine and sincere. This does not mean we should be brutally honest with our clients but rather that we find sensitive and tactful ways to communicate clearly, accurately, and honestly. Being congruent is an important element in transmitting genuineness and sincerity. Our verbal and nonverbal messages must be consistent and compatible, providing clients with unambiguous messages.

Communicating genuineness, sincerity, and congruence. We can best communicate these variables by being real people in our sessions, not just blank slates. We can laugh with our clients, feel sad with them when they hear bad news, and even get tears in our eyes when they experience a great loss. As long as our interventions are intentional and have a helpful purpose, we can share our reactions with our clients, provide them encouragement, and let them know our reservations about potentially harmful choices. Of course, we must respect their right to self-determination, unless they present a clear danger to themselves or others, but I believe it is easier for clients to form a positive working alliance with a real human being than with an anonymous and inexpressive one. More information will be provided later in this chapter on appropriate clinician self-disclosure.

6. Persuasiveness and credibility

Description.   Clinicians who have credibility with their clients have what Kottler and Brown (2000) referred to as benevolent power or interpersonal influence. In their description of this dimension, they stated, "Interpersonal influence is that dimension of counseling that involves the application of expertise, power, and attractiveness in such a way as to foster self-awareness and constructive change" (pp. 94–95). When clients perceive their clinicians as admirable and believable, those clients are more likely to use their clinicians as role models and to take reasonable risks to achieve their goals. Interpersonal influence is particularly likely to develop if clients perceive some similarity between their clinicians and themselves; this connection can inspire clients and give them hope that they, too, can achieve personal and professional success. This role modeling can be particularly important for our nontraditional clients, people who have not yet become acculturated to this society or who have had little exposure to mental health services. People such as these may feel considerably reassured by knowing that their clinicians have a cultural background or belief system that is similar to their own.

Communicating persuasiveness and credibility.   Although we do not want to exaggerate the power differential between ourselves and our clients, we do need to inform our clients of our training and credentials. This can easily be done through a written consent to treatment form, given to clients before they begin treatment, or through a brief verbal description of the clinician's professional background. Our training, our degrees, and our licenses all enhance our credibility. Interpersonal influence is also likely to develop when clinicians know what they are doing, have a sense of direction, give structure to the sessions, and show understanding of their clients and their concerns.

7. Optimism

Description.   When people seek counseling or psychotherapy, they often feel discouraged and sometimes even hopeless and suicidal. Counseling may be their last resort, perhaps one that makes them feel inadequate and defective in some way. Understanding these feelings and countering them with hope and optimism can make a great difference in treatment outcome. This involves giving people the message that treatment can make a difference in their lives and can help them achieve realistic and attainable goals. Focusing on people's strengths and accomplishments, rather than their failures and disappointments, can also engender optimism.

Communicating optimism.   The communication of optimism will only make a difference for people if it is realistic and linked to their specific goals. Clinicians need to be honest with clients about the time and effort involved in effective treatment. However, they can also provide assurances. Consider these examples:

- "Depression feels like it will never go away but in reality, therapy is usually very successful in helping people feel less discouraged."
- "I can see that you have already taken some important steps to help yourself stop drinking. I think we can find some ways to help you build on the gains you have made."

In addition, treatment should encourage and emphasize successes and reinforce and celebrate those. Establishing a series of small, readily achievable goals that build on each other can establish a pattern of successes.

8. A sense of structure and direction

Description.   Mental health treatment is such a complex and ambiguous process that even experienced clinicians are sometimes unsure how to help someone. Although this feeling is understandable and although we usually seek to work collaboratively with our clients, we must keep in mind that we are the experts on mental health treatment. People come to us for help they have not been able to provide for themselves. We are responsible for giving structure and direction to the sessions, for developing sound treatment plans, for helping clients formulate realistic goals, and for seeking consultation or making a referral if we need help in assisting our clients. Having a sense of structure and direction is important in helping our clients move forward and in sustaining their hopefulness and optimism.

Communicating a sense of structure and direction.   Most clinicians today, especially those in mental health settings, keep written records that pave the way for treatment to move smoothly from one session to the next. The foundation for these records is generally a list of clear, achievable, and measurable goals, developed in collaboration with the client. Once goals have been agreed upon, clinicians can develop a treatment plan based on their knowledge of the individual client, that person's concerns and diagnosis, and treatment systems and strategies that have demonstrated success with similar clients. Treatment plans are typically reviewed with clients so that they can be fine-tuned if necessary and the client's agreement to treatment can be obtained. Weekly progress notes, records of tasks that have been suggested to the client, and accomplishments made each week also give the treatment a sense of direction and structure.

9. Support, encouragement, reassurance, and affirmation

Description.   One of the most challenging skills for clinicians is encouraging and reassuring clients without judging them. Saying to a client, "You did a good job of getting your work done on time" may seem benign and even helpful. However, once we put ourselves in the role of evaluating our clients, we emphasize the power differential between our clients and ourselves. This can lead clients to place greater emphasis on pleasing the clinician than on pleasing themselves and can make them apprehensive that, if we can judge them positively, we can also judge them negatively. In general, we want to enable clients to provide themselves the support, encouragement, reassurance, and affirmation they need rather than looking to us for that help.

Communicating support, encouragement, reassurance, and affirmation.   Many strategies are available to facilitate clinicians' efforts to enable clients to become their own cheerleaders. Probably most important is directing clients' attention to their accomplishments and helping them to praise themselves. Clinicians might say, for example,

- "You must have been very proud of yourself when you turned in all your work on schedule this week."
- "It sounds to me like you achieved all your goals this week."
- "How did you feel when you got a positive response when you talked to your mother differently?"

Helping people identify the steps they took to achieve their successes can be particularly empowering and can help to reinforce their positive changes. Clinicians might say,

- "What did you do differently this time?"
- "Let's review the steps you took so you can repeat them the next time."
- "How did you manage to make that happen?"

Acknowledging the effort clients expended to achieve their goals is yet another way to affirm and reinforce their efforts. Being specific and concrete when providing this affirmation can help clinicians avoid the pitfall of sounding judgmental. For example, the clinician might say, "Although you didn't get your desk organized as you had hoped, you did spend three hours more time on that project than we had planned and have nearly reached your goal."

Helping clients develop their own affirmations, short meaningful slogans that they repeat to themselves, is another way for them to give themselves support and reassurance. Typical affirmations include:

- "I know I can do this."
- "I have the skills I need to deal with my family successfully."
- "That is my depression talking, but I can talk back to it."

Finally, helping people identify useful resources can provide an additional source of support and self-confidence. For example, the woman who fears her husband's violent behavior can develop a step-by-step plan to protect herself, while the man who is having difficulty maintaining his sobriety can list and rehearse new thoughts and actions to help him control his harmful impulses.

10. Ability to address problematic client behaviors and attitudes

Description.   People are not always willing and cooperative clients. Many clients are mistrustful, unmotivated, and easily frustrated, having only a limited capacity for insight. Whether fear, rage, or despair drives their reactions, they sometimes present challenging barriers to effective treatment. I believe nearly everyone wants to find ways to lead happy and fulfilling lives. However, sometimes those feelings are deeply buried. To provide successful treatment, clinicians need strategies to circumvent or reduce barriers to treatment without shaming or attacking their clients. Because this is such an important clinical issue, additional sections of this chapter will be devoted to strategies for dealing effectively with client emotions, thoughts, and actions that get in the way of treatment.

ILLUSTRATION OF STRATEGIES TO DEVELOP A POSITIVE THERAPEUTIC ALLIANCE

The following dialogue encompasses the important clinician characteristics and behaviors discussed previously. Notice that all 10 important clinician characteristics are illustrated in this brief interview.

Example

Clinician 1:   Alice, I know you were worried about Mother's Day. How did that go for you? (**Trustworthiness, caring**)

Alice 1:   I guess I should talk about Mother's Day. Boy, I really lost it.

Clinician 2:   You lost it? (**Empathy**)

Alice 2:   Yes. I don't know why I can't just get used to it. Every Mother's Day is a disaster. My son never called, my daughter called at midnight, my husband tossed a card at me as he ran off to play golf, and there I was making dinner for my mother. Well, it's over for another year. What's the point of dwelling on it?

Clinician 3:   And yet I hear great sadness when you talk about it. (**Empathy, good listening skills, caring and concern, genuineness**)

Alice 3:   Yes, you're right. I spent most of the day crying. But nobody knew. Whenever anyone was around, I just put on that happy face.

Clinician 4:   Having to keep your sadness to yourself must have made it even harder. (**Empathy, caring**)

Alice 4:   I guess so, but I'd feel really stupid if my family knew how badly I felt. Who am I to think that everybody should give up what they want to do and pay homage to me, just because it's Mother's Day?

Clinician 5:   It sounds like you don't think you deserve anything special. But I know how committed you are to your family, how hard you are working now to plan for your daughter's wedding, to help your son pay for graduate school, and to help your husband launch his new business. (**Good listening, genuineness, persuasiveness**)

Alice 5:   But I can't be doing enough or they would have done something special for me on Mother's Day.

Clinician 6:   Am I hearing you say that you feel like a failure as a wife and mother because your family didn't do much for you on Mother's Day? (**Empathy, good listening**)

Alice 6:   Yes, I guess that is the way I feel.

Clinician 7:   That concerns me. You're devaluing yourself because of your family's behavior on one day rather than deciding for yourself the value of what you do for your family. (**Caring and concern, genuineness and sincerity, affirmation**)

Alice 7:   I can see what you're saying, but how do I change how I feel?

Clinician 8:   These feelings seem insurmountable to you. And yet I can think of several ways we can work together to perhaps make a shift in those feelings. One place to start is by identifying and checking out the thoughts you have that underlie those feelings of worthlessness. Another approach would be to talk about ways to communicate your thoughts and feelings to your family. Perhaps you have other ideas. (**Persuasiveness and credibility, optimism, structure and direction, encouragement, ability to address problematic behaviors and attitudes**)

Alice 8:   Well, they both sound worth a try. Let's start with the first one; it would be too hard for me to share my feelings with my family right now.

Clinician 9:   All right. Let's go back to a time on Mother's Day when you felt especially sad. . . (**Structure and direction, addressing problematic behaviors and attitudes**)

Many of the clinician statements, illustrating important clinician qualities, are brief and deceptively simple. However, integrating these qualities into the therapeutic process is an art that usually requires considerable practice. The exercises at the end of this chapter will afford you the opportunity to practice integrating interventions such as these into your own counseling.

IMPORTANT CLIENT CHARACTERISTICS

Thus far in this chapter, we have focused on the important characteristics and interventions that clinicians contribute to the development of a positive working alliance, as well as the characteristics of that alliance. Of course, the clients themselves bring with them attitudes and characteristics that exert a strong influence over the quality and development of the therapeutic alliance.

Clinicians have two ways to help people develop and make use of those qualities that will assist them in engaging productively and collaboratively in the therapeutic alliance. Clinicians can identify those strengths that people bring with them into treatment, and they can try to reinforce and build up those qualities in their clients. The following client qualities have been linked to successful treatment (Seligman, 2001):

- Maturity—being responsible, well informed, and reasonably well organized
- Capacity to trust others and form caring and stable relationships
- Ability to establish appropriate interpersonal boundaries, being neither too dependent on others nor too isolated from others
- Capacity for introspection and insight
- High frustration tolerance and ability to delay gratification
- Motivation toward accepting help and making positive changes in oneself
- Positive but realistic treatment expectations
- Good self-esteem and feelings of empowerment (pp. 541–542)

ROLE INDUCTION

Clinicians can teach people how to be successful clients and how to engage productively in a collaborative working alliance. This process of orienting people to the treatment process is known as *role induction*. A study conducted by Acosta, Yamamoto, Evans, and Skilbeck (1983) found that people who received a pretreatment orientation to counseling or psychotherapy were more motivated and optimistic, had a better understanding of the treatment process, and were more willing to participate actively in treatment.

Although it is a learning process for the client, a role induction should not be done in a didactic style; rather, it should be an interactive process, a dialogue. Clinicians not only transmit information but also model those important qualities that are essential to the development of a positive working alliance and elicit and explore client reactions to the information provided. From the very first contact, even a telephone call to schedule an appointment, clinicians should keep in mind the importance of forming a sound treatment partnership with the client. All interactions with the client should have, as an underlying objective, the enhancement of the treatment alliance.

Role induction typically occurs during the first session or two of the treatment process. In role induction, the clinician explores the client's preconceptions of the treatment process, clarifies the nature of that process, and helps the client develop realistic expectations and an accurate understanding of treatment. An initial session, including a role induction, might include the following 10 steps (Seligman, 2001, p. 29):

1. Initial exploration of presenting concerns
   - Immediate precipitant of client's seeking treatment
   - Nature, duration, and symptoms associated with presenting concerns
2. Discussion of client's expectations for treatment procedures and outcome
3. Explanation of how treatment promotes positive change and description of concerns that usually respond well to treatment
4. Description of the collaborative nature of treatment
   - The positive working alliance
   - Roles and responsibilities of the clinician
   - Roles and responsibilities of the client, including the importance of self-disclosure
   - Discussion of client's reactions to and questions about the collaborative nature of treatment
5. Ethical aspects of the therapeutic relationship
6. Practical information on treatment
   - Information on how to contact the clinician
   - Fees, appointment schedule, cancellation policy
   - Obtaining third-party payments
7. Further exploration of presenting concerns
8. Transition to gathering relevant background information (see section on intake interviews for details)
9. Linking of relevant background information to presenting concerns
10. Conclusion of session
    - Summarization of session
    - Suggestion of tasks for client to complete
    - Opportunity for client reactions and questions
    - Scheduling of next appointment

This may look like a great deal to accomplish in one session. Having some of the role induction information in written form, perhaps as part of the clinician's consent to treatment form, can streamline the process. Suggesting that clients review the written information at home, after it has been explained in the session, can solidify understanding of the treatment process. In addition, only a preliminary exploration of presenting concerns and background usually is done in the first session, paving the way for subsequent in-depth discussion of those areas in later sessions. Finally, keep in mind that it is fine if these 10 steps require more than one session, as long as they are included in the early stages of the treatment process. The exercises at the end of the book will provide you the opportunity to conduct an initial session and to address strong client emotions, the next topic in this chapter.

DEALING WITH STRONG NEGATIVE CLIENT EMOTIONS

Clients often bring strong emotions with them into treatment, emotions such as rage, suicidal thinking, and despair. Often, these extreme reactions occur in response to a crisis or upsetting event. These emotions may feel overwhelming to the clinician just as they typically do to clients and those around them. In addition, these emotions may interfere with the development of a positive therapeutic alliance and with the role induction process. In order to provide successful treatment and safeguard our clients and those who might be affected by their strong feelings, we must find effective ways to address and modify these powerful emotions and to help people deal with the crises that may have triggered these feelings.

This section of the chapter reviews ways to help people manage and change three types of strong emotions often seen in clinical settings: suicidal ideation, anxiety and upset associated with a crisis or critical incident, and strong anger. The models presented here can be adapted and used to help clients deal with other strong and harmful emotions.

SUICIDAL IDEATION

Estimates suggest that approximately 25,000 to 35,000 people commit suicide each year in the United States. Not only is suicide the cause of many deaths, but it has a profound negative impact on many other people. Family members, friends, colleagues, neighbors, and fellow students of the person who has committed suicide may experience loss, guilt, self-blame, and other negative emotions.

Clinicians suffer, too, when a client commits suicide. Recently, in a class of 10 relatively new counselors, the topic turned to suicide and strong feelings began to emerge. I was surprised to learn that of the 10 people in the class, 4 had experienced the suicide of a client. According to Westefeld et al. (2000), 97% of psychology trainees reported working with suicidal clients, 29% had at least one client who attempted suicide, and 11% had a client commit suicide.

Suicidal thinking is far more common than completed suicides. All clinicians, even counselors in elementary schools, need to be on the alert for the presence of suicidal ideation. Whether or not we believe a person is likely to act on the suicidal thoughts, the devastating impact of a suicide mandates that we take suicidal thinking seriously and take effective steps to prevent self-injury.

Working with a suicidal person can be frightening and confusing to clinicians. Having a model or plan for addressing suicidal thinking, such as the one that follows, can provide helpful reassurance to both client and clinician.

Step 1. Determine the Presence of Suicidal Ideation

Before we can address suicidal ideation, we need to determine whether such thoughts are indeed present and the level of risk to the person experiencing the suicidal thoughts. Although suicide attempts and completed suicides cannot be predicted with good accuracy, being aware of common indicators of suicide potential and looking for those in our clients can be a good place to begin a suicide assessment.

Risk factors.   The following factors, grouped in categories, have been associated with suicidal ideation (Carney & Hazler, 1998; Motto, Heilbron, & Juster, 1985; Westefeld et al., 2000):

Biological

- Age—suicide is particularly common among adolescents and people over 65
- Changes in eating and sleeping patterns
- Gender—males are more likely to kill themselves than are women, although women are more likely to make suicide attempts
- Serious physical illness, especially a terminal illness

Psychological

- Depression
- Flat affect
- External locus of control—being more strongly influenced by external signs of approval than by inner values and self-assessment
- Psychotic disorders
- Feeling of hopelessness and helplessness
- Low self-esteem
- Questioning the meaning of life, one's own identity
- Social isolation, lack of support systems

Cognitive

- Extensive cognitive distortions
- Ideas of reference or persecution—having pervasive, unwarranted thoughts that people are criticizing you, talking about you, or seeking to harm you
- Inflexibility in thinking
- Negative self-talk
- Self-centeredness
- Suicidal ideation
- Verbalizing thoughts of wanting to disappear or cease to exist
- Thoughts of invulnerability

Behavioral

- Giving away possessions (especially in adolescents)
- Negative outcome of previous efforts to obtain help
- Substance misuse
- Talking, writing, or drawing about suicide and death

Environmental

- Availability of lethal methods, especially guns
- Coming from a culture that is competitive and goal directed, especially if that culture views suicide as honorable (suicide rates are especially high in the United States, Japan, and Sweden, and among Native Americans)
- Occupational problems, especially loss of position or prestige
- Living in an urban, metropolitan region
- Having a socioeconomic status that is middle class or above—risk increases with financial resources
- Experiencing significant marital/family conflict

- History of suicide, substance abuse, or depression in one's family
- Unusual stress, loss, or threat of loss

The SAD PERSONS Scale.   More than 20 "recognized suicide prediction scales" have been identified in the literature (Cochrane-Brink, Lofchy, & Sakinofsky, 2000, p. 445). One of the simplest is the SAD PERSONS scale. Its validity and reliability have not yet been well established (Juhnke, 1994). Used cautiously, however, this scale affords clinicians a rapid and helpful way to assess the likelihood that someone will make a suicide attempt. The SAD PERSONS scale is an acronym, with each letter representing one of the important factors to consider when assessing for suicidal ideation. Developed by Patterson, Dohn, Bird, and Patterson (1983), this scale includes the following items (Juhnke & Hovestadt, 1995, p. 32): sex, age, depression, previous attempt, ethanol abuse, rational thinking loss, social supports lacking, organized suicide plan, no spouse, sickness.

Asking about suicidal ideation.   When you believe a person may have suicidal thoughts, particularly when at least two of the risk factors in the SAD PERSONS scale are present, you should inquire, matter-of-factly, about the presence of such thoughts. You might say, "Have you ever felt so bad, you thought about hurting or killing yourself?" Raising this question gives the client permission to express suicidal thoughts and is likely to reduce any shame associated with having such thoughts. Talking about suicide will almost always decrease, rather than increase, its likelihood.

Step 2. Determine Level of Risk

Having suicidal thoughts is very common; you may even have had such thoughts yourself. The nature and intensity of these thoughts and the availability of means for killing oneself determine whether a person is in danger. Information on level of risk can be obtained by asking, "Do you have those thoughts now? When you have those thoughts, how likely do you think it is that you actually would harm yourself?"

Determine whether the person has a plan and the means to commit suicide.   The likelihood of an attempted or completed suicide is strongly related to the presence of a plan and means to commit suicide. You might ask the person, "When you thought about killing yourself, how did you think you would go about doing it? Do you have those means available to you? Did you think about a particular day and time when you might kill yourself?"

Review the history.   People who have a history of suicide in their families or who have made prior suicide attempts are more likely to consider suicide as a solution to their problems. Ascertaining the presence of suicidal thinking and behavior in the client and in the family can provide further information about the level of risk. Questions that might give you this information are, "As far as you know, has anyone in your family thought about suicide, made suicide attempts, or even killed themselves? Have you had thoughts about killing yourself in the past? How long/how often have you had those thoughts? Have you made suicide attempts or harmed yourself in the past? When, how, and under what circumstances?"

Step 3. Assess for Coping Mechanisms

Determining the presence of coping mechanisms in suicidal and depressed people can be a challenge. Be sure to use empathy and provide support, reassurance, caring, concern, and optimism (all discussed earlier in this chapter) when exploring resources with people who have suicidal thoughts. If they perceive themselves as having few resources or coping mechanisms, they can become even more discouraged. You might ask questions such as, "When you have suicidal thoughts, what do you do to help yourself? How does it work? What gives you a reason to stay alive and keep trying to feel better? When you have had other crises or strong feelings of upset in the past, what have you done to help yourself?"

Step 4. Explore Person's Concept of Suicide and Death

People have a reason for considering suicide. That reason may not seem logical to us but understanding the client's reasoning can be useful in preventing the suicide. Three common reasons for suicide are:

1. *Hopelessness and wish to escape from pain*   (If things get too bad, I'll kill myself.)
2. *Manipulation of another person*   (If you don't change or do what I want, I'll kill myself or scare you with a suicide attempt.)
3. *Revenge*   (I'll kill myself and then you'll be sorry for what you did to me.)

Asking people about their concept of suicide and death can also be helpful. People may have been raised to think of suicide as honorable, or they may believe that, when they are dead, they will go to heaven and find peace. On the other hand, they may have been raised with religious beliefs that prohibit killing oneself, and they may view suicide as a sacrilegious behavior.

Step 5. Process and Organize the Information

Now that you have finished gathering information on the person's suicidal thinking, you can summarize that information by answering the following questions:

- What suicide risk factors are present?
- Is suicidal ideation present?
- What is the level of risk?
- What plan, if any, does the person have for committing suicide?
- What factors in the person's background or family history might predispose the person to a suicide attempt?
- What coping mechanisms has the person used successfully in the past? What coping mechanisms seem to be readily available to the person now?
- What seems to be the person's primary reason for considering suicide?
- What views does the person have of suicide, death, and the afterlife?

The information you have gathered and thought about can be organized into two broad categories:

What factors contribute to the likelihood that this person will commit suicide? What factors can protect this person from committing suicide?

Step 6. Analyze and Synthesize the Information

Now that you have obtained, thought about, and organized the information, you can take a deeper look at that information and consider its connections and implications. Particularly important is understanding the dynamics of the suicidal thinking. The following questions will facilitate your analysis:

- Assuming that suicidal ideation is present, what patterns does it follow? Is it chronic or acute? How long has it been present? Is it worse at particular times of day or under certain circumstances? What life events seem to trigger suicidal ideation for this person?
- How are the risk factors linked to the suicidal ideation? For example, is a depressive disorder or chronic alcohol dependence creating feelings of hopelessness, are previous treatment failures making the person feel like nothing will help, or is a marital separation leading the person to crave both revenge and escape from pain?
- What is the meaning or the message of the suicide plan? For example, is the person contemplating shooting himself in the parking lot of the company from which he was fired? Is he considering taking an overdose of pills right before his parents are due home from work so that they will realize how unhappy he is? Plans such as these are intended to give a message.
- How are background factors contributing to the likelihood that a person will commit suicide? Perhaps a man whose mother committed suicide believes that her action condones his behavior. Perhaps previous suicide attempts brought the person sympathy, attention, and other secondary gains. Identify background factors that need some attention in treatment, not only to prevent them from contributing to the likelihood of a suicide attempt, but also to help the person identify and work through unresolved past concerns.
- What is your understanding of the person's views of suicide, death, and the afterlife? Here is an important opportunity for you to use your multicultural counseling competencies to understand the context of the suicidal thinking. The person's cultural and religious background may be compatible or incompatible with the concept of suicide. For example, a Japanese American man may view suicide as an honorable behavior after he has experienced a loss of face; this viewpoint is probably consistent with his cultural heritage and may increase the likelihood that he will commit suicide. On the other hand, a suicidal woman from a Jewish background may be aware that suicide is antithetical to the tenets of her faith; this may help to reduce the likelihood that she will make a suicide attempt. Ideas for helpful interventions will begin to emerge with understanding of a person's multicultural background.

Step 7. Make Sense of the Suicidal Ideation

Now you are ready to understand the underlying purpose and meaning that suicide has for your client, the last step before formulating your interventions. The basic question you are answering here is, "What makes suicide an acceptable and appealing alternative for this person?" Your answer should reflect a deep understanding of this person as well as an integration of the information you have gathered and processed.

Step 8. Develop Interventions

You should now be ready to develop interventions to address and reduce the suicidal ideation and behavior and improve the person's coping skills. The following suggestions will help you determine how best to accomplish these goals:

- You have already identified factors that are important in determining the level of suicide risk. How might those factors be changed to reduce the level of risk?
- What might be done to interfere with any plans to commit suicide and to separate the person from the means? For example, the adolescent's parents might be notified that she has been taking their Valium and now has more than 50 pills hidden in her drawer. The person with guns might be encouraged to remove the ammunition and guns from the home and leave them with a trusted friend.
- Having determined whether the primary motivation for the suicidal ideation is escape, manipulation, revenge, or another purpose, what better ways might the person accomplish the same purpose? For example, cognitive therapy might help alleviate emotional pain, while training in communication skills might help people find healthier ways to get attention, give others a message, or communicate anger.
- You have already identified coping skills that the person used successfully in the past. What is preventing your client from coping effectively at the present time? How can you help the person make effective use of previously successful coping skills? Perhaps the client turned to support systems in the past but now lives far from family and friends. Perhaps the client views the current crisis to be of greater magnitude than any previously experienced. Develop interventions to help the person overcome these barriers to effective coping.
- What coping skills does the person seem likely to develop easily? Teaching those coping skills that are most likely to be acceptable to the client will, of course, make them most likely to be used successfully. For example, a person who is generally very well organized might benefit from looking at the current situation step by step to figure out how to handle it best. A person who tends to be quiet and private might benefit from reading about the current problem or learning meditation and relaxation strategies. Development of coping skills can emerge from information on the four elements in the BETA format: background, emotions, thoughts, and actions. The following provides information

on frequently used approaches in suicide prevention, grouped according to whether they draw primarily on emotions, thoughts, or actions.

Emotions

- Make a referral for medication, particularly medication to reduce depression or psychotic thinking.
- Allow person to express feelings, but also teach ways to contain and control emotions.
- Establish yourself as a support system by scheduling follow-up telephone calls and future appointments.

Thoughts

- Dispute the client's motivation for committing suicide.
- Use statements such as the following to give people a different perspective:
  - "Perhaps we can find other ways to lessen that great pain you are experiencing."
  - "Perhaps your friends will feel sorry about making fun of you, but you won't be alive to enjoy that. While they are graduating from school and going onto college, you will be lying in your grave."
- Dispute cognitive distortions.
- Teach client positive affirmations to solidify changes in thinking.
- Help person find a reason to stay alive.
- Focus on strengths and accomplishments to build up self-esteem and clarify identity.
- Emphasize any religious or cultural beliefs that might discourage suicide.
- Help person learn more effective ways to make decisions and solve problems.

Actions

- Develop a verbal or written safekeeping contract, agreed to (and signed if written) by both client and clinician. An example is the following written agreement: "I will not either accidentally or on purpose hurt or kill myself no matter how bad things might get and no matter how badly I feel." People who are highly suicidal may not agree to an open-ended contract but may be willing to agree to a time-limited contract of 24 or 48 hours, with a daily telephone call to renew the contract. This strategy reassures clients that the clinician is concerned about them and is trying to help.
- Teach the client improved communication skills.
- Collaborate with the client in the development of a list of coping strategies that can be used if suicidal thoughts or impulses arise. This should be a lengthy list, giving the client many options, and might include any or all of the following:
  - Go to the local emergency room.
  - Call a hot line.
  - Call your therapist.
  - Call a trusted friend or family member.
  - Go to a public place, like a shopping mall, where you know you will not harm yourself.
  - Engage in relaxation or meditation.

- Do something physically active (e.g., taking a walk, working out, doing sit-ups).
- Do something to make yourself laugh (e.g., read a humor magazine, watch a funny movie or television program).
- Remind yourself of the reasons you have to stay alive (e.g., look at photographs of your children).
- Plan a pleasurable trip or activity.
- Make use of your improved communication skills to tell someone or write about your bad feelings.
- Take steps to further develop your support systems (e.g., join a 12-step program, call an old friend, or suggest meeting a new friend for dinner).
- Ask someone to stay with you until you believe you are safe.
- If necessary, go to the hospital.

Step 9. Monitor Progress

Because of the immediate risk presented by suicidal ideation, ongoing evaluation of the client and the impact of treatment is essential. If rapid progress is not evident, changes may be indicated in the treatment plan. Ongoing consultation with a colleague, supervisor, or psychiatrist and documentation of all information and interventions are important to protect both the client and the clinician.

Example of Ways to Address Suicidal Ideation

Sydney, a 62-year-old divorced man, has had a moderately successful dental practice for many years. However, he has struggled with depression and frequent suicidal thoughts for more than 40 years. Sydney's mother reportedly suffered from long-standing depression and eventually did take her own life. Sydney described his father as " alcoholic" until his death at age 63. This client has been diagnosed with a progressive neurological disease that is already affecting his ability to perform his work. He has low self-esteem and few support systems, deriving his primary sense of himself from his work. The loss of his work feels devastating to him.

Sydney reports that he is currently at high risk of making a suicide attempt and has lethal drugs readily available. On the other hand, Sydney has never made a suicide attempt, largely because of his concern about the impact it would have on his two sons, now ages 27 and 24. Sydney is still troubled by the impact his mother's suicide had on him and does not want to make his children suffer as he did. In addition, he was deterred from suicide in the past because he did not want to tarnish his reputation in the community, nor did he want his ex-wife to view him as a failure.

Sydney coped with past stressors such as his divorce and downturns in his business by reading and consulting with experts, including lawyers and accountants. He has no strong religious beliefs, but was raised in the Jewish religion. He thinks of suicide as "an end to all this pain and struggle."

The following interventions were used to help reduce Sydney's depression and suicidal ideation:

Emotions

- Discuss the suicide of Sydney's mother and the impact it had on him; help him to finally come to terms with that.
- Emphasize his wish not to hurt his children in any way.
- Provide Sydney support via frequent telephone calls and reinforcement of his efforts to help himself.

Thoughts

- Dispute Sydney's reasons for committing suicide.
- Help Sydney find more reasons to stay alive.
- Focus on the many accomplishments he has had over the years.
- Emphasize Sydney's religious background (Jewish) and Judaism's negative messages about suicide.
- Help Sydney find solutions to the problems inherent in his diagnosis with a neurological condition.

Actions

- Develop a safekeeping contract with Sydney.
- Draw on previous coping strategies; suggest that Sydney read about career development in the later years and the impact of suicide on the survivors.
- Encourage regular exercise, as sanctioned by Sydney's physician.
- Facilitate development of Sydney's support system.

CRISIS INTERVENTION

In addressing suicidal ideation, we drew on the BETA format to facilitate the development of interventions. To illustrate another useful model, the modified version of Bloom's taxonomy, introduced in chapter 6, is used here to help clinicians deal with other strong client emotions.

People often enter treatment because of crises in their lives. Crises take many forms and may be viewed in terms of the following categories:

- An actual or threatened loss such as a bereavement, a job loss, or a divorce
- An important decision point such as whether to accept a marriage proposal, adopt a child, end a troubled relationship, or move an elderly and ill parent into a nursing home
- A traumatic event such as a rape, an automobile accident, a terrorist attack, or a hurricane or other natural disaster

Although these crises certainly vary in terms of their nature and magnitude, a standard protocol can help clinicians treat all people who are dealing with crises or critical incidents.

When helping people deal successfully with crises, clinicians generally focus their attention on the current situation and take a more active role than they might usually assume (Srebalus & Brown, 2001). They typically collaborate with clients in establishing short-term objectives that are intended to either minimize the negative consequences of a crisis or prevent a negative outcome, while helping the clients regain equilibrium. In learning to cope successfully with a crisis, people commonly develop new strategies for handling problems and may become more empowered and self-confident than they had been.

Bloom's taxonomy, along with the BETA format, illustrate the steps in the process of helping people cope with crises. You will see that many similarities exist between this format and the steps that were suggested previously for suicide prevention.

Modified Version of Bloom's Taxonomy Applied to Crisis Intervention

1. **Content** (What are the facts?)

   - Obtain a clear description of the situation.
   - Note the presence of risk factors: biological, psychological, cognitive, behavioral, environmental.
   - Determine whether the person is in danger.
   - Determine what the person has already done or plans to do to cope with the crisis.
   - Review the relevant history.
   - Assess for coping mechanisms that the person has used to deal with prior crises or difficulties.
   - Explore the significance that the crisis has for the person.

2. **Process**

   a. Comprehend   (What do I know and understand about these facts?)

   - What is the nature of the crisis?
   - What risk factors are present?
   - What is the current level of danger?
   - What has the person tried to do to address the crisis?
   - What coping mechanisms has the person used effectively in the past?
   - What does this crisis mean to the person?

   b. Organize   (What principles, categories, and generalizations help me to understand this information?)

   - What factors contribute to the difficulty the client is having in coping with this crisis?
   - What factors are protecting or helping the person in this time of crisis?
   - What immediate decisions and actions are needed?
   - What are the viable alternatives?
   - What are the available resources?
   - What has worked and what has not worked in coping with crises of this nature?

c. Analyze/synthesize   (How are these facts related and what inferences can I draw about their connections?)

Take a deeper look at the information and consider its connections and implications. Begin to think about ways to empower the client and enable that person to see options more clearly. Focus especially on the following:

- ways to enable client to make urgent decisions and take immediate steps
- the underlying significance of the crisis for the person
- implications of the crisis for the person's life
- the link between the current crisis and prior history, especially previous crises
- options available for dealing with the crisis
- coping skills available to the client

d. Interpret   (What does all of this mean, and what sense does all of this make?)

The basic question to answer here is, "What has made handling this crisis particularly difficult for this person?" Perhaps the crisis is reminiscent of an earlier and very painful crisis, perhaps it is only one of a long series of crises, perhaps it is life threatening, or perhaps it calls into question the meaning and value of the person's life. These and many other factors and patterns contribute to making a crisis feel insurmountable. Draw on all the information you have obtained about both the person and the crisis in determining the answer to this question. Once you have been able to figure out an answer to that question, you can move forward with interventions that are likely to help.

e. Application   (What approaches seem most likely to be effective in helping the client cope with this crisis?)

Once you and the client have developed a clear picture of the nature of the crisis, the impact it has had on the client, and sound strategies for coping with the crisis, client and clinician are ready to address the crisis. Clinicians should be careful not to rush or pressure the client unnecessarily; that can compound the stress for an already fragile person. Typically, the process of helping someone cope with a crisis includes the following steps:

Background

- Help the client see the connection between the current crisis and that person's history.
- Develop a list of coping skills that the person has used effectively in the past.

Emotions

- Using strategies presented in chapter 3, facilitate the person's awareness and expression of emotional reactions to the crisis.
- Help the client manage and change emotional reactions as needed.

Thoughts

- Identify any distorted cognitions related to the crisis. Common examples include, "I am unable to handle this," "I am powerless," "This is a hopeless situation," and "There is nothing I can do about this."

- Using strategies presented in chapters 4 and 8, help the person identify and modify the distorted cognition.

Actions

- Teach new coping skills if needed.
- Identify coping skills that the person used successfully in the past and facilitate their application to the present situation.

The following behavioral coping skills are especially likely to be useful to people in crisis:

- relaxation
- visual imagery, focusing on empowerment and success
- decision-making skills
- clarifying priorities
- dividing large tasks into manageable actions
- developing and drawing on support systems
- affirmations
- use of a safe place
- thought stopping

f. Evaluation   (How has my work gone? What can I learn from this?)

For several reasons, evaluation is a crucial component of helping people cope with crises. The crises themselves may be long lasting and may change and evolve over time, necessitating changes in coping skills. Examples of this include coping with chronic and life-threatening illnesses, going through a separation and divorce, and dealing with the decline and eventual death of a family member. In addition, the full emotional impact of a crisis may not be felt until the crisis is long past. Posttraumatic stress disorder, for example, may begin months or even years after the end of a crisis and may continue indefinitely, exacerbated by reminders of the crisis. Clinicians dealing with people in crisis need to include long-term follow-up, education on the warning signs of posttraumatic stress disorder, and prevention strategies in their treatment plan. Continual evaluation of treatment effectiveness is clearly essential when helping people cope with crises.

Example of Ways to Help People Cope with Crises

The following example, using the case of Eileen Carter whom you have met previously throughout this book, illustrates the application of this format for helping people cope with a crisis. As you review this case, think about what other questions and strategies you would incorporate into your work with this client.

1. Content.   Eileen Carter recently received a call from her older brother, informing her that their mother had been hospitalized following a heart attack. This raised both practical and emotional issues for Eileen. She believed she had no one to care for her son, if she did go to visit her mother nearly 200 miles away. She was taking a college course and did not want to fall behind in her class or have to drop the class. In addition, she and her mother had a very conflicted relationship.

2. Process

a. Comprehend

Nature of the crisis—Eileen's mother had been hospitalized following a heart attack. Eileen felt torn between her loyalty to her family of origin and her current commitments to her son and her education.

Risk factors—Eileen was afraid that her mother might die while they were still at odds. This situation brought back to her many painful memories of her childhood, the abuse she had experienced from her stepfather, her mother's failure to protect Eileen, and the rage she had felt at both parents. However, she also remembered the closeness she had felt to her mother and her biological father before his death. Another risk factor is that Eileen's absence from college might jeopardize her academic progress. Finally, some risk exists that, under stress, Eileen might relapse into feelings of self-hatred as well as unhealthy behaviors such as abuse of drugs and alcohol and flight into self-destructive relationships.

Level of danger—Eileen is not in any physical danger. However, she had to address the crisis quickly, because of her mother's tenuous health.

Efforts to address the crisis—Eileen has not yet taken any steps to address the crisis, other than discussing the situation with her counselor.

Past coping mechanisms—Until the birth of her son, Eileen coped via escape into drugs and unhealthy relationships. However, with her marriage and birth of her son, she has begun to learn improved problem solving and decision making. She has begun to confide in other women and to use relaxation strategies. Prayer provides her another way to cope.

Meaning of crisis—Her mother's heart attack brought home to Eileen the fact that she could not avoid dealing with her past indefinitely. Now that she was a mother herself, she felt greater empathy for her mother. However, she was uncertain whether she wished to reconcile with her mother.

b. Organize

Factors contributing to difficulty of crisis—Eileen's conflict with her mother, her troubled and difficult childhood, her commitment to doing well in her college course, her reluctance to leave her son with his father or another caregiver.

Factors that are helping and protecting client—Eileen's recent realization of the importance to her of family and the mothering role, her own intelligence.

Immediate decision/action—Whether to visit her mother, whether to reconcile with her, whether to miss one or more college classes, whether to leave her child with a caregiver.

Alternatives—Visiting her mother or refusing to make that visit. Her visit could take many forms, ranging from a brief casual visit to a lengthy reconciliation.

Resources—Eileen's husband's reassurance that he could take care of their son for a few days, the financial resources to allow her to visit her mother, a friend in class who could take notes for her, a good relationship with her course instructor.

Coping strategies likely to work in this situation—Decision making, information gathering, awareness of feelings, identification and modification of cognitive distortions.

c. Analyze/synthesize

The immediate impact of the crisis—Initially, Eileen felt overwhelmed by unhappy memories of her background and of the unanticipated pressure on her to reconcile with her mother.

The underlying significance of the crisis for the person—This experience called into question Eileen's feelings about her family of origin. She had distanced herself from her mother in anger and, although the two had resumed contact, had not planned on reconciliation yet. However, she now thought that this might be her last chance to reconnect with her mother before that woman's death. Eileen's ambivalence about visiting her mother led her to view herself as a "bad and unloving person" and contributed to her already low self-esteem.

Implications of the crisis for the person's life—Eileen would have to make practical arrangements for her son and for obtaining notes from her class. Far more important was her recognition that if she reconciled with her mother and her mother survived her heart attack, this would have an impact on Eileen's current family life. She wasn't sure whether she wanted to make space in her current life for her family of origin or whether she wanted Junior to have contact with his grandmother.

The link between the current crisis and prior history—Since her marriage, Eileen had tried to shut out the pain of the years between the death of her father and the birth of her son. However, the call from her brother brought back to her all the difficulties of those years and the guilt and anger she felt.

Options available for dealing with the crisis—Eileen could refuse to see her mother at this time, perhaps precluding any opportunity for reconciliation. On the other hand, she could visit her mother. How much time she spent with her mother and how she interacted with her mother were unanswered questions that depended on both Eileen's and her mother's choices.

Coping skills available to the client—Although she tended to devalue her coping skills, Eileen had both internal and external resources. Her husband was supportive of whatever decision she made about visiting her mother, her son reminded her of the importance of family, and her contacts at school could help her avoid missing too much in her class. She was motivated to take care of herself for the sake of her son and had begun to develop improved self-esteem and problem-solving skills. Her faith had helped her through many difficult situations.

Ways to enable Eileen to make necessary decisions—Because of the urgency of this decision, short-term counseling, focused on the benefits and drawbacks of visiting her mother, seems most likely to help Eileen. In addition, reminding her of the strengths she had demonstrated, especially in recent years, could motivate Eileen to deal effectively with her current crisis.

d. Interpretation.   Many factors have made handling this crisis particularly difficult for Eileen, including the potential urgency of the situation, her mother's neglectful behavior after the death of Eileen's father, Eileen's mistreatment by her stepfather, the unhealthy ways in which she had coped with the difficulties in her family of origin, her cutoff from that family, her strong commitment to her son and her education, and the value she placed on her current family. In addition, Eileen, now a mother herself, identified with her mother and recognized how painful it must be to cope with a life-threatening illness without the support of one of your children. At the same time, Eileen feared that if she returned to her hometown, the pain and problems of her adolescence would overwhelm her once again and she would not be able to move forward with her life.

e. Application/interventions   Now that we have made some sense of Eileen's inability to make a decision, we can identify interventions that are likely to help her move forward. The following are some that will probably be helpful.

Background

- Help Eileen see the impact of the past on her current crisis.
- Enable her to see that she has learned and grown from her past experiences and that she is able to make more mature choices now.
- Help her to develop a more balanced and sympathetic picture of her mother, encompassing both her strengths and her weaknesses.
- Facilitate Eileen's efforts to develop a list of the coping skills that she has used successfully.

Emotions

- Help Eileen vent her fears and anxieties and learn ways to reduce and modify her strong emotions.
- Normalize Eileen's upset about this situation but help her see that the intensity of her emotions is getting in the way of making a sound decision.
- Encourage Eileen to use prayer and her faith to counteract her hopelessness and help her find the best decision.
- Help her use her love and dedication to her son to enable her to develop some empathy for her mother and perhaps even to forgive her.
- Enable Eileen to value her own needs and to care for herself as well.

Thoughts

- Help Eileen clearly identify her options for dealing with the current situation and then explore and evaluate each one to facilitate decision making.
- Explore Eileen's cognitions regarding her fear of falling back into her old self-destructive patterns; identify, dispute, and modify any distorted cognitions.
- Use meditation and imagery to enhance Eileen's efforts to make decisions.

Actions

- Encourage Eileen to find solutions to the practical problems presented by this situation, including child care and missed classes.
- Teach Eileen communication skills that she might use with her mother and role-play her anticipated interactions with her mother.
- Encourage Eileen to use relaxation, affirmations, and thought stopping to help her cope more effectively with her current crisis.

f. Evaluation.   Counseling should continue, either after Eileen visits her mother or while she comes to terms with her decision not to visit her mother. Eileen needs to deal with the long-term implications of her decision for herself and her current family, with the resurfacing of painful and guilt-ridden memories of her past, and with her doubts about herself as daughter and mother. Coping with this situation and getting her life back on track can be an experience that further empowers Eileen. It can help her clarify her priorities, improve her relationships, and value herself even more.

UNDERSTANDING AND ADDRESSING CLIENT RAGE, ANGER, AND VIOLENT IMPULSES

Anger is a universal emotion and can provide useful information and energy when understood and managed. On the other hand, clients with anger problems can present a challenge for clinicians. Anger can cause clients both interpersonal and legal problems, particularly when it leads to violence. Anger directed toward the clinician has the potential of eliciting strong negative reactions; clinicians may respond to the anger with fear, discouragement, and reciprocal anger. Such responses on the part of a clinician can undermine the therapeutic relationship, reduce treatment effectiveness, and exacerbate rather than alleviate the client's problems. Clearly, clinicians need to be able to identify the early signs of clients' anger; help them recognize, curtail, and modify those strong emotions; and channel them in positive directions.

Modified Version of Bloom's Taxonomy Applied to Anger

The modified version of Bloom's taxonomy is used here to illustrate ways of helping clients learn anger management. Both general information about the treatment of anger and the example of Henry, a 54-year-old Caucasian male, are presented.

1. Content.   (What are the facts?) Anger manifests itself in a wide variety of ways under a broad range of conditions. Anger may be a pervasive and enduring aspect of a person's personality, or it may flare up only in transient and stressful situations. The diverse ways in which anger is expressed can complicate diagnosis and treatment. As Tavris (1989) pointed out, ". . . there are different angers, involving different processes and having different consequences to our mental and physical health. No single remedy fits all" (p. 22). Anger is not a mental disorder in itself but can be a component of many disorders (Deffenbacher & McKay, 2000). Looking at the components of anger is a good way to gather factual information about a person's anger.

Physiological

• *Identify the client's unique pattern of anger arousal.* Anger activates the sympathetic nervous system and releases epinephrine and norepinephrine into the bloodstream, producing a variety of physiological changes and sensations. Primary changes include accelerated heart rate, elevated blood pressure, increased blood sugar in the muscles, pupil dilation, speeding up or cessation of long-term bodily functions such as digestion, blocking of physical pain, an urge to scream, and a rush of energy through the entire body. According to Stosny (1995), "Anger is the only emotion that activates every organ and muscle group of the body" (p. 56). Clinicians need to gather information about what the client experiences when anger is beginning and what signals the client recognizes as the anger rises into out-of-control rage.

Henry initially was unaware of any physical cues connected to his anger. However, after paying attention to his bodily sensations, he described a feeling of a rotating ball in the pit of his stomach as the first internal signal that something might be distressing him. Next, he typically experienced tension in his forehead, an increase in his heart rate, and an urge to yell, which would lead to outbursts of rage he later regretted.

• *Determine whether any organic or physiological factor is creating or fueling the anger.* While it has physiological manifestations, anger is not usually generated by a biological condition. However, some conditions, such as brain injury and epilepsy, have been connected with anger. Ascertain whether the client has experienced head trauma, hormonal fluctuations, or other medical conditions that might be generating or compounding factors.

• *Determine level of substance use.* Use of alcohol and substances such as PCP and other stimulants can worsen anger problems. Assess the client's level of substance use and identify any connection between substance use and incidents of angry outbursts.

Cognitive

• *Identify the client's thought patterns underlying the anger.* Anger typically arises from how one interprets or thinks about an event. Usually, anger begins with a perception of pain or injury and a feeling of distress. Another person or group is often seen as the cause of the pain, and that becomes the target for the anger.

For example, Henry reported that his days frequently got off to a bad start because his 8-year-old son Johnny was so disorganized that he would rarely be ready for school on time. This caused Henry to become anxious and upset and to scold Johnny for his lateness. Even after he dropped Johnny off at school, Henry ruminated on the boy's actions and saw his son as having ruined Henry's day.

Anger is particularly likely to escalate when such blame is combined with the perception that another person is acting out of malice or a deliberate intention to inflict pain and when strong feelings of injustice arise (Beck, 1999). Henry fueled his anger by seeing Johnny as a "spoiled brat" who maliciously delighted in frustrating and angering his father. Clearly, identifying and paying attention to thought patterns linked to anger are critical.

Emotional

• *Assess the client's patterns of emotional experience.* "All emotions, including anger, have what amount to goals that they press hard to achieve" (Fein, 1993, p. 18). Understanding the goals of a person's anger can deepen understanding of that emotion. This can be accomplished by obtaining a clear picture of the client's experience of anger, including the timing, nature, frequency, duration, and intensity of that emotion.

Henry's anger became most intense when his child or wife did not comply with his wishes. At the start of treatment, his anger toward his wife was almost constant, an ever-present rumble that periodically erupted. His anger toward his son, while similarly intense, was interspersed with warm feelings, usually when Henry was not in Johnny's presence.

• *Identify the problem signaled or suppressed by the emotional response.* Anger often reflects difficulties related to one's sense of self and one's personal boundaries. It can express the frustration connected to these difficulties and cover up emotions that are hard to acknowledge and express. Emotions commonly suppressed by anger include shame, loneliness, sadness, and grief. Stosny (1995) described anger as "ice on a wound" (p. 59). Of course, ice may numb pain temporarily but eventually becomes a source of pain itself. In identifying the problem signaled or covered up by the anger, the clinician needs to pay attention to the client's sense of self and to the client's relationships with others.

Henry's anger was a reaction to his perception of himself as unlovable and powerless. His anger gave him a false sense of power. It protected him from experiencing the pain connected to his longing for power, closeness, and acceptance and the hopelessness he felt about ever achieving what he wanted in his relationships.

• *Determine the level of motivation for change.* Clients present for treatment at various stages of readiness to work on an issue (more on this in chapter 9). DiGiuseppe (1995) found that many people with anger problems focus on changing others and have little motivation to change themselves.

When Henry initiated treatment, he was not motivated to change his anger toward his wife. He believed that ceasing to be angry with her would condone and encourage her unacceptable behavior. However, he was distressed at seeing his son copying Henry and becoming enraged with his friends. Henry's recognition of the harm he was doing to his son was a strong motivator for him.

Behavioral

• *Determine the functions that anger serves.* The behavior of becoming angry attracts attention and changes our interactions with others. According to Potter-Efron and Potter-Efron (1991), anger can provide communication, power and control, intimacy regulation (managing both distance and connection), status, self-defense, and problem solving.

Henry's anger was a form of communication. It also served as a way of both exerting power and control and regulating the intimacy between his wife and himself.

• *Determine the reinforcers.* While anger has long-term negative consequences, there may also be immediate payoffs. For example, Henry was able to stay in a marriage without having to risk emotional closeness with his wife. He was also able to coerce his son into complying with his commands.

• *Determine the costs.* Despite its short-term gains, anger can have a long-term negative impact on all areas of one's life, including physical health, emotional well-being, relationships, occupational and economic success, and legal status. Henry became aware of the negative impact of his anger on his son and their relationship.

Environmental

• *Review the client's history of experiencing and expressing anger in family and community.* According to Beck (1999), "People continuously monitor and mimic one another's emotional reactions without realizing they are doing so" (p. 147). Many families experience multigenerational patterns of destructive anger. In our environment, we experience terrorism, prejudice, road rage, and other forms of anger and violence. Despite the rampant anger and hatred, people always retain the choice of expressing themselves in different and more positive ways.

2. Process.   Once the information about a client's experience of anger has been gathered, that information can be processed. This will continue to be illustrated using the example of Henry and the modified version of Bloom's taxonomy.

a. Comprehension/organization.   What do I know and what do I understand about these facts? What principles, categories, and generalizations help me to understand this information?

• *Initial experience of anger*—What are the warning signs of anger for this client? What is the client's level of awareness of these signs? Is the anger related to substance use?

- *Arousal pattern*—How does anger accelerate for this client? What successful and unsuccessful strategies has this person used to interrupt the anger arousal?
- *Emotional basis of anger*—What personal needs underlie the anger? What boundary issues are involved in the anger? What emotional strengths does the person demonstrate?
- *Cognitive acceleration of anger*—What thoughts and underlying beliefs fuel the anger? What level of insight does the client have into how thoughts affect the problem?
- *Environmental factors*—What experiences, especially in the family of origin, have shaped this person's understanding and use of anger? What environmental factors contribute to maintaining or inhibiting the person's anger? What positive experiences or models are available for learning new responses?
- *Behavioral strategies*—How does this person express and respond to anger?
- *Functions/reinforcers*—What is this person trying to accomplish through his or her expression of anger? Are there any beneficial effects of the anger?
- *Negative impact*—What problems is the anger causing or aggravating? What potential exists for self-harm or harm to others?
- *Level of self-awareness*—What insight does this person have into the problem and his or her sense of self? What responsibility does this person accept for the problem?
- *Level of motivation*—What is the person's readiness to change?

b. Analysis/synthesis.   How are these facts related and what inferences can I draw about their connections?

After obtaining and organizing information on a person's anger, clinicians can develop an understanding of the client's major areas of anger-related concern and how they fit into the overall picture. Answering the following questions will facilitate development of a successful treatment approach for a client.

- *What is the pattern of anger escalation and how clear is the person about the signs of initial and rising anger?* In other words, does this person go from 0 to 100 mph in a second, or does the client experience a slow, prolonged buildup of anger, accompanied by rumination?
- *What self-perceptions contribute to the anger?* Understanding if clients see themselves as wounded or inadequate helps clinicians to understand the emotional pains the person experiences and where healing needs to occur.
- *What cognitive strategies and perspectives does this person employ?* Perfectionism and demandingness often fuel anger. Many angry people rely on long lists of shoulds to direct their own behavior and judge others' behaviors. They often have conditional beliefs such as, "If he loved me, he would never disappoint me," or "If I were a responsible individual, I wouldn't have made that mistake" (Ellis, 1977).
- *What background and family of origin issues contribute to this person's current anger problem?* Consider the lessons presented and learned about how to handle anger as well as the impact of early experiences in shaping one's view of self, understanding of relationships, and beliefs about anger. For example, if a client

had a violent parent, does the client view the parent as admirable or is the client determined not to be like the angry parent?

- *Does this client recognize the negative impact of the anger?* So often what a person strives to achieve with anger becomes even more elusive, thus generating further anger unless the cycle can be clarified and interrupted. Awareness of the negative consequences of anger can increase motivation to change.
- *What are the person's overall levels of self-awareness and life skills?* When skill deficits contribute to the problem, appropriate training, such as communication or assertiveness skills or parenting classes, can reduce anger.
- *What is motivating the client to change, and how can that motivation and interest in treatment be encouraged?*
- *Is the anger a deviation from the person's usual way of operating, or is the anger reflective of long-standing patterns of thoughts and actions?* If the anger reflects a change, understanding and addressing what led to this shift is essential. If, however, the anger is a long-standing pattern, a more comprehensive approach to treatment is probably indicated.
- *What risks to self or others are presented by the anger?* Does the clinician need to warn others of potential danger?

c. Interpretation.   What does all of this mean, and what sense does all of this make?

Now that the clinician has developed a deep understanding of the anger and its connection to the person's view of self, others, and the world, it is possible to understand the meaning the anger has for the person.

Henry was an intelligent, self-employed, though unsuccessful, photographer who had a long history of anger, anxiety, and depression. He described his father as an "angry alcoholic" and a "bully." Henry's mother was usually withdrawn and depressed but occasionally would rage at Henry and his three younger siblings. Henry reported he was anxious and angry as a child and was a bully himself. He played contact sports and enjoyed the aggressive interactions. As a young adult, Henry abused drugs and alcohol. He described his wife as depressed and emotionally unavailable and reported that his son Johnny exhibited signs of depression and periodic temper outbursts.

By bullying people, both as a child and as an adult, Henry experienced a sense of potency that led him to feel good about himself and see himself as better than others. This viewpoint led him to believe that others should welcome his direction and appreciate him. Consequently, Henry became enraged and contemptuous when others did not appreciate his frequent criticisms and reprimands and did not recognize them as his effort to relate to them. At a deeper level, Henry both craved the closeness denied him in childhood and feared it, in case his powerful facade might be shattered and his negative view of himself, recognized and confirmed. As a result, after his anger peaked, he would usually engage in emotional or physical cutoff.

Since he was repeating long-standing multigenerational patterns of behavior and relationships, Henry did not recognize that his anger led others to engage in the very behaviors that were most frustrating to him: his wife's emotional withdrawal and his son's stubbornness. Henry lacked knowledge of healthy parenting and relationship strategies. However, his love and concern for his family provided the motivation for him to continue in treatment.

d. Application.   What approaches seem most likely to be effective in reducing the client's angry feeling, thoughts, and actions and helping that person learn new and more positive ways to deal with anger? The following offers an array of treatment options:

Physiological

- Recommend referral for medication, physical examination, and substance use evaluation.
- Teach recognition of signs of rising anger. Potter-Efron (1994) suggests an anger thermometer as a metaphor to help a client recognize the signs of rising anger from the lowest through the highest stages.
- Use imagery in session to have a client reexperience a recent anger-provoking incident. This can provide access to cognitions as well as to physical signs of anger.
- Teach relaxation strategies, such as progressive relaxation, imagery, meditation, and simple diaphragmatic breathing to interrupt rising anger.
- Teach the client to call a time-out when anger rises into the danger zone, doing so in a way that does not seem like abandonment of the other person.
- Teach stress management. Anger and rumination accelerate in relation to the level of stress present at the time of the provocative situation. Living a balanced life with minimal stress and ample support facilitates anger management.
- Encourage the client to exercise regularly. Exercise is an important component of stress management and also is important in alleviating symptoms of depression related to anger.
- Offer stress or anger inoculation training. Develop a hierarchy of anger-evoking situations and use cognitive skills to formulate new responses. Practice these in treatment sessions.

Emotional

- Empathy and respect can prevent an angry client from becoming entrenched in an angry defensive position.
- Self-esteem training. Helping people identify and value their strengths can counteract their resentment and jealousy of others.
- Compassion training. Stosny (1995) identified compassion as "an emotional regulator incompatible with contempt and anger" (p. 10). Learning to have compassion for others as well as for oneself can contribute to reduction of angry emotions.
- Emotional self-regulation. This is another strategy that can slow down the progression of anger and facilitate use of anger management strategies.
- Focus on enhancing motivation. It is important to build a positive therapeutic alliance with shared and meaningful goals.

Cognitive

- Journals. Keeping a journal of angry thoughts and events or a mood diary provides a basis for identifying cognitive distortions and monitoring progress.
- Cognitive therapy. This is one of the most effective approaches for helping people identify and challenge the distorted thinking that underlies counterproductive anger.

- Bibliotherapy. Some people benefit from reading relevant self-help books such as *The Dance of Anger* (Lerner, 1985), *The Feeling Good Handbook* (Burns, 1999), *Angry All The Time* (Potter-Efron, 1994), and *Anger Kills* (Williams & Williams, 1993).

Behavioral

- Help the client recognize the costs of anger and how it detracts from goal achievement.
- Incorporate assertiveness training, communication training, and empathy training into treatment.
- Model and teach problem solving. When anger is used to gain power and control and to solve problems in living, teach the client a more effective approach to problem solving.
- Encourage the client to take parenting training.
- Introduce behavioral experiments. Encouraging a client to experiment with a new response, despite cynicism about its probability of success, can change beliefs and perspectives and lead to new behavioral responses.

Environmental

- Enable the client to build healthy relationships and support systems.
- Help the client to identify and solve problems in living.
- Consider referrals to relevant resources, such as Alcoholics Anonymous or other self-help and support groups.

Determining which interventions to use depends on the nature of the problem and sometimes involves a process of trial and error. For Henry, treatment was lengthy and involved interventions from most of the categories. The following outlines the interventions used with Henry:

Physiological

- Henry was referred for *antidepressant medication* and physical and substance use *evaluations*.
- Teaching *recognition of signs of rising anger* proved helpful to Henry.
- *Imagery* helped Henry gain insight into his thoughts and his physical experience of anger.
- Henry learned *relaxation strategies,* especially diaphragmatic breathing.
- At first, Henry used angry withdrawal and thought that he was employing *time-outs.* After much work, he learned the use of constructive time-outs.
- Henry reduced the stressful areas of his life in order to *achieve greater balance.*
- Henry was not much interested in structured *exercise* but did start walking his dog on a regular basis.
- Henry put significant effort into *stress inoculation training,* creating and practicing new responses to provocations.

Emotional

- *Empathy* was an essential element in Henry's treatment. It enhanced the therapeutic alliance, thereby increasing his motivation to change.

- *Self-esteem training* was woven into the course of treatment, and Henry gradually became aware of his many strengths.
- *Compassion training* helped Henry to talk about his injuries from a vulnerable, as opposed to a morally righteous, viewpoint and to develop more compassion and empathy toward others.
- *Emotional self-regulation* was integrated into the entire treatment process.
- Henry's *motivation was enhanced* by the development of the therapeutic alliance and an emphasis on how Henry's improved anger management might benefit his son.

Cognitive

- Henry did not want to keep a daily journal but would *write about his anger* when it flared up.
- Henry responded well to *problem solving* since he prided himself on his intelligence and clear thinking.
- Via *cognitive therapy*, Henry slowly learned to change his counterproductive thinking.

Behavioral

- Helping Henry to *recognize the costs of anger* had a powerful impact on him.
- *Assertiveness and communication training* helped Henry become less aggressive and find a middle ground.
- Henry learned *new ways of parenting* such as natural and logical consequences.
- Henry did *behavioral experiments* in his interactions with his wife. He was quite surprised by the outcome of these experiments, both in his wife's responsiveness and in his own warm feelings toward her.

Environmental

- Working with Henry to *build healthy relationships and support systems* was a central focus of treatment.
- As treatment progressed, Henry became more successful in *applying problem-solving strategies to issues in his world;* this led to a sense of mastery and improved self-esteem.

e. Evaluation.   How has my work gone? What can I learn from this?

Continued monitoring of progress and reevaluation of the treatment plan is necessary in helping people with anger-related concerns. Relapse is common and strategies need to be provided to help people cope with backsliding.

Henry and his clinician noted reductions in frequency, duration, and intensity of Henry's anger both with his son and his wife. When Henry reported that his new calmer responses were becoming automatic, a major part of his goals had been accomplished.

Henry's therapist made sure she had supervision and peer consultation to help her manage any negative feelings that she might develop toward Henry and to deal with times when his anger was directed at her. It took quite awhile before Henry was able to express negative feelings toward his therapist in direct and calm ways; his eventual success in that area was another sign of progress. Talking about disappointment or frustration without being sarcastic or demeaning was another new skill for Henry. Continued follow-up helped ensure that Henry maintained the gains he had accomplished through treatment.

CLINICIAN SELF-DISCLOSURE AND IMMEDIACY

In this section, we shift our focus from clients' expression of emotions to clinician self-expression. Knox, Hess, Petersen, and Hill (1997) found that, although self-disclosure was infrequently used by clinicians, clients gave this intervention high marks for helpfulness and reported that it had a considerable impact on them. Edwards and Murdoch (1994) arrived at a similar conclusion: "Theory and research have suggested that counselor self-disclosure can be an effective technique if used for purposes that benefit the client" (p. 385).

Why, then, do clinicians make such limited use of an apparently helpful intervention? The answer is that clinician self-disclosure is a risky intervention that has both pros and cons (Simone, McCarthy, & Skay, 1998). Clinician self-disclosures can greatly enhance the therapeutic process, create a sense of collaboration and immediacy, build rapport, and introduce helpful new perspectives and reactions. On the other hand, clinician self-disclosure can blur the client-clinician boundaries, shift the focus from the client to the clinician, and exploit the client.

Although I believe that the great majority of clinicians act in ethical and professional ways and are dedicated to helping others, my clients have told me about the following:

- The psychologist who gave her client a running progress report on the clinician's relationship with her partner and spent a session in tears when her partner ended their relationship
- The counselor who asked her client, a wedding planner, for advice on her daughter's wedding
- The social worker who asked his client, a personal trainer, to lend him weights and help him establish a weight-lifting program

These examples may sound far-fetched to novice clinicians who are well versed in the ethics of counseling and psychology, but all are true. Although you may never be tempted to engage in such extreme boundary violations, even lesser instances of inappropriate clinician self-disclosure can be damaging to the therapeutic alliance and lead to premature termination of treatment. Novice clinicians seem especially likely to overuse self-disclosure because of their eagerness to form a bond with their clients. Keeping the following guidelines for appropriate uses of clinician self-disclosure in mind can help you make positive use of this powerful tool and avoid its pitfalls.

Guidelines for Beneficial Use of Clinician Self-Disclosure

Many have studied and written about the appropriate use of clinician self-disclosure. Knox et al. (1997), for example, found that clinician self-disclosure is particularly likely to be helpful under the following circumstances:

- When the client is discussing important personal issues
- When the self-disclosure is perceived as intended to normalize or reassure
- When the self-disclosure consists of "a disclosure of personal nonimmediate information" (p. 274) about the clinician (e.g., "When I began college, I, too, had difficulty avoiding all the distractions and focusing on my studies. Many students experience that.")

Theory and research suggest the following guidelines to help clinicians make the best use of self-disclosure:

- Self-disclosures must be made for the *primary purpose of helping the client.* Clinicians should never share personal information in order to help themselves feel better or to use the client as a sounding board or source of information.
- *Keeping the focus on the client* rather than the clinician greatly increases the likelihood that the self-disclosure is intended to help the client.
- Clinicians should *think through their reasons for making a self-disclosure* and be able to articulate them; if they are unsure about the reason for or value of a self-disclosure, they should refrain from making the self-disclosure. Self-disclosures should not be made just to fill up time or make conversation, unless that is a therapeutic purpose.
- Clinician self-disclosures should be *used sparingly* and should be *clear and concise;* this minimizes the likelihood that they will distract the client or shift the treatment focus from the client to the clinician. Less is better in terms of clinician self-disclosures.
- *Careful timing and wording* of self-disclosures can ensure that they are well integrated into the treatment process. They should be relevant to the immediate discussion and should echo repeated language and key issues expressed by the client so that the relevance of the self-disclosures is evident.
- Using the *present tense* when making self-disclosures is likely to increase the relevance and immediacy of the statement.
- Self-disclosures should be *relatively impersonal.* Edwards and Murdock (1994) found that the most frequent topic for clinician self-disclosure was professional issues such as the credentials or experience of the clinician. The least common area of clinician self-disclosure was sexuality. This clearly reflects the continuum of self-disclosure, from the relative benign and impersonal topic of the clinician's professional background to the highly charged and usually inappropriate topic of the clinician's sexual attitudes and behaviors. Self-disclosures that are moderately personal rather than impersonal or very personal seem to be most meaningful to clients.
- Be sure to *incorporate the essential therapeutic conditions* into all self-disclosures. Using empathy, as well as reflection of meaning, and highlighting the connection between the clinician's self-statement and the client's concerns increase the relevance and meaningfulness of the self-disclosure.
- *Client self-determination, pride, and empowerment should be fostered* by clinician self-disclosures; they should not shame or attack clients.
- *Be honest and authentic* when offering self-disclosures. Maintaining credibility is an important component in successful clinician self-disclosures.

- Make self-disclosures that are likely to *empower clients* and increase their range of choices; don't shame or blame them or limit their options unless they present a danger.
- Be aware that clinician self-disclosure is most likely to be *effective with clients who have good ego strength* (Simone, McCarthy, & Skay, 1998).

Appropriate Purposes of Clinician Self-Disclosure

Clinician self-disclosure, following the previous guidelines, can accomplish many purposes. The following are some of the most important objectives of self-disclosure:

- *Providing clinically important information about the counselor or therapist.*
  - Informing the client of the clinician's training, experience, and theoretical orientation
  - Providing information about the beliefs and biases of the clinician and the treatment setting ("This is a church-based agency and does not provide information on abortion as an option in dealing with an unwanted pregnancy.")
- *Building and deepening the therapeutic alliance.* Self-disclosure can be especially helpful to clients whose backgrounds are different from those of the clinician, particularly when the client is from a traditionally oppressed group. Clinician self-disclosure can highlight similarities in the face of apparently extreme differences and can enable clients to become more familiar and comfortable with the clinician.
  - Increasing client's perceptions of the similarity between the client and the clinician ("You know, like you, I came to the United States as a teenager and had to deal with many changes.")
  - Increasing clinician credibility, trustworthiness, and attractiveness
  - Humanizing the clinician ("I was so upset when the terrorist attacks occurred that I had to stop my work for the day.")
- *Teaching and demonstrating new or alternative insights, emotions, thoughts, and attitudes.*
  - Modeling self-disclosures
  - Introducing new perspectives and reactions ("I think I would have been very hurt if my best friend said that to me.")
  - Encouraging reality testing ("I know you are eager to attend that college, but I'm concerned that you have not paid enough attention to their admission requirements.")
  - Providing feedback ("You have worked very hard to resolve your difficulties through counseling.")
- *Empowering the client.*
  - Normalizing a client's reactions ("You seem dismayed that you felt angry when your supervisor cursed at you, and yet I think I would have felt angry about that too.")
  - Providing appropriate reassurance ("It sounds like you did everything you could to make the project a success.")
  - Instilling hope ("I know you feel pretty hopeless when you have a panic attack, and yet I know from both the research and my work with other people that it is possible to learn to manage and even prevent these attacks.")

- Emphasizing client strengths and resources ("It sounds like your resource-fulness and quick thinking really made a difference when the caterer dropped the birthday cake.")
- *Promoting immediacy.* Immediacy can have a very beneficial effect on the treatment process when progress seems stalled or when the client seems to have strong feelings such as attraction, dependence, or mistrust toward the clinician.
  - Promoting discussion of client-clinician interactions; these often mirror the client's interactions with people outside of treatment ("You know, when you raise your voice and gesture like that, it makes me think that you are very angry even though you say you are not feeling anger.")
  - Focusing on the treatment process ("You have come late for our last three sessions. I'm concerned that you are not really invested in our work together.")

Examples of Clinician Self-Disclosure

Consider the following examples of self-disclosure. Each pair of examples illustrates one of the five major purposes of clinician self-disclosure. However, one follows the guidelines for appropriate self-disclosure while the other violates one or more of those guidelines. In the exercises at the end of this chapter, you will have the opportunity to identify the purposes of self-disclosure statements, to assess whether or not they follow the guidelines, and to develop some of your own self-disclosure statements.

1. *Purpose: Providing clinically important information about the counselor or therapist.*
   - I believe ending a marriage is a very serious matter and that we should do all we can to improve a marriage before deciding it should end.
     Assessment: This clinician places great importance on the institution of marriage and communicates this attitude to clients. It is acceptable because it allows them to seek a different clinician if they are not comfortable with this approach, and to understand the clinician's point of view if they do continue treatment with this person. It does not shame, criticize, or blame the clients but rather enables them to make an informed choice.
   - You are putting your own needs in front of those of your children in deciding to end your marriage. Divorce is always devastating to children. Don't your children's feelings matter to you?
     Assessment: This self-disclosure is countertherapeutic because it does blame and criticize clients. It misrepresents the research findings on the impact of divorce on children and does not allow the client to make choices.
2. *Purpose: Building and deepening the therapeutic alliance.*
   - You may be surprised to know that I, too, am a cancer survivor. It was one of the most difficult experiences I have ever had, as it probably is for you. What has it been like for you?
     Assessment: Although this is a very personal statement, it introduces an important similarity between the client and clinician, increases clinician credibility, and can instill hope. It is concise, is stated in the present tense, and keeps the focus on the client.
   - You know, I, too, had cancer. Was that ever tough for me! I still think about the pain of the surgery, the nausea and vomiting from the chemotherapy, and the fear that I would die. You're lucky they have new drugs now that control

the nausea; it shouldn't be so bad for you and you should have a better prognosis. I still worry that the cancer will catch up with me.

      Assessment: While this statement also identifies a similarity between client and clinician, it is too wordy and personal, and it shifts the focus from the client to the clinician. In addition, rather than communicating empathy, it minimizes the client's concerns.

3. *Purpose: Teaching and demonstrating new or alternative insights, emotions, thoughts, and attitudes.*

   • I can hear you trying very hard to forgive your wife for her infidelities and her physical abuse of your children. I know that forgiveness is very important in your value system. However, from what you have said, she has never tried to change her behavior. If I were in your situation, I would probably want to put most of my energy into taking care of my children and myself rather than spending so much time trying to understand my wife. What reactions do you have to that?

         Assessment: This statement gives the client feedback and presents alternative thoughts and behaviors. The clinician is also trying to help the client become more concerned about the harm this situation may do to his children. It incorporates reflection of feeling and meaning, is authentic, and maintains a focus on the client, although it does give the client implicit advice.

   • Week after week, you focus on your unsuccessful efforts to forgive your wife. And yet I think we're losing sight of who is really important here. I was abused as a child, and I know the lifelong damage that can do. You need to face the fact that your wife is never going to change and do what a father is supposed to do, protect his children.

         Assessment: While the second statement has the same purposes as the first statement, it seems to be a harmful statement because it violates several guidelines. The clinician's reference to his own abuse is too personal and highly charged for this context. In addition, the statement shames and attacks the client and fails to incorporate the essential therapeutic conditions.

4. *Purpose: Empowering the client.*

   • You seem embarrassed about calling your physician last night when you had chest pains. If I'd had open-heart surgery not long ago, I would have been on the telephone to my physician as soon as I had pains like that. And I'm impressed that, even though you were scared, you used your deep breathing to relax, you made a list of your questions, and you talked calmly with your physician until you got the information you needed.

         Assessment: This statement is designed to normalize the client's reactions and to provide appropriate reassurance. The statement also emphasizes client strengths and resources. Although the statement may be too lengthy, it does follow other important guidelines. It communicates empathy, keeps the focus on the client, and is honest and authentic.

   • Why were you so reluctant to disturb your physician? They expect emergency calls. Don't be like my brother who was so afraid to bother anybody that he waited to get help until he had a heart attack that did permanent damage. Next time, get on that phone right away.

         Assessment: Again, this self-disclosure is too personal. It takes the focus off the client and is using scare tactics and demands to change client's behavior.

While the clinician is probably motivated by genuine concern for the client, these tactics tend to detract from the client's feelings of power. In addition, the clinician failed to communicate empathy for the client.

5. *Promote immediacy.*

- I'm feeling uncomfortable about our work together lately. You seem to be giving me all the credit for your progress, just as you did now when we discussed your good grades. You are ignoring the hard work you have done in treatment. I wonder if you often devalue yourself in this way?

  Assessment: This statement is intended to focus on the treatment process and promote discussion of the client's difficulty in accepting credit for her accomplishments. This probably will raise her awareness of a pattern of behavior that she manifests in many settings. This statement also should contribute to her feelings of empowerment and can strengthen and build the therapeutic alliance. The statement is concise, uses the present tense, keeps the focus on the client, and is encouraging rather than shaming.

- I know you had planned to talk about your problems studying for finals, but I have something I want to bring up first. I noticed that you always tell me how wonderful I am and never say much about how great you are. Well, I think you are pretty wonderful, too, and I wish you could be more aware of it.

  Assessment: This clinician is caring and supportive toward the client and is seeking to empower the client. However, the intervention is poorly timed, detracting from the topic the client has on her mind. It is vague and general rather than concise and clear, and it does not encourage dialogue about the immediate client-clinician interaction or about the client's patterns of behavior. In addition, the clinician sounds judgmental, a behavior to avoid even if the judgment is a positive one.

Client Requests for Clinician Self-Disclosure

Typically, clinician self-disclosures are initiated by the person providing treatment. However, sometimes clients ask clinicians to disclose information about their own values, beliefs, experiences, and lifestyle. In responding to such requests, clinicians should keep in mind the guidelines and purposes presented previously. Several additional considerations are also relevant under these circumstances.

- *Refusing to self-disclose can detract significantly from the trust and credibility inherent in the therapeutic alliance.* Even sidestepping client questions can be experienced as a rejection. For example, in response to a client's question about their marital status, some clinicians do not directly answer the question but instead ask something like, "What makes it important to you to know my marital status?" or "What is leading you to ask such a question?" or "What would it mean to you if I were married?" While the answers to these questions might well be important, clinicians who respond to a question with a question run the risk of being perceived as manipulative and as exaggerating the power differential in the therapeutic relationship.
- *Provide only as much information as is requested.* Just as young children who ask where babies come from do not generally want a lecture on biology, so do most

clients want only minimal information. For example, if a client asks whether you are married or have children, a yes or no response is enough. Avoid providing details on the genders and ages of your children or the number of marriages you have had unless clients specifically request that information.

- *Avoid making assumptions about what clients want to know.* Several years ago, I had to take a month off from my practice for some surgery. I gave all clients the same minimal information: "I will be away from my practice for the next month in order to have surgery for a medical condition." (Of course, I also gave them people to contact in the event of an emergency.) A few asked no questions and quickly resumed discussion of their own concerns. Most asked a few questions about my medical condition and treatment; once reassured that I was not in danger, they seemed satisfied. One expressed great concern about my health; after responding briefly to her questions, I helped her to recognize the link between her anxiety about my situation and the death of her mother from what was supposed to be minor surgery. People vary greatly in terms of what they want to know about their clinicians; let them tell you what they need.

- *Answer first, then explore.* Like the client who was reminded by my surgery of the unexpected death of her mother, people's questions typically reflect their own interests and concerns. Once you have provided at least a brief response to their questions, you may well decide it is therapeutic to explore the thoughts and emotions behind their questions. Feel free to gently explore questions as in the following example, "No, I don't have children. I know that parenting is one of your important concerns. What does it mean to you that I don't have children?"

- *Think carefully before responding to a client's questions.* Sometimes clients request information that we think may be harmful to them or may undermine the therapeutic process. This seems to arise particularly with adolescent clients who might ask, "Did you ever use drugs?" or "Didn't you have sex when you were my age?" Questions such as these may create a dilemma for you. You want to be honest, but you also want to serve as a positive role model for your clients and discourage self-destructive choices. There is no formula for responding to questions such as these. However, this is a time to draw on your in-depth understanding of the client. Think about the meaning of the question for the client as well as the probable effect your response will have on the client and then craft a response that is most likely to have a positive impact in light of that information.

  For example, to the question on your use of drugs, you might decide to reply, "Yes, like you, I wanted to be accepted by my friends and so I did smoke pot for awhile. However, I felt it was getting in the way of my school work, so I got up my courage and told my friends that I didn't want to do drugs with them anymore. To my surprise, my decision didn't really hurt our friendship at all."

- *Remember that you have rights, too.* Sometimes clients ask us questions we do not want to answer. Perhaps the question is personal and addresses information we choose not to provide. Perhaps we believe that it would be countertherapeutic to respond to that particular question. We must still treat the client with respect and acknowledge the legitimacy of their questions. We also usually should process with the clients our decision not to provide requested information and to explore the meaning this has for them as well as the emotions it elicits. However, we do not need to provide the answers. This is illustrated in the following examples:

- I don't want to color your decision about your pregnancy by telling you my beliefs about abortion. I hope you understand that I think it would be better to keep our focus on your choices.
- I realize you are very curious about me, but your questions are making it difficult for us to address your concerns. Remember, during our first session, I discussed with you your role as a client. I encourage you to shift your focus to your issues rather than to me so we can help you resolve your concerns.
- I'm glad to hear that you like my office but I don't understand how it is relevant to our goals for me to tell you how much rent I pay here. If I am missing a connection, please help me understand it.
- I would rather not discuss my sexual orientation with you. I prefer to keep my personal life and my professional life separate. How do you react to my decision not to answer your question?

Clearly, the issue of clinician self-disclosure is a complex one. However, following the guidelines and models provided here should help you to deal effectively with this issue.

CLIENT RELUCTANCE

Despite appropriate clinician self-disclosure and use of other strategies to foster clients' involvement in treatment, people are not always willing or able to participate fully in the treatment process. Their reluctance to talk openly about themselves and take constructive steps to resolve their concerns can impede the therapeutic process and prove frustrating to clinicians. This dynamic has been known by many terms over the years, including *defensiveness, resistance, reluctance, reactance,* and *noncompliance.* Clients who present with considerable reluctance may be described as difficult, oppositional, unmotivated, or challenging. I will use the term *reluctance* because it is a relatively neutral term and does not imply criticism of clients for having difficulty engaging in treatment.

Clinicians identified client reluctance and its potentially negative impact on the treatment process more than 100 years ago. Freud believed that resistance, manifested by the client's opposition to bringing unconscious material into awareness, reflected "the client's innate protection against emotional pain" (Cowan & Presbury, 2000, p. 411). Reluctance also has been viewed as reflective of a negative transference to the clinician, stemming from impairment in early childhood attachment to caregivers. For many years, client reluctance has been seen as undesirable.

However, our attitudes toward this process and even the terminology used to describe this process have changed considerably over the years. Today, reluctance is viewed as a common and understandable aspect of treatment. Although most clinicians probably still wish they did not need to contend with client reluctance, they seem to have much more empathy for this reaction and also take more responsibility for helping people get past their reluctance and engage productively in the treatment process.

Reluctance is particularly prevalent in people who are involuntary clients; perhaps they are court-mandated to treatment, required to seek help as a condition of maintaining their employment, or seeking help at the insistence of a concerned or unhappy parent or partner. Reluctance is also common in people who are mistrustful of others, shy and fearful, or dubious about the value of treatment. Reluctance is common and understandable, too, in people whose cultural backgrounds do not encourage counseling and psychotherapy and who believe they have little in common with their clinicians. Strong reluctance can also be found in people who are invested in proving that someone else is to blame for their problems, in demonstrating that they are incorrigible, in defeating the clinician, or in proving others wrong.

Conceptualizing Reluctance

In teaching both novice and experienced clinicians to understand and cope with reluctance in their clients, I encourage them to take an optimistic but realistic attitude. Assume that all people want to feel better and have more rewarding lives, but just have not yet found a way to make those changes. Of course, we will not be successful in reaching all of our clients, but taking an optimistic but realistic stance seems most likely to help us find a way to reduce reluctance. Looking at reluctance through the lens of our modified version of Bloom's taxonomy can help us better understand that process and determine appropriate interventions.

The case of Delaney, a 14-year-old Japanese American adolescent, will be used to illustrate the application of the taxonomy to dealing with reluctance. Delaney had been referred for counseling because of her declining grades and withdrawn behavior. Delaney was the youngest of three children born to a Japanese mother and an American father who met while the father was working in Japan. Delaney and her two brothers were born in Japan but moved to the United States when Delaney was 7. Delaney's father was emotionally and physically abusive toward her mother and had frequently behaved in an inappropriately sexual way toward Delaney. On several occasions, Delaney had observed her mother talking to a man Delaney did not know and behaving in secretive ways.

Delaney's reluctance is processed in the following example, according to an abbreviated version of Bloom's taxonomy. Understanding the reluctance clearly leads to identification of ways to address it that are likely to succeed.

1. Content.   Reluctance is the process of acting in ways that seem to obstruct the progress of treatment. Reluctance can take many forms. The following are some of the most common.

Violating rules

- arriving late for sessions or failing to attend scheduled sessions
- failing to pay for treatment in a timely way
- not completing suggested tasks or activities
- making excessive demands on the clinician (e.g., telephone calls, extra time)

Withholding communication/restricting content

- focusing the session on extraneous material such as the weather, the traffic, humorous anecdotes, the problems of a friend, or anything else not related to the treatment goals
- talking excessively about facts and ideas; avoiding expression of emotion

- overtalking so that the clinician has little opportunity to intervene and ignoring what the clinician does say
- avoiding discussion of important experiences, emotions, thoughts, and behaviors
- evading questions or responding with "I don't know" or "I don't remember" to clinician's questions
- dwelling on past concerns and avoiding exploration of the relationship of past to present concerns
- talking about the same topics or issues again and again without attempting to make any changes
- silence or withdrawal
- asking many questions not germane to the treatment process

Hostility and manipulation

- verbal attacks or constant criticisms of the clinician or the treatment process
- externalizing blame for one's difficulties
- being angry, belligerent, argumentative, or defiant
- discounting the value of whatever the clinician says or suggests
- seductive behavior toward the clinician
- threatening harm to oneself or another person

These and many other client behaviors and attitudes can impede the therapeutic process and can prove very frustrating to clinicians.

Delaney avoided discussing personal information in counseling. When her counselor asked her direct questions, she replied with, "I don't know" or "I don't remember." When she did talk, it was typically about singers or actors she admired. She failed to complete the few simple tasks the counselor had suggested to her and often asked how much longer she had to meet with the counselor.

2. Comprehension and organization.   Just as all people have defenses, all clients probably have mixed feelings about beginning counseling or psychotherapy. Change is difficult and, even if our current ways of coping are ineffective or painful, giving them up for the unknown can be frightening. The question is not whether a client has reluctance about the treatment process but how strong that reluctance is and whether the reluctance is greater than the motivation to make positive changes. Also important is noting times when the reluctance is particularly strong; this is typically a sign that treatment is focusing on important and highly charged issues that need attention. Once clinicians have identified signs of reluctance (listed previously), they can determine whether the client's behavior in treatment is impeding the treatment process. If that is the case, then understanding the motivation behind the reluctance is important in determining the best way to address it.

The following are common reasons that clients manifest a high degree of reluctance:

Negative thoughts or feelings about the clinician and the treatment process

- lack of trust
- lack of understanding of counseling or psychotherapy
- belief that the clinician will not understand or accept them

- a view of treatment as a punishment or source of shame
- fear of change
- disinterest in change and comfort with the known
- discomfort with self-disclosure, expression of emotion

Feelings or thoughts about the self

- shame or guilt about own behavior or situation
- wish to gain power or control over another
- need to assert independence or separateness
- fear of success
- need to protect their own view of reality
- need to prove that they are hopeless and beyond help

Feelings or thoughts about others

- wish to protect another person
- desire to prove another person wrong by ensuring that treatment is ineffective

An important aspect of understanding the client's reluctance is looking at the clinician's reactions to the client as well as the interactions between the clinician and the client. Reluctance can be annoying and frustrating to hard-working clinicians who are doing their best to help a client. The clinician's feelings of anger and irritation can inadvertently manifest themselves during treatment. The clinician may appear short-tempered or impatient with a client. Empathy may diminish while questions and harsh confrontation increase in an effort to compel the client to change. Needless to say, this will probably exacerbate the client's reluctance and create a vicious cycle in which client reluctance leads the clinician to have negative reactions that, in turn, exacerbate the reluctance. Clinicians need to recognize any ways in which they are contributing to the reluctance and take steps to modify their own behaviors and attitudes.

Delaney's reluctance primarily took the form of withholding communication and restricting content. Her noncompliant behaviors were passive rather than active; she was not hostile and manipulative. She complied, at least superficially, with the treatment process but did not really engage in that process.

Reasons for Delaney's reluctance to engage in treatment included all three areas listed previously:

- *Feelings and thoughts about treatment*—Delaney mistrusted her clinician and did not believe that counseling could help her. She also worried that her clinician would not maintain her confidentiality and would tell her parents about her sessions.
- *Feelings and thoughts about herself*—Delaney was uncomfortable with self-disclosure and expression of emotion and felt fearful and ashamed when encouraged to talk about herself.
- *Feelings and thoughts about others*—Delaney appeared to be protecting her family by refusing to engage in any discussion of her parents, their interactions with each other, and their relationships with her. The only comments she made about her family focused on how wonderful her mother was and how entertaining her brothers were.

3. Analysis and synthesis.   In analyzing and making sense of Delaney's reluctance, the counselor considered a range of factors:

- The nature of Delaney's reluctant behavior (withholding/restricting content), providing only superficial positive information about her family, and avoiding any mention of her father and the interactions within her family
- The probable reasons for her reluctance
  - Delaney's cultural background, which might, at least in part, explain her need for privacy and lead her to withhold information that might reflect badly on her family
  - The great change Delaney experienced when relocating from Japan, where she had grown to school age, to the United States, where she felt out of place and different from her peers
  - The decline in Delaney's grades, several years after the family's relocation to the United States, suggesting an additional problem that had developed fairly recently

4. Interpretation.   Interpretation of reluctance is the process of making sense of that behavior. Clinicians review their analysis and synthesis of the material they have gathered on the nature and dynamics of the client's reluctance and try to understand that process. The basic question to be answered is, "What purpose does the reluctance serve for this person?"

Delaney's self-doubts, as well as behaviors she perceived as potentially shameful in her family, seemed to be the primary causes of her reluctance. Multicultural factors certainly played a part in her attitude toward counseling, as did her family's relocation. Her lack of knowledge about counseling and her mistrust of that process were additional factors in her reluctance. In addition, more recent factors, not yet determined, also seemed to contribute to Delaney's reluctance. All this information suggested that the motivation behind Delaney's reluctance was protection of herself and her family from humiliation and pain, probably stemming from family relationships.

5. Application and intervention.   Many strategies have been suggested for addressing and reducing client reluctance. The following are some of the more common of these:

Increasing client comfort with the treatment process

- establishing mutually agreed-upon goals
- increasing use of empathy
- providing information on the nature and purposes of treatment (role induction)
- using relaxation and other strategies to reduce anxiety
- giving the client more control over the treatment process
- developing the therapeutic alliance
- focusing on the positive
- teaching the client useful skills and strategies such as assertiveness and other communication skills
- finding motivations or incentives for the client to engage productively in treatment

Normalizing the reluctance

- helping clients recognize that ambivalence about treatment is common
- giving clients permission to talk about their conflicted feelings
- viewing the reluctance as an important source of information

Using indirect treatment strategies

- paradoxical intention ("I'd encourage you to sit quietly until words come to you that want to be spoken.")
- visual imagery
- bibliotherapy (suggesting reading about the value of counseling)
- doing something unexpected
- modeling appropriate self-disclosure
- focusing on nonverbal cues
- suggesting that client review tapes of sessions
- using humor
- using metaphors or reframing ("I can see by your silence that you have a great deal to think about.")
- becoming more silent
- piquing client's curiosity
- suggesting that positive change will happen ("When you are ready, you will be able to talk about this more freely.")
- discussing the benefits of avoiding change

Directly challenging the reluctance

- providing data to demonstrate client reluctance ("Were you aware that you have been late five out of six sessions?")
- using challenge or confrontation to point out the self-destructive nature of the reluctance ("You say that you want to get along better with people and yet you refuse to follow through on the suggestions I make.")
- setting limits ("I will need to suspend our sessions until you establish a schedule for paying the money you owe for your treatment.")
- interpreting the reluctance to the client to facilitate the client's efforts to reduce blocks to progress ("I wonder if your reluctance to talk about your family is a way to protect them.")
- disputing the client's negative perceptions of treatment ("You tell me that treatment has been a waste of your time. That surprises me since your grades have improved, you have stopped purging, and you have made a new friend.")
- establishing a treatment contract
- raising anxiety

Clearly, many types of helpful interventions are available to clinicians who are trying to reduce client reluctance. However, clinicians should generally guard against using the following potentially harmful interventions:

- letting reluctance go on and on without addressing it
- personalizing the reluctance ("I want you to stop harassing me with your constant telephone calls.")

- getting into a power struggle with the client
- allowing yourself to be abused or manipulated by a client
- blaming and attacking the client
- giving the client full control of the treatment process
- greatly reducing expectations of what can be accomplished by the treatment process
- quickly moving toward referring the client to another clinician or terminating the treatment process

In light of the analysis and interpretation of Delaney's reluctance, directly challenging the reluctance seemed to be the least desirable approach. This intervention is likely to increase her fear and sense of shame and make her even more reluctant to engage in treatment.

Normalizing the reluctance and using indirect treatment strategies might be helpful after Delaney had developed some trust in the clinician and in the treatment process. However, even those approaches run the risk of making Delaney feel manipulated, uncomfortable, and under pressure to comply with the clinician's requests.

Interventions that seem most likely to reduce Delaney's feelings of fear and shame are those that increase her comfort with the treatment process. Consequently, her clinician increased the use of empathy in treatment, making sure not to be intrusive or overly personal. The clinician gave Delaney greater control over the treatment process, letting her set the agenda for each session after educating her on appropriate issues for discussion. Her clinician focused on Delaney's strengths and accomplishments, such as her academic success in the first few years after the family's move to the United States. In addition, her counselor taught Delaney some study skills and communication skills that helped her perform better at school and engage more successfully in group projects. This helped Delaney see that her counselor did have caring and concern for her and was unlikely to humiliate or pressure her.

Subsequent interventions normalized Delaney's reluctance and encouraged her to discuss her ambivalence about getting help. Indirect interventions such as suggesting that positive change was possible and using stories, metaphors, humor, and bibliotherapy eventually enabled Delaney to share with the counselor the problems in her family.

Following a step-by-step process to understand client reluctance using the modified version of Bloom's taxonomy can help clinicians not only reduce reluctance but even use it as an important source of information about a person and the way the person deals with new and challenging situations. The exercises in the following Learning Opportunities section provide you an opportunity to practice applying the taxonomy to examples of client reluctance.

LEARNING OPPORTUNITIES

This chapter was designed to help you build on your knowledge of technical skills for addressing and modifying clients' emotions. It also introduced an array of conceptual skills that can provide you with a better understanding of how to make positive use of and modify strong emotions in the treatment setting. These include the following:

- initiating and developing a positive therapeutic alliance
- understanding the client and clinician characteristics that contribute to a strong therapeutic alliance

- role induction
- crisis intervention
- addressing suicidal ideation
- dealing with client anger and violence
- clinician self-disclosure
- dealing with client reluctance

The following exercises afford you the opportunity to apply the conceptual skills that have been presented in this chapter. This section will include written exercises, discussion questions, exercises and an assessment tool to use in your practice groups, and activities to address in your journal.

Written Exercises/Discussion Questions

1. Many modern clinicians and researchers believe that the treatment alliance between the client and clinician is more important than the treatment plan that is used. Does this point of view surprise you? Why or why not? What evidence can you present that supports or refutes this position?
2. Beginning on page 213, you will find a list of 10 dimensions that characterize clinicians who are skilled at developing therapeutic alliances with their clients. For each of the following clients, identify two or three clinician qualities from that list that you believe will be especially conducive to the development of a good working alliance with that client:
   a. A 7-year-old boy who has lived in several foster homes has recently been reunited with the parent who neglected him as an infant.
   b. A 56-year-old man was recently fired from his job because of arguments with supervisors and coworkers. He believes he was fired because of his high salary.
   c. The husband of a 27-year-old woman with two young children recently left her because the woman with whom he was having an affair became pregnant. This client is very depressed and humiliated.
3. Assume that you inadvertently scheduled two clients at the same time. How will you deal with this? Identify the characteristics you will model in order to maintain a positive therapeutic alliance with both people.
4. Ada has been a challenging client for you. Your first two sessions have largely been monologues by Ada, blaming her parents and friends for her difficulties and reiterating her hopeless feelings. At the end of the second session, Ada asks you whether you like her. How will you respond to her question, keeping in mind the importance of communicating caring and genuineness to clients?
5. Your client is Nathan, a 17-year-old male. He was recently diagnosed with a sexually transmitted disease, although he had been sexually involved with only his girlfriend. When he confronted his girlfriend about this, she acknowledged that she had been sexually involved with many of his friends. Nathan went home and consumed a bottle of aspirin along with a quart of vodka. Although he survived this suicide attempt, he continues to wish he were dead. Nathan's father abuses alcohol and is unemployed. Nathan has few friends, except for his girlfriend, and has never been a strong student. He had been involved in sports but was dropped from the team because of his many absences. Develop your understanding of Nathan's suicidal ideation by applying the modified

version of Bloom's taxonomy to the information you have on Nathan. Then formulate a plan that seems likely to reduce the risk that Nathan will commit suicide.

6. Beverly, a 76-year-old woman, has lived her entire life with her twin sister Valerie. Valerie recently had a stroke and is on life support systems. The doctors say it is unlikely that she will recover and encourage Beverly to request that the life support systems be removed. Valerie did not have a living will but spoke often of not wanting to live unless she had dignity and quality of life. Beverly is devastated by Valerie's stroke and feels unable to make a decision. Following the guidelines beginning on page 231, analyze the nature of Beverly's crisis and develop a plan to help her cope with this situation.

7. Discuss the probable benefits and drawbacks of the following clinician self-disclosures:
   a. That's interesting. I also am a marathon runner. I find it really helps me stay well, both physically and mentally.
   b. I grew up in Peoria, too. I think your brother was in my high school class.
   c. I have a perfume allergy and ask that you not wear strong perfume to our appointments.
   d. I'm impressed that you got here on time. The weather really slowed me down this morning.
   e. You really look terrific in that red outfit.

8. How would you respond to the following client requests for you to disclose information about yourself?
   a. Did you ever feel like killing yourself?
   b. I brought my wife to our last session so that I could get your feedback on her. What did you think of her?
   c. Because of her accident, my wife suffered brain damage and has become a quadriplegic. I'm only 28 years old and want to have a life. Would you divorce your wife if you were in my situation?

9. Considering the types of clients you expect to work with, what sort of client reluctance do you think you are most likely to encounter? What do you think will be the three or four approaches you will be most likely to use to address reluctance?

10. Clinicians seem to be increasingly aware of the importance of role induction in getting the treatment process off to a good start. What do you see as the advantages and disadvantages to role induction? For what types of clients do you view a role induction as especially important? Under what circumstances are you likely to omit doing a role induction?

Practice Group Exercises—Dealing with Strong Client Emotions While Building the Therapeutic Alliance

Divide into your practice groups.   In this chapter, as in the previous one, you will have the opportunity to practice your conceptual skills and further refine your technical skills. As usual, continue to tape-record both the practice session and the subsequent discussion.

Purpose of exercise.   In chapter 3 you learned skills that will help you promote dialogue with your clients and assist them in expressing, understanding, and modifying their emotions. In this practice group exercise, you will build on what you learned in chapter 3. This exercise will encompass the following skills:

Technical skills

- ability to make good use of encouragers (restatement, paraphrase, summarization)
- ability to make accurate and helpful reflections of feeling
- ability to identify and make good use of nonverbal communication

Conceptual skills

- initiating treatment
- demonstrating characteristics that will build a sound therapeutic alliance
- understanding and working with a challenging client

Role-play exercise.   In each dyad, one person will assume the role of clinician and the other will assume the role of client. This interaction should be viewed as an initial treatment session. Those in the client role may determine their specific concerns, as long as their presentation reflects *one* of the challenging issues discussed in this chapter:

- a client in crisis
- a suicidal client
- an angry or potentially violent client
- a highly reluctant client

Those of you in the clinician role may discover that you have some strong emotional reactions to this role play. You may feel frustrated or irritated, and you may even feel some anger toward your partner for being such a difficult client. Keep in mind that this is a role play, not a genuine interaction between the two of you, and try to make the most of what may be a challenging learning experience.

Clinicians in this exercise have three major goals:

- to demonstrate those characteristics that promote the development of a sound therapeutic alliance
- to demonstrate effective use of the skills learned in chapter 3 (encouragers, reflection of both verbal and nonverbal emotions)
- to begin to address effectively the concerns and issues presented by this challenging client (e.g., suicidal ideation, anger, strong reluctance)

Time schedule.   If possible, allow 3 hours for this exercise, with the four role plays and their processing each taking 45 minutes. If you do not have this much time, do only two role plays, one for each dyad. Each person will then have the opportunity to be either client or clinician but will not be able to experience both roles.

- Allow 20–25 minutes for each role-played interview.
- Take about 10 minutes to provide feedback to the person in the clinician role. As you have done with other exercises in this book, begin the feedback process with

the person in the clinician role, focus on strengths first, and offer concrete suggestions for improvement. Remember to make this a positive learning experience. Feedback should focus on the areas listed in the Assessment of Progress Form.

- After you have given the clinician feedback, take about 10 minutes to discuss the issues presented by the client according to the information on addressing that topic presented earlier in this chapter. Identify those treatment strategies that are most likely to be helpful in dealing with the client's strong emotions.

Assessment of Progress Form 7

1. What clinician characteristics were used to initiate the session and build a positive treatment alliance?

    a. Which of these seemed particularly successful? What made them effective?

    b. What else might the clinician have done to further develop the treatment alliance?

2. Describe the clinician's use of the following skills:
    a. Encouragers (restatement, paraphrase, summarization)

    b. Reflection of feeling

    c. Attention to nonverbal messages

3. Which of the clinician's interventions seemed particularly successful?

4. How might the clinician have improved on his or her interventions?

5. What was the clinician's strategy in dealing with the challenging situation presented by the client?

    a. What interventions were especially effective in addressing the challenging situation?

    b. How might the clinician have dealt even more effectively with that situation?

6. Summary of feedback:

Personal Journal Questions

1. Which of the 10 important clinician characteristics (described beginning on page 213) do you believe you will be able to use well in developing positive therapeutic alliances with your clients? Which ones do you think will be the most difficult for you to use and why?

2. If you have been in therapy yourself, did your clinician conduct a role induction with you? If yes, was that helpful to you? If not, in what ways, if any, do you think that process would have been helpful to you?

3. What do you think it would be like for you to work with a suicidal client? What do you think would be the most difficult aspect of that process for you? What skills do you have that would help you work with that client?

4. What do you think it would be like for you to work with an angry and potentially violent client? What do you think would be the most difficult aspect of that process for you? What skills do you have that would help you deal with that client?

5. Listen to the tape recording of the role-played interview in which you participated as part of this chapter. Respond to the following questions about that recording:
   a. How did you feel about working with a challenging client? Did your feelings interfere with your ability to provide effective treatment?
   b. What do you view as your greatest accomplishment during this role play?
   c. What progress did you make toward achieving the goals you identified in your previous journal entry?
   d. What goals do you have for your next role play?

6. What is the most important thing you learned from this chapter and its exercises?

SUMMARY

This chapter focused on conceptual skills associated with helping clients identify, express, understand, and alter their strong emotions. Continued use was made of the modified version of Bloom's taxonomy to promote learning of the skills presented in this chapter. Particular attention was paid to establishing a positive therapeutic alliance, conducting a role induction, making helpful self-disclosures, dealing with strong client emotions such as suicidal ideation and rage, and client reluctance to engage productively in treatment.

Chapter 8 will focus on conceptual skills associated with thoughts. Included in that chapter will be information on assessment, defining clients' central concerns, diagnosis, and treatment planning.

CHAPTER 8

Using Conceptual Skills as Frameworks for Clinicians' Thoughts

INTRODUCTION

Most of the chapters in this book have focused on characteristics of the client, helping clinicians to understand and address clients' backgrounds, emotions, thoughts, and actions. Chapter 4, for example, looked primarily at understanding, analyzing, and modifying clients' cognitions. Chapter 7 focused on changing strong and self-destructive client emotions and developing a sound therapeutic alliance.

This chapter, however, takes a somewhat different slant on the treatment process. As the third chapter in the Conceptual Skills section, it focuses on thoughts, the third element in the BETA format (background, emotions, thoughts, and actions). However, rather than focusing primarily on the clients' thoughts, most topics in this chapter will focus on the clinicians' thoughts. The purpose of this chapter is to help clinicians clarify and develop their own thoughts about their clients and then to use those thoughts to further the treatment process. Information in this chapter, as well as the concluding exercises, will incorporate these new skills into what you have already learned about technical and conceptual skills. This will help you progress in your ability to provide effective treatment to your clients.

Chapter 8 will cover the following topics:

- *Assessment*—Chapters 2 and 6 have already provided quite a bit of information about client assessment. These chapters presented the steps in an intake interview, provided tools such as the genogram and lifeline to facilitate information gathering, and helped you analyze the information you obtained according to the modified version of Bloom's taxonomy. While the intake interview is the most important tool in the assessment process, sometimes it does not yield all the information you need to understand clients fully enough to develop a sound treatment plan. This chapter will present the mental status examination and also will discuss the appropriate use of tests, inventories, and structured observations to facilitate the assessment process.

- *Defining memories*—Just as people have earliest memories that reflect the way they view the world (discussed in chapter 2), so do many people have memories of important incidents that give shape and direction to their lives and their view of themselves. Identifying and understanding the significance of these memories is an important aspect of the assessment process and facilitates treatment planning.

- *Case conceptualization and problem definition*—Once you have completed the assessment process, you should be ready to identify your clients' focal concerns and develop a comprehensive understanding of how these concerns are connected to the rest of their lives. Several formats, including the modified version of Bloom's taxonomy, will be used to illustrate the processes of problem definition and case conceptualization. This section of the chapter will pave the way for the next two parts of this chapter.

- *Diagnosis*—Diagnosis is one of the most important tools of today's clinicians. Using the current version of the *Diagnostic and Statistical Manual of Mental Disorders* (2000a) to make a multiaxial diagnosis for a person enables clinicians to tap into and make use of a wealth of information on the treatment and prognosis of mental disorders.

- *Treatment planning*—Developing a structured treatment plan is the next step in the process of successfully helping our clients. This section will present structured formats for treatment planning. Development of a treatment plan affords both clients and clinicians many benefits:
  - It enables them to anticipate the direction of their work together.
  - It facilitates their use of successful treatment procedures.
  - It enables them to evaluate and modify their work together as needed.
  - It maintains hope and optimism that they will achieve their goals.

ASSESSMENT

Assessment is the process of building a comprehensive picture of a person's background, personality, emotions, thoughts, and behavioral patterns from a broad vantage point, sampling pertinent sources of information (Kottler & Brown, 2000). This typically entails use of a variety of tools to gather information. Assessment almost always includes an intake interview, often includes a mental status examination as well as tests and inventories, and sometimes includes a structured observation. Assessment is a comprehensive and integrative process, combining information gleaned from several sources into a meaningful whole.

The intake interview, described in chapter 2, is usually the first step in the assessment process. The mental status exam, described in the following section, is often incorporated into the intake interview.

MENTAL STATUS EXAMINATION

The mental status examination has become an important tool for clinicians. Although some specific questions may be used to clarify aspects of a client's mental status, the term *examination* is misleading. In reality, most of the information for a mental status exam is inferred rather than obtained from a formal evaluation. That information is garnered from the clinician's observations of and interactions with the client. Few specific procedures are required of the clinician when conducting a mental status examination; the clinician needs only to listen and observe carefully the client's presentation, keeping in mind the categories encompassed by a mental status exam.

The mental status exam is important in many ways:

- It deepens clinicians' understanding of their clients.
- It enables clinicians to systematically assess their clients' areas of strength and weakness.
- It facilitates the process of diagnosis.
- It enables clinicians to develop individualized treatment plans that are likely to be effective.
- It allows clinicians to assess progress in their clients by tracking changes in mental status.

Mental health agencies, as well as managed care groups, are increasingly asking clinicians to provide mental status information in order to assess clients' needs for services and the appropriateness of the services that are provided.

Categories in a Mental Status Exam

Information derived from mental status examinations is generally presented on a checklist or in a few descriptive paragraphs. Categories included in a mental status exam vary but typically include some or all of the items in the following list (Seligman, 1996a):

1. Appearance
   - Overall appearance
   - Nature and appropriateness of clothing in light of the weather and the context
   - Cleanliness and grooming
   - Distinguishing physical characteristics
2. Behavior
   - Eye contact
   - Habits or mannerisms such as restlessness, nail biting, gum chewing, or blinking

- Movement retardation, agitation, or difficulties in motion
- Sensory difficulties such as problems in vision or hearing
3. Speech
   - Clarity of articulation and communication
   - Rate of speech (pressured, slowed, or normal)
   - Unusual or idiosyncratic speech or word usage
   - Speech reflective of cultural or ethnic background
4. Emotions and overall affect
   - Observable emotions, both immediate and underlying
   - Range and lability (amount of change) of emotions
   - Appropriateness of emotional responses
   - Quality of emotions (e.g., flat and blunted, intense, flamboyant)
5. Orientation to reality
   - Aware of time (hour, day, month, year)
   - Aware of place (where interview is being conducted)
   - Aware of persons (who client and clinician are)
   - Aware of situation (what is happening)
6. Concentration and attention
   - Alertness (responsive, lethargic, or distracted)
   - Ability to sustain attention
   - Ability to follow a train of thought and maintain focus on a topic
   - Ability to provide clear and relevant responses
7. Thought processes
   - Capacity for abstract thinking
   - Clarity of thoughts (coherent and logical or reflecting confusion, tangential thinking, and loose associations)
   - Repetitions and perseverations
   - Responses rapid or delayed
8. Thought content
   - Suicidal ideation
   - Thoughts of violence, aggression, or rage
   - Obsessions or compulsions
   - Intrusive recollections of traumatic or other upsetting experiences
   - Other prominent thoughts
9. Perceptions
   - Hallucinations (auditory, visual, olfactory, tactile, other)
   - Bizarre or nonbizarre (within the realm of possibility) delusions
   - Ideas of suspicion, persecution, or reference
   - Other unusual beliefs or perceptions
10. Memory
   - Adequacy of immediate memory (less than a minute)
   - Adequacy of short-term memory (e.g., information provided at the beginning of the interview)
   - Adequacy of medium-term memory (e.g., client's activities a week ago)
   - Adequacy of long-term memory (e.g., childhood experiences, educational/ occupational history, important world events during person's lifetime)

11. Intelligence
   - Educational level
   - Adequacy of fund of information
   - Level of vocabulary
   - Overall intelligence
12. Judgment and insight
   - Decision-making ability
   - Problem-solving ability
   - Awareness of and insight into own self and difficulties
   - Ability to defer action and control impulsivity

The Mini-Mental Status Exam

A variation of the mental status examination is the mini-mental status exam. This is most likely to be used to assess people who show signs of severe cognitive difficulties such as loss of contact with reality, dementia, and other forms of cognitive impairment. The mini-mental status exam is similar to a general mental status exam but is more structured and is designed specifically to assess cognitive functioning. Psychiatric nurses and psychiatrists are more likely to use the mini-mental status exam than are counselors and other nonmedical clinicians.

A typical mini-mental status exam includes the following categories, illustrated by the sort of exercises or questions that might be used to assess that category of functioning:

- *Orientation*—What is the day/month/year/season?
- *Registration*—Clinician names three common objects such as "shoe, hat, dog" and then asks the client to immediately repeat the list of three items.
- *Attention and concentration*—The clinician might ask the client to spell a word backwards or to count backwards from 100 by 7s.
- *Recall*—Midway into the session, the clinician might ask the client to name the three objects that were presented at the beginning of the session (see Registration, listed previously).
- *Language*—Client is asked to provide the names for common objects such as a chair and a pencil, to repeat a sentence, or to follow a three-stage command such as, "Open the cabinet, take out a pad of paper, and put it on the desk."

Other exercises typically incorporated into a mini-mental status exam include writing a sentence and copying a design.

Example of a Mental Status Examination

Below is a mental status examination, describing Eileen Carter, the client who has been presented throughout this book, when she first sought treatment:

Appearance—Eileen Carter is a tall, slender African American woman. She was casually and appropriately dressed and appeared well groomed. She has no distinguishing physical characteristics.

Behavior—Eileen initially had some difficulty making eye contact, but her eye contact improved as the interview continued. Some mannerisms, such as clasping and unclasping her hands and chewing on her fingernails, suggested anxiety. Agitation also was noted in her movements. Otherwise, no unusual mannerisms or sensory difficulties were evident.

Speech—Eileen spoke rapidly but clearly. Although she occasionally mispronounced words, she made herself understood without difficulty.

Emotions/affect—Sadness and tearfulness characterized Eileen's presentation, except when she was talking about her son. A dysphoric mood seems to have been present for many years, exacerbated by current disappointments. Eileen's affect was appropriate to the content of the session.

Orientation to reality—Eileen was oriented to time, place, person, and situation (oriented $\times$ 4).

Concentration and attention——Eileen had no difficulty following the direction of the interview. She was alert and responsive, provided relevant responses, and maintained attention.

Thought processes—Eileen was capable of thinking in a logical and coherent way and seems to have a sound capacity for abstraction. However, she sometimes responded to questions too rapidly; her answers seemed driven more by anxiety than by careful thought. She repeated many times the importance to her of her son and her education.

Thought content—Although Eileen expressed considerable anger toward her husband and described strong feelings of guilt within herself, she did not seem to present a danger to herself or anyone else.

Perceptions—No indications of hallucinations, delusions, or other unusual perceptions were evident during the interview with Eileen.

Intelligence—Eileen completed her GED after leaving high school at age 17. She has recently begun to take college courses. Her fund of information and vocabulary reflect her limited education. However, her depth of thought and interest in learning suggest she is of average to above average intelligence.

Judgment and insight—Eileen seems to have a good awareness of her difficulties and accepts responsibility for the part she has played in her problems. She is trying to change past patterns of impulsivity and poor judgment but needs help in learning problem-solving and decision-making skills.

Now that you have read this mental status exam, think about how it has organized the information you already have about Eileen. You can probably imagine how you could use this information, along with information from the earlier intake interview that was conducted with Eileen, to determine effective ways to help her. Later sections of this chapter discuss the processes of formulating diagnoses and developing treatment plans. A diagnosis and treatment plan facilitates your use of information from an intake interview and mental status examination to determine effective ways to help Eileen and other clients.

Although the mental status exam is a powerful and useful tool, it does entail your making judgments about clients' levels of functioning. Be cautious during this process and be sure that you are making good use of your multicultural counseling skills, discussed earlier in this book. Using tentative language and factoring in information on your clients' cultural backgrounds will help you avoid premature and inaccurate conclusions. At the end of this chapter, you will have the opportunity to draw on both your knowledge of assessment and your understanding of multicultural factors as you prepare mental status examinations.

USING TESTS AND INVENTORIES AS PART OF THE ASSESSMENT PROCESS

Incorporating tests and inventories into the assessment process requires careful thought, decision making, and planning on the part of the clinician. Both clients and clinicians probably bring with them some preconceptions about the use of tests and inventories. These may be either positive or negative. Some people view standardized inventories as an objective, reliable, and helpful source of information, while others are apprehensive about the use of such tools, believing that they stereotype and judge people. Both of these viewpoints are valid; standardized inventories can enhance the treatment process by providing new information and promoting useful discussion. At the same time, these tools can indeed contribute to misunderstanding of clients and to the clients' low self-esteem and the belief that they are poorly understood and unappreciated by the clinician.

In order to emphasize the benefits that testing can yield and minimize its drawbacks, clinicians should be clear about what they hope to accomplish via testing and should be aware of their own reactions to incorporating testing into the treatment process. They also should discuss the prospect of testing and its potential benefits and drawbacks with their clients.

Maximizing the Benefits of Testing

Asking themselves the following seven questions will help clinicians determine whether testing can enhance their work with a particular person and what types of tests and inventories are most likely to be useful (Seligman, 1994):

1. What knowledge, insight, or information am I seeking?
2. Have I first reviewed available sources of information, such as intake interviews, mental status examinations, psychological and academic records, and previous tests and inventories administered to this client, to determine whether they can provide the needed information?
3. Does it seem likely that tests and inventories can provide important knowledge that is not available from other sources?
4. How is the client likely to benefit from and react to the use of tests and inventories?
5. How will the treatment process and the therapeutic alliance be affected by the use of tests and inventories?
6. What tests and inventories are most likely to yield the desired information? The selection process should be sure to take account of the client's multicultural, socioeconomic, and educational background to maximize the likelihood of selecting instruments that yield valid, reliable, and meaningful information.
7. How should those tests and inventories be integrated into the treatment process?

Types of Tests and Inventories

Clinicians should be familiar with the array of tests and inventories available to them, so that they can choose instruments that are likely to provide the information they are seeking. Reference books, such as *Tests in Print* published by the Buros Institute of Mental Measurements, *Test Critiques* published by the Test Corporation of America, and the *Mental Measurements Yearbook* published by the Mental Measurements Yearbook, along with catalogues issued by test publishers, can help you identify appropriate tests for your purposes.

Five broad categories of assessment tools are available (Seligman, 1994). A brief description of these follows. However, reference books and test catalogues should be used to provide additional information about specific tests and inventories.

- *Measures of ability* include tests of achievement, aptitude, and intelligence. These are primarily used in school settings for academic purposes. School psychologists, school counselors, and career counselors most often administer these tests. Individual intelligence tests, such as the Stanford-Binet Intelligence Scale, the Wechsler Intelligence Scale for Children, and the Wechsler Adult Intelligence Scale, are also used by clinical and counseling psychologists to assess intellectual functioning, work habits, and personality. Ability tests that you have probably taken include the Scholastic Aptitude Test and the Graduate Record Examination.
- *Interest inventories* are widely used by counselors and psychologists, particularly those engaged in career counseling. These inventories are typically combined with expressed interests (what people say their interests are) and manifest interests (what interests are reflected in people's activities) to develop a composite and comprehensive picture of people's likes and dislikes. This information can help people to better understand and address their academic and occupational dissatisfaction, to make wise choices of academic programs and occupations, and to develop their awareness of unexplored areas of interest. The Self-Directed Search and the Strong Interest Inventory are widely used interest inventories.
- *Personality inventories* include comprehensive measures of people's personalities, inventories of self-esteem and values, and measures of specific aspects of personality such as depression, dissociation, suicidal ideation, alcohol use, and anxiety. These inventories are helpful in promoting client self-awareness, in identifying emotional strengths and difficulties, in characterizing personality style, and in tracking changes in a particular variable such as depression or anxiety. Well-known comprehensive personality inventories include the Minnesota Multiphasic Personality Inventory (MMPI), the Millon Clinical Multiaxial Inventory (MCMI), and the Myers-Briggs Type Indicator (MBTI) (McCaulley, 1990). More narrowly focused inventories such as the Beck Depression Inventory and the Beck Anxiety Inventory are particularly useful to clinicians in mental health settings who want to determine the severity of people's affective symptoms and assess the progress of treatment.
- *Measures of career development* assess such variables as decisiveness, work-related attitudes, and knowledge of careers. These assessment tools are often incorporated into computer-based assessment and information programs designed

to facilitate career development. Computer-based programs typically also include computerized interest inventories and career information systems and may also include inventories to assess abilities. These assessment tools are particularly likely to be available at high schools and colleges and at career counseling programs.

- *Nonstandardized approaches* to assessment also are sometimes used by clinicians. These are generally checklists and informal questionnaires that have not yet demonstrated their validity and reliability. They are used primarily to promote thought and discussion rather than for assessment purposes.

Conceptualizing the Testing Process for Eileen Carter

Eileen Carter will be used here to illustrate how you might decide whether to use tests and inventories with a particular client and how to select the specific instruments to use with that client. Although we already have considerable information about Eileen from the intake interview (chapter 2) and the mental status exam, there are significant gaps in the information she has been able to provide. Consequently, her clinician is considering whether tests and inventories might provide additional useful information to both client and clinician.

Let's look at the answers to the questions presented on page 270 as they pertain to Eileen:

1. What knowledge, insight, or information are you seeking?

   Eileen spoke openly about her background and present life situation. However, her years of involvement with drugs and alcohol, as well as her limited work experience and education, make it difficult to help her clarify her interests and develop sound future goals. In light of her wish to continue her education, tests and inventories that give Eileen and her therapist a clearer picture of her interests and abilities would probably help Eileen determine areas of strength and interest. Exploring these could give more direction to her college coursework and increase her motivation and sense of accomplishment.

   Just as Eileen has little sense of her interests and abilities, so does she also have little sense of her own personality. Her background provides evidence of much strength. However, Eileen tends to denigrate herself and has little awareness of her personal assets. Personality inventories might present an objective view of those assets and give her language she can use to think of herself in more specific positive terms.

2. Have available sources of information, such as the intake interview, the mental status examination, psychological and academic records, and previous tests and inventories administered to this client, been reviewed first to determine whether they can provide the needed information?

   An intake interview and a mental status examination have already been conducted with Eileen; both were fruitful sources of information. However, no other tests or records are available on Eileen as an adult. High school grades, tests, and inventories probably have little validity because of the difficulties Eileen was experiencing at that time. Eileen today is very different than she was as an adolescent.

3. Does it seem likely that tests and inventories can provide important knowledge that is not available from other sources?

   Based on the answers to the previous questions, it does seem likely that tests and inventories can provide useful information that cannot be obtained from other sources. However, especially because of Eileen's cultural background and her limited interest in education as an adolescent, care must be taken in both the selection and the interpretation of the inventories.

4. How is the client likely to benefit from and react to the use of tests and inventories?

   Because of her recent interest in education and her self-referral for counseling, Eileen probably will have considerable interest in inventories and their results. The use of tests and inventories seems likely to enhance her self-awareness and self-esteem. On the other hand, the clinician should keep in mind the possibility that the use of these tools will reawaken negative reactions that Eileen had to testing as an adolescent, and she may feel judged and categorized by these tools. It is also possible that, because of her hunger for learning, Eileen will overemphasize the importance of the test results and take them too literally.

5. How will the treatment process and the therapeutic alliance be affected by the use of tests and inventories?

   Because of the potential risks inherent in using tests and inventories with Eileen, the results of those instruments should be used primarily to promote discussion and suggest new avenues for exploration. They should not be used to provide definitive answers and direction. As a vehicle for discussion, the information provided by tests and inventories can help Eileen to recognize her strengths and interests, encourage self-exploration, and possibly enhance her self-esteem.

6. What tests and inventories are most likely to yield the desired information?

   Because the goal of Eileen's testing is promoting discussion and self-esteem, instruments should be selected, at least initially, that do not have right and wrong answers but instead encourage self-awareness and exploration. Two well-established inventories that meet these criteria are the Myers-Briggs Type Indicator, a personality inventory that focuses on the normal rather than the pathological personality, and the Strong Interest Inventory, a broad-based interest inventory.

7. How should those tests and inventories be integrated into the treatment process?

   Time should be taken to develop a positive therapeutic alliance with Eileen before suggesting that she complete any inventories. In addition, Eileen needs to make rapid decisions about remaining in college; progress should be made toward resolving the current crisis before inventories are used to promote discussion. When the possibility of taking personality and interest inventories is presented to Eileen, she should be given ample information about these tools and their benefits and potential drawbacks so that she can play an active and informed role in deciding whether to take the inventories. Empowering Eileen is an important goal, and that effort should be incorporated into her treatment as much as possible. Similarly, Eileen should play an active role in the interpretation of the inventories. In addition, information already provided by Eileen on her interests and personality style should be reviewed and integrated into the discussion of the inventories. This should enable her to view the results of the inventories as providing a more accurate and comprehensive picture of herself than she has already provided to the clinician.

Results of inventories taken by Eileen Carter.   Eileen's Myers-Briggs Type Indicator (MBTI) showed that her preferences were ISFJ, reflecting the following personality styles:

- *I/Introversion*—Eileen generally focuses on her inner world and prefers being alone or with a small number of close friends or family members to being with a large group. This was a high score.
- *S/Sensing*—She is focused on facts and information and tends to be practical. However, this score was low. This suggests that Eileen also frequently uses intuition and sometimes experiences conflicts between her practical side and her intuitive side.
- *F/Feeling*—This was another high score, suggesting that Eileen is understanding and supportive, values her relationships with others, and tends to make decisions subjectively, based on her values and on the welfare of others, rather than on objective evidence and impartial analysis.
- *J/Judging*—This was a relatively low score. Eileen tends to prefer her life to be clear, structured, and well organized. However, she can be spontaneous and sometimes has difficulty meeting deadlines and following through on plans, especially when her need for structure conflicts with her wish to please and be close to others.

Eileen's overall MBTI profile is ISFJ. According to Kroeger and Thuesen (1988), people with this personality type emphasize duty and responsibility and focus their energy outward, in the service of others. They are matter-of-fact, serious, and thorough in their activities and diligently pursue their goals. They take parenting very seriously, are loyal to their partners and friends, but sometimes allow others to take advantage of them. As students, they prefer courses that are organized and practical.

This profile is consistent with and provides some clarification of what we already know about Eileen. She is dedicated to her family and is a caring and responsible parent. She has a small circle of friends and feels most comfortable with people she knows well. She currently is torn between two strong feelings, her love for her son and the joy she has discovered through attending college. She is eager to satisfy her J side and make a decision, but has difficulty making an objective assessment of her options and determining a sound plan because of the emotional conflict she is experiencing.

On the Strong Interest Inventory (SII), Eileen manifested very high interest in the Social (S) theme and moderately high interest in the Artistic (A) and Conventional (C) areas. Occupations that reflect both her MBTI personality type (ISFJ) and her SII code (SAC) include librarian, preschool teacher, medical technician, dental hygienist, and licensed practical nurse. A clear pattern of interests emerges from these scores. Eileen would probably most enjoy working in a helping capacity, perhaps with children, and perhaps in an educational or medical setting. This information, too, is compatible with what we already know about Eileen; her enthusiasm for education and for helping others and her enjoyment of children are reflected in these scores. Discussion of these personality and interest inventory results may well help Eileen develop a clearer picture of herself and identify occupations that are likely to be particularly rewarding to her.

The Use of Observation as an Assessment Tool

Clinicians use informal observations of their clients throughout the treatment process, beginning with their first telephone contact. We observe clients' tone of voice, their style of dress, their physical mannerisms and movements, their greeting, and much more. However, sometimes clinicians find it helpful to conduct a formal and structured observation of clients in addition to their informal observations. School counselors, school psychologists, and other mental health professionals who work with children are most likely to conduct structured observations.

Structured observations are particularly useful when clients meet the following criteria:

- They are unable to verbally disclose much information about themselves because of their age, their reluctance, their limited self-awareness, or their limited intelligence or communication skills.
- They present with behavioral difficulties such as hyperactivity, aggressiveness, or social withdrawal.
- They are in a classroom or other setting in which they can readily be observed.

Usually, the clinician prepares for an observation by developing a list of behavioral categories that will facilitate the assessment. For example, assessment of a child suspected of having an attention-deficit/hyperactivity disorder might include the following categories:

- Number of times child gets up from seat without permission
- Number of times child speaks out in class without being called on
- Number of times child engages in inappropriate conversation or physical interaction with another child
- Approximate number of minutes or percent of class time that child remains on task

Observational information such as this can be useful in promoting understanding of a child, especially when discrepancies exist in information already available.

CONCEPTUALIZING THE MEANING OF DEFINING MEMORIES

Yet another approach to assessment is the use of defining memories. Alfred Adler (1931), an early psychoanalyst, wrote about the importance of earliest memories, discussed in chapter 2. According to Adler, those memories that stood out in people's minds as their earliest memories were usually reflective of their lifestyles, their views of themselves, and their interactions with others. Adler emphasized that what mattered was not the reality of the memories but, rather, the way they have been preserved in people's minds.

Although early memories have special significance, people have other memories that shape who they are. Important memories often are preserved in our minds in an almost photographic way; some elements of the memory stand out sharply and clearly while others are lost in the background. This has been described as a *frozen moment*. Probably all of us have such memories that come to us often and reflect a turning point in our lives. Think about memories that are important to you and visualize them to have a better sense of the defining moments in your life. Memories of these defining moments or critical incidents come in many forms.

- They may be what we would consider *traumatic experiences*. Alonzo, for example, remembers being severely beaten by an older boy in his neighborhood. Ben, who is allergic to nuts, remembers the near-fatal reaction he had the first time he ate peanut butter.
- They may be *peak experiences* that leave an indelible impression. Jenna vividly recalls winning the academic achievement award when she graduated from fifth grade, while Denuta remembers her excitement and apprehension when her family left Poland for the United States.
- These defining memories also may reflect moments that seem *insignificant to others but are very meaningful to us*. Lulu remembers the first day her parents let her go to the playground alone and how independent and brave she felt, climbing on the play equipment without supervision. Gerard remembers the day his father accidentally ran over a squirrel that had run into the road. For Gerard, his view of his father and the dangerousness of life were embodied by that incident.

Application of Bloom's Taxonomy

Once again, the modified version of Bloom's taxonomy can be helpful in determining the significance that particular memories have for a person. That information can then be used to promote self-awareness and to guide the treatment process.

Content.   The first step is eliciting one or more memories that stand out in a person's mind. Using two or three memories typically provides a clearer and more reliable picture. Clinicians can ask people to simply recall and describe these important memories, or they can actually ask people to visualize or imagine themselves in the memory and then report what they are seeing, feeling, thinking, and doing. Several meaningful memories provided by Eileen Carter, the client who has been highlighted throughout this book, illustrate how the use of memories can enhance the treatment process.

Eileen presented three memories that stood out in her mind:

1. She recalled a time when, as an adolescent, she had been sexually involved with a man who had a motorcycle. Both had been using drugs and alcohol that evening when the man took her for a ride on his motorcycle. Along the way, they stopped to get gas for the motorcycle. They noticed that a woman who was getting gas had left her purse in the car while she paid for the gas. Eileen's boyfriend grabbed the purse and the two of them sped off on the motorcycle. Eileen vividly recalled this incident and her mixture of feelings: exhilaration at their successful crime but also shame that she had participated in such an experience.
2. Eileen remembered the first day of her first class at college. She felt a strong mixture of anticipation and anxiety. She had trouble finding a parking place and so had not had time to purchase her books before class; when the teacher referred to a page in the book and many of the other students pulled out their books to follow along, Eileen felt ashamed that she didn't have a book with her. However,

when the student sitting next to her moved closer to Eileen so they could share a book, Eileen thought that perhaps college would be a positive experience after all.

3. Of course, for Eileen, the birth of her son was a defining moment. However, even during that experience, her reactions were mixed. She felt great joy and a sense of belonging and purpose in her life because of the birth of her son. At the same time, she remembers thinking, "Now I must stay with my husband; I can never be free again."

Comprehend.   Clarifying the emotions, thoughts, and actions associated with each memory can facilitate comprehension of these defining moments. For Eileen, the emotions, thoughts, and actions associated with each memory include the following.

Memory 1—Theft of purse:
Emotions—Exhilaration, shame
Thoughts—I must be a terrible person to enjoy committing a crime.
Actions—Fled the scene of the crime, did not report the crime.

Memory 2—First day at college:
Emotions—Fear, shame, and hope
Thoughts—I don't belong here, I don't think I can succeed at college, but I really want to and perhaps people will help me enough so that I can succeed.
Actions—Did continue in college, with recognition of her need to be better prepared and to ask others for help.

Memory 3—Birth of son:
Emotions—Joy but also a sense of being trapped
Thoughts—Now my life has meaning; I have someone to love who loves me, but I have lost my freedom in the process. Why can't I be contented with what I have?
Actions—I gave birth to my son and resolved to stay with my husband.

Organize.   The information obtained from the content and the comprehension of the memories can be organized according to themes. The following themes are reflected in Eileen's memories:

- *Conflicting emotions*—Joy is mitigated by guilt, shame, or regret.
- *Conflicting choices*—Part of Eileen is drawn toward socially acceptable behavior (obeying the law, becoming a wife and mother) but another part of her longs to break free and defy social conventions.
- *Low self-esteem*—A confused sense of self.
- *Other-directedness*—Concern with how she is perceived by others.

Analyze and synthesize.   The conflicts in Eileen's memories reflect the split in her life. During her adolescence and early adulthood, she made some self-destructive choices: she misused drugs and alcohol, she became dependent on men who abused her, she had and aborted two unwanted pregnancies, she rejected her family, and she even engaged in criminal behavior. However, all that changed with her marriage and the birth of her son. According to Eileen, "I became a totally different person." In reality, however, external influences have always largely determined Eileen's life. In her youth, she molded herself in the image of her peer group, behaving in socially unacceptable ways even though they felt shameful to her. Now, she has molded herself into the image of the middle-class wife and mother, dressing and acting the part as much as possible. Never has she figured out who she is, nor has she been able to integrate the two sides of her personality into a rewarding whole.

Interpret.   The conflict described previously seems to be at the root of Eileen's current difficulties. She believes that she should be the perfect wife and mother, never deviating from what she perceives as the boundaries of that role. Not only is she driven by a desire to be well regarded by others and achieve a socially acceptable role for herself, she is also driven to counteract her own painful childhood experiences. She wants her son to have the good parenting and stable home she missed and does not want him to experience the turmoil and self-doubts she experienced. However, the side of Eileen that is a free spirit and that longs for independence and achievement has found college to be a great source of gratification. While college appears to be a healthy and growth-promoting choice for Eileen, the side of her that adheres rigidly to her prototype of the perfect wife and mother is uneasy about her decision to attend college. Reconciling her wish to attend college with her view of herself as a perfect wife and mother became especially difficult for Eileen when that choice conflicted with her husband's preferences. Also difficult for her was the realization that, because of her husband's lack of cooperation, Eileen would occasionally need child care for her son while she attended college. Eileen's self-doubts, her sense of shame, her reliance on others to tell her how to lead her life, and her lack of healthy role models in childhood all made it extremely difficult for her to integrate the two sides of herself and find a healthy and rewarding balance of roles in her life.

Application and intervention.   This analysis of the defining moments in Eileen's life provides important insights that inform the treatment process. Clearly, Eileen needs help in the following areas:

- understanding and accepting both sides of her personality
- integrating the two sides of her personality into a healthy self-image
- developing the ability to act on that positive and integrated self-image
- making choices that are rewarding to her, that take account of both societal norms and the needs and values of her loved ones, and that reflect her own creation of her life rather than an unfulfilling effort to fit into a stereotype.

As you can probably see, eliciting and analyzing defining memories can be a fruitful source of information and can contribute greatly to the treatment planning process. Exercises at the end of this chapter will afford you the opportunity to identify and analyze several of your own important memories and to apply the modified version of Bloom's taxonomy to clusters of important memories presented by others.

The next section will focus on obtaining an in-depth understanding of clients and identifying their focal concerns or problem. This process is similar to analyzing important recollections. Having learned to analyze memories will make it easier for you to work collaboratively with clients to understand them more fully and obtain a clear and treatment-ready definition of their concerns.

CASE CONCEPTUALIZATION AND PROBLEM DEFINITION

I recently met with Jean, a 37-year-old woman in crisis, who was seeking counseling. Jean was married and had two sons, aged 10 and 12. She had been diagnosed with ovarian cancer about a month before we had our first session. Jean was understandably upset about her diagnosis and was having difficulty making treatment decisions. In addition, she reported that her children, both diagnosed with attention-deficit/hyperactivity disorder, had become almost uncontrollable and very disruptive in the classroom. Jean's husband, who had a history of alcohol abuse, had resumed drinking and was often withdrawn and uncommunicative. Jean was apprehensive about telling her mother of Jean's diagnosis; her mother, who was in her 70s, had a heart condition and was not in good health. Jean's father had died of prostate cancer 12 years earlier.

Jean very much believed in the value of counseling and psychotherapy and, as a result, had seen many mental health professionals to help her deal with her current crisis. She had met with the school psychologist to discuss her sons' behavior, social workers at the continuing care facility where her mother lived, an alcohol counselor, a family therapist, and a specialist in helping people cope with cancer. By the time she saw me, Jean was overwhelmed, not only by the many stressors in her life but also by the conflicting interactions she had with all these mental health professionals. Apparently, each one had viewed Jean's situation from the perspective of his or her own mental health specialization. This was not surprising, since Jean' presented her concerns differently to each one.

In the worlds of counseling and psychotherapy, more is often not better. More problems, more clinicians, more interventions, and even more sessions can exacerbate a person's difficulties rather than ameliorate them. What is necessary is to develop a clear description of a person's problems and a conceptualization of the case, considering all symptoms, difficulties, and areas of concern. Once the problem has been clearly described and the case holistically conceptualized, appropriate interventions can more easily be identified. According to Mayfield, Kardash, and Kivligham (1999, p. 504), "Client conceptualization is an important skill. . . . In forming a client conceptualization, counselors take in a vast array of client data (symptoms, familial background, etc.) and organize this information into a model of the client." According to Loganbill and Stoltenberg (1983, p. 235), "case conceptualization involves the integration of cognitive, behavioral, emotional, and interpersonal aspects of the client, which can be synthesized into a comprehensive understanding of his or her current functioning." Case conceptualization entails understanding a person's story, making sense of that person's life, and formulating a central issue. In case conceptualization, clinicians seek to answer core questions such as, "What might cause this person to feel/think/act as he or she is?"

Research suggests that beginning clinicians often have difficulty with case conceptualization (and I suspect that is a challenge for many advanced clinicians as well). Pfeiffer, Whelan, and Martin (2000), for example, looked at how doctoral students in psychology made decisions about the nature of clients' difficulties. Early in the treatment process, the doctoral students formulated a hypothesis as to clients' central concerns. This can be a helpful starting point if clinicians then consider both confirming and disconfirming information. However, confirmatory bias led these clinicians to focus on information that supported their hypotheses and to overlook discrepant information. Schwitzer (1996,

p. 259) agreed with this finding and concluded, "Novice clinicians, especially, typically lack the conceptual structures and extensive general knowledge of counseling required for making effective decisions. . ." Keep in mind that you might find the skill of case conceptualization to be a challenging one. However, the work you have already done on understanding background and context (chapter 5) and clients' strong emotions (chapter 6) should facilitate the development of your case conceptualization skills.

Information Needed for Case Conceptualization

Before you can accurately and clearly conceptualize a case, you must gather information on the client and on that person's context. Intake interviews, the mental status examination, tests and inventories, observations, and previous client records all provide information that contributes to a useful case conceptualization.

Several models have been developed to facilitate the process of case conceptualization. These will be discussed in the next section. First, we will review the essential ingredients of all case conceptualizations. The following information should be obtained about a person before moving forward to develop a case conceptualization:

- overt and presenting concerns
- covert and unacknowledged difficulties
- current lifestyle
- relevant background information
- nature, intensity, and impact of characteristic emotional responses
- helpful and dysfunctional thoughts, especially those that are recurrent or pervasive
- constructive and self-destructive actions, especially habits, impulsive behaviors, and violent and self-injurious behavior
- context of person and problems
- support systems and resources
- multicultural considerations
- barriers to change, including reluctance, transference, defensiveness, secondary gains, lack of information, or misunderstanding of the treatment process
- other factors that worsen symptoms or block progress
- client's accomplishments, strengths, and assets
- other factors that enhance functioning or promote progress

Models of Case Conceptualization

Several models of case conceptualization are presented here, along with illustrative examples. In working with your clients, you can use one of the following models or develop a model of your own. Models that are helpful in facilitating case conceptualization typically meet the following three criteria:

- They organize a broad range of client information into a small number of categories.
- They present a concise understanding of the client.
- They facilitate the processes of diagnosis and treatment planning (discussed next in this chapter).

The Learning Opportunities at the end of this chapter will give you experience in case conceptualization and allow you to apply one or more of the following models.

Concept Mapping

Concept mapping is a way of organizing many salient client statements into a small number of categories and then identifying the connections and patterns among those categories (Mayfield, Kardash, & Kivligham, 1999). This process begins with a listing of important client statements. The case of Jean, the woman diagnosed with ovarian cancer presented previously, will be used to illustrate this process. Initially, the multiple categories listed on page 280 will be used as follows to organize important statements made by Jean.

Overt and presenting concerns
1. I'm having great difficulty coping with my diagnosis of ovarian cancer.
2. I'm feeling depressed and anxious.
3. My family is not helping me but is actually making my situation worse.

Covert and unacknowledged difficulties
4. My husband and I sleep in separate bedrooms and rarely spend time together.
5. Our house is always in chaos.
6. I know that alcohol is bad for me, but I need something to help me relax.
7. At least I have some time off from work; I couldn't deal with that pressure, too.
8. I usually feel like I'm swimming against a strong current and just managing to hold my own.

Current lifestyle
9. We live in a three-bedroom apartment on the outskirts of town.
10. The house is much too small for us and is always a mess.
11. My husband works at home.
12. I'm employed as a teacher's aide in an elementary school.
13. Every day it's just get up, get the kids off to school, go to work, make dinner, get everybody to bed.
14. We manage, but I don't see the light at the end of the tunnel.

Relevant background information
15. My father, two of my mother's sisters, and a close friend all died of cancer.
16. My mother and I have never been close.
17. My mother has been treated for depression for many years.
18. My father doted on me. I was devastated when he died.
19. My mother always told me I didn't have much going for me so I'd better get married as soon as I had the chance.
20. My parents worked really hard to make ends meet; I wanted a different life for myself but I don't have it.

Nature, intensity, and impact of characteristic emotional responses
21. I'm a lot like my mother; I may even have inherited her depression.
22. I've always had trouble making decisions. Now I have a life-or-death decision to make and I just can't figure out the right thing to do.

23. I've been crying at least two or three times a day.
24. I've even thought about killing myself, but that seems stupid when I'm working so hard to survive cancer. Maybe I should just let the cancer kill me.
25. I almost never get angry but every once in awhile I really explode.

Helpful and dysfunctional thoughts, especially those that are recurrent or pervasive
26. I always thought something awful would happen to me; I'm just an unlucky person.
27. I'm a strong person, but I'm feeling like I can't handle any more.
28. I must have done something pretty bad to deserve this.
29. If I die, it will destroy everyone, my husband, my children, and my mother.
30. I often wish this would all just end.

Constructive and self-destructive actions, especially habits, impulsive behaviors, and violent and self-injurious behavior
31. A few drinks are the only thing that gets me through the day.
32. I just live from moment to moment, never really looking down the road.
33. Sometimes my children are so difficult, I really lose my temper and hit them so hard they can't breathe.
34. I avoid my husband as much as possible.

Context of person and problems
35. Other than a few people I see at work, I don't talk much to anyone, not even my family.
36. I do have confidence in my physicians, but when they disagree about my treatment I just feel lost.
37. I do my job all right, but I sometimes feel like I'm just going through the motions, and that's not fair to the kids I work with.
38. At least money for my medical care isn't a problem; we do have good health insurance and sick leave at work.
39. It's taking care of my family that worries me.

Support systems and resources
40. I really haven't had any close friends and associates since I lost my father and my friend Josie.
41. I have a younger brother but he's pretty useless, always after some wealthy woman or some get-rich-quick scheme.
42. My mother can't even take care of herself, let alone help me.
43. My husband acts like he's the one with cancer, not me, always complaining about how badly life has treated him and turning to the bottle.
44. My husband should be taking care of me instead of vice versa.
45. I've tried to get my kids to help out around the house, but it's more trouble than it's worth.

Multicultural considerations
46. I was raised Jewish but haven't been to synagogue since my father died.
47. I know that gynecological cancers are more common among Jewish women and my aunts both died of breast cancer. Could this be hereditary? Does that mean I'm destined to die of this disease, too?

48. My parents were always very concerned about prejudice against Jews but, of course, they grew up during the Second World War.

49. There aren't any other Jewish families in our neighborhood. I tell my children not to talk about their religion so they won't be discriminated against. We even celebrate Christmas like everyone else in the neighborhood. That really feels hypocritical.

Barriers to change including reluctance, transference, defensiveness, secondary gains, lack of information, or misunderstanding of the treatment process

50. I think that counseling is a place where people tell you the right things to do.

51. I've talked to lots of therapists but they all tell me something different; how do I know who to listen to?

52. I don't like to sit around and talk about things; I want to get moving.

53. My doctors say I should have decided about my treatment two weeks ago.

54. I don't have a lot of time so I hope this counseling thing isn't going to take too long.

Other factors that worsen symptoms or block progress

55. I was barely hanging on before my diagnosis; I don't know how I can handle one more thing.

56. I wish someone would just make the right decision for me.

57. My husband and children are driving me crazy; I feel like running away from home.

Client's accomplishments, strengths, and assets

58. Even though my mother treated me badly all my life, I never cut her off and I'm still helping her.

59. My children may drive me crazy, but I love them and I'd do anything for them.

60. I'm the teacher's aide in the toughest class in the school, but somehow I do all right and the teacher really seems to appreciate me.

61. I was a pretty good student all through school.

62. I am a strong person and have coped with a great deal.

63. I'll do anything I can to help my family and myself.

Other factors that enhance functioning or promote progress

64. My prognosis is pretty good.

65. My job is stable.

66. My husband and I may have our differences but we're going to stay together.

Organization of these statements into a concept map with fewer categories yields the following:

Family of Origin/Family Dynamics—(items 3, 15, 16, 17, 18, 20, 21, 41, 42, 43, 46, 48, 58, 59)—Jean came from a hard-working Jewish family. She describes her father as loving and helpful, her mother as critical and demanding, and her brother as self-centered. She believes she may have inherited both cancer and depression from her family. Current family includes two very active sons and a distant husband who abuses alcohol. Jean seems to be the mainstay in her current family just as she was the good child in her family of origin.

Stressors in Current Life—(items 1, 7, 22, 29, 36, 37, 39, 44, 53, 54, 57)—The primary stressors in Jean's life are her diagnosis with ovarian cancer, her need to make a rapid decision regarding her treatment, and her fear of death as a result of cancer. She also experiences stress as a result of her children's behavior, her husband's withdrawal and use of alcohol, and the demands of her job.

Factors Exacerbating Difficulties—(items 2, 4, 5, 6, 8, 9, 10, 11, 19, 25, 26, 27, 28, 30, 34, 35, 40, 45, 47, 49, 51, 55)—Jean lost both her father and a good friend, apparently the strongest members of her support system. At present, she seems to have no helpful support systems, she lives in a chaotic environment, has little free time, and views herself as having primary responsibility for her family. She is not involved with her religion and, in fact, conceals her Jewishness from others. She is experiencing depression and anxiety, contributing to her difficulty in making important decisions.

Strengths, Coping Strategies, and Behaviors—(items 7, 12, 14, 23, 24, 31, 32, 33, 38, 50, 52, 56, 60, 61, 62, 63, 64, 65, 66)—Jean is an intelligent person who is hard working and action oriented. Although she wishes she could escape from her difficult situation, she is willing to do all she can to help herself and her family. She has consulted many specialists to figure out how to help herself. At the same time, she is not introspective, looks to others to give her answers, becomes impatient and angry, and uses alcohol to relieve her anxiety.

Interrelationships of Concept Map—Jean's recent diagnosis with cancer and issues related to that diagnosis are the core of Jean's concerns. However, these stressors have been worsened by the underlying problems in her family of origin and current family, as well as by the secondary stressors she is experiencing, including her work situation, her limited support system, and her depression and anxiety. Her typical efforts to help herself have been moderately effective but may not be up to the challenge of coping with cancer.

Case Conceptualization—Jean is coping with a great many difficulties, including the immediate stressor of cancer and long-term stressors from both her current family and her family of origin. In many ways, Jean's current life replicates patterns in her family of origin; she is the responsible one, she seeks to please the other family members, and she copes with cancer and depression. As in her family of origin, she has limited resources and support systems. However, in her family of origin, she was rewarded with the love of her father. Her husband apparently has not shown her caring in the same way, and Jean seems angry and resentful about this. Nevertheless, she seeks to push her needs aside, is committed to her family, and keeps trying. Unfortunately, the added stress of cancer has been almost too much for her, and her already tenuous coping skills are letting her down, allowing her depression and anxiety to surface and leaving her immobilized and searching frantically for answers.

The process of organizing a broad array of diverse client statements into broad categories, then into narrower categories, and finally into a case conceptualization is one approach to deepening your understanding of a client and moving toward a diagnosis and treatment plan. Clinical factor analysis is another approach.

Clinical Factor Analysis

Emmerson and Thackwray-Emmerson (1992) developed an approach to case conceptualization that involves an analysis of clients' statements. Their model "attempts to translate the principles of statistical factor analysis into an applicable clinical process of identifying factors or themes in therapy to assist in case conceptualization" (p. 404). It consists of the following steps:

1. Construct a list of client's emotional statements over the course of at least one session. Client's voice quality, body language, and statement content are all used to indicate emotional statements.
2. Rate the level of emotional intensity and reactivity of each statement using the symbols L for low, M for medium, and H for high. These symbols equate to numbers: L = 1, M = 2, H = 3.
3. Group statements that have a common theme.
4. Analyze and name each theme as succinctly and clearly as possible. Each theme will be viewed as a factor, representing the statements it includes.
5. Average the emotional intensity ratings for each factor.
6. Rank the factors according to their emotional intensity ratings and use this ranking to develop a case conceptualization and to identify and prioritize client needs.

An application of clinical factor analysis to a session with Jean, the client in the previous example, yielded the following rank-ordered factors, listed along with their average emotional intensity ratings:

- Cancer and related treatment issues—3.0
- Feeling overwhelmed by my life—2.77
- Concern about my children's welfare—2.65
- My relationship with my husband—2.53
- Limited support systems—2.23
- Job-related stress—2.03

This list clarifies treatment priorities and facilitates development of a sound treatment plan.

The Inverted Pyramid Heuristic

Schwitzer (1996) suggested an inverted pyramid heuristic to facilitate case conceptualization. This model provides a stepwise method for understanding people's concerns. When applied to Jean, this model looks like the following:

Step 1. Problem Identification and List of Client Concerns
   Diagnosis with ovarian cancer • Need to make treatment decision • Fear of dying
   Depression • Anxiety • Overactive children • Aged, ailing mother • Stressful job
   Husband withdrawn, abusing alcohol • Limited support systems • Self-doubts
   Tendency to look to others for answers • Difficulty with problem solving, insight
   Concern about children's future • Pessimism • Some abuse of alcohol • Weak coping

Step 2. Organize Concerns into Logical Thematic Groupings or Constellations
   Medical concerns • Lack of family support and closeness
   Emotional dysfunction • Coping with many demands

Step 3. Theoretical Views of Thematic Groupings
   Self-doubts and other-directedness (**Humanistic Perspective**)
   Impaired attachment, poor role models (**Psychodynamic Perspective**)

Overreliance on nonproductive and impulsive behaviors (**Behavioral Perspective**)

Seeking perfection in self, others, options (**Cognitive Perspective**)

Step 4. Narrowed Inferences: Underlying Difficulties

Limited sense of self, derived from pleasing others

Lack of support and validation, sharpened by cancer diagnosis

This approach to case conceptualization is a complex one, requiring knowledge of theoretical models and considerable insight. However, it, too, facilitates efforts to hone in on central client concerns.

Stevens and Morris's Format for Case Conceptualization

The format for case conceptualization developed by Stevens and Morris (1995) consists of 14 components, reminiscent of a mental status exam. However, these components are carefully sequenced, moving from the observational to the inferential. This enables clinicians to gradually deepen their understanding of a person. The 14 components include:

1. Relevant background information (e.g., age, physical appearance, living arrangements, education, medical history, family background, cultural and religious background)
2. Nature and severity of presenting concerns and current stressors
3. Content of sessions, especially important themes
4. Verbal style of presentation (e.g., tone of voice, fluency, quantity and rate of verbalization)
5. Nonverbal behavior (e.g., eye contact, facial expressions, body movements, posture)
6. Nature, intensity, duration, and range of client's emotions and their relationship to verbal content
7. Clinician's experience of and reactions to client
8. Client-clinician interactions and roles in treatment process
9. Results of tests and inventories, mental status exam, behavioral assessments, records, creative products
10. Multiaxial diagnosis according to the *Diagnostic and Statistical Manual of Mental Disorders*
11. Inferences and assumptions, including a working model of the client's difficulties and factors that contributed to their development
12. Short- and long-term treatment goals, growing out of a clinical understanding of client's difficulties
13. Identification of interventions that will lead to accomplishment of goals
14. Evaluation of outcomes

This model will not be illustrated here because it repeats much of the material that already has been presented. However, you might draw on what you know about Jean to develop your own illustration of this model.

The Modified Version of Bloom's Taxonomy

The now-familiar modified version of Bloom's taxonomy can also be used as a structure to facilitate the development of a case conceptualization. The learning opportunities at the end of this chapter will afford you the opportunity to prepare case conceptualizations according to Bloom's taxonomy and several of the other models presented here.

DIAGNOSIS

Diagnosis of mental disorders, based on the latest edition of the *Diagnostic and Statistical Manual of Mental Disorders (DSM)* (American Psychiatric Association, 2000a), is one of the most essential clinical skills. According to Hinkle (1994, p. 174), "At the foundation of effective mental health care is the establishment of a valid psychodiagnosis." An accurate diagnosis, derived from a careful and valid case conceptualization, contributes to the treatment process in many ways (Seligman, 1996a).

- Diagnosis of a mental disorder provides important information about the symptoms associated with that disorder as well as the probable course of the disorder.
- Information provided about a diagnosis in the *DSM* can deepen the clinician's knowledge and understanding of age, gender, familial, ethnic, and cultural factors related to that diagnosis.
- Helping people to recognize that they have a mental disorder can reduce their guilt and self-blame, promote greater self-awareness, provide reassurance that they are not alone in their difficulties, and increase both their hopefulness and their engagement in the treatment process.
- With knowledge of a client's diagnosis, clinicians can make good use of the extensive research literature on treatment effectiveness to determine those treatment systems and strategies that are most likely to ameliorate a particular mental disorder.

Knowledge and appropriate use of diagnosis also can help clinicians in many important ways:

- Diagnostic terminology is a common language that enables clinicians from all specializations and theoretical orientations to communicate with each other and with insurance companies providing payment for their services.
- Records of diagnosis, treatment plans, and treatment outcomes provide a way for clinicians to demonstrate accountability, determine their areas of effectiveness and weakness, improve their work, and protect themselves in the event of malpractice lawsuits.

Clearly, knowledge of diagnosis and the *DSM* can be very beneficial to clients and clinicians. At the same time, the use, validity, and reliability of the *DSM* still needs improvement. Imprecisely defined disorders, clinician subjectivity and lack of knowledge of the *DSM*, and the frequent need to make rapid diagnoses to satisfy mental health agencies and insurance companies can lead to erroneous diagnoses. Clinicians should be sure they have the training and supervision they need to make accurate diagnoses.

Although a detailed presentation of the *DSM* is beyond the scope of this book, an overview of that volume will be provided here to introduce readers to the skill of diagnosis and the range of mental disorders. A more detailed discussion of the *DSM* is provided in other readings (Seligman, 1996a; Seligman, 1998).

Multiaxial Assessment

The *Diagnostic and Statistical Manual of Mental Disorders* provides a multiaxial format for diagnoses. This format consists of five axes or perspectives that afford clinicians the opportunity to view clients holistically.

> **Axis I: Clinical Disorders and Other Conditions That May Be a Focus of Clinical Attention**—Nearly all of the mental disorders are listed on this axis, including some of the most common diagnoses such as mood disorders, anxiety disorders, adjustment disorders, and substance-related disorders.
>
> **Axis II: Personality Disorders and Mental Retardation**—As indicated by the title of this axis, only two categories of disorder are included on axis II, personality disorders and mental retardation (along with borderline intellectual functioning, also reflecting impairment in intellectual functioning). Axis II encompasses disorders that, by definition, are long-standing, often lifelong. Axis I, on the other hand, includes disorders that tend to be time-limited, although many of them may continue for many years.
>
> **Axis III: General Medical Conditions**—This axis includes medically verified physical conditions as well as physical signs and symptoms that may be related to or are having an impact on people's emotional functioning.
>
> **Axis IV: Psychosocial and Environmental Problems**—This axis is the place where clinicians list the stressors in people's lives. This axis may include the following:
> - recent and circumscribed stressors such as a relocation or job loss
> - enduring stressors such as coping with a chronic illness or an abusive marriage
> - stressors that occurred many years ago but that are still relevant to a client's mental condition such as a combat experience that led to prolonged post-traumatic stress disorder
>
> **Axis V: Global Assessment of Functioning (GAF) Scale**—On this axis, clinicians rate a client's current level of functioning on a 1–100 scale. The higher the number, the better is the functioning. This axis is useful in assessing the severity of people's difficulties, determining the nature and level of treatment they require, and measuring their progress during treatment.

The following is the multiaxial assessment for Eileen Carter, the client who has been presented throughout this book:

Axis I:
     309.28 Adjustment Disorder with Mixed Anxiety and Depressed Mood
     300.4 Dysthymic Disorder, moderate
     304.80 Polysubstance Dependence, Prior History
Axis II: Dependent Personality Traits
Axis III: 424.0 Mitral Valve Prolapse

Axis IV:
- Problems with primary support group: Conflict with husband
- Educational problems: Barriers related to continuing education

Axis V: GAF = 63 (current)

In this multiaxial assessment, axis I reflects Eileen's anxiety and discouragement in response to her husband's efforts to stop her from attending college (Adjustment Disorder), her long-standing moderate depression (Dysthymic Disorder), and her prior history of misusing multiple drugs and alcohol. Her tendency to be other-directed, to defer to the men in her life, and to involve herself in unhealthy relationships is reflected on axis II as dependent personality traits. Axis III alerts the clinician to the presence of a medical problem, mitral valve prolapse, which can produce symptoms resembling an anxiety attack. Axis IV identifies the current stressors in Eileen's life. Finally, axis V, indicating that Eileen has a Global Assessment of Functioning Score of 63, suggests that she has some mild-to-moderate symptoms but is functioning fairly well overall.

Determining the Presence of a Mental Disorder

Although nearly everyone who presents for counseling or psychotherapy has problems or difficulties, not everyone has a mental disorder. Determining whether a mental disorder is present and, if it is, identifying the nature and severity of that disorder is essential to effective treatment. The latest edition of the *Diagnostic and Statistical Manual of Mental Disorders* (*DSM-IV-TR*) (American Psychiatric Association, 2000a) defines a mental disorder in the following way:

> In *DSM-IV*, each of the mental disorders is conceptualized as a clinically significant behavioral or psychological syndrome or pattern that occurs in an individual and that is associated with present distress (e.g., a painful symptom) or disability (i.e., impairment in one or more important areas of functioning) or with a significantly increased risk of suffering death, pain, disability, or an important loss of freedom. (p. xxxi)

This definition suggests the following series of questions that can help clinicians determine whether a mental disorder is present:

- Does the person manifest "clinically significant symptoms" such as depression, anxiety, or impulsive and harmful behaviors?
- Have the duration and severity of the symptoms been such that the person meets the criteria for one of the mental disorders listed in the *DSM*? Although several of the disorders in the *DSM* such as major depressive disorder, brief psychotic disorder, and adjustment disorder have a minimum duration of days or weeks, the most common minimum duration for mental disorders is six months. In addition, although some people with mental disorders will have axis V GAF scores that are above 70, most people with mental disorders have GAF scores that are below 70, reflecting at least mild impairment.
- Is the person experiencing one or more of the following?
  - Significant present distress (e.g., overwhelming sadness, suicidal ideation, agitation and anxiety)
  - Disability or impairment in functioning (e.g., problems in concentration, impaired performance at work or home, exhaustion)

- Risk of suffering death, pain, disability, or an important loss of freedom (e.g., extreme restriction of food intake, criminal activity, suicidal ideation, use of harmful substances)

Meeting these criteria suggests that a mental disorder may well be present. However, presenting symptoms that reflect what the *DSM* calls an "expectable and culturally sanctioned response to a particular event" (p. xxxi) should generally not be viewed as constituting a mental disorder. For example, many women from Hispanic cultural backgrounds present attitudes and behaviors that suggest a dependent personality disorder. However, if these women enjoy their traditional role, function well in that role, and have adaptive flexibility, they should not be viewed as having a mental disorder but, rather, as thinking and acting in ways that reflect the norms of their culture. Multicultural counseling competence is necessary for skillfulness in both diagnosis and treatment.

The 17 Categories of Mental Disorders

In addition to the multiaxial assessment format, the *DSM* provides 17 categories of disorders, allowing clinicians to identify, describe, and better understand the nature of people's difficulties. A thorough description of these categories is beyond the scope of this book. Readers are referred to other sources for that information (American Psychiatric Association, 2000a; Seligman, 1998). However, a brief overview of those 17 categories is presented here so that you will have some understanding of the nature of the mental disorders included in the *DSM*.

Disorders Usually First Diagnosed in Infancy, Childhood, or Adolescence

This is the most heterogeneous category in the *DSM* because it is organized according to typical age at onset rather than similarity of symptoms. This is an important category for school counselors, school psychologists, and other clinicians who focus their work on the treatment of children, adolescents, and families. This category also has importance for clinicians who only treat adults; although disorders in this category generally begin during the first two decades of our lives, they may continue into and through adulthood, often in a somewhat altered form. In addition, many adults have a history of mental disorders in childhood. Understanding the implications of these diagnoses for adults can be invaluable to clinicians.

Clinicians working with young people are most likely to encounter three disorders in this category: attention-deficit/hyperactivity disorder (ADHD), conduct disorder, and oppositional defiant disorder (ODD):

- *Attention-deficit/hyperactivity disorder*—Difficulty in concentration and attention and impairment in social, academic, and occupational functioning characterize people with ADHD. Those with the hyperactive-impulsive type of this disorder tend to be in constant motion and often interrupt or intrude on others. Those with the inattentive type of ADHD tend to be careless and distractible, having difficulty with organization and careful listening.
- *Conduct disorder*—This disorder is reflected by a persistent pattern of violating laws, rules, and social norms. People with this disorder typically engage in be-

haviors that are aggressive, destructive, deceitful, and seriously disobedient (e.g., repeatedly running away from home overnight).

- *Oppositional defiant disorder*—ODD is often a precursor of conduct disorder and involves less serious violations of rules and norms. People with this disorder typically are temperamental, argumentative, angry and vindictive, touchy, and deliberately disobedient. They can present quite a challenge to their parents and teachers.

Other prevalent disorders included in this first section of the *DSM* are mental retardation, learning disorders, motor skills disorder, communication disorders, tic disorders, elimination disorders, separation anxiety disorder, and reactive attachment disorder. Less common disorders in this section are pervasive developmental disorder (e.g., autistic disorder, Asperger's disorder), feeding and eating disorders of infancy or early childhood, selective mutism, and stereotypic movement disorder.

Delirium, Dementia, and Amnestic and Other Cognitive Mental Disorders

Disorders in this section reflect cognitive impairment (brain injury or malfunction), generally have a medical cause (e.g., Alzheimer's disease, stroke, a neurological disease, head injury, HIV disease), and nearly always include memory impairment. Neurologists or psychiatrists rather than nonmedical clinicians usually diagnose these disorders.

Mental Disorders Due to a General Medical Condition Not Elsewhere Classified

Disorders in this category reflect mental and emotional symptoms that are the physiological consequences of a medical condition. This category does not encompass people's emotional reactions to upsetting medical symptoms or diagnoses but rather the direct physiological consequences of medical conditions. Like the previous category of disorders, a physician generally should diagnose these disorders.

Substance-Related Disorders

This important category of the *DSM* includes harmful use of drugs or alcohol (*substance abuse* and *substance dependence*) and the side effects and emotional symptoms stemming from the harmful use (*substance-induced disorders*). To make a diagnosis from this category, clinicians need to determine what substances are misused, whether the pattern meets the criteria for abuse or the more severe dependence, whether physiological dependence is present, and which secondary or induced disorders (if any) are present. Common induced disorders include intoxication, withdrawal, and substance-induced mood disorders, anxiety, or psychotic symptoms. Misuse of drugs and alcohol is rampant in the United States and can be found in almost every setting, ranging from elementary schools to geriatric facilities. Consequently, knowledge of this category of the *DSM* is important to all clinicians.

Schizophrenia and Other Psychotic Disorders

Schizoaffective disorder, schizophrenia, delusional disorder, brief psychotic disorder, and other similar disorders are included in this category. These psychotic disorders all are characterized by impairment in awareness of reality. Symptoms commonly associated with these disorders include hallucinations, delusions, disorganized speech, and catatonic or disorganized behavior. Hallucinations are sensory experiences that are in-consistent with reality (e.g., hearing voices when no one is present, feeling insects crawling all over one's body when none are present, believing incorrectly that one emits a foul odor). Delusions are beliefs that also are not consistent with reality and can include a variety of themes such as persecution, grandiosity, and romantic rela-tionships. Because medication is the primary treatment for most psychotic disorders, their diagnosis tends to fall to psychiatrists. However, nonmedical clinicians are often part of a treatment team for people with psychotic disorders.

Mood Disorders

Mood disorders are probably the most common disorders encountered by clinicians in both inpatient and outpatient settings. One or both of the following symptoms charac-terize mood disorders:

- *Depression,* reflected by such symptoms as sadness, excessive guilt, hopeless-ness, irritability, loss of pleasure in usual activities, impaired eating and sleep-ing, thoughts of death
- An abnormally *elevated mood* (mania or hypomania), typically reflected by such symptoms as grandiosity, anger and irritability, rapid and pressured speech, di-minished need for sleep, and unwise and even dangerous decisions and behav-iors (e.g., investing all one's savings in rejuvenating a long-abandoned oil well)

The nature, severity, and duration of the symptoms of depression and/or elevated mood determine whether the disorder is a

- *Major depressive disorder*—This disorder is characterized by at least two weeks of severe depression.
- *Dysthymic disorder*—Characterized by moderate depression, dysthymic disor-der, by definition, lasts for at least two years in adults and one year in youth.
- *Bipolar disorders*—These disorders include a combination of elevated and de-pressed mood episodes.

Determining the precipitant of an episode of a mood disorder can be especially in-formative; episodes can be caused by seasonally related changes in available light, by hormonal changes experienced postpartum, by an actual or perceived rejection, or by many other factors.

Anxiety Disorders

Like mood disorders, anxiety disorders are a common reason for people to seek treatment, especially in outpatient settings. Symptoms of anxiety usually are both emotional (e.g., worry, hypervigilance, fear, apprehension) and physical (e.g., shortness of breath, heart palpitations, trembling, chills, intestinal discomfort). Clinicians should be sure to rule out a medical cause for these symptoms before diagnosing an anxiety disorder.

Anxiety disorders in the *DSM* include:

- *Panic disorder*—The primary characteristic of this disorder is attacks of over-whelming panic, at least some of which are unexpected and have no apparent cause. This experience can lead people to worry about having additional attacks and to avoid places they believe might trigger such attacks (agoraphobia).

- *Agoraphobia without a history of panic disorder*—This disorder is characterized by avoidance of certain places or situations out of a fear of having paniclike symptoms, although the person has not meet the criteria for a panic disorder. People with severe forms of agoraphobia may be housebound, relying on others for all their transactions with the outside world.
- *Specific phobia*—This disorder is characterized by an excessive fear of a particular stimulus, leading to avoidance behavior that causes impairment. A strong anxiety response results, should the person inadvertently encounter the stimulus. Common types of specific phobias include inordinate fear of dogs, insects, snakes, heights, thunderstorms, injections, and flying.
- *Social phobia*—Like other phobias, social phobia involves an excessive fear; here, it is the fear of humiliation or embarrassment in social or performance situations. Fear of public speaking is a common type of social phobia.
- *Obsessive-compulsive disorder*—This disorder involves recurrent obsessions (intrusive thoughts) or compulsions (driven behaviors) that cause significant distress or impairment. Common obsessions focus on fear of contamination, persistent doubts, need to have things in a particular order, and unacceptable sexual or aggressive urges. Common compulsions, including washing and checking, typically neutralize and counteract the obsessions. Although people are generally aware of the unreasonable nature of their obsessions and compulsions, they feel unable to curtail those symptoms.
- *Posttraumatic stress disorder (PTSD) and acute stress disorder*—Both of these disorders involve maladaptive responses to traumatic experiences such as rape, a war experience, a natural disaster, or an accident. People with these disorders persistently reexperience the trauma in thoughts or dreams, avoid reminders of the trauma, withdraw from others, and experience anxiety symptoms. Acute stress disorder begins shortly after the traumatic experience and lasts no longer than a month while PTSD typically lasts longer and may have a delayed onset.
- *Generalized anxiety disorder (GAD)*—GAD involves pervasive and excessive anxiety and worry, lasting at least 6 months. Both emotional and physical symptoms of anxiety are present.

Somatoform Disorders

These disorders might be thought of as psychosomatic disorders, although clients tend to find that term offensive. In somatoform disorders, people believe they have a serious medical illness or physical symptom and may experience associated pain and disability. However, medical examination and testing provide no evidence for the presence of the physical symptoms or disorder. Probably the best known types of somatoform disorder include *hypochondriasis* (belief that one has a serious disease, based on misinterpretation of physical symptoms) and *conversion disorder* (reflected by a sensory or motor dysfunction such as blindness or paralysis). *Body dysmorphic disorder,* a somatoform disorder in which people are preoccupied with a slight or imagined defect in appearance, has received increasing attention in recent years and may well be on the increase.

Factitious Disorder

People with this disorder also present with unverified medical and/or psychological difficulties. However, the difference between people with somatoform disorders and those with factitious disorders is that people with factitious disorders are deliberately producing or pretending to have their symptoms, usually in order to assume a sick role and receive attention, care, and sympathy. In *factitious disorder by proxy,* a type of factitious disorder, people produce or feign symptoms in another person, typically a child or disabled person under their care, so that they can indirectly gain the benefits of being in the sick role.

Dissociative Disorders

These disorders are characterized by what the *DSM* (American Psychiatric Association, 2000a) terms "a disruption in the usually integrated functions of consciousness, memory, identity, or perception" (p. 519). Probably the best known of these disorders is *dissociative identity disorder,* previously known as multiple personality disorder. Identity fragmentation and two or more distinct identities characterize this controversial disorder. Other dissociative disorders include *dissociative amnesia, dissociative fugue,* and *depersonalization disorder.*

Sexual and Gender Identity Disorders

This category includes three distinct groups of disorders:

- *Sexual dysfunctions*—This group encompasses problems in sexual response (desire, arousal, or orgasm) as well as pain during sexual activities. Important to the accurate diagnosis of these disorders is information on the duration, circumstances, and medical or psychological causes of these disorders.
- *Paraphilias*—People with these disorders manifest harmful or self-destructive sexual responses, urges, or behaviors. Their sexual fantasies and desires focus on objects, suffering, and humiliation, or children or others who do not consent to the sexual activity. Common paraphilias include *pedophilia* (sexual urges or actions involving children), *voyeurism* (sexual urges related to observing other people unclothed or engaged in sexual activities), *sexual masochism,* and *sexual sadism.*
- *Gender identity disorder*—In this disorder, people have both a long-standing discomfort with their assigned gender and a strong identification with and wish to be the other gender.

Eating Disorders

The two eating disorders in this category, anorexia nervosa and bulimia nervosa, are particularly common among adolescent and young adult women but are on the increase among both younger and older women and men.

- *Anorexia nervosa*—The primary characteristic of this disorder is a body weight that is less than 85% of the expected body weight for a person of that size.

Anorexia nervosa may be characterized by either restricted eating or by binge eating with accompanying purging via self-induced vomiting or other means.

- *Bulimia nervosa*—This disorder always includes recurrent episodes of binge eating and may or may not include compensatory purging. Both people with bulimia nervosa and those with anorexia nervosa may engage in binge eating and purging, but only those with anorexia have the symptom of a very low body weight.

Sleep Disorders

Increasing attention has been paid to sleep disorders over the past decade because of the growing awareness of the emotional difficulties that can cause and be caused by these disorders. Sleep disorders reflect a wide range of difficulties in achieving an adequate and restful sleep and include the following, along with their most characteristic symptoms.

- *Insomnia*—persistent difficulty falling asleep or remaining asleep
- *Hypersomnia*—persistent oversleeping
- *Narcolepsy*—sudden attacks of sleep
- *Breathing-related sleep disorder*—abnormal respiration during sleep
- *Circadian rhythm sleep disorder*—incompatibilities between one's biological clock and one's lifestyle such as recurrent jet lag
- *Nightmare disorder and sleep terror disorder*—recurrent troubling dreams
- *Sleepwalking*

Diagnosis of these disorders often necessitates an evaluation of people's sleeping patterns in a hospital or other setting in which they can be assessed and observed.

Impulse-Control Disorders Not Elsewhere Classified

Many disorders in the *DSM,* including eating disorders, substance-related disorders, and the disorders included in this category, are characterized by a buildup of tension or arousal discharged via some harmful or dysfunctional behavior that provides a sense of pleasure or relief. Although guilt may follow the behavior, problems in impulse control lead to repetitions of the harmful behavior. Impulse-control disorders not elsewhere classified includes the following, along with their most characteristic symptoms.

- *Intermittent explosive disorder*—characterized by impulsive and aggressive outbursts
- *Kleptomania*—impulsive theft of items that are not needed or that have little value
- *Pyromania*—impulsive fire setting
- *Pathological gambling*—gambling to a harmful extent
- *Trichotillomania*—impulsive pulling out of one's own head or body hair

Adjustment Disorders

These are among the mildest of the mental disorders. In an adjustment disorder, people respond with distress or impairment to a stressor such as a developmental event (marriage, graduation from school), a negative event or experience (diagnosis of a serious disease, living in poverty), a disappointment (end of a romantic relationship, job loss), or another type of stressor. Symptoms of adjustment disorders are generally mild to moderate in severity, begin within 3 months of the stressor and, by definition, last no longer than 6 months after the termination of the stressor and its consequences. These are relatively common disorders that usually respond well to treatment and can lead to personal growth.

Personality Disorders

These are long-standing, pervasive disorders that are evident by adolescence or early adulthood and sometimes much earlier. People with personality disorders tend to have poor coping skills, limited insight and empathy for others, and inflexibility. They have a persistent pattern of dysfunctional thoughts, emotions, and actions that typically cause impairment and distress in all aspects of their lives.

The *DSM* includes the following 10 personality disorders, listed along with their essential characteristics.

- *Paranoid personality disorder*—The hallmark of this disorder is distrust and suspiciousness of others.
- *Schizoid personality disorder*—Lack of involvement and interest in social relationships as well as a restricted range of emotions characterize people with schizoid personality disorders.
- *Schizotypal personality disorder*—This disorder is characterized by distorted perceptions and thoughts, poor interpersonal skills and relationships, and odd or unusual behavior.
- *Antisocial personality disorder*—With conduct disorder as a precursor, this disorder is characterized by lack of concern for the rights and feelings of others and repeated violations of societal rules and norms, often manifested in criminal behavior.
- *Borderline personality disorder*—People with this personality disorder manifest self-destructive instability and impulsivity in behaviors, emotions, and relationships. They often have multiple associated disorders such as eating disorders, substance-related disorders, and mood disorders.
- *Histrionic personality disorder*—A need to be the center of attention, volatile emotions, unstable relationships, and self-dramatization characterize this disorder.
- *Narcissistic personality disorder*—Like people with histrionic personality disorders, those with narcissistic personality disorders also crave attention and admiration. They have an exaggerated sense of their own importance, along with feelings of entitlement.
- *Avoidant personality disorder*—People with this disorder tend to be socially isolated like those with schizoid personality disorders. However, those with avoidant disorders shun social activities not out of lack of interest but because of their fear of rejection, their negative self-image, and their reluctance to risk embarrassment.

- *Dependent personality disorder*—People diagnosed with dependent personality disorder usually have a strong need for protection and nurturance, reluctance to take initiative or responsibility, and feelings of helplessness and dependency.
- *Obsessive-compulsive personality disorder*—Rigidity, order, perfectionism, and control characterize people with this disorder and typically impair both interpersonal and occupational functioning.

Other Conditions That May Be a Focus of Clinical Attention

Problems named in this section of the *DSM* are not considered mental disorders, although they may be a focus of treatment. These conditions are used to describe concerns of people without mental disorders who seek treatment or to label prominent problems needing attention in clients who also have coexisting mental disorders. Categories of conditions include *psychological factors affecting medical condition, medication-induced movement disorders, relational problems, problems related to abuse or neglect,* and miscellaneous groups of additional conditions (e.g., *noncompliance with treatment, bereavement, academic or occupational problem, religious or spiritual problem, acculturation problem,* and *phase of life problem*).

Examples of Multiaxial Assessments

Most people need extensive study of and experience with the *DSM* before they can use that valuable tool with ease and accuracy. However, the introduction you have received to the *DSM* in this book should give you some basic understanding of the multiaxial assessment format, the wide array of mental disorders in the *DSM,* and the implications of diagnoses for treatment. Review the following brief descriptions of clients, along with their multiaxial assessment. You will probably find that this information is much more meaningful to you now than it was before you read this section. Exercises at the end of this chapter will afford you the opportunity to develop some preliminary multiaxial assessments. I strongly encourage you to take coursework or training in the *DSM* and to further your reading on this important topic via such books as *Selecting Effective Treatments* (Seligman, 1998) and *Diagnosis and Treatment Planning in Counseling* (Seligman, 1996a).

Case 1.   Ralph is a firefighter who was present at the September 11, 2001 collapse of the World Trade Center. Although he was not injured, several of his colleagues were killed on that day despite Ralph's heroic efforts to rescue them. Since September 11, he has experienced considerable anxiety, difficulty concentrating, and hypervigilance, as well as intrusive and recurrent images of the towers collapsing. He has found it difficult to fight fires in tall buildings and has become detached from his work. This has left him feeling very isolated because his colleagues at the fire station are his only friends. Ralph has been a loner as long as he can remember. Although he often fantasizes about having close friends, he is fearful that others would reject him if they knew him well and so he tends to reject others before they have the chance to reject him. He views himself as having poor social skills and rarely risks meeting new people.

Multiaxial Assessment of Ralph

Axis I   309.81 Posttraumatic stress disorder, chronic, moderate
Axis II   301.82 Avoidant personality disorder
Axis III   Ralph reports no medical problems
Axis IV   Problems related to the social environment, other psychosocial, and environmental problems: Present at collapse of World Trade Center, deaths of colleagues
Axis V   60

Case 2. Wendy, age 8, was referred for counseling because of her refusal to attend school for the past month. Her parents are currently separated, and Wendy tells her counselor that she needs to stay home to take care of her mother and make sure she is all right. Wendy reports that something awful will happen to her mother unless Wendy is with her. Wendy becomes very upset when separated from her mother, even when her mother needs to take a shower. According to the history, Wendy's father had been verbally and physically abusive toward his wife and sexually abused Wendy until recently. However, Wendy refuses to talk about this and changes the subject whenever she is asked about her father. Wendy's mother reports that Wendy has been diagnosed with asthma.

Multiaxial Assessment of Wendy

Axis I   309.21 Separation anxiety disorder, severe
            995.53 Sexual abuse of child
Axis II   V71.09 No mental disorder on axis II
Axis III   Mother reports that Wendy has been diagnosed with asthma
Axis IV   Problems with primary support group: Reported sexual abuse by father, observed father's abuse of mother, parents' separation
Axis V   55

Case 3. Sara, age 15, was brought to counseling by her mother after Sara told her mother that she had ingested 15 aspirins in an effort to kill herself. Sara has been feeling very sad for the past eight months, since her older sister and only sibling left for college. (Sara has never felt this way before.) Sara reported that she could no longer stand being without her sister. Sara reports difficulty falling asleep almost every night and states that "nothing is fun anymore," even riding her beloved horse. Sara also reports feeling guilty and rejected because of her sister's decision to attend college across the country. Sara has a thin and frail appearance with unusually heavy hair growth on her arms. Sara has lost over 30 pounds in the past six months and now weighs only 75 pounds. Although Sara assists her mother in making dinner for the family and does the grocery shopping, Sara said that she wanted to have a "more athletic" appearance and so deliberately has been eating very little. Sara also is coping with severe acne. Although her schoolwork is satisfactory, Sara's grades have dropped from an A− average to a C+ average and she rarely spends time with friends, other than sending them instant messages.

Multiaxial Assessment of Sara

Axis I   296.23 Major depressive disorder, single episode, severe, without psychotic features, with melancholic features
            307.1 Anorexia nervosa, restricting type, severe
Axis II   V71. 09 No diagnosis on axis II
Axis III   Reports severe acne, appears markedly underweight
Axis IV   Sister's departure for college
Axis V   20

TREATMENT PLANNING

A multiaxial assessment using the *DSM* is the most essential information you need to develop an effective treatment plan. Effective treatment plans succeed in helping clients resolve their difficulties, ameliorate their symptoms, and develop coping skills that assist them in dealing with future difficulties. Like diagnosis, treatment planning is a crucial tool for today's clinicians. Treatment plans have the following benefits (Seligman, 2001, p. 504):

1. A carefully developed treatment plan, based on a sound understanding of the client, an accurate diagnosis, and knowledge of the research on treatment effectiveness, provides assurance that the counseling or psychotherapy has a high likelihood of success.
2. Written treatment plans allow clinicians to demonstrate their accountability and effectiveness. Sound treatment plans can assist clinicians in obtaining funding for programs and in receiving third-party payments for their services. Treatment plans also can provide a defense in the event of allegations of malpractice.
3. Use of a treatment plan that specifies goals and procedures can help clinicians and clients to track their progress. They can determine whether goals are being met as planned and, if not, they can make appropriate revisions in the treatment plan.
4. Treatment plans also provide structure and direction to the therapeutic process. They help clinicians and clients to develop shared and realistic expectations for treatment and promote hope and optimism that progress will be made.

Formats for Treatment Planning

Treatment planning, like diagnosis according to the *Diagnostic and Statistical Manual of Mental Disorders* (American Psychiatric Association, 2000a), has become an essential tool for clinicians. However, no standard or universal format for treatment planning exists. Each third-party payer and each mental health agency seems to have its own preferred format for treatment planning. These vary according to the nature and amount of information requested. I have developed a 12-step format for treatment planning (Seligman, 1996a) that is presented here, along with a sample of an abbreviated treatment plan used by third-party payers.

DO A CLIENT MAP

The DO A CLIENT MAP is a 12-step comprehensive format for treatment planning. The first letters in each of the 12 steps spells out DO A CLIENT MAP, thereby serving as a mnemonic device to facilitate recall of the elements of the treatment plan. The name, CLIENT MAP, also reflects the purpose of a treatment plan, to map out the clinician's work with a particular person or group of people. Just as when we are taking a trip, a map facilitates the journey, reduces the likelihood of getting lost, enables us to get back on track after we have taken a detour, and successfully gets us to our destination.

The DO A CLIENT MAP consists of the 12 steps presented next. Following this list are guidelines that should be kept in mind for each step when developing a treatment plan. Information needed to complete the treatment plan comes from the intake interview with the client (see chapter 2), the mental status exam (discussed earlier in this chapter), and any relevant and available inventories or records.

The DO A CLIENT MAP

1. Diagnosis
2. Objectives
3. Assessments
4. Clinician
5. Location of treatment
6. Interventions
7. Emphasis
8. Number of people seen in treatment
9. Timing
10. Medication
11. Adjunct services
12. Prognosis

Guidelines for completing the DO A CLIENT MAP

1. **Diagnosis**
   - Be sure to complete all five axes of the multiaxial assessment for a client, according to the format provided in the *DSM* and described earlier in this chapter.
2. **Objectives**
   - Ideally, objectives should be formulated collaboratively, with client and clinician working together to identify important treatment goals.
   - When formulating specific objectives, consider the *DSM* diagnosis, presenting problems, and both observable and reported symptoms. Objectives may go beyond a person's diagnosis but should certainly address any identified mental disorders and their associated symptoms.
   - Objectives should be specific, measurable, and achievable by the client. Breaking large goals down into small, realistic objectives maximizes the likelihood of success.
   - All treatment plans should include short-term goals that can be accomplished in a few days or weeks. If treatment will be longer than that, the plan also should include medium-term goals that can be accomplished in a few months. If treatment will be lengthy, long-term objectives also should be established.
   - To avoid overwhelming the client, each group of objectives (short-term, medium-term, and long-term) should initially include approximately three to six items. Other objectives can be added as progress is made.
   - Information on developing goals or objectives has been presented in chapter 5; review that section for additional information.

3. **Assessments**
   - Identify any important missing information that might be obtained through assessment. Examples of such information include medical factors that might play a part in the client's emotional difficulties, the client's intellectual and academic abilities, and additional diagnostic information.
   - Consider both outside sources of assessment (e.g., physicians, neurologists, gynecologists, school psychologists) and assessments that you might administer (e.g., personality inventories, interest inventories, measures of learning style and ability).
   - Determine those assessment tools and resources that are likely to provide the missing information and enable you to develop a more effective treatment plan. Additional information on this process is provided earlier in this chapter.

4. **Clinician**
   - Determine whether the client has a strong preference as to the characteristics of the clinician. Client preferences should be considered when selecting the clinician.
   - Determine those clinician characteristics that are likely to contribute to the development of a sound collaborative therapeutic relationship with the client. Consider not only the clinician's skills and experience but also the clinician's gender, age, multicultural background, and life experiences.

5. **Location of treatment**
   - Evaluate the client's living situation, support system, self-care, and financial resources as well as that person's motivation to get help, contact with reality, level of suicidal ideation, and propensity toward violent and aggressive behavior.
   - Based on this information, determine whether the client is currently in a safe situation and is likely to keep regular appointments at an outpatient treatment facility. If the client is not in a safe situation, presents a danger to self or others, or lacks personal resources or support systems, consider a treatment program that provides a higher level of care, such as a day-treatment program or an inpatient treatment program in a psychiatric hospital.
   - Once the level of care has been determined, decide on the specific treatment program that is most appropriate for this client in light of the factors identified previously.

6. **Interventions**
   - Drawing on the current research on effective treatment of the client's problems or mental disorders, identify the treatment system (e.g., psychodynamic, cognitive-behavioral, person-centered, multimodal) that seems most likely to succeed in helping this client reach the objectives that have been identified.
   - For each identified objective, determine specific strategies that are compatible with the treatment system selected and that seem likely to achieve that objective. Begin with interventions designed to achieve short-term objectives and then develop a tentative list of interventions designed to address longer term objectives.

7. **Emphasis**
   - Consider both client and treatment approach to determine how the treatment process might best be adapted to and individualized for a particular client. For example, think about whether:

- treatment will emphasize the past, present, or future.
- it will be structured primarily by the clinician or by the client.
- it will be exploratory or seek accomplishment of specific tasks.
- it will be confrontational or reinforcing.

8. **Number of people in treatment**
   - Viewing people in context can help determine whether they are likely to benefit most from individual, family, or group treatment or some combination of those. Assess whether the client's concerns are:
     - primarily individual and internal.
     - intertwined with family dynamics and the attitudes and behaviors of family members.
     - characterized by deficits in social skills and interpersonal relationships, a lack of support and positive role models, or limited understanding of what is healthy and normal behavior.
   - Use this information to determine whether the primary mode of treatment should be individual, family, or group counseling or psychotherapy.
   - Determine whether combining two or more modes of treatment (e.g., individual counseling and family therapy) is likely to be more powerful than either alone.
   - Determine the client's readiness for group or family treatment. For example, people who are fragile and fearful, who have feelings of rage toward their families, or who have extremely poor social skills often benefit from an initial course of individual treatment before group or family treatment is added.
   - Finally, decide on whether and when individual, group, and family treatment will be part of your client's treatment.

9. **Timing**
   - Determining the optimal timing for the treatment process involves making a series of decisions:
   - Decide whether standard 45–50 minute sessions are appropriate for this client or whether, because of the setting, the age of the client, the level of motivation, or the symptoms, a shorter or (occasionally) longer session seems preferable.
   - Determine whether the standard weekly appointment is appropriate for this client, whether the urgency or risk inherent in the person's situation suggests more frequent meetings, or whether the person is relatively high functioning and able to work independently, perhaps needing less frequent sessions.
   - Determine the approximate number of total sessions needed to achieve the objectives that have been identified.
   - Determine the pacing of the treatment process. People with urgent concerns, clients at risk, and healthy and motivated clients probably benefit most from a fairly rapid pace, while clients who are apprehensive about treatment, vulnerable, or well defended usually require a more gradually paced treatment.

10. **Medication**
    - Based on current research, determine whether the client's mental disorder(s) are likely to benefit from a combination of medication and psychotherapy.
    - If it seems that medication would enhance the treatment process, determine the client's attitude toward the possibility of taking psychotropic medication.

- If medication seems indicated and the client is receptive to a medication evaluation, refer the client to a psychiatrist in whom you have confidence and with whom you can work collaboratively.

11. **Adjunct services**
    - Because treatment typically progresses more rapidly if clients are engaged in positive and growth-promoting activities between sessions, clinicians should usually incorporate adjunct services into the treatment plan. To identify those adjunct services that are most likely to enhance the treatment process, assess the following dimensions of the client's life:
        - basic survival needs (e.g., a safe environment, food, housing, warm clothing)
        - legal and medical needs and resources
        - health, weight, exercise, physical activity
        - employment and finances
        - use of drugs and alcohol
        - rewarding relationships and leisure activities
        - peer support and role models
        - life skills, education, and information
        - cultural, religious, and spiritual resources
    - Identify problems, deficits, or areas of unmet need.
    - Determine adjunct services that can address these needs, such as the following:
        Basic survival needs—government assistance, aid to dependent children, subsidized housing
        Legal and medical needs and resources—legal aid, health insurance, low-cost medical and dental programs
        Health, weight, exercise, physical activity—exercise classes, weight control programs, clubs focused on particular sports (e.g., hiking, in-line skating)
        Employment and finances—assistance with resume writing, job seeking, financial planning
        Use of drugs and alcohol—Alcoholics Anonymous, program for adult children of alcoholics, other 12-step programs, Rational Recovery
        Rewarding relationships—leisure activities, support groups, workshops in communication skills or assertiveness, volunteer experiences, community recreation courses
        Peer support and role models—relevant peer support groups such as Parents Without Partners, Tough Love, and Overeaters Anonymous
        Life skills, education, and information—classes on parenting skills, use of the Internet
        Cultural, religious, and spiritual resources—involvement with a religious or spiritual community, meditation classes, reading on cultural background

12. **Prognosis**
    - Review the literature to determine the usual prognosis for treatment of the client's mental disorders.
    - Review information on the severity of this client's particular mental disorder(s) and the client's response to any previous treatment. Prognosis may be less positive if the client has more than one mental disorder or has not had a favorable response to previous treatment.

- Consider the client's motivation for treatment and the likelihood that the client will follow through on treatment recommendations.
- Based on all this information, determine the prognosis for effective treatment of each of the client's problems or mental disorders.
- If prognosis is positive (excellent, very good, good), move forward to implement treatment plan, being sure to evaluate progress frequently.
- If prognosis is questionable (fair, poor, guarded), consider revising objectives, interventions, or recommendation for medication to develop a more promising treatment plan.

EXAMPLES OF TREATMENT PLANS

The following treatment plan was developed for Eileen Carter, the client discussed throughout this book. It follows and illustrates the DO A CLIENT MAP format.

Diagnosis

Axis I: 309.28 Adjustment Disorder with Mixed Anxiety and Depressed Mood
            300.4 Dysthymic Disorder, moderate
            304.80 Polysubstance Dependence, Prior History
Axis II: Dependent Personality Traits
Axis III: 424.0 Mitral Valve Prolapse
Axis IV: Problems with primary support group: Conflict with husband
            Educational problems: Barriers related to continuing education
Axis V: GAF = 63 (current)

Objectives

Short term:
1. Eileen will identify at least two plans for continuing her education while maintaining her commitment to her family, as measured by written descriptions of plans.
2. Eileen will achieve a reduction of at least three points in her level of depression as measured by the Beck Depression Inventory (BDI).
3. Eileen will achieve a reduction of at least three points in her level of anxiety as measured by the Beck Anxiety Inventory (BAI).
4. Eileen will achieve at least a one point improvement in her self-esteem as measured by a 1–10 self-rating scale.
5. Eileen will report at least a one point improvement in satisfaction with her interactions with her husband as measured by a 1–10 self-rating scale.

Medium-term objectives:
6. Eileen will finalize and begin to implement plans for continuing her education as measured by self-report.
7. Eileen's score on the BDI will be in the normal mood range.
8. Eileen's score on the BAI will be in the normal range.

9. Eileen will report improved and at least satisfactory self-esteem, as reflected by a 1–10 self-rating scale.
10. Eileen will report improved and satisfactory skills in communicating with and interacting with her husband as reflected in journal entries.
11. Eileen will report improved ability to make decisions as reflected by a decision list in her journal.

Long-term objectives:
Long-term treatment is not anticipated for this client, so long-term objectives are not needed at this time.

Assessments

- Beck Depression Inventory
- Beck Anxiety Inventory
- Self-esteem self-rating scale
- Informal 1–10 self-rating scale of Eileen's satisfaction with her interactions with her husband
- Journal
- Strong Interest Inventory, to assess career interests

Clinician. Eileen expressed a strong preference for a female clinician about her age or somewhat older. She also thought she might feel more comfortable talking to an African American woman, but was willing to work with a clinician who was Caucasian. In addition, her clinician should be knowledgeable about family dynamics, have multicultural counseling competencies, and be able to provide information on parenting and career and educational development.

Location. Because Eileen is in a safe situation, has considerable emotional health, and is motivated to obtain help, an outpatient treatment setting is clearly the preferred location. Eileen might feel especially comfortable in a treatment setting focused on helping women with their concerns.

Interventions

Treatment system—Cognitive and behavior therapy
Specific interventions—(numbers after each intervention link intervention to objective)
- Identification, assessment, and modification of distorted cognitions (2, 4, 7, 9)
- Information gathering and brainstorming to generate possible ways to continue education (1, 4, 6, 9)
- Teaching assertiveness and communication skills (2, 3, 4, 5, 7, 8, 9, 10, 11)
- Relaxation and visualization (1, 3, 8)
- Identification of strengths and coping skills (2, 4, 6, 7, 9, 11)
- Decision-making training (11)
- Clarification of interests and related and realistic career goals (1, 4, 6, 11)

Emphasis.   Because treatment goals include empowering Eileen and developing her self-confidence, she will be encouraged to structure and take the lead in her own treatment as much as possible. Considerable support from the clinician will facilitate that process. Although treatment will focus largely on Eileen's present concerns, some attention will be paid to past issues to prevent resumption of drug and alcohol use and to help Eileen forgive herself for mistakes she made in the past.

Numbers.   Most of Eileen's treatment will involve individual counseling. However, some couples sessions with her husband might help them to understand each other better and communicate more effectively. In addition, once she has made some progress, Eileen might benefit from group treatment, perhaps with women about her own age who are seeking to balance family, career, and individual goals.

Timing.   Once-a-week sessions of 45–50 minutes seem appropriate for Eileen. The frequency of sessions can be increased if she needs to make some rapid decisions. Treatment of approximately 20–30 sessions is anticipated. Treatment can progress at a rapid pace because Eileen is eager to move forward with her life and because she seems relatively healthy at present.

Medication.   Because of the nature of her diagnoses and Eileen's reluctance to take any drugs, a referral for medication seems contraindicated at the present time. In addition, helping Eileen take credit for her progress in treatment is important; a medication referral may lead her to credit the medication for her improvement instead of herself. However, if her depression does not respond to treatment fairly quickly, the question of medication should be revisited.

Adjunct services

- Exercise class to alleviate anxiety and depression and promote relaxation, self-esteem, and contact with others
- Involvement in a neighborhood baby-sitting co-op to increase free time and contact with others

Prognosis.   Although dysthymic disorders and personality traits can be treatment resistant, Eileen is motivated and has many personal resources. Consequently, the prognosis for successful treatment is at least good if not very good.

The treatment plan you have just read is detailed and comprehensive, providing a clear plan for Eileen and her clinician. Many clinicians prepare treatment plans of this nature for their own use. However, the following shorter treatment plan is more typical of that required by mental health agencies and insurance companies.

Example of Abbreviated Treatment Plan

The following format for treatment planning has been adapted from those used by several third-party payers. It has been completed with information on Eileen Carter.

MENTAL HEALTH OUTPATIENT TREATMENT REPORT

Client name: Eileen Carter   **Date of birth:** 4/17/79
Therapist: Merle Young, Ph.D.   **Date of plan:** 6/3/03

Client's initial reason for seeking treatment and current clinical condition: Ms. Carter sought treatment because she was upset at her husband's request that she leave college. She presented with mild anxiety as well as moderate and long-standing depression. She successfully cares for herself and her family and has been attending college but otherwise is rather isolated. History of substance-related problems and unstable relationships contribute to depression, low self-esteem, and interpersonal difficulties.

Mental Status: Ms. Carter is oriented x 4. She appeared tearful and worried; emotions were appropriate to the topic. Some mild impairment in concentration and attention was noted. Judgment and decision making also reflect mild impairment.

Indicate presence of any symptoms below, manifested by this client:

_____ Danger to self
_____ Danger to others
_____ Thought disorder
_____ Potential for loss of impulse control
_____ Potential for decompensation into more serious illness
_____ Potential for decompensation into behaviors dangerous to self or others
_____ Perceptual disorder
_____ Disordered behavior
__x__ Disturbed affect
_____ Disorientation
_____ Impaired memory
__x__ Impaired judgment
_____ Current substance abuse or dependence

Client's strengths:

SOCIAL
_____ Supportive family
_____ Network of friends
_____ Use of community resource
_____ Leisure activities
__x__ Other—commitment to family

PHYSICAL

___x___ Good health

___x___ Good personal hygiene

___x___ Good grooming

___x___ Appropriate use of medical resources

_____ Other

EMOTIONAL:

_____ Good emotional control

_____ Copes well with stressors

___x___ Good reality testing

___x___ Other—highly motivated

BEHAVIORAL

_____ Adaptive flexibility

_____ Sound problem solving

_____ Seeks and uses help well

___x___ Other—no longer makes harmful use of drugs or alcohol

Diagnoses:

Axis I: 309.28 Adjustment Disorder with Mixed Anxiety and Depressed Mood
             300.6 Dysthymic Disorder, moderate
             304.80 Polysubstance Dependence, Prior History
Axis II: Dependent Personality Traits
Axis III: 424.0 Mitral Valve Prolapse
Axis IV: Problems with primary support group: Conflict with husband
             Educational problems: Barriers related to continuing education
Axis V: GAF = 63 (current)

Treatment Plan: Describe current treatment goals and focus of treatment—Goals of treatment include alleviation of depression and anxiety; improved decision making, family relationships, and self-esteem. Treatment will be primarily cognitive-behavioral in nature, modifying distorted cognitions and improving coping. Skill development will promote better communication and decisions. Some attention will be paid to past issues, particularly to prevent relapse of substance-related disorder.

Frequency, duration, and expected number of sessions until completion of treatment: Approximately 25 weekly sessions, 50 minutes in length, are anticipated.

Medication: Not indicated at the present time.

Adjunct treatment: Exercise class, peer support group.

Prognosis: Describe client's anticipated level of functioning after treatment—Overall prognosis is good to very good. Considerable reduction in depression and anxiety is anticipated along with improvement in decision making, communication skills, self-confidence, coping skills, and relationships.

LEARNING OPPORTUNITIES

This chapter focused on the thinking skills that clinicians need to clearly and accurately conceptualize the nature and dynamics of their clients' concerns and plan effective ways to help them. These skills give both clinicians and clients a focus and direction to treatment, promote collaboration and hope, and contribute immeasurably to a mutually rewarding outcome. The conceptual skills in this chapter include:

- Appropriate use of assessment
  - the mental status examination
  - selection and use of tests and inventories
  - client observation
- Identification and therapeutic use of defining memories
- Case conceptualization and problem definition
  - concept mapping
  - organization of key client statements
  - clinical factor analysis
  - inverted pyramid
  - Stevens and Morris format
- Diagnosis using the *Diagnostic and Statistical Manual of Mental Disorders*
- Treatment planning
- DO A CLIENT MAP
- Brief treatment plans

The following exercises, like those in previous chapters, afford you the opportunity to apply the conceptual skills presented in this chapter. This section includes written exercises, discussion questions, exercises and an assessment tool to use in your practice groups, and activities to address in your journal.

Discussion Questions

1. The term *mental status examination* is misleading because it does not require an actual examination. What would be a better term for this process of gathering information to formulate a picture of a person's overall functioning?
2. Clinicians often disagree on the value of incorporating tests and inventories into the treatment process. Discuss the pros and cons of using these tools as part of the assessment and treatment process.
3. What categories of tests and inventories seem most useful to you and why? Least useful and why?
4. Discuss the benefits and disadvantages of the following five approaches to case conceptualization, presented earlier in this chapter. Which seems to have the most overall usefulness to clinicians and why?
   - concept mapping
   - organization of key client statements
   - clinical factor analysis
   - inverted pyramid
   - Stevens and Morris format

5. Diagnosis using the *Diagnostic and Statistical Manual of Mental Disorders* (DSM) has become an essential clinical tool. However, as recently as 25 years ago, nonmedical clinicians typically had little formal training in diagnosis, and many chose not to make diagnoses. How do you explain this great change? What advantages and drawbacks do you see in the establishment of diagnosis as a mainstay of clinical practice? What do you think clinicians can do to maximize the advantages and minimize the drawbacks of that process?

6. Treatment planning is another essential clinical tool. What do you see as the most challenging elements in the treatment planning process? What can you do to facilitate the process of treatment planning?

7. Some agencies and clinicians emphasize the importance of sharing a multiaxial assessment and treatment plan with the client. What are your reactions to this policy? What advantages and disadvantages are inherent in this policy?

Written Exercises/Discussion Questions

The following exercises and questions are based on the case of Amy, age 13.

Presenting Concerns.   Amy's school counselor suggested that Amy needed some special help for academic, emotional, and behavioral difficulties. Amy's school performance was one to two standard deviations below grade level. In class, Amy usually seemed disinterested and involved in daydreaming, staring out the window, or passing notes to a classmate. When a subject did catch her attention, she tended to blurt out answers. During the elementary school years, her teachers described her as constantly in motion, frequently falling, dropping things, or forgetting things. Amy was tall and heavy for her age and seemed uncomfortable with her body. She rarely completed homework assignments; when she did, they were incomplete and carelessly done.

Amy manifested a strong need for approval from her teachers and classmates. She often asked people if they liked her, if she was talking too much, or if she was annoying them. She was aware that both her grades and her behavior in school were often unsatisfactory, and that troubled her. At the same time, she seemed unable to make any successful efforts to change. Amy had experienced some anxiety and sadness for many years, and these symptoms seemed to have worsened over the previous 6 months.

Background.   Amy is the child of Julia, a Latina woman, and Claude, an African American man. Both came from lower socioeconomic families, where alcohol misuse was rampant. Despite their difficult family backgrounds, both Julia and Claude completed high school and earned scholarships to continue their schooling. Julia was employed as a nurse and met Claude when he was completing a medical residency in the hospital where she worked. In addition to Amy, the couple has a son, Eduardo, who is an outstanding student and athlete in the fourth grade. Julia and Claude have had little contact with their families of origin since they completed high school. However, about 6 months ago, Julia allowed her younger brother Diego to live with them after he completed an inpatient drug treatment program. After about 4 months, Claude found some cans of beer in Diego's room. He also suspected Diego of behaving inappropriately toward Amy, although he had no clear evidence of this. Claude insisted that Diego move out. Julia disapproved of this decision, and she and Claude have had many arguments about this issue. Both Claude and Julia are very concerned about Amy, but their primary ways of dealing with her are to urge her to try harder in school, to tell her that they are ashamed of her poor grades, and to hire more tutors to help her.

Client Statements.   In the course of her first two sessions with a counselor, Amy made the following statements:

1. I guess I'm here because I can't keep up with the other kids.
2. Things have been pretty bad lately between my mom and dad.
3. School is really boring; I can hardly stay awake.
4. If I could have anything I wished for, I'd look like Britney Spears and go out with one of the Backstreet Boys.
5. I have a dog and a cat. Most people are surprised at how well they get along, but I made them be friends.
6. I wonder if I'll ever have a boyfriend.
7. My brother is the smartest kid in his class, and my parents are very proud of him.
8. My parents are really ashamed of my bad grades; I wish I could be better, but no matter how hard I try, I never do very well in school.
9. My parents both work really hard; I pretty much take care of myself.
10. My uncle Diego stayed with us for awhile. I don't like him at all. He did some really bad stuff.
11. My parents fight a lot, but I know they really love each other.
12. At home, I watch television most of the time; I like the cartoon shows and MTV.
13. I have a really pretty bedroom; my mom and I decorated it with pink roses and I have a ruffled bedspread.
14. I saved all my dolls from when I was a kid and keep them on my bed. They keep me company, and my cat and dog sleep with me, too.
15. My mom gave me a key last year so I can just let myself into the house, make myself a snack, and watch television.
16. My mom has a big family, four brothers and three sisters, but she says they're "not a good influence" so we don't see them much.
17. The other girls are starting to have boyfriends and to talk about having sex and getting married.
18. I don't know if I ever want to get married; I might just want to stay with my mom and dad.
19. My dad said I could go to a really good college after high school and then spend a year in Europe after I finish college, but I don't like school much.
20. I did like a few things we did in school this year; we saw the movie *Romeo and Juliet* and we read a book called *Of Mice and Men*. They're both about love and friendship and how much people need those things. I know I do.
21. We acted out part of *Romeo and Juliet* at school. I tried to get the part of Juliet, but the kids laughed when I tried to read all those old English words. The teacher just put me in a crowd scene.
22. I have one good friend, Lily. She's 18 and helps out with me and my brother sometimes. She gave me some perfume once, and sometimes she brings me ice cream or cookies.

23. Holidays can be really good at our house, as long as my mom and dad are getting along. My mom makes homemade soup like her mom, and she makes ribs for my dad. Otherwise, we eat takeout most of the time.

24. I wanted to go out for the soccer team, but my mom said I needed to spend my time on schoolwork. I probably wouldn't be very good at soccer anyhow.

25. Did you know that I could swim? I didn't even know it but when our school went on a picnic, I went in the pool and I could swim really well. I don't know how I learned to do that.

26. I don't look like anybody in my family. My mom says I'm big and tall like her father, but I never met him. My mom is short and so's my dad and my brother. And their skin color and hair are different from mine.

27. I wish I could have long hair, but my hair just looks like a mess if I let it grow out.

28. My mom took me shopping to buy some school clothes but it was hard to find anything to fit me. We finally had to go to the women's department. I kept hoping nobody would see me there.

29. We're not very religious. My parents used to take me to church sometimes when I was younger, but I guess I would make too much noise and they would usually have to leave early. Now we don't go anymore. But my parents believe in God, and so do I. I think God punishes you if you do bad things.

30. My mom talks a lot like I do, and she likes pretty things. She's really pretty herself. Once somebody thought we were sisters. I wish I had a sister, just like me.

31. My dad is real quiet, except when he gets mad. He's so tired when he comes home from work, he just wants his supper and a good book or some television.

32. My brother is more like my dad, pretty quiet. My mom says he is very smart and might become a doctor or a lawyer. I wish I could be smart like that, but my mom says I shouldn't complain or be jealous.

33. We live in a big house. My brother and I have our own rooms. Our garage has space for three cars, even though we only have two cars.

34. One of my aunts died of cancer. I think about that a lot. What if one of my parents got cancer?

35. I remember when my brother was born. I really missed my mom, even though she was only in the hospital for 2 days. My dad took me to visit her.

36. Then when my brother came home, he wasn't much fun. My mom told me that after awhile I said, "Can you take him back now?"

37. Maybe the worst day of my life was the day my uncle Diego moved in. I thought it would be fun, but I didn't know what he would be like and the problems he would cause between my parents. I wish he'd never come.

38. Once my dad got so mad, he hit the wall. It almost broke his hand. He was really sorry he did that.

39. Another bad thing was once when I got lost in Sears. I was only about 4, and I guess I just walked off and my mom didn't notice. I thought I'd be lost forever but she found me.

40. I don't know what I'll be when I grow up. I love animals. Maybe I'll have a pet shop or be a veterinarian. So I could help animals.

Questions.   In responding to these questions, you may provide additional details about Amy, as long as that information is consistent with the information you already have about her. Some of these questions are quite challenging and call for the use of new skills and ways of thinking. Unless you already have some clinical experience, I recommend that these questions be discussed in class or in a study group rather than being completed individually.

1. Prepare a mental status examination for Amy.
2. What tests or inventories, if any, would you incorporate into your treatment of Amy? The questions on page 270 can help you answer this question.
3. Do you think it would be fruitful to observe Amy in class? If so, what categories of information would you include in your observation?
4. Select one of the critical incidents or defining memories presented by Amy. Analyze it according to the modified version of Bloom's taxonomy. What important information does that provide about Amy and your plans for working with her?
5. Develop a case conceptualization for Amy using at least one of the following models:
    *   Bloom's taxonomy
    *   concept mapping
    *   organization of key client statements
    *   clinical factor analysis
    *   inverted pyramid
    *   Stevens and Morris format
6. Formulate a tentative multiaxial assessment for Amy.
7. Develop a treatment plan for Amy, according to the steps in the DO A CLIENT MAP.

Practice Group Exercises

Divide into your practice groups. In this chapter, as in the previous two chapters, you will have the opportunity both to practice your conceptual skills and to further refine your technical skills. As usual, continue to tape-record both the practice session and the subsequent discussion.

Purpose of Exercise.   In chapter 4, you learned skills that are intended to help you identify, assess, analyze, dispute, and modify clients' distorted cognitions. In this practice group exercise, you will build on what you learned in chapter 4. This exercise will encompass the following skills:

Technical Skills
*   reflection of meaning
*   eliciting, analyzing, and modifying distorted cognitions
*   other technical skills to promote problem resolution, including information giving, thought stopping, positive self-talk/affirmations, and paradoxical intention

Conceptual Skills
*   mental status examination
*   analysis of defining memories
*   case conceptualization

- diagnosis
- treatment planning

Role-play Exercise.   As usual, in each dyad, one person will assume the role of clinician and the other will assume the role of the client. The presenting problem in this role-play should be a critical incident or defining memory of an event in the life of the client. The person in the client role may present an actual incident in his or her life or may role play another person. Presenting an actual incident in your life may have personal benefits for you and is likely to lead to a more powerful counseling session. However, this has risks and so you should, of course, think about what and how much you are willing to disclose about yourself and be sure to take care of yourself. If you decide to role-play another person, you may continue the role you assumed for the practice group exercise in the previous chapter or you may create a new role for yourself.

Clinicians in this exercise have the following major goals:

- to continue to demonstrate those characteristics that promote the development of a sound therapeutic alliance
- to use reflection of meaning to elicit and explore the incident or memory
- to elicit, analyze, and dispute any cognitive distortions underlying the person's presentation of the incident or memory
- to use one of the technical skills presented in chapter 4 (e.g., thought stopping, affirmations, information giving) to help the client and bring the session to a close

Observers play a particularly important role in this exercise. They should take careful notes on key client statements so that they can take an active part in the discussion of this case following the role play. This discussion will afford participants the opportunity to apply the skills presented in this chapter to an actual case.

Time Schedule.   Ideally, this role play should extend over two 2-hour periods. However, the exercise can easily be modified so that it requires only one 2-hour period or even half that time. What determines the amount of time this exercise requires is how many role plays are completed. Whether or not group members have the opportunity to assume client or clinician roles, they will play an active part in this exercise.

Each role play should follow this schedule:

- Allow 20 minutes for each role-played interview.
- Take about 10 minutes to provide feedback to the person in the clinician role. As you have done with other exercises in this book, begin the feedback with the person in the clinician role, focus on strengths first, and offer concrete suggestions for improvement. Remember to make this a positive learning experience. Feedback should focus on the areas listed in the following Assessment of Progress Form.
- Following the role-played interview, take about one-half hour to discuss the following in your small group:
  - a conceptualization of the case, developed according to one of the models presented earlier in this chapter.
  - the treatment plan for this client. (The diagnosis should not be discussed because the person in the client role may be presenting an actual concern.)

Assessment of Progress Form 8

1. What strategies did you use to build a positive treatment alliance?

2. Describe your use of the following skills:
   a. eliciting and exploring the incident or memory

   b. reflections of meaning

   c. eliciting, analyzing, and disputing cognitive distortions

   d. use of other technical skills

3. Which interventions seemed particularly successful?

4. How might you have improved on your use of these interventions?

5. Summary of feedback:

Personal Journal Questions

1. List three critical incidents or defining memories that have had an important impact on your life. Briefly analyze the meaning one of them has for you according to the modified version of Bloom's taxonomy.
2. What apprehensions do you have about learning and applying the skills of diagnosis and treatment planning? What can you do to reduce those apprehensions?
3. If you could create the perfect test or inventory for assessment of yourself, what would that instrument be like and what information would it provide?
4. Write a mental status examination for yourself.

5. Describe what you found to be the most difficult skill in this chapter and explain what made it challenging for you.
6. What is the most important thing you learned from this chapter and its exercises?
7. How can you use that information or skill in your work?

SUMMARY

This chapter focused on conceptual skills associated with thinking. Unlike most other chapters in this book, most of the skills presented here were not intended for direct use with clients but rather for clinicians to use in better understanding their clients and conceptualizing their concerns. Particular attention was paid to conducting a mental status examination, making appropriate use of tests and inventories, understanding and analyzing important memories, conceptualizing a case, and formulating a diagnosis and treatment plan.

Chapter 9 will focus on conceptual skills associated with actions. Included in that chapter is information on stages of change, structuring treatment sessions, assessment of progress, and termination of treatment. Chapter 9 also will provide information on referral and collaboration in treatment, session notes, generating solutions, and researching your own practice in order to become a more effective clinician.

CHAPTER 9

Applying Conceptual Skills to Actions for Positive Change

INTRODUCTION

Chapter 8 focused on thinking skills, the third element in the BETA model. It presented ways of thinking about people and their difficulties that can help clinicians gain a full and deep understanding of their clients and develop effective treatment plans.

This chapter, the last in the section on conceptual skills, focuses on actions, the fourth element in the BETA framework. This chapter emphasizes actions that clinicians take, in collaboration with their clients, to implement treatment plans and move the treatment process forward to a rewarding outcome. This chapter provides you with the remaining skills presented in this book. Knowledge of the skills described and illustrated throughout this text give you the essential skills you need to provide effective treatment to your clients.

This chapter will cover the following topics:

- *Stages of change*—People's readiness for change, when they begin counseling or psychotherapy, is an important determinant of the nature of the treatment that will be helpful to them and the eventual treatment outcome. Particularly important is adapting the introductory phase of treatment to a client's level of motivation and readiness for change.

- *Referral and collaboration*—Successful treatment today often entails a collaboration of the clinician and other professionals, including school counselors, social workers, psychiatrists, neurologists, and even lawyers and physicians. Understanding when and how to make a referral to another specialist and knowing ways to work cooperatively with that person can considerably enhance the treatment process.
- *Structuring interventions, sessions, and the treatment process*—Each intervention and session has a pattern to it. This may be a random pattern that evolves differently and haphazardly over the course of each session, or the pattern may reflect the clinician's efforts to plan a productive session. Deliberate structuring of sessions for therapeutic benefit is another action that clinicians can take to increase treatment effectiveness. Similarly, the treatment process itself has a structure. Planning the overall structure of that process in a thoughtful way and then following that plan, of course with some flexibility, is another way of enhancing treatment.
- *Progress notes*—Progress notes help clinicians identify issues that need continued attention, assess the strengths and weaknesses of the treatment process, determine the optimal structure of future sessions, modify the treatment plan as needed, and track progress toward goal attainment.
- *Generating solutions*—The treatment process often is replete with problems, both those presented by clients and those encountered by clinicians. Having strategies for addressing and resolving those problems can accelerate the treatment process.
- *Assessing and terminating treatment*—Treatment ends, sometimes because clients have achieved their goals and no longer have a strong need for clinical help and sometimes for other reasons. Clinicians and clients need criteria for determining when termination is appropriate and, if it is, for making the termination process a beneficial ingredient in the overall treatment process.
- *Using research to enhance your practice and your professional development*—Skilled clinicians constantly seek ways to learn promising new strategies and further develop their clinical abilities. Probably the most important way for them to accomplish this is through research, both by reading the professional literature and by researching the strengths and weaknesses of their own practice. This section will present ways for clinicians to benefit from involvement in research and to continue their professional development.

STAGES OF CHANGE

In many settings, a substantial percentage of the clients are not initially eager for assistance. This is particularly likely in correctional settings, substance abuse treatment programs, and inpatient treatment programs. People who have been court referred or strongly encouraged to seek help by a dissatisfied supervisor, a concerned teacher, or an unhappy family member also tend to be reluctant clients. Even among people who voluntarily seek counseling or psychotherapy, some will have little understanding of the treatment process and no interest in personal change.

Of course, clinicians do encounter motivated and enthusiastic people in all treatment settings. These people recognize that they have difficulties, take some responsibility for their problems, believe they would benefit from help in making changes, and are willing, at least initially, to engage in treatment.

Clearly, clinicians should not treat both groups of people in identical ways. Rather, counselors and psychologists are more likely to succeed at developing a collaborative treatment alliance, establishing mutually agreeable goals, and getting the treatment process off to a positive start if they can meet clients where they are. Assessing a client's stage of readiness for treatment and matching treatment strategies to that stage of readiness is essential to effective treatment (Miller & Rollnick, 1991).

Assessment of Readiness for Change

An array of factors should be considered when assessing a person's readiness for change via counseling or psychotherapy. These include:

- the referral source (self or other)
- the presenting concerns (symptoms and precipitants)
- the multiaxial assessment according to the *Diagnostic and Statistical Manual of Mental Disorders* (discussed in chapter 8)
- the severity of the symptoms and their impact on the person's life
- the person's expressed level of distress and motivation to change
- the person's level of insight, self-awareness, and empathy

In general, people with a high level of readiness for change are those who are self-referred, have an identifiable cause or precipitant for their difficulties, a mild to moderately severe emotional disorder that is having an impact on their personal and professional functioning, and some capacity for insight, self-awareness, and empathy. On the other hand, people who are mandated or pressured into seeking treatment, who have long-standing difficulties with no apparent precipitant or stressor, who have either very mild or very severe difficulties, and little capacity for insight into themselves or others are far more likely to have a low level of readiness for change.

Stages of Change Model

Prochaska and Norcross (1999) delineated six levels of readiness for change in a model known as the Stages of Change Model (SOC) or the Transtheoretical Model of Change (TTM). Suggested strategies are presented for each of the six levels of readiness for change:

1. *Precontemplation*—People in this stage do not recognize a need for change and consequently have no intention of making changes in their emotions, thoughts, or actions in the foreseeable future. They will probably be reluctant to disclose information about themselves and are unlikely to engage in goal setting.

Strategies: Clients must recognize the need for change before they can be engaged in the treatment process. Strategies should focus on raising doubts about the effectiveness of people's current behaviors. Looking at the results of their choices and whether their actions are meeting their needs is a good place to begin discussion.

2. *Contemplation*—People in this stage recognize that they have some difficulties and they have some preliminary awareness of the need for personal change. However, they have not yet decided whether to invest themselves in the process of changing. They may be dubious about their ability to successfully change, they may not know effective ways to make changes, or they may not even be aware that alternatives to their current emotions, thoughts, and actions exist.

Strategies: As with people in the precontemplation stage of change, clinicians can promote motivation toward change by helping clients see the drawbacks and risks of continuing their current behaviors and choices. Helping people become more hopeful about the prospects of change also can facilitate progress. This can be accomplished by making them aware of the availability of effective procedures for change, strengthening their optimism and confidence in their ability to make positive changes, and educating them about better choices they might make.

3. *Preparation*—People in this stage of change not only recognize the importance of making some changes in their lives, but they are even planning on making some changes within the next month. They may not know exactly how or what they want to change, but they are ready to move forward.

Strategies: Clinicians can build on the commitment these people have already made to change. Helping them to develop specific, achievable, and meaningful goals; identifying the best routes to change; and formulating an action plan, including a time line and initial steps toward successful change, can propel these clients forward in their efforts to change.

4. *Action*—People in this stage are ready to make some positive changes; in fact, they have already taken steps to change their environment, emotions, thoughts, or actions. However, they are still struggling to find the most effective ways to change. They may have established unrealistic goals, may not know where to begin to tackle sizable goals, or may expect too much of themselves.

Strategies: Congratulating people in this stage for moving forward and helping them develop positive feelings about their progress can solidify the gains they have already made. Additional strategies that build on those gains include: developing goals; breaking down sizable goals into manageable pieces; identifying steps toward change that are small, specific, and realistic; and giving a logical sequence to clients' steps toward change. Encouraging continued progress via rewards, reinforcements, and other methods can prevent loss of momentum and backsliding.

5. *Maintenance*—In this stage, people have already made many positive changes and have achieved most or all of their objectives. They have developed a repertoire of new emotions, thoughts, and actions that are healthy and growth promoting. They are seeing gratifying changes in their lifestyles. However, relapse continues to be a risk, and signs of relapse may even be present.

Strategies: Solidifying gains is the most important process in this stage. People may lack confidence that they can persist in the changes they have made, may not yet have encountered challenges to their newfound successes, or may be having difficulty coping with the challenges they have encountered. Identifying and addressing risk factors, alerting people to the signs of relapse, and helping them develop the coping skills they need to ward off threats to progress can strengthen their resolve to maintain positive change and give them confidence that they can stay on track. Developing both intrinsic and extrinsic sources of support and motivation can further enhance the likelihood that gains will be maintained.

6. *Termination*—In this final stage, clients have satisfactorily attained their goals, made positive changes, and learned new attitudes and skills that can maintain and perhaps even build on progress already made. Clients in this stage typically are confident that they can cope more effectively with life's challenges and know how to find help if they feel overwhelmed or begin to revert to their former unhealthy behaviors and attitudes. Treatment is a success for both client and clinician.

Strategies: More will be said about the termination process later in this chapter. In general, treatment for people in this last stage of the change process entails identification, consolidation, and reinforcement of gains. In addition, clients and clinicians may look to the future in order to help clients establish goals they are now likely to achieve on their own, using the knowledge and skills they have acquired through their treatment.

Of course, treatment does not always have such a positive ending. Miller and Rollnick (1991), applying the Stages of Change Model to people with addictive behaviors, suggested that the final stage is sometimes Relapse, rather than Termination. If that is the case, helpful strategies include strengthening clients' motivation, reinforcing their ability to change, helping them to reinstitute the successful coping skills they learned, and bolstering their morale.

Examples

The following three clients represent three different levels in the Stages of Change Model. Notice how the interventions planned for these people address the stage each is in when he or she seeks treatment. The Learning Opportunities at the end of this chapter will afford you the experience of identifying the appropriate stage of change for several clients and suggesting interventions that match their level of readiness for treatment.

• *Client 1*—Lita was court-mandated to a treatment program providing help with anger management. She frequently engaged in explosive and aggressive behavior. One night when her partner returned home several hours later than promised, Lisa began pelting her with dishes and shoes. A neighbor called the police, who took Lita into custody. She explained her behavior by stating that she believed her partner had been with her former girlfriend. Lita viewed her behavior as justified in light of her suspicions and her partner's late arrival. Lita is in the Precontemplation stage of change.

Strategies: Lita's therapist encouraged her to examine her long history of explosive behavior, along with the consequences of that behavior. Her actions had cost her several relationships that had been important to her, she had been beaten on more than one occasion when someone retaliated, and she was now threatened with imprisonment.

• *Client 2*—Roberto, age 9, had been diagnosed with mild mental retardation and an attention-deficit/hyperactivity disorder. Since he began school, he had difficulty paying attention, often interrupted his classmates to blurt out answers, and often broke or lost items of importance. Although he was in a special program designed to address his special needs, he did poorly in school and had difficulty forming friendships with his peers. He recognized that he needed to make some changes and, with the help of his parents and teachers, had developed a list of changes he needed to make. However, Roberto felt overwhelmed by the long list and felt discouraged about the process of change. Roberto is in the Preparation stage of change.

Strategies: Roberto and his counselor reviewed the list of desired changes, shortened the list, and identified the two most important goals: completion of his homework and not blurting out answers in class. They then agreed on two small steps Roberto could take with the help of his family and teachers to initiate the change process. These steps (checking with his teacher at the end of each day to ensure that he had written down his assignments correctly and drawing a hand on the outside of his notebook to remind him to raise his hand when he had something to say in class) were specific, meaningful, and readily attainable.

• *Client 3*—Khorn, a Cambodian woman, had worked hard in treatment to deal with the terrible experiences she had in her native land and to adjust to life in the United States. She was much less anxious, was sleeping better, had found employment, and had begun to form some friendships outside of her immediate family. However, her difficult background and the enormous changes she had experienced left her feeling uncertain that she would be able to maintain the gains she had made. Khorn was in the Maintenance stage of change.

Strategies: Khorn's therapist helped her to identify support groups and community resources that would promote Khorn's efforts to maintain her gains. In addition, her therapist worked with Khorn to list her gains and coping skills. They discussed hypothetical situations that might cause her to resume her unhealthy thoughts and behaviors and identified ways she might cope successfully with those challenges. In addition, her therapist helped her develop warning signs of relapse, along with ways she might seek help to prevent a full relapse. This entire process was done in a way that would further empower Khorn, reinforce the many gains she had made, and consolidate them to make them readily accessible to her.

REFERRAL AND COLLABORATION

Effective use of referral and collaboration is another important way to promote positive change. Clinicians generally spend 50 minutes a week or less in face-to-face contact with a client. However, positive growth and change are ongoing processes that are encouraged not only by therapy but by many factors in people's daily lives. If we can help people build into their lives additional factors that enhance their development and coping skills, the treatment process is likely to be more effective and efficient. In addition, as powerful as counseling and psychotherapy are, clinicians and their treatment procedures clearly have limitations that perhaps can be alleviated through additional sources of help.

Today, counseling and psychotherapy are increasingly collaborative procedures. For example, residents in a correctional setting where I served as a consultant were assigned to a treatment team, composed of the following members:

- a psychiatrist who monitored and prescribed medication
- a counselor who was responsible for individual psychotherapy
- a peer helper, typically someone with a history of criminal behavior and drug or alcohol problems, who was now recovering and helping others with similar difficulties
- a clinical psychologist who provided a deeper understanding of the clients via psychological testing
- a life skills trainer who taught the program residents to manage money and keep a budget, locate appropriate housing, and develop other basic skills needed to function effectively in society
- a job placement specialist who helped people become aware of their work-related skills and interests, apply for employment, and successfully begin working as they made the transition from prison to community

In addition, residents of this correctional program had the opportunity to participate in Alcoholics Anonymous and other self-help programs, to engage in team sports, to work out regularly, and to take classes in communication skills, relationship building, and parenting.

Of course, most programs and clinicians do not offer such an extensive array of services. However, clinicians are increasingly recognizing the advantages of a multifaceted treatment plan and so are collaborating with other programs and clinicians to enrich the services available to their clients.

Determining the Need for Referral or Collaboration

When you are thinking about including another source of help in a client's treatment plan, consider the following six questions:

1. Does this person need professional services that I cannot provide?
   - Should the person have a medication evaluation?
   - Does the person need a psychological evaluation to clarify the diagnosis or determine whether a specific disorder is present (e.g., mental retardation, learning disorder, dementia)?
   - Does the person need a medical evaluation to determine whether physical conditions are contributing to symptoms?
   - Does the person need to be detoxified from drugs or alcohol, or does the person need frequent screenings to determine whether that person has used drugs or alcohol?
   - Would the person benefit from family counseling, career counseling, or group therapy?
   - Are there other psychological services such as eye movement desensitization and reprocessing, hypnotherapy, or biofeedback that might enhance treatment?

2. Does the person seem likely to benefit from participation in a self-help or peer support group? Such groups are especially useful to people with the following types of concerns:
   - drug or alcohol problems
   - eating disorders
   - other impulse-control disorders
   - chronic or life-threatening medical problems
   - major life changes (e.g., separation/divorce, bereavement, suicide of a close friend or family member, having a child with a severe emotional or other problem)
   - traumatic experiences (e.g., war experience, natural disaster, physical or sexual abuse, or severe family dysfunction)
3. Does the person need more friends and social contacts, and is the person ready to interact with others? If so, participation in groups that reflect the person's interests, such as book discussion groups, hiking clubs, karate classes, or quilting groups, can provide possibilities for interaction and friendship.
4. Does the person have a need for increased physical activity? If so, joining a health club or participating in a team sport or organization designed to promote a particular sport can have emotional and physical benefits as well as provide opportunities for interaction.
5. Does the person have a need for government or social services?
   - Does the person lack financial resources for basic needs?
   - Does the person need help in locating and paying for safe and affordable housing?
   - Is the person seeking to reenter the workforce but facing barriers such as child care, limited skills, or lack of appropriate clothing?
   - Does the person have a disability that limits mobility and employment?
   - Is the person an immigrant or from another culture, and might that person benefit from either a closer connection with representatives of that culture or from services designed to help people from diverse cultural backgrounds?
   - Is the person over the age of 65?
   - Does the person need legal assistance but cannot afford a lawyer?
   - Does the person have medical problems but cannot afford medical care?
6. Does the person need help in acquiring information and skills that cannot easily be provided during the course of counseling or psychotherapy? Training in such areas as effective parenting, nutrition, study skills, and self-defense can be beneficial to some people.

Planning the Referral or Collaboration

Once clinicians have determined that a client is likely to benefit from professional or other services that are not provided as part of the counseling or psychotherapy, they need to plan the integration of those services into the treatment process. This should be done collaboratively; generally the clinician will suggest a referral and then will discuss the benefits and possible disadvantages of the referral with the client. Unless the clinician believes that the referral is essential to continuing treatment, such as a physical or medication evaluation, the final decision about whether to accept a referral is the client's.

The timing of the referral often is critical to its eventual outcome. Particularly risky is a premature referral, placing clients in situations that are threatening and uncomfortable for them. Referrals generally should not be made until clients have developed a strong collaborative alliance with their clinicians as well as the self-confidence and coping skills that will enable them to effectively manage their discomfort and benefit from the referral. Unless the client has an urgent need for outside help, clinicians should take the time to get to know their clients, establish and begin to implement a treatment plan, and become confident that the referral will be a successful and beneficial experience for the client. A failed referral, especially one that raises clients' self-doubts, can harm the client and jeopardize the therapeutic relationship.

Determining whether to have direct contact with the referral source is another important decision for the clinician. Sometimes the answer is obvious. For example, a clinician is unlikely to establish direct contact with the director of a bridge club the client is joining, but would almost certainly contact the psychiatrist who is seeing a client for a medication evaluation. At other times, the answer may require thought. For example, should the clinician contact the gynecologist of a woman who has been sexually abused and who has been apprehensive about her upcoming medical appointment? What about contacting the person who oversees workers compensation benefits for a client who has had a traumatic work-related injury? Contact should probably be made with these people but only after thought and discussion with each client.

Of course, disclosure of any information about clients, even the fact that someone is a client, requires the clients' consent, unless ethical or legal standards mandate disclosure of information to prevent harm. When clients agree that the clinician and a referral source should be in communication to facilitate collaborative work and shared decision making, clients should sign a written release that permits mutual disclosure of relevant information.

A close collaboration is especially important between clinician and psychiatrist or other physician. The two need to confer about the impact of medical treatment on emotional symptoms and whether the psychotropic medication is ameliorating symptoms or causing side effects. Although the physician may be the expert on medication, often the clinician has the most contact with the client and is in the best position to describe the client's symptoms and learn about the impact of the medication. By maintaining communication with a psychiatrist or other physician, clinicians can help prevent clients from discontinuing medication in harmful ways, failing to comply with medical recommendations, and giving up hope that medication can benefit them. Finding a helpful medication for a client often entails a process of trial and error. Enabling clients to understand that process and keeping physicians informed of clients' emotional and physical reactions to a medication can contribute greatly to effective treatment.

Application

Now that you are familiar with some of the options and guidelines for referral and collaboration, you can use the following important questions to guide the referral process:

- Would some type of referral enhance this person's treatment?
- If so, what type of referral or outside service should that be?
- How do I think the referral will enhance the client's treatment?
- When should the referral be made?
- Should I, the clinician, obtain the client's permission and contact the referral source?
- What information do I need from the client or from the referral source to determine whether the referral is accomplishing what I hoped it would?

The following cases illustrate the application of these questions to specific clients:

Client 1—Sheila is a 69-year-old woman who has severe arthritis. She has driven little since her husband died 6 months ago and is concerned about transportation to her medical appointments. Her sadness about her husband's death has been exacerbated by her own medical condition. She knows that she needs to establish a more rewarding life for herself but feels hopeless about the future.

- Would some type of referral enhance this person's treatment?
  - Yes, Sheila is coping with many serious difficulties and probably would benefit from some outside sources of help. She clearly needs more help than counseling alone can offer.
- If so, what type of referral or outside service should that be?
  - support group for people diagnosed with arthritis
  - sources of information on arthritis and its treatment
  - information about low-cost transportation to help people get to medical appointments
  - bereavement support group
  - classes or groups focused on activities of interest to Sheila
  - medication evaluation due to Sheila's depression
- How do I think that the referral will enhance the client's treatment?
  - provide support, information, social contacts, and rewarding activities
  - improve mood
- When should the referral be made?
  - Referrals for medication, arthritis support and information programs, and low-cost transportation should be made almost immediately.
  - Referrals for the bereavement support groups and activity groups should be made later, once the immediate crisis has subsided.
- Should I, the clinician, obtain the client's permission and contact the referral source?
  - The psychiatrist should certainly be contacted.
  - Depending on Sheila's preferences, the clinician might also contact the arthritis and bereavement support programs.
  - Activity group leaders probably need not be contacted unless Sheila believes it would help her if the clinician paved the way for her to begin the activity groups or classes.
- What information do I need from the client or from the referral source to determine whether the referral is accomplishing what I hoped it would?

- scores from administrations of the Beck Depression Inventory to monitor changes in level of depression
- feedback from the psychiatrist on medication recommendations
- self-reports from Sheila on the support, information, and activity programs

Client 2—Chantha is an 18-year-old girl who arrived in the United States from Southeast Asia about 5 years ago. Although language and cultural differences clearly play a part in her difficulties, other concerns also are relevant. Chantha left high school in the 10th grade and has had a series of unrewarding and unsuccessful jobs since that time. She reports great difficulty in learning and concentrating, dating back to her early childhood. She is living with her family and has few outside friendships or activities. She reported some experimentation with drugs, a great source of shame to her. In addition, she reports seeing deceased family members, especially when using drugs.

- Would some type of referral enhance this person's treatment?
  - Determining the nature of Chantha's difficulties, as well as ameliorating them, is challenging because they seem to be multidetermined. Outside sources of help are clearly indicated.
- If so, what type of referral or outside service should that be?
  - A thorough evaluation of Chantha's mental health and learning and intellectual abilities is indicated; this should be done by a clinician with strong multicultural competencies and knowledge of Chantha's language and culture. Particular attention should be paid to determining whether current drug use, an attention-deficit disorder, a learning disorder, and a psychotic disorder are present.
  - The evaluation might indicate the need for a medication referral.
  - Career assessment and counseling and job placement would be beneficial to Chantha.
  - In addition, Chantha needs help in regaining her once strong connection to her culture of origin and also becoming part of her new culture. More active involvement in activities related to both cultures might be very helpful to her.
- How do I think that the referral will enhance the client's treatment?
- A careful assessment of Chantha's abilities will facilitate effective treatment planning and identification of job possibilities and activities that might provide her with successful experiences.
- When should the referral be made?
  - The assessment should be conducted as soon as Chantha is willing to invest time in that process and appreciates the value it might have for her.
  - If a referral for a medication evaluation is needed, that, too, should occur early in the treatment process.
  - Other sources of help can be gradually phased in; the clinician should be careful not to overwhelm Chantha with many new and possibly anxiety-provoking experiences.
- Should I, the clinician, obtain the client's permission and contact the referral source?
  - Contact should be made with the person who is conducting the assessment to clarify the reasons for the assessment and with the psychiatrist, if a medication referral is needed.

- Contact probably should also be initiated with the person helping to facilitate Chantha's career development.
- Contact will probably not be initiated with the other referral sources.
- What information do I need from the client or from the referral source to determine whether the referral is accomplishing what I hoped it would?
  - A complete written report of Chantha's psychological assessment is needed.
  - The psychiatrist could supply a verbal report of any medications that were prescribed and their anticipated effects.
  - A verbal assessment from the career counselor probably would be useful.
  - Chantha's description of the benefits and drawbacks of the other referral sources will probably be sufficient.

STRUCTURING INTERVENTIONS, SESSIONS, AND THE OVERALL TREATMENT PROCESS

Make progress and solidify gains. These are the principles that guide the structure of the treatment process. If treatment rushes forward in a haphazard way without moving toward goal attainment or reinforcing gains, both clients and clinicians are likely to feel that they are floundering or walking through a maze without end. On the other hand, treatment that focuses almost exclusively on maintenance of gains can feel like running in place; it may be rewarding for a time but will ultimately feel limiting and unfulfilling.

Consider the following client statement, followed by three possible clinician responses:

Amalia: That role play we did on talking to my supervisor was really helpful. I did talk with her and made progress in resolving the billing problem, but then my computer crashed and I felt helpless and overwhelmed again.

Clinician 1:   What did you do about feeling helpless and overwhelmed again?

Clinician 2:   So you really felt good about your talk with your supervisor.

Clinician 3:   So you were successful in problem solving with your supervisor but lost some of your confidence when your computer crashed. Let's look at both sides of that. What did you do that worked so well in talking to your supervisor?

As you can see, the first clinician response ignores the progress Amalia has made, while the second one overlooks her subsequent loss of confidence. However, the third clinician attends to both the effective skills that Amalia used as well as their fragility; she felt overwhelmed again when another crisis occurred. This intervention is most likely to help Amalia see that she did make successful use of new thoughts and behaviors and to facilitate her application of those new skills to other situations.

The guiding principle of *making progress and solidifying gains* can be used at all levels of intervention: a single clinician statement, a segment of a session, an entire session, and the complete treatment process. This principle promotes hope and optimism in clients. It enables them to see that they are learning new ways of feeling, thinking, and acting and are achieving some success through these changes. This is empowering and encourages them to meet new challenges and continue to move forward toward their goals. Use of this format in an intake or initial session can increase people's motivation toward treatment and initiates a sense of accomplishment, even in the first hour of treatment. Later in this chapter, we will discuss the application of this principle to the termination process.

When structuring interventions, sessions, and the overall treatment process, clinicians should keep the following two principles in mind. These were discussed in an earlier chapter.

- *Collaboration with the client is essential.* The client's presenting concerns and goals, accomplishments and disappointments, motivation and fears all should be considered as both client and clinician work together to determine the direction of the treatment process.
- *Clients and clinicians should have established clear, meaningful, and measurable goals.* Those goals should be reflected in the direction of progress and the gains that are reinforced.

Structuring the Intervention and Treatment Segment

Although, of course, not all interventions will follow the format of *making progress and solidifying gains,* keeping that framework in mind can help clinicians ensure that clients take pride in and learn from their accomplishments while continuing to move forward toward their goals. This framework also can provide a sense of closure and completion to the treatment process.

Let's consider Amalia, the client introduced earlier. Through the course of treatment, Amalia described herself as a person with many self-doubts who blamed herself when anything went wrong. She avoided dealing with problems because she feared that confronting them would only reveal her inadequacies. She and her therapist had been addressing Amalia's distorted cognitions that contributed to her self-blame. In addition, her therapist had been teaching her communication and assertiveness skills to help her deal with problems more immediately and effectively.

Amalia's job involved processing, checking, and paying the bills for a large organization. In the previous incident, she had failed to back up her computer records and consequently had lost documentation substantiating the validity of bills submitted by a particular vendor. Amalia dealt with this by discarding bills from that vendor for nearly 6 months, until the vendor threatened to contact the president of the company. With help from her therapist, Amalia planned and role-played ways to present this situation to her supervisor; Amalia accepted responsibility for the problem and acknowledged her errors but avoided her usual pattern of excessive and generalized self-blame. In addition, she developed two possible solutions to the problem that she offered to her supervisor. She made a commitment to her therapist that she would contact her supervisor within two days.

Amalia successfully followed the plan she had developed with her therapist. She contacted her supervisor promptly, presented the problem clearly and concisely, took appropriate responsibility for the current situation, and offered possible solutions. Although her supervisor was dismayed that Amalia had not addressed this problem sooner and strongly advised her of ways to avoid future situations of this nature, she did not attack, humiliate, or fire Amalia as Amalia had feared. In fact, her supervisor commended Amalia for her creative solutions to the problem and for taking responsibility for her errors.

Although this experience was a powerful learning experience for Amalia, her long-standing self-doubts remained strong. When her computer crashed again, the anxiety associated with her previous computer problem rushed back to her. At least temporarily, she lost sight of her accomplishments and reverted to her former pattern of guilt, fear, and self-blame.

For most people, once they have made progress in overcoming a problem, it becomes easier for them to draw on their history of successes to rebound from a setback. Keeping this in mind enabled Amalia's therapist to reinforce her gains and continue her forward movement. After identifying both Amalia's accomplishments with her supervisor and the deeply ingrained negative responses Amalia had to the second computer failure, the therapist began by collaborating with Amalia to reinforce and strengthen her gains. Discussion focused on Amalia's courage in finally addressing this problem, her follow-through on the plan she had developed, her use of assertiveness skills, her willingness to accept appropriate responsibility without either making excuses for herself or devaluing herself, and her ability to formulate tentative solutions to the problem. Rather than praising Amalia lavishly, the therapist enabled Amalia to identify her own strengths in this incident and take pride in her successful use of new skills.

Attention then shifted to the recent computer failure and Amalia's automatic reactions of self-blame and hopelessness. The therapist helped Amalia to recognize the relatively minor consequences of this situation and enabled her to transfer successful use of her new skills to this situation. Amalia recognized that she needed additional training and probably also needed a more powerful computer to help her accomplish her job. She planned and role-played a dialogue with her supervisor in which she would request both of these. Throughout the process, her therapist coached her on ways she could continue to use, and even build on, her new skills. With plans in place for Amalia to talk to her supervisor, this segment of the session was concluded.

This segment of the session with Amalia included the following seven steps:

1. follow-up on plans and new learning from previous session
2. identification of new presenting concern
3. reinforcement of accomplishments and application of new skills
4. exploration of new presenting concern
5. establishment of link between new skills and new concern
6. application of new skills to current concern
7. development of specific plans to address current concern

The interweaving of new learning and current concerns, the application of effective skills to those current concerns, and the development of plans to use the skills to resolve the current concerns make a powerful treatment package. Such a structure can characterize a single intervention, a segment of a session, an entire session, a series of sessions, or an entire therapeutic interaction. However, it probably lends itself best to structuring a segment of a session.

Structuring the Session

Let's broaden our perspective and look at an entire counseling session. Whether it is a 20-minute meeting in a school counselor's office, a 50-minute session in a private practice or community mental health center, or a 90-minute group or family counseling session, all treatment sessions have a beginning, a middle, and an end. In addition, all sessions have a sense of flow or movement, perhaps smooth and productive, perhaps rocky and erratic. Having a prototype in mind for the format of a session can increase the likelihood that the session will be a smooth and productive one.

Many outlines for clinical sessions have been developed. Two useful ones, developed by Judith Beck and Allen Ivey, are presented here. Clinicians can use these as a basis for developing their own session formats that take account of the nature of their clients, the clinical setting, the length of the sessions, typical client concerns, and treatment goals.

Judith Beck (1995), a cognitive therapist, advocates the importance of having a clear and consistent structure to treatment sessions. The following 10-step format is typical of Beck's sessions:

1. Collaborate with the client to establish a meaningful agenda for the session.
2. Determine and measure the intensity of the person's mood.
3. Identify and discuss current concerns.
4. Establish clear and meaningful goals for the session.
5. Embed the current concerns in context, focusing especially on similar concerns that the client has handled successfully.
6. Help client to identify connections between current concerns and past difficulties.
7. Draw on past successes and promote development of new skills that will help person resolve current concerns.
8. Suggest tasks to be completed between sessions.
9. Summarize the session.
10. Elicit client feedback on the session.

Allen Ivey and his colleagues (Ivey, Ivey, & Simek-Morgan, 1997), in a similar effort to develop a prototype for a clinical interview, suggested that a treatment session should include the following five steps:

1. Establish rapport and structure the interview.
2. Gather information on concerns, strengths, and resources.
3. Define desired outcomes.
4. Generate alternatives and address obstacles to successful resolution of difficulties.
5. Generalize and transfer learning.

Although Beck and Ivey have very different theoretical orientations, with Beck advocating cognitive therapy and Ivey advancing the growth of developmental counseling and therapy (DCT), considerable similarity is evident in their session prototypes. Both include the following three stages:

1. Beginning
   - Development and strengthening of rapport
   - Review of previous session and outcome of homework tasks
   - Assessment of current mood
   - Presentation of immediate concerns and issues
   - Identification of desired outcomes
2. Middle
   - Identification and reinforcement of accomplishments and new learning
   - Exploration of immediate concerns and issues

- Linking of immediate concerns and issues to context (history, other concerns, accomplishments, and new learning)
- Development of ways to resolve and manage current concerns
- Learning and practicing relevant skills that can promote personal growth and resolution of current concerns

3. End
- Consolidation of learning
- Development of a detailed plan to continue addressing remaining concerns
- Suggestion of relevant between-session tasks
- Summarization of session
- Eliciting client feedback and wrapping up session

Structuring the Treatment Process

Just like the session, the treatment process has a beginning, middle, and end. The point at which one phase of treatment stops and another begins is usually unclear and treatment often needs to dip back temporarily into an earlier phase. However, keeping these three stages in mind can help ensure the success of treatment. Considerable progress needs to be made toward achievement of the goals of each stage before treatment can successfully move on to the next stage. The objectives and procedures of the treatment process can be conceptualized as follows:

1. Beginning
- Provide information on the treatment process, including ethical guidelines, clinician's training and theoretical orientation, school or agency policies, and the appropriate roles of client and clinician.
- Explore client's immediate reasons for seeking treatment, expectations for treatment, and presenting concerns.
- Begin to develop rapport and a collaborative therapeutic alliance.
- Gather information on client's background, emotions, thoughts, and actions, usually via an intake interview.
- Develop a diagnosis and/or case conceptualization.
- Establish clear, meaningful, and measurable treatment goals.

2. Middle
- Determine treatment systems and strategies that are likely to promote client development and ameliorate client's concerns.
- Apply treatment systems and strategies to client issues.
- Teach client skills that can lead to growth and problem resolution.
- Track progress and revise treatment plan as needed.
- Reinforce and promote generalization of learning and progress.

3. End
- Determine that client has achieved adequate realization of goals.
- Determine that no new goals warrant treatment at present.
- Consolidate, reinforce, and generalize learning and new skills.
- Provide relapse prevention strategies.
- Share feedback regarding the treatment process and conclude treatment process.

PROGRESS NOTES

Having a prototype in mind for each session will facilitate the writing of progress notes (also known as process notes or session notes). The growing emphasis on accountability, concern about malpractice suits, and especially clinicians' goals of providing the best possible treatment to their clients, have combined to make progress notes an important component of the treatment process.

Clear, concise, and accurate progress notes have many advantages. They can

- remind the clinician of the nature of previous sessions with a client.
- remind the clinician of topics and tasks from a previous session that should be addressed in a future session.
- facilitate assessment of the effectiveness of treatment interventions.
- allow the clinician to track the overall progress or movement of the treatment process and determine whether adequate progress is being made.
- provide a vehicle for communication with other mental health treatment providers.
- help the clinician document the treatment process and demonstrate that appropriate treatment has been provided, if legal or ethical questions are raised about the treatment.

Progress notes can be made in a chart, in a computer file (as long as confidentiality is maintained), or simply on a blank piece of paper. Progress notes should include the date of the session, the name (and sometimes the birth date) of the client, information on the content and process of the session, and the signature of the clinician who wrote the progress notes. Progress notes should be brief and concise, containing essential information about the session. Paring down the rich content of a session to a brief but informative paragraph or two is usually the most challenging aspect of progress notes.

Formats for the content of progress notes vary. Some clinicians have developed their own structure for these notes while others follow formats used by their schools or agencies. Several standardized formats also have been developed.

SOAP Format

Widely used, especially in medical settings, is the SOAP format (Law, Morocco, & Wilmarth, 1981). This acronym represents four elements in the progress notes (subjective, objective, analysis, plans). Descriptions of these elements follow, along with a question that reflects the substance of that element. Answering the questions associated with each element will help you develop a progress note for a given session.

Subjective—This section includes the clinicians' impressions of the client and the session, addressing such topics as the nature of the therapeutic alliance, the client's mood and level of functioning, and progress made since the prior session.
Question: What were your impressions of the client during this session; particularly, what progress or backsliding was evident?
Objective—This provides information on the content of the session and any important experiences or concrete changes in the client (e.g., taking a new job, applying to college).

Question: What was the focus of this session, and what new information did you learn about the client?

Analysis—Here, clinicians make sense of the subjective and objective information presented, interpreting or commenting on the significance of that information.

Question: What is the significance of your observations and the information provided during this session in terms of your understanding of the client and the direction of treatment?

Plans—In this last section of the progress note, clinicians develop both short- and long-range treatment plans. Particular attention is paid to suggested between-session tasks, important topics that need to be discussed further, other issues needing attention or follow-up, and plans for future interventions.

Question: What tasks did you suggest to the client, and what are your plans for the next session with this client?

The following is an example of a progress note, following the SOAP format:

December 2, 2002—7th individual session with Gregory O'Malley (D.O.B. 7/14/75)
Gregory arrived late for the session, avoided making eye contact, and seemed anxious and uncomfortable throughout the session (S). He reported that he had three drinks, following an unsuccessful job interview, and was disappointed that he had only been able to maintain his sobriety for two months. Conflict with his wife escalated as a result of Gregory's drinking (O). Despite some good initial use of stress management and other coping skills, Gregory was unable to maintain his abstinence from alcohol when confronted with stress and perceived rejection. He continues to need help in both understanding the risk of relapse and strengthening his coping skills. I helped Gregory identify the triggers for his relapse and taught him to make better use of relaxation and stress management skills (A). Gregory agreed to practice the skills reviewed in this session and to attend an extra AA meeting each week. The next sessions should follow up on these plans and continue to strengthen his ability to remain alcohol-free. Attention should also be paid to his interactions with his wife. Clinician: Diana Rodriguez, Ph.D., Licensed Psychologist

STIPS Format

Another format for progress notes is the STIPS format (Prieto & Scheel, 2002). Here, too, an acronym represents the five elements in the progress notes:

Signs and Symptoms: This first part of the progress note describes the client's current level of functioning, along with clinical symptoms and significant changes from the previous session. This is almost like a very brief mental status examination.

Topics of Discussion: The issues discussed in the session, as well as any changes in the client's issues, are recorded in this section.

Interventions: Here, clinicians describe the treatment system and specific interventions used in the session to address the client's concerns.

Progress and Plan: This section of the progress note describes indications of client improvement as well as difficulties encountered in the session and other obstacles to client progress. Plans for the next session also are included here.

Special Issues: New issues are included here, along with critical client dynamics such as suicidal ideation, dangerousness, or loss of contact with reality.

Think about which of these models for progress notes you prefer and which seems most likely to help you in your work. Both the SOAP and STIPS formats are better suited to clinical than school settings, but they can be used in modified or abbreviated ways in all settings. Perhaps you will decide to revise one of these models or develop one of your own that is well suited to your clinical setting, or perhaps your school or agency has its own model for progress notes. The exercises at the end of this chapter will afford you an opportunity to write some progress notes.

GENERATING SOLUTIONS TO CLIENTS' PROBLEMS

Thus far, this chapter has presented four topics that emphasize the importance of identifying and addressing clients' difficulties: the stages of change model, referral and collaboration, structured formats for treatment sessions, and progress notes. Understanding people's primary concerns and providing them some help with those problems are essential to building a sound therapeutic alliance and promoting client motivation and progress.

Treatment is most likely to be successful and empowering if client and clinician work together to address the client's concerns. However, sometimes people ask clinicians to solve their problems for them or tell them what to do. Such clients might ask:

- My teacher picks on me. What should I do?
- My supervisor gives my colleagues credit for work I have done. What should I do?
- My wife leaves her crafts projects all over the house; it looks like a mess. What should I do?
- I'm pregnant and my boyfriend says the baby isn't his. What should I do?

These are only a few of the many requests for advice that clinicians receive from their clients. Because we want to help our clients, because we probably have some good ideas as to what they should do, and because it is gratifying to us to find solutions to problems that have stumped others, we may be tempted to reply with a suggestion: "You should talk to your teacher," "You should inform your supervisor of the contributions you make," "You need to express your feelings to your wife," or "You need to determine whether or not he is the father."

Pitfalls of Advice Giving

Whether or not these are useful and helpful ideas, clinicians should be extremely cautious about moving into an advice-giving role for several reasons:

- Self-determination is a core value in the mental health professions; assuming that we know what is best for our clients violates their right to self-determination.
- Telling clients what they should do can communicate a lack of confidence in their ability to solve their own problems.
- Even if the advice is helpful in the short run, telling people what is best for them does not teach them to solve their own problems; instead, they learn that asking another person what to do is the best strategy when confronted with a problem.

- Many people have a "yes, but . . ." reaction when others tell them what they should do: "Yes, but I have already talked to the teacher," or "Yes, but I know in my heart that he is the father of my child." Perhaps the client has already tried the clinician's suggestion, perhaps the advice is not right for the client, or perhaps the client does not really want to be told what to do. Often, one "yes, but . . ." response leads to another, until the clinician feels discouraged and drained of ideas, as in the following example:

  Client: My teacher picks on me. What should I do?

  Clinician: You should try to discuss this with the teacher.

  Client: Yes, but she's so busy, she never listens to me.

  Clinician: What about scheduling an after-school appointment with her?

  Client: Yes, but I have to catch the bus right after class.

  Clinician: Can you arrange to meet with her on your lunch break?

  Client: Yes, but she has lunch then, too.

  Clinician: Can one of your parents pick you up so you can stay late at school one day?

  Client: Yes, but it's hard for them to get time off of work.

  As you can see, this is not a productive dialogue.

- If the client follows the advice and it turns out not to be helpful, then the client may blame the clinician for providing harmful direction. This can lead the client to lose confidence in the clinician and the treatment process and can even lead to the premature termination of treatment.

- Although some clients appear to want the clinician to give them advice and suggestions, they may not really want that sort of help and may undermine the help that is provided. There are several possible reasons for this sort of interaction. Perhaps the clients want to prove to another person that therapy is not helpful to them, perhaps they need to be in control, or perhaps their self-doubts make it difficult for them to believe that anything can help them. For a variety of reasons, clients sometimes sabotage the treatment process and seek to demonstrate that it cannot help them. Giving clients advice makes it especially easy for them to demonstrate that treatment is not working for them.

Alternatives to Advice Giving

What then should a clinician do when a client requests advice? Two general principles should guide your thinking when you respond to clients' requests for advice:

- *Build on strengths that people already have.*
- *Facilitate people's efforts to solve their own problems*—so they develop the confidence and skills they need to continue to resolve their own difficulties.

Many specific strategies are available to help clinicians implement these principles in their work. The growth and development of brief, solution-based therapy has provided the basis for some of these (de Shazer, 1988; O'Hanlon & Weiner-Davis, 1989). The following list includes strategies that clinicians can use when asked or tempted to give advice. These will be illustrated with reference to the statement made by Juan: My wife leaves her crafts projects all over the house; it looks like a mess. What should I do?

Help people identify strategies they have used successfully to resolve past problems and concerns. Facilitate application of those strategies to the present problem.

- Juan, the man in this example, had a business colleague who annoyed him with loud music and distracting telephone conversations. Juan initiated a conversation about the problem, beginning with identification of his colleague's strengths and then collaborating with him to find a solution. They agreed that the music and telephone calls would be restricted to the afternoon, allowing Juan some quiet time in the morning for his most intensive work projects. Initiating a conversation with his wife, emphasizing the many strengths in their relationship, expressing his concerns in a nonblaming way, and then seeking a compromise reflected transfer of the skills that Juan used successfully in the past to the present situation.

Brainstorming solutions to the problem can be a creative and productive way to help people resolve their own difficulties. Both client and clinician participate in developing a list of potential strategies to address a particular problem. Both viable and frivolous ideas should be included to stimulate discussion and allow client the opportunity to think about and evaluate the advantages and disadvantages of each suggestion.

- Juan and his therapist developed the following list of possible solutions:
    1. I suggest that we turn the spare bedroom into a craft room for my wife.
    2. I clean up after her each evening.
    3. I talk to my wife about this problem and ask her for possible solutions.
    4. I leave my woodworking supplies all over the house so that my wife can see how annoying it is when the house is a mess.
    5. I buy my wife a dog so that she won't have so much time to spend on crafts.
    6. I just live with this situation and focus on my wife's many strengths.
    7. I offer to help my wife finish her craft projects so that she can put them away.

  Clearly, not all of these solutions are good ideas. However, the goal of the brainstorming process is to generate possibilities that can then be evaluated and modified until a good solution emerges.

Review what the client has already done to resolve the problem and encourage new approaches. Before seeking advice from a clinician, people have usually made considerable effort to resolve their own difficulties. However, people's repertoire of strategies tends to be limited, and they typically do more of the same rather than seeking new solutions. Bringing a new perspective into a well-worn situation and interrupting repetitive and nonproductive sequences of behaviors can be therapeutic and can help people see new and hopeful possibilities.

- Juan's usual way of dealing with his wife's tendency to leave her crafts projects around the house was to nag and criticize her for her sloppy behavior. Although she might put her projects away temporarily, she would inevitably fall back into her old behaviors. Juan responded to this by nagging more and becoming even more angry and critical. This not only failed to resolve the problem but also escalated conflict and tension between Juan and his wife. At the clinician's suggestion that he consider a new approach, Juan decided that he would try to praise his wife whenever he saw a slight improvement in the organization of her crafts and withhold his criticism.

Teach new skills or behaviors that clients can use to resolve their difficulties. Sometimes, people simply lack the skills or knowledge they need to address their concerns successfully. Learning these skills can provide them with new and more effective strategies and also can help them feel empowered and optimistic about their ability to resolve their concerns.

- Juan's usual way of operating was to be in charge and to tell people what to do. He perceived this as an effective way to communicate and to get things done. However, it was not effective in changing his wife's behavior. Other ways of communicating seemed to him to reflect weakness and to give away power, stances that were unacceptable to him. His therapist gave him some reading on win-win situations and assertive communication and practiced these skills with him in their sessions. Juan recognized that other styles of communication could maintain his sense of power and control and yet enable him to negotiate successfully with others.

Finding exceptions or times when problems seem improved can direct people's attention to viable solutions. Most problems wax and wane in severity. If people can identify what circumstances contribute to amelioration of the problems, perhaps they can intensify or build on those circumstances.

- Juan noticed that his wife was particularly likely to engage in multiple unfinished crafts projects when she was experiencing considerable stress in her job, and when Juan found his job very stressful and worked long hours. He made a deliberate effort to become more aware of the stress in both of their lives, and to take steps to spend more time with his wife and avoid bringing his business worries home with him.

Reframing a problem or concern can help people see it in a new way; this, in turn, can enable them to develop solutions that might not have seemed possible before.

- Juan very much valued the warmth and comfort of his home and had viewed his wife's crafts projects as detracting from the beauty of their home. However, when his clinician suggested that her projects reflected his wife's creativity and domestic leanings, Juan came to see them in a more positive light.

Clearly, many alternatives to advice giving are available to the clinician. Helping clients to expect positive change can enhance the use of these alternatives. Clinicians can promote this attitude by using what solution-focused clinicians refer to as solution talk or possibility language. Juan's therapist, for example, asked questions that implied a successful resolution to the problem such as, "When this problem is solved, how do you think it will affect your relationship with your wife?" or "If you weren't feeling annoyed about the condition of your home, what do you think you would be feeling instead?" Emphasizing clients' strengths and coping behaviors, focusing on actions rather than thoughts or emotions, and using words that suggest change such as "different," "unexpected," "new," and "possible" all communicate the likelihood of change. Particularly powerful are interventions that are compatible with the client's worldview, that use images and metaphors to change perceptions, and that are indirect and empowering.

ASSESSING AND TERMINATING TREATMENT

Counseling and psychotherapy have many endings: the end of each session, the end of work on a particular problem or issue, the premature ending of a treatment process, and the successful conclusion of a therapeutic relationship. These can be glossed over and ignored, they can be handled in troubling and destructive ways, or they can be made a rewarding part of the therapeutic process.

Consider the following brief dialogues at the end of a counseling session:

Example

Dialogue A

Client: You know, I think I've gotten what I needed out of counseling. I feel ready to end treatment.

Clinician: I'm glad to hear that. Don't hesitate to call if you feel a need for counseling in the future. It's been a pleasure to work with you, and I wish you well.

Dialogue B

Client: You know, I think I've gotten what I needed out of counseling. I feel ready to end treatment.

Clinician: You've certainly made progress in your career, but we haven't addressed the difficulties you've been having with your sister. You really should do some work on that before you finish counseling.

Dialogue C

Client: You know, I think I've gotten what I needed out of counseling. I feel ready to end treatment.

Clinician: I can hear the pride in your voice when you say that. Let's go back to our original goals once more so that we can really pinpoint the progress you have made and what you have learned through this process. We can also think about what continuing goals you might have that you want to address either in counseling or after we complete our work together.

The differences among these three dialogues are probably clear to you. Only the third dialogue views the possibility of termination as a learning experience. The following hallmarks of the dialogue facilitate that process:

- The clinician neither agrees nor disagrees with the client's perception that he is ready to end counseling.
- Rather, the clinician creates a situation that will enable the client to identify and reinforce new learning and accomplishments and to determine, in a thoughtful and careful way, whether this is indeed the right time for counseling to end.
- The conclusion of the treatment process is viewed as an opportunity for growth and positive change; it is seen as a transition, either to continued counseling with revised goals or to the client's independent efforts to maintain progress and continue positive development.

- Discussion of termination is a collaborative process that continues to reflect positive counseling.

Concluding Sessions

Similarly, the end of a session can be a learning experience or can miss important opportunities to help people make positive changes and achieve their goals. Consider the following dialogues, all reflecting the last few minutes of a treatment session:

Example

Clinician: We have just a few minutes before the end of our session.
Client: I haven't told you about an argument I had with my mother; that was another really stressful experience I had this week.

Response A
Clinician: Unfortunately, our time is up for today. I'll see you next week at this same time.

Response B
Clinician: Our sessions will be most productive if you bring up important issues early in each session. However, I do have a free hour following our session so let's just talk for a few minutes about your argument with your mother before we wrap up.

Response C
Clinician: It sounds like you are identifying a theme of stressful experiences as the focus of our session this week.
Client: Yes, it seems like everyone in my life is just out to give me a hard time.
Clinician: How about, for next week, you jot down at least two stressful interactions you have with people between now and our next session and how you handled them. Then we can be sure to give this topic some more time next week.

Once again, the differences among the three dialogues are probably evident to you. The first clinician response does maintain the boundaries of the session, generally important in clinical work. However, the client may well perceive that clinician as abrupt and disinterested. The second clinician seems much more compassionate and flexible but, by allowing the client extra time, may inadvertently encourage the client's efforts to prolong sessions. The third clinician maintains the boundaries of the session but does so in a way that acknowledges the importance of the client's issues and encourages continued learning between sessions. Response C observes the following principles, closely related to those principles listed previously that should characterize the end of the counseling process:

- The clinician creates a situation that promotes new learning and accomplishments.
- The conclusion of the session is viewed as an opportunity for growth and positive change; it is seen as a transition to both the next counseling session and to

the client's independent efforts to maintain progress and continue positive development between sessions.

- The conclusion of the session is a collaborative process that continues to reflect positive counseling.

Implementing Guidelines for Concluding a Session

Notice how these and other guidelines for effective treatment are incorporated into the following dialogue, bringing productive closure to a session. As you read the dialogue, try to identify what makes it effective.

> **Clinician:** We have about 5 minutes until the end of this session. How would you summarize what you learned from this session?
>
> **Client:** I saw that, both with my colleague and my daughter, I jumped to the conclusion that they had some bad feelings about me just because they weren't especially talkative. I didn't know that my daughter had a fight with her best friend that day and maybe my colleague had a bad day too, because she was fine the next day. I seem to be my own worst enemy sometimes.
>
> **Clinician:** So you could see that you tended to make negative assumptions about what people were thinking about you. What did you learn about how you could change this pattern?
>
> **Client:** I think just being more aware of it will help. And if it's someone I'm close to, I can talk with him or her about what is going on.
>
> **Clinician:** How would you feel about trying out these new strategies this week?
>
> **Client:** That sounds like a good idea.
>
> **Clinician:** Perhaps you could make some notes about one incident in which you became aware that you might have an inaccurate perception and took steps to check it out.
>
> **Client:** Yes, I can do that.
>
> **Clinician:** All right. I'll write that down on the back of our appointment card. Our time is up for today. See you again next week at this same time.

The conclusion of this session is consistent with the principles listed previously. The following clinician behaviors contribute to the success of this dialogue:

- Clinician reminds client that session has only a few minutes remaining.
- Clinician encourages client to take primary responsibility for summarizing the session.
- Emphasis is placed on client's learning of new thoughts and actions.
- Learning is reinforced via repetition.
- A between-sessions task is suggested to build on new learning.
- Clinician checks out client's willingness to complete suggested task; task would be modified if it were not acceptable to the client.
- Task is written down to encourage completion.
- Although client-clinician collaboration is emphasized, the clinician maintains control of the session; the clinician ends the session on schedule and reminds client of the next appointment.

The learning opportunities at the end of this chapter afford you the opportunity to practice using these guidelines to end a treatment session.

Concluding Treatment

Bringing a productive and rewarding conclusion to the entire treatment process is generally more complex and challenging than concluding a treatment session. The two ingredients that are key in facilitating the termination of treatment are:

1. a clear and up-to-date statement of treatment goals
2. an open, trusting, and collaborative treatment alliance between client and clinician

Reasons for termination.   Termination of treatment typically occurs in one of four ways (Seligman, 2001):

- *Clinician's choice*—Clinicians may be changing jobs or retiring and so may need to terminate treatment with their clients. Alternatively, the agency or school where treatment is occurring may be changing its mission, may have had financial and staff cutbacks, or may have changed the managed care plans with which it is affiliated. These circumstances, too, may require clinicians to end their work with some or all of their clients.
- *Client's choice*—Clients sometimes terminate treatment before clinicians believe they are ready to end their work. Most premature terminations occur early in the treatment process, before the development of a sound therapeutic alliance and clear and meaningful goals. The following are some common reasons why clients end treatment prematurely:
  - Clients don't believe that treatment can help them.
  - They may find it threatening to take an honest look at their concerns.
  - They may have financial or logistical concerns that make it difficult for them to remain in treatment.
  - They may believe they have gotten what they need from treatment even though their clinician may not share that perception.
- *Mutual agreement/negative outcome*—Occasionally, clients and clinicians agree that treatment should end because it is not effective. This can occur when the clinician cannot provide the sort of treatment the client needs, when the client-clinician match is not a positive one, or when all efforts to engage the client in productive treatment are unsuccessful. Referrals to other agencies or treatment providers should be offered to the client in cases such as these.
- *Mutual agreement/positive outcome*—The ideal culmination of the treatment process occurs when both client and clinician agree that treatment has been successful, that the client has satisfactorily achieved her or his goals, that the therapeutic alliance has been a positive one, and that the client is ready to complete treatment. Often clients telegraph their readiness to end treatment. They may cancel sessions for unimportant reasons. They may have little to talk about in sessions. Or the focus of the sessions may shift from a presentation of troubling emotions and painful experiences to talking about interpersonal successes and

rewarding activities. Clues such as these suggest that clinicians might broach the topic of termination and begin to explore whether the time is right for ending the treatment process.

Determining whether the time is right for termination.   Before introducing the idea of concluding the treatment process, clinicians should ask themselves the following questions:

- Have the clients achieved most or all of their goals?
- If new issues have been introduced that were not incorporated into clients' initial goals, have the clients made satisfactory progress in resolving those issues?
- Have the clients developed a repertoire of adaptive, coping, communication, problem-solving, and decision-making skills they can use to resolve future concerns?
- Have the clients established healthy sources of gratification and pleasure in their lives?
- Have the clients established healthy and rewarding relationships that are compatible with their personalities?
- Do the clients have a sense of well-being, and are they practicing strategies and habits that will continue to enhance their physical and emotional well-being?
- Are the clients giving messages that they may be ready to complete treatment?

If you answer all or most of these questions affirmatively, then the clients are probably ready to complete their treatment.

Effecting a successful termination.   Regardless of whether treatment has been successful or unsuccessful and regardless of who is initiating the end of treatment, termination should be viewed as a process, not an event. Facilitating clients' transition out of treatment can make a big difference in their ability to use what they learned in treatment and continue to create rewarding lives for themselves. The following procedures can help make termination of treatment a positive process:

- *Allow ample time* to discuss whether termination is appropriate and to complete the termination process. If possible, three or more sessions should be allocated to the process of concluding treatment.
- *Facilitate clients' expression of thoughts and emotions about the idea of terminating treatment.* Typically, clients have a mixture of positive and negative responses. They may feel apprehensive about their ability to maintain their gains without the clinician's help, and they may feel sad at the loss of contact with the clinician. They may feel angry that treatment is ending, even if it is their choice. On the other hand, they may also feel proud of their accomplishments, glad to be free of the commitment of time and money that treatment entails, and eager to move forward with their lives. Clinicians should be sure to normalize these mixed reactions and give clients the permission and opportunity to expression both positive and negative thoughts and emotions.
- *Take the time to identify and process your own reactions to the termination process,* either on your own or with a supervisor or colleague. Clinicians, too, often have strong and conflicted reactions to the termination of treatment, especially if treatment has not been fully successful or if it has been long-term treatment

that has culminated in considerable client growth and development. If the treatment process has been a disappointing one, clinicians may fault themselves for not having been more helpful to their clients and may even doubt their abilities as clinicians. If a strong bond between client and clinician has developed in the context of successful treatment, clinicians may regret that they will probably not have the opportunity to see their clients blossom and make effective use of all they have learned in treatment. Just as parents have mixed emotions when they see their grown children off to college, marriage, or employment, clinicians too can have bittersweet reactions to the launching of a client. As long as clinicians are aware of their responses to the termination process and deal with those feelings in appropriate and professional ways, these mixed reactions can be viewed as a normal and understandable aspect of termination.

- *Collaborate with clients in identifying their accomplishments during treatment.* This process usually is most meaningful to clients if their perceptions of accomplishments are elicited first and are written down. Once clients have finished their report of their accomplishments, clinicians can suggest additional gains and, if accepted by the clients, these can be added to the list. Reviewing the list later can remind clients of all that has been gained through treatment.
- *Compare accomplishments with goals.* This can help clients to see even more clearly the progress they have made since entering treatment. Even people who are leaving treatment prematurely usually find they have made some progress; the process of identifying difficulties and seeking help can be an important accomplishment in itself. People who are concluding successful treatment typically discover that they have achieved many but not all of their original goals and that they also have made gains that they had not anticipated at the inception of treatment.
- *Look forward to the future.* Discussion might focus on ways in which clients can continue to use and build on their new skills and move forward to accomplish new goals or those that were not completely realized during treatment. Writing down these goals and strategies can help clients to keep them in mind and to continue the positive movement that began during treatment.
- *Ask clients for feedback on the treatment process and the work of the clinician.* Learning more about themselves as clinicians and about what clients perceive as the successful and unsuccessful components of treatment can be useful information. Clinicians can use that information to research their practice (discussed in the next section of this chapter) and continue to improve their knowledge and skills.

Once these procedures have been completed, usually over the course of several sessions, it is time to say good-bye to the client. A handshake, or even a hug, is often appropriate, along with congratulations to the clients for their hard work and successes. In addition, clinicians should remind clients that counseling and psychotherapy are resources that can be helpful to them again in the future if they run into difficulties they cannot handle effectively on their own. Ending the treatment process on a positive note and, if appropriate, leaving the door open for future contact can be reassuring to clients and help them terminate treatment with feelings of pride and hopefulness.

Illustration of Part of the Termination Process

Eileen Carter, a woman who was having considerable difficulty balancing her own needs and those of her husband and son, has been used throughout this book to illustrate many of the skills and concepts presented here. Once again, she will provide the focus of this example of part of the termination process. Assume that Eileen and her therapist have agreed that she has achieved most of her goals and is now ready to terminate treatment. The following illustrates part of a session and reflects the guidelines and principles listed previously.

Example

> **Clinician 1:**   Now that we've decided to end our work together for the foreseeable future, I'd like us to take a look at the results of your treatment.
>
> **Client 1:**   That sounds like a good idea.
>
> **Clinician 2:**   How about if you start by describing some of the accomplishments you see yourself as having made through treatment, and I'll write them down.

- Most important, I found ways to continue my education while still meeting the needs of my husband and son. I got some financial aid from the college, and I'm using the day care at the college for my son when I am in class.
- My husband and I understand each other better. He finally realizes how important college is to me, and I can understand why he was worried that my taking college classes might jeopardize our marriage.
- I feel more like I belong at college. Before, I felt like an impostor, hiding my background from the other students who all seemed so young and innocent. Now I have been using some of my experiences in my writing. People have been really interested in what I went through and how I got myself on track.
- I feel more confident about myself as a mother and wife, too. I seem to be less caught up with my own feelings and more tuned into my husband and son. I'm able to relax more with both of them, and we have more good times together.
- I feel like I've forgiven myself for all those mistakes I made when I was younger. I wish I hadn't gone through all that, especially the abortions, but I don't feel that hatred I had toward myself in the past.

> **Client 2:**   That's about all I can think of.
>
> **Clinician 3:**   There are a few more that occur to me. Let me tell you what they are and you can decide whether to include them in our list.

- You seem much less depressed and anxious. We saw a big change when we compared the depression and anxiety inventories you had taken at the beginning of counseling with the ones that you took last week.
- You have made some women friends, both at college and in your neighborhood.

- Your college grades have improved now that you have become more open and comfortable in your writing. Having a clearer career direction has also helped you to be more successful in your courses.
- You've begun an exercise program and have been trying to eat more healthfully.
- You've also started to reestablish contact with your family of origin.

Client 3: Yes, you're right, I have done all of that, but I'm still not where I want to be in terms of my relationship with my mother and in getting regular exercise.

Clinician 4: We can talk about that in a few minutes, but first I'd like to compare your goals with the ones we wrote down when you first began counseling. Here is a copy of the list we developed together.

Client 4: Wow, some big changes. I didn't even know if I wanted to stay married then, and now I really am committed to my marriage. I can see I had many doubts about myself and was pretty sure I would have to give up college, or at least put it off for many years. My mood is much better and I have become more confident in myself as I had hoped. But when we wrote up these goals, I was so focused on the immediate problems, I didn't even think about dealing with my past or making new friends or improving my health. We've accomplished even more than I had hoped.

Clinician 5: You must feel very proud to see all you have accomplished.

Client 5: I really am. But it seems like I have new goals now. Does that mean I'm not really ready to finish counseling?

Clinician 6: Let's talk about that. What are those new goals?

Client 6: I'm not exercising as much as I would like, and I'm just beginning to deal with my family of origin. Then pretty soon I have to make a final decision on my major at college. This is a never-ending process.

Clinician 7: That's true. We always have new goals and issues to address, but that doesn't necessarily mean you need to continue counseling at this time. How do you feel about your ability to handle some of those issues yourself?

Client 7: I can certainly try. I have narrowed down my choice of major. And my exercising is going in the right direction. Dealing with my mother is another issue, though.

Clinician 8: That seems like the hardest one for you. What do you think you could do to improve your relationship with her?

Client 8: I could analyze my thoughts like we did here and make sure I was thinking clearly about the situation. I could use some of those communication skills I used so well with my husband. And I could talk to my best friend Betty; she has problems with her mother, too.

Clinician 9: So it sounds like you have quite a few strategies to help you achieve your goals without counseling.

Client 9: Yes, I can see that I do. If I really get stuck, can I come in for a few more sessions?

Clinician 10: Yes, of course, but I hope you'll remember all those skills you already have. Before we finish our session today, I'd like us to talk about the counseling process and our work together. It would help me to hear from you about what was especially helpful to you and how we might have improved on the counseling process.

Client 10:   It's hard to say. It has certainly helped me. I always felt that you were there for me and your support meant a lot, but you wouldn't really tell me what to do. You'd just help me figure it out for myself. I liked that decision-making strategy you taught me, and practicing new ways to talk to my husband really helped.

Clinician 11:   So you learned quite a few new skills from our work together. What would have made our work together even better?

Client 11:   I can't really think of anything.

Clinician 12:   Let's see if I can help you identify a few things that might have improved our work. During our first few sessions, you seemed uncertain about whether counseling would be helpful. Can you remember what triggered those feelings?

Client 12:   Yes, I guess so. I was really in a crisis when I first came to see you, and I wanted you to jump right in and tell me what to do. I felt that you didn't understand how urgent my situation was.

Clinician 13:   So it felt like you needed more direction at that time?

Client 13:   Yes that's it. Also, I wasn't sure how you reacted when I told you about my abortions. I was crying then and all you did was hand me a tissue.

Clinician 14:   What would have helped you at that time?

Client 14:   Maybe just a pat on the shoulder or more acknowledgment of how badly I was feeling.

Clinician 15:   I can understand how that would have been helpful to you. What other ways can you think of for improving our counseling?

Client 15:   I can't come up with anything else.

Clinician 16:   We have talked before about the differences in our backgrounds and your initial concern that I couldn't really understand you because I was white and had so much more education than you did. Those feelings became especially strong after I returned from vacation. What thoughts do you have now about that aspect of our work together?

Client 16:   You're right. That was a barrier between us, especially after I heard you had gone to Africa on your vacation. I thought, there you were spending lots of money to see animals but not really understanding the African culture. That did bother me.

Clinician 17:   What happened to those feelings?

Client 17:   You seemed to sense how I was feeling, and we talked about it. You really did seem to accept and understand me as an individual and didn't just stereotype me. Eventually those feelings got to be much less and I felt good about how open I could be with you. Maybe it even helped me to relate to some of those college students who seemed so different from me.

Clinician 18:   So what started as a barrier wound up being helpful, although it was important that we did talk about our differences.

Client 18:   Yes, that's true.

Clinician 19:   As we planned, our next session will be our last session. How would it be if, during the week, you review the list of accomplishments we made up and start to write down some of those future goals that we began to discuss? You can add to or change any of the items on those lists and we can discuss them in our last session.

Client 19:   That sounds fine.

Clinician 20:   I'll write that down on your appointment card. And if you have any further thoughts about the strengths and weak areas in our work together, I'd be interested in hearing more about that, too.

Client 20:   All right, see you next week.

Now that you have read this excerpt once, go back over it, keeping in mind the guidelines for termination that were presented on pages 343–344. See if you can find the lines of dialogue that reflect each of those guidelines. If you discover that any of them were missing or were not addressed well, think about how you might have improved on this dialogue.

USING RESEARCH TO ENHANCE YOUR PRACTICE AND YOUR PROFESSIONAL DEVELOPMENT

Now that we have reviewed information on terminating the treatment process, you are almost ready to conclude your learning of new skills from this book. However, you have one more step to take, which is self-evaluation.

Counseling and psychotherapy are vital and evolving fields. They are rich with exciting research, informative professional journals, and stimulating national and international conferences and training opportunities. You might already feel overwhelmed by all there is to learn about your profession and the constant challenge of acquiring important new knowledge and skills.

In order for clinicians to provide excellent service to their clients and take pride in their work, they must become lifetime learners, always excited about the advances in counseling and psychology. At the same time, clinicians, of course, cannot become knowledgeable about all of the new developments in their field. How then can clinicians continue to enhance their knowledge and skills in meaningful ways without becoming overwhelmed? The following guidelines can help you to answer this question for yourself.

Develop Your Professional Specialization

Finding your niche, your area of specialization in the profession, is an important step. Probably your area of specialization will evolve as you gain experience and discover new interests and opportunities, so you do not need to regard your current interests as fixed. However, identifying a circumscribed area of interest will help you to build a reputation in your field and develop strong skills.

My own areas of specialization have evolved considerably over the years. After college, I became a high school English teacher and began working with school counselors to educate students about harmful drugs and provide help to those students who were already misusing drugs or alcohol. This led me to seek a master's degree in school counseling.

However, by the time I finished my master's degree, I also had become interested in career development and family dynamics. Those interests led me to enter a doctoral program so that I could learn more, not only about my continuing interest in substance-related disorders and their treatment, but also about career development and family therapy. While pursuing doctoral study, I developed an interest in multicultural counseling; my first publications focused on the two areas of multicultural counseling and career counseling (Seligman, 1977, 1979, 1980). These interests grew out of areas that had been emphasized in my doctoral studies.

After finishing my doctorate, I combined teaching and practice, training graduate students in psychology and mental health counseling. These experiences led me to develop a strong interest in understanding mental disorders and developing effective treatment plans. Those areas have become my most enduring and important areas of specialization, reflected in four books (Seligman, 1986, 1990, 1996a, 1998) and many articles and presentations on those topics. Finally, issues in my own family as well as concerns of my clients led me to develop a special interest in helping people cope more effectively with serious illness (Seligman, 1996b). At present, my primary professional interests include diagnosis and treatment planning, counselor education, helping people cope with chronic and life-threatening illnesses, systems and strategies of counseling and psychotherapy, and multicultural counseling.

Probably, your professional development will follow a pattern that is similar to mine. Your interests will evolve and change over time with some enduring and others fading; your interests will be sparked by many experiences, both personal and professional; and you will continue to relish the excitement of our stimulating and always changing profession.

Think about what you currently view as your area of professional specialization. This specialization can be defined in many ways:

- *Age*—(e.g., children in elementary school, adolescents, people over 65)
- *Presenting problems*—(e.g., infidelity, career concerns, anger and aggression, drug and alcohol abuse, bereavement, chronic and life-threatening illnesses)
- *Mental disorders*—(e.g., personality disorders, mood disorders, anxiety, attention-deficit/hyperactivity disorders, conduct and oppositional defiant disorders, dissociative disorders)
- *Type of counseling setting or treatment facility*—(e.g., counseling in a middle school, a community mental health center, a university, a rehabilitation facility, or a women's center)
- *Treatment approaches*—(e.g., cognitive-behavioral therapy, psychoanalysis, eye movement desensitization and reprocessing, play therapy, or Gestalt therapy)

Researching Your Own Practice

Once you have identified one or more areas of specialization, you can begin to conduct research on your own practice. The first step is to assess the present status of your work in the following way:

- determine what you do that is effective and successful
- determine what you do that is not usually effective
- determine what important unanswered questions you have about your work, your clients, and their difficulties

Many tools and approaches are available to help you research your practice (McLeod, 1994). These include:

- *Structured inventories*—Many inventories have been developed to help clinicians assess the effectiveness of their work. Administered to clients at predetermined points in the treatment process, these self-report measures yield a quantitative measure of clinical outcome.
- *Single-subject design*—Empirical research also can be conducted on a single client, following principles established for single-subject design.
- *Qualitative research*—Structured or semi-structured interviews, conducted with a small number of clients, can yield useful qualitative information about the nature, strengths, and weaknesses of one's clinical work. This approach to research can be individualized to yield the sort of information that is especially useful to a particular clinician.
- *Goal attainment scaling*—In this process, clinicians obtain data on their success in helping clients achieve their goals (Cytrynbaum, Ginath, Birdwell, & Brandt, 1979; Zaza, Stolee, & Prkachin, 1999). Once goals have been selected, they can be weighted based on their relative importance. Expected outcomes and an anticipated time frame for goal attainment are then determined. Finally, goal attainment is rated on a − 2 to + 2 scale, reflecting how the actual outcome compares with the anticipated outcome. A composite score reflects overall treatment effectiveness.
- *Informal assessment*—Unstructured discussions, incorporated into the termination process, also can yield valuable information on clinician and treatment effectiveness. Patterns in feedback can point to strengths as well as areas needing improvement.

Example of Research on Own Practice

Thomas, an African American man who was a counselor in a middle school, used a checklist, qualitative interviews, and informal assessment to research his practice. He came up with the following evaluation of his work:

- *Determine what I do that is effective and successful:* I generally think I do a good job but I seem to work especially well with African American boys. I am direct and straightforward with them, drawing on Glasser's Reality Therapy to help them assess whether their behaviors are helping or hurting them. I make sure to follow up with them, once they have made a commitment to make some changes. I confer with their teachers and parents and think holistically about the young people with whom I work. All of these procedures seem helpful.
- *Determine what I do that is not usually effective:* I don't do as well forming a therapeutic alliance with students who are not motivated to succeed at anything, whether it is academics, athletics, or friendships. Reality Therapy doesn't seem to work as well with them either. I may be missing some underlying depression and am expecting too much from them.
- *Determine what important unanswered questions I have about my work, my clients, and their difficulties:*
  - Have I made an accurate assessment of my strengths and weaknesses as a counselor?

- How does depression look in young people in early adolescence?
- What approaches seem effective in reducing their depression and increasing their motivation?
- What does the literature say about using Reality Therapy with young people who are depressed?
- How do the teachers and parents regard my work? Would they benefit from even more contact with me?

Thomas can now move onto the next phase of researching his practice, gathering additional information to support or refute his conclusions and to provide some answers to his questions. He can go about this in a variety of ways:

- He might interview a small group of teachers and parents to elicit their perceptions of his work and how he might be even more helpful to them.
- He might ask his colleagues and supervisor about their perceptions of his work.
- He might complete a brief checklist after each student he sees, listing the student's concerns, the strategies Thomas used to help the student, and his impression of the effectiveness of his work. He could later compare this information with the student's attendance record and grades. This can help Thomas determine whether his hypotheses about the quality of his work are accurate and obtain further clarification of his strengths and weaknesses as a counselor.
- Thomas might do some additional reading, specifically on diagnosis and treatment of depression in adolescents and on the use of Reality Therapy to address depression in young people.

Turn to the Literature

Over the past 10 years, researchers in counseling and psychology have produced a substantial body of literature, clarifying the nature of people's difficulties and mental disorders and identifying effective ways to treat them (Seligman, 1998). Particularly important has been the research conducted by the American Psychological Association's Task Force on empirically supported treatments (Waehler, Kalodner, Wampold, & Lichtenberg, 2000). Empirically supported treatments have been defined as "specified interventions designated as having demonstrated efficacy for individuals with specific psychological disorders" (p. 657). This task force conducted meta-analyses of large numbers of empirical research studies and identified nearly 60 treatment strategies that had convincingly demonstrated their effectiveness. Becoming skilled in those strategies that have proven value and that are relevant to your practice is particularly important in maximizing your effectiveness as a clinician.

Clearly, the professional literature is an important source of information for clinicians interested in improving the power of their work. However, the large body of literature available to clinicians is overwhelming to most. How then do you make good use of available information to better your work? The following guidelines should help you to narrow your focus:

- Join one or more national professional associations such as the American Psychological Association, the American Mental Health Counselors Association, and the American Counseling Association.
- Join divisions or special interest groups offered by national professional associations that reflect your identified areas of specialization.

- Read the journals and newsletters issued by the professional associations you have joined.
- Become familiar with the names and concepts that are especially important to your work and seek out additional relevant information and training.

This book is only a beginning in your development into a clinician with strong conceptual and technical skills. Participating actively in your profession, becoming familiar with the literature that is pertinent to your areas of specialization, and continuing your professional development through training and by researching your practice and conferring with your supervisors and colleagues will help you become a clinician who makes a positive difference in people's lives.

LEARNING OPPORTUNITIES

This chapter focused on actions, primarily those that clinicians need to know how to perform as part of their work. The action-oriented conceptual skills presented in this chapter include:

- understanding the Stages of Change Model and adapting treatment to a client's readiness for change
- making referrals to and collaborating with other clinicians and helping professionals
- structuring interventions, sessions, and treatment plans
- keeping progress notes
- helping clients generate solutions to their concerns
- concluding sessions and ending the overall treatment process
- using research to enhance your practice

The following exercises afford you the opportunity to apply the conceptual skills that have been presented in this chapter. This section will include discussion questions, written exercises, role-play exercises and an assessment tool to use in your practice groups, and topics to write about in your journal.

Written Exercises/Discussion Questions

1. Review the case of Amy, beginning on page 310 of chapter 8. In what stage of change is Amy? What information led you to that conclusion? In light of her stage of change, what principles and approaches would initially guide your work with Amy?
2. What types of referral sources, if any, do you think would be helpful to Amy? What is the logic behind your recommendations?
3. Review the following progress note. Then rewrite it in the STIPS or SOAP format or in another structured format for progress notes.

Amy came to her session about 10 minutes late and looked upset and disheveled. Once she began talking, it was difficult to stop her. She had a great deal on her mind. She talked about her fear when her dog was lost for two days, her parents' possible divorce, her discomfort with her uncle Diego, and the departure of her best friend for summer camp. She also talked about her unsuccessful efforts to lose weight and how badly she felt when a boy in the neighborhood called her "Pimples." She seemed more anxious than depressed but her mood changed rapidly; positive feelings were evident only when she talked about the return of her dog. I tried to provide Amy with considerable empathy and support but that failed to slow her down and I wasn't even sure she heard me some of the time. Finally, we started to review her diet and exercise plan but she really hadn't made any progress with that. My suggested tasks seem to have been too ambitious. She may need more time to vent but that doesn't seem very productive; I need to help her focus on realistic ways to make small changes and move forward.

4. Based on the session with Amy just described, create a dialogue that might occur during the last 5 minutes of that session. Follow the principles presented on pages 339–341 for bringing a session to a positive close. Be sure to include a task assignment in your dialogue.

5. This chapter provided information on the typical ingredients of the beginning, middle, and ending phases of the treatment process. Based on the case of Amy, discuss or write down a list of goals and interventions for each of the three phases of treatment.

6. Although clinicians generally avoid giving clients direct advice, certain situations warrant advice giving as part of the treatment process. How would you decide whether or not to give a client advice? What client characteristics, problems, or elements in the therapeutic relationship would make it likely that you would give a person advice? What client characteristics, problems, or elements in the therapeutic relationship would make it unlikely that you would give a person advice?

7. Assume that you have a lengthy and positive therapeutic relationship with a client. You have come to like the client personally and look forward to your sessions. The client is someone you could envision having as a friend. Now it is time to terminate your successful work together, and you are feeling sad about that. How would you deal with your reactions to the termination process? What, if anything, would you say to the client about your feelings? Describe the thinking that led you to these conclusions.

Discussion Questions

1. The concept of identifying a person's level of readiness for change (stage of change) and then using interventions that are particularly well suited to that stage of change has had a considerable impact on the fields of counseling and psychotherapy in recent years. Why do you suppose this concept has been so well received? What impact do you think the concept of stages of change will have on future research and treatment?

2. What are the differences between a resistant client and one who is at the precontemplation stage of change?

3. What do you believe to be the ideal model for collaboration between a nonmedical psychotherapist who is providing counseling and a psychiatrist who is providing medication for the same client? What are the differences in the roles of these two people? What overlap is likely to exist? How would you handle the situation if a psychiatrist seemed to be doing therapy with a client whom you had referred only for a medication evaluation?

4. The following clients request advice from you. Drawing on what you have learned about ways to help people generate solutions to their own problems, discuss how you would respond to each of these people and what strategies seem most likely to help them.
    - I don't really enjoy my work but at least I feel comfortable with my colleagues and supervisor. I'm afraid that my disability will make it hard for me to find another job where I feel so well accepted. What do you think I should do?
    - I found a lump underneath my arm. Do you think I should ask a physician about it or just wait awhile and see if it goes away?
    - I've been working really hard at losing weight and I've got my weight down to 92 pounds. My parents say I look too thin but I'd like to lose another 10 pounds. I've stopped eating dinner. Do you think I should cut out breakfast as well?

5. In your capacity as a college counselor, you have been working with a client who tells you that she has been using cocaine to such an extent that both her work and her academic performance are seriously impaired. What decisions would you make about referring this client for other sources of help and about continuing your work with the client? What is the logic behind your decisions? How would you present your decisions to the client?

6. Assume that you decided to refer the woman in the previous example to a substance abuse treatment program. However, the client told you that she would not take the referral and would not return to see you after this session. How would you use the remaining 30 minutes of your session with her?

7. What obstacles are clinicians likely to face as they begin to research their practice? What can they do to minimize these obstacles and facilitate the process of researching their practice?

Practice Group Exercise 1

Divide into your practice groups. In this chapter, as in the previous three chapters, you will have the opportunity to both practice your conceptual skills and further refine your technical skills. This chapter includes two role play exercises. As usual, continue to tape-record both the practice session and the subsequent discussion.

Exercise 1. In chapter 5, you learned skills to help you facilitate clients' efforts to make behavioral changes. In this exercise, you will build on what you learned in chapter 5. This exercise will encompass the following skills:

Technical Skills

- goal setting
- concreteness and specificity
- suggesting homework tasks

Conceptual Skills

- adapting the treatment session to the client's stage of change
- structuring the session
- concluding the treatment session

For purposes of this exercise, each person in the group should assume a different stage of change when he or she is in the client role. For example, if a group has four members, each person should assume one of the following four stages of change, making sure that all four stages are represented: precontemplation, contemplation, preparation, and action. When in the client role, each person should present a problem behavior.

Clinicians in this exercise have the following major goals:

1. Structure the session according to the 10-step model presented earlier in this chapter and repeated here:
   - Collaborate with the client to establish a meaningful agenda for the session.
   - Determine and measure the intensity of the person's mood.
   - Identify and discuss current concerns.
   - Establish clear and meaningful goals for the session.
   - Embed the current concerns in context, focusing especially on similar concerns that the client has handled successfully.
   - Help the client to identify connections between current concern and past difficulties.
   - Draw on past successes and promote development of new skills that will help the person resolve current concerns.
   - Suggest tasks to be completed between sessions.
   - Summarize the session.
   - Elicit client feedback on the session.
2. Adapt the treatment process to the client's stage of change.
3. Make use of the technical skills presented in chapter 5 to establish goals for the session.
4. Make use of concreteness and specificity to rapidly obtain a clear picture of the problem behavior.
5. Suggest a task to be completed between sessions.
6. Bring appropriate closure to the session, following guidelines presented in this chapter.

Clearly, the clinician in this role play has a challenging task.

Observers can facilitate their efforts to provide feedback by dividing up the parts of this exercise to focus on during the role play. For example, one observer might focus on the first two goals listed previously while the second observer focuses on the remaining four goals.

Time Schedule. Completion of this exercise requires approximately 3 hours. Of course, reducing the number of role plays from four to two can shorten this exercise, like most of those in this book. Each role play should follow this schedule:

- Allow at least 30 minutes for each role-played interview.
- Allow 15 minutes for feedback and processing of each role play.

Assessment of Progress Form 9a

1. In what ways did you adapt the treatment process to the client's stage of change? How effective was that? What would have improved upon that adaptation?

2. How well did the session follow the 10 steps in the format for structuring sessions? Which steps worked especially well? How might the process have been improved?

3. Describe the process of goal setting. Were goals clear, relevant, and specific? How might the goal setting have been improved?

4. Describe and assess your use of concreteness and specificity.

5. Assess the appropriateness of the homework task that you suggested to the client. Was the task clear, relevant to the client's problem behavior, and readily achievable? Was the client engaged in the process of formulating the homework task? How might the process of suggesting a homework task have been improved?

6. Describe the way you brought closure to the session. What were the strengths of that process? How might that process have been improved?

Practice Group Exercise 2

You and your partners have probably gotten to know each other very well through the many role-played interviews you have done over the course of the training experiences presented in this book. This exercise will afford you the opportunity to use the skills you have learned in this chapter to bring closure to your work together.

Purpose of Exercise.   The clinician in this role play has the following goals:

- to bring a positive close to your work with your partner
- to identify and reinforce the clinical strengths and gains that your partner has made over the course of this training experience
- to determine two technical or conceptual skills that your partner wants to improve
- to share feelings about the end of the role plays
- to say good-bye

Although the person in the clinician role should, as usual, be in charge of the session, collaboration is an important element in this exercise as it nearly always is when treatment ends. This should not be a problem-solving session. The clinician is primarily a facilitator for this exercise, promoting the client's expression of thoughts and feelings in reaction to the end of this training experience. A high level of clinical skills should be maintained throughout this process, with participants applying what they have learned throughout the training.

When group members assume the client role, they should be themselves for this session, talking about their learning in the small group and processing their reactions to the end of the learning experience. In addition, this session should provide an opportunity for growth and positive change. It is a transition, as participants move onto other training experiences or into the practice of counseling and psychotherapy.

Time Schedule.   This will probably be a relatively brief role play. Each role play should follow this schedule:

- Allow 20 minutes for each role play.
- Following the interview, the entire group should contribute to the development of a list of the strengths of the person who had just been in the client role. This should take approximately 10 to 15 minutes.

Assessment of Progress Form 9b

1. List the strengths and gains that you and your group observed in you over the course of this training experience.

2. List two technical or conceptual skills that warrant your continued attention.

Personal Journal Questions

1. If you were to seek counseling or psychotherapy for your own personal growth and development, what stage of change would you be in? How do you explain that?
2. This chapter has focused on actions and behaviors rather than background, emotions, or thoughts. How well did that mesh with your natural style of intervention?
3. What aspects of this chapter appealed to you and came easily to you?

4. What aspects of this chapter were unappealing and presented you with a considerable challenge?
5. What do you currently view as your areas of specialization? Have they evolved over time, remained stable, or are you only now beginning to think about your areas of specialization?
6. If you were to research your practice, how would you go about doing that? Assess your current practice (even if it has only been role-played interviews) according to the following format:
   - Determine what you do that is effective and successful.
   - Determine what you do that is not usually effective.
   - Determine what important unanswered questions you have about your actual or anticipated work, your clients, and their difficulties.

SUMMARY

This chapter focused on conceptual skills associated with actions. As in the previous chapter, most of the skills presented here were designed for clinicians to use in better understanding and treating their clients. Particular attention was paid to the stages of change, referral and collaboration, progress notes, structuring sessions and the treatment process, generating solutions to clients' concerns, concluding sessions and the treatment process, and researching your own practice.

The next and last chapter affords you an opportunity to review and apply much of what you have learned during the course of this training experience. Chapter 10 also provides you the opportunity to synthesize and integrate the feedback you have received as well as your own perceptions of your clinical skills so that you can continue to develop into an outstanding clinician.

PART IV
Solidifying Technical and Conceptual Skills

CHAPTER 10

Reviewing, Integrating, and Reinforcing Learning

INTRODUCTION

The purpose of this final chapter is to help you accomplish the following goals:

- Reevaluate your clinical strengths.
- Gain understanding of the transition from novice to expert clinician, and assess your progress along that path.
- Review the learning you have acquired through the information and exercises provided in this book.
- Raise your awareness of how much you have learned through your study of this material.
- Enhance and increase the learning you have acquired.
- Take another opportunity to practice your conceptual and technical skills.
- Reinforce your learning.

This chapter consists of three major sections. The first section once again presents the checklist of clinician strengths, initially presented in chapter 1. Rerating your abilities on this checklist will help you identify the progress you have made while you have been using this book to develop your technical and conceptual skills. The first section of this chapter also presents an overview of some of the research on the process of becoming an expert clinician and the important characteristics of that clinician.

The second part of this chapter presents an intake interview with a man who has both immediate and long-standing difficulties. A series of learning opportunities follow that interview, enabling you to review and apply many of the skills presented in this book to that case.

The third section includes additional learning experiences. Most important is a presentation of all the self-evaluation forms you have used throughout this book. This affords you another opportunity to assess your skills, identifying strengths as well as areas continuing to need attention. Use of these forms should give you an even clearer picture of yourself as a clinician and help you target your continuing efforts to improve and refine your skills. A final series of personal journal questions concludes this chapter, enabling you to further reflect on and synthesize the material you have studied and learned.

CHECKLIST OF CLINICIAN STRENGTHS

Chapter 1 presented a list of clinician strengths. You were asked to assess yourself, using that checklist. For each item, you used a + to indicate a strength, a − to reflect a weakness or a quality you have not yet developed, or a ? to indicate uncertainty about whether or not an item describes you. Before you look back at your self-ratings from chapter 1, complete the following checklist, using the same directions. As was suggested in chapter 1, you might also ask a trusted friend, colleague, supervisor, or family member to identify those items on the list that he or she perceives as your strenghts.

Checklist of Clinician Strengths

_____ Able to ask for help
_____ Able to deal with ambiguity and complexity
_____ Able to express oneself clearly, both orally and in writing
_____ Able to give credit to others for their accomplishments
_____ Aware of own political, spiritual, interpersonal, and other values
_____ Can see details as well as the big picture
_____ Can draw on and learn from past experience
_____ Caring
_____ Creative
_____ Comfortable with networking and collaboration
_____ Emotionally stable
_____ Empathic and able to identify emotions in self and others
_____ Ethical and respectful of laws, rules, standards, and boundaries but also able to exert efforts to change harmful standards
_____ Flexible and resourceful
_____ Hard working
_____ High frustration tolerance
_____ Insightful and psychologically minded
_____ Intelligent
_____ Interested, curious, an eager learner
_____ Maintains balance in own life

_____ Maintains own physical and emotional health
_____ Manifests good interpersonal skills and has some close relationships
_____ May have own concerns, but is addressing them and does not impose them on others
_____ Respectful and appreciative of others and their differences
_____ Self-aware and honest with oneself
_____ Serves as a role model and inspiration to others
_____ Sound capacity for attention and concentration
_____ Willing to listen to feedback and make changes as needed

Once you have completed and reviewed the checklist, compare it with the checklist you completed on pages 9–10 in chapter 1. What similarities do you see in your completion of the two checklists? What ratings have changed? Have you now marked more items with a + and fewer items with a ? or a −? That is a good indication that you perceive yourself as having made progress.

However, you may find that you have even more items marked with a ? or a −. Don't let that discourage you. As we take a closer look at our skills and acquire a better understanding of the skills of the effective clinician, we may recognize that our skills are not as strong as we originally believed they were. This is a painful, but common, step in the process of becoming an expert clinician and probably does not mean that your skills have really declined. This can actually be viewed as progress because, now that you can more accurately assess the quality of your skills, you can more easily find ways to improve them.

Look at the three steps you identified on page 10 to help you minimize your weaknesses, build on your strengths, and get to know yourself better. What progress have you made on those steps? What results have you gotten? Should you continue to work on those same steps, or do you now recognize other steps that would promote your professional growth? Keep the answers to these questions in mind as you continue reading and completing the exercises in this chapter, providing you even more information on your progress thus far and ways to continue your professional development.

CHARACTERISTICS OF THE EXPERT CLINICIAN

Although you probably do not yet think of yourself as an expert clinician, you may find it useful to learn how the literature describes such a clinician. That should give you a better understanding of the evolution you may experience as you develop from novice to skilled or even expert clinician and provide you with some ideas of ways to accelerate your progress toward increasing your clinical expertise.

Etringer, Hillerbrand, and Claiborn (1995) have taken an in-depth look at the transition from novice to expert clinician. In general, they found that the biggest distinction between novice and expert is in conceptual skills such as those presented in part III of this book. Etringer, Hillerbrand, and Claiborn list the following as specific qualities of the expert clinician:

- can develop and use strategies to monitor and regulate their own cognitive activity

- have good awareness of what they do and do not know
- have a knowledge base that is not only broad and deep but also detailed and well integrated
- able to organize information into abstract, problem-relevant structures and categories
- have good memory skills in their areas of expertise and can use them to recognize patterns
- can use existing knowledge to solve new problems
- able to generate, assess, and either accept or reject hypotheses and then use those hypotheses to move toward conclusions
- can engage in forward reasoning and analysis and synthesis
- can start with existing information and then move toward a future-oriented goal or can start with a series of problems and move toward a diagnosis

These findings can be summarized as follows:

> The expert clinician is characterized by being able to process and synthesize information, noting discrepancies and highlights along the way, and then use theoretical and conceptual frameworks to make sense of that information and generate diagnoses, goals, and treatment plans to resolve issues and solve problems.

Sawatsky, Jevne, and Clark (1994) wrote another useful study on the process of becoming an expert clinician. They refer to that clinician as "empowered" and provide an interesting view of the process of becoming empowered or expert. According to Sawatsky et al., clinician development is a cyclical process of seeking and experiencing dissonance, responding to that dissonance, and learning from the process. Dissonance can come from many sources, including realizing that we have weaknesses in our knowledge or skills, encountering challenging clients and problems, and receiving feedback from supervisors, colleagues, and clients. Using dissonance as a learning experience often entails some risk taking as we acquire and experiment with new skills and strategies. Anxiety is inherent in this process and, unless at disabling levels, usually is a promoting rather than an inhibiting factor.

The journey from novice to expert clinician is often an erratic and gradual one that continues, and usually accelerates, long after formal coursework has been completed (Skovholt & Ronnestad, 1992). Over time, learning comes increasingly from interpersonal encounters rather than from data, from clients rather than from mentors, and from within rather than from without.

Successful negotiation of the cyclical process described here will ultimately lead clinicians to develop the following characteristics (Leach, Stoltenberg, McNeill, & Eichenfield, 1997; Sawatsky et al., 1994; Skovholt & Ronnestad, 1992):

Self-Awareness

- a sound capacity for self-reflection
- awareness of their own motivations, needs, attitudes, values, personalities, and perceptual styles

Self-Efficacy

- eagerness to engage in continual self-reflection and growth
- a sense of empowerment
- professional individuation, reflected in an integration of professional and personal selves
- reasonable confidence in their own judgment
- a sense of control over their responses
- ability to welcome dissonance as a learning experience
- consistency and congruence between both their beliefs and values and their theoretical framework and strategies
- flexibility and psychological health reflected in emotions, thoughts, and actions
- awareness of ethical standards

Strong Knowledge Base and Conceptual Skills

- a broad and deep knowledge of events, concepts, and skills in their field
- ability to use that knowledge base to construct their own knowledge and to organize information
- ability to acquire and apply new learning and skills from many sources, including role models, clients, and the professional literature
- acceptance and appreciation of human diversity

Think about yourself in relation to these profiles of expert or empowered clinicians. Try to be honest with yourself. You will probably find that you do indeed already possess many of the qualities of the expert clinician. You will also probably find that you need further learning and development in many of these areas. As part of the process of continual self-evaluation that characterizes advanced clinicians, the personal journal questions at the end of this chapter will afford you the opportunity to assess yourself in relation to the previous descriptions of the expert clinician.

INTAKE INTERVIEW OF SAMUEL GOLD

Now that you have reviewed some of the characteristics and abilities of the skilled and expert clinician, you have the opportunity to demonstrate some of those skills. The following exercise, which includes an intake interview and a series of questions and procedures applied to the client presented in the interview, allows you to use many of the technical and conceptual skills you learned through the course of this book. Begin by carefully reading and thinking about the case of Samuel Gold.

The client, Samuel (Sam) Gold is a 34-year-old Jewish man who is self-referred for treatment. He is about 5′ 7″ tall and slender. He has dark hair and a beard and is dressed casually in a tee shirt, jeans, and running shoes. Sam appears tense and talks rapidly but clearly.

Clinician 1:   What brings you in for treatment, Sam?
Client 1:   Do you want the long story or the short story?
Clinician 2:   Whichever you would prefer.

Client 2:   Let's start with the short one, and I'm sure we'll get to the long one soon. About 3 weeks ago, I was diagnosed with lymphoma. Now I'm facing months of chemotherapy and other treatments and who knows what the outcome will be. I'm only 34. I should be dealing with raising a family like all my friends, not with thoughts about dying.

Clinician 3:   This must be very frightening and upsetting to you.

Client 3:   Yes, it sure is. But then, in a funny way, it isn't.

Clinician 4:   So your feelings about this are really mixed?

Client 4:   Yes, you might say that. I guess I always knew I'd get cancer or some terrible disease.

Clinician 5:   What made you think that?

Client 5:   A couple of things. First, I had been feeling lousy for 6 or 8 months—tired, run-down, just not myself. I'm not a real high-energy person but this was worse than usual. And the one thing I do on a regular basis is run; that's been part of my life for years. I couldn't even get myself to do a mile or two, let alone my usual five or ten. Something had to be wrong. I went through a bunch of docs and then finally found one smart enough to figure it out.

Clinician 6:   So you hadn't been feeling well for quite a few months and suspected you had a medical problem going on.

Client 6:   Yeah, but that wasn't all . . .

Clinician 7:   It wasn't all?

Client 7:   Yeah. This might sound strange, but I'm just not a lucky person. Bad things keep happening to me. So it really wasn't such a surprise when they told me I had cancer. I guess we got into the long story even faster than I thought.

Clinician 8:   It probably would be useful to put your diagnosis with cancer in context, so how would you feel about giving me some background information that is probably part of the long story?

Client 8:   Sure. I know we only have 45 minutes but I'll try to make a very long story short. I have to start with my great-grandparents. All four sets of great-grandparents came to the U.S. from Eastern Europe, Poland, or whatever it was then, in the early 1900s. Came through Ellis Island. Jews had been treated pretty badly in that part of Europe, so they came here to get away from that. I guess the men came first, hooked up with relatives who were already here, found jobs and places to live and then sent for the women and children. I think a couple of the grandparents came over as very young children and the other two were born here. They settled in urban areas in the northeast U.S.—New York, Philly, Hartford. They were poor when they got here, couldn't bring much out with them. But I guess they were pretty industrious. The great-grandparents became merchants of one kind or another and tried to make a decent home for the kids, get them a decent education.

Clinician 9:   It sounds like you believe they had quite a struggle but tried hard to realize their values of family and education.

Client 9:   Yes, that's really the Jewish tradition, of religion, family, and education all being important. And you can see this pattern of each generation doing a little better than the last one—until they got to me. But I'm getting ahead of myself, and I really want to tell you the whole story. The grandparents did a little better than their parents. My mother's father became a pharmacist and his wife was an elementary school teacher. My father's father was an accountant. His wife never worked, but she did lots of volunteer work in New York City. So then we get to my parents. When they met, my father was a medical student at Columbia University, and my mother was a graduate student in social work. She was spending the summer in New York, taking some courses but really getting away to sort out her life. Sounds like a perfect match except for one little problem: She's already married and has a husband and baby back in Connecticut. She's miserable; her husband's abusive and she can't stand him. So she starts seeing my father and gets pregnant. Sounds like a soap opera, doesn't it?

Clinician 10:   It's a pretty complicated story. How does all of this affect you?

Client 10:   Now we get to the part about me. I'm the little surprise, the pregnancy that messes up this great romance. This was back in the 60s when everybody is having sex but you're still not supposed to. Hard to hide when you get pregnant. So my parents move in together, my mother gets a quickie divorce, and they get married as soon as they can. They don't tell my father's parents about my mother's first marriage, just make believe it never happened. My father's parents, the rich accountant and his wife, make them a big party to celebrate the marriage. Nobody mentions the ex-husband and kid in Connecticut, and now my parents are supposed to live happily ever after. Of course, my mother gives up custody and all contact with her daughter and never talks about any of this to anyone except my father. And by now he's doing his residency and is never home.

Clinician 11:   This was certainly a very hard way to start a marriage.

Client 11:   Yeah, too difficult. Now, remember that I'm making a long story short. My mother gets very depressed, tries to kill herself, and is put in a psychiatric hospital. I get farmed out to my father's parents who have no time for a kid, and so I'm in child care before I can even walk. Well, the story keeps going downhill. After a couple of tries at reconciliation, my parents get a divorce, my mother never really recovers and has been in therapy, on medication, and in and out of the hospital her whole life. My father finishes medical school, becomes a top New York City cardiologist, gets married again, has a few more kids, and only remembers me long enough to call me and ask how my grades are.

Clinician 12:   You've certainly had a very difficult family background. How did you cope with all this?

Client 12:   How did I cope? Not very well. I felt a lot of pressure on me to bring something good out of this mess. I guess I was pretty precocious as a child, played the piano and the violin when I was very young, wrote music. The next Mozart, they thought. Send him to special schools, put even more pressure on him. So I started causing trouble, not doing my homework, not practicing my music, then cutting class, smoking pot, running away, having sex with anybody I could. Then they started in with the therapists who were supposed to fix me. The only one who did me any good was the one who just sat there and played chess with me for the whole time. I didn't want to be fixed, so I wouldn't say a word.

Clinician 13:   Perhaps you were working very hard to be your own person and to be noticed for yourself.

Client 13: I'm sure that was at least part of it. But now I'm 34 years old and I'm still doing it. I dropped out of high school, made some money off of some pyramid schemes, got a GED, tried a couple of colleges. Bard was too unstructured, City College was too structured, and the community college was too boring. Finally, after many years, I put all the pieces together and got a college degree. And I do the same thing with women and jobs. Just go from one to another and when the going gets tough, I get going.

Clinician 14: For many years, then, you've been looking for a niche that fits you, but you haven't been able to find it. How has that made you feel?

Client 14: Like a real loser. Dad keeps paying the bills and bailing me out when I get into trouble; at least he does that for me. But that almost makes things worse. Each time he bails me out, he says, "Samuel, I hope you can learn something from this. I hope the next time will be different." But it never is. I know he's very disappointed in me. His other kids, younger than I am, are these great successes. His son is a lawyer and his daughter is in an M.D./Ph.D. program. And then there's Samuel, the failure.

Clinician 15: You sound disappointed with many of the choices you have made in your life.

Client 15: You can say that again. I've always felt pretty bad about myself. I don't know if I inherited my mother's depression but I've felt depressed most of my life too.

Clinician 16: What is your depression like for you?

Client 16: I have trouble falling asleep. It's so bad, I hate to even try to go to sleep, so I stay up watching late night television, commercials interspersed with a few minutes of programming. Sometimes it makes me sleepy enough so I can conk out but usually it just leaves me so tired in the morning that I can't get my work done. I worry a lot, ruminate about all my past failures and the ones I know are still to come. I feel guilty about the mess I've made of my life but I haven't been able to change it. I feel pretty hopeless. I guess I'm not as bad off as my mother. I've never tried to kill myself and, most of the time, I have a job, but it still feels like I'm trapped in a tunnel with no way out.

Clinician 17: It does sound like you have been very depressed. What has your life been like lately?

Client 17: I hesitate to say this; I don't want to jinx myself. But actually things were getting slightly better before I was diagnosed with cancer.

Clinician 18: How so?

Client 18: I've been dating a decent woman for a change. Vicki is her name. She's a history teacher, very bright with lots of interests. We can actually carry on a conversation, a first for me with women. She's never been married either. And she's even Jewish, which makes all the relatives happy. I've been in the same job now for over a year, working in publicity for an arts complex. It's pretty creative and they put up with me wearing whatever I want and making my own schedule.

Clinician 19: So both personally and professionally, your life has been looking up. What impact did your medical diagnosis have on all that?

Client 19: I figured Vicki was going to drop me as soon as I told her, but she seems to be hanging in with me. She even went to a couple of doctor's appointments with me. The people at work have been pretty supportive, too, giving me time off and helping me figure out my medical coverage. Even my father came through. He told me which oncologist to see, he read my medical reports, and he helped me make some decisions about my treatment. His name really opened doors for me and I've gotten in to see the top docs at Sloan-Kettering. I guess my dad figures if I die there's no hope I'll ever amount to anything.

Clinician 20:   You sound surprised that people have tried to help.

Client 20:   Yeah, I guess I am. You know, the thought of marrying Vicki even crossed my mind. The docs told me my treatments might make me sterile and then suggested I bank some sperm in case I ever wanted to have children. A few years ago, I wouldn't have cared, but now I'm going to do it. I sure can't imagine myself as a husband and father, though. How would I even know how to be a decent husband and father?

Clinician 21:   You sound pretty doubtful about your ability to handle those roles, and yet I hear some excitement about that, too. Sometimes dealing with a life-threatening illness can lead us to reevaluate our lives and make some changes in our goals and priorities.

Client 21:   Really! I guess that's what happened. Now if I can just survive this, there may still be some hope for me. Before, I never felt like I had much hope or reason to go on. Now, I think I do. I don't want to die of cancer, and I want to see if I can do something more with my life after I'm through with all my treatments.

Clinician 22:   I'm hearing some goals there. Sounds like you want to use your new perspective on your life to try to make some positive changes.

Client 22:   You got it.

Clinician 23:   Our time is just about up. We've covered quite a bit of ground and still have lots more to talk about in future sessions but I wonder if there is anything else you want to be sure to mention before we wrap up for today?

Client 23:   Not right now. It looks like I did tell you the short story as well as the long story after all.

Clinician 24:   And they both fit together. You've been through a great deal in your life, and something inside you kept you alive and still fighting. Even though you will probably have even more to deal with as you cope with cancer and its treatments, I think it is important for us to remember how much you have dealt with, along with the glimmer of hopefulness you are feeling now.

Client 24:   Yeah, I guess I do have some things going for me even now. Let's schedule another appointment.

LEARNING OPPORTUNITIES

The case of Samuel Gold is a lengthy and complex one. To understand Sam as fully as possible, you need to consider many factors, including:

- the content of this dialogue
- Sam's presentation and style of talking
- his cultural and religious background
- the intergenerational messages and models he received
- the backdrop of the times in which he and his family members grew up

- his life history
- his immediate presenting concern (his diagnosis with lymphoma)

Consider all of these factors as you complete the following exercises. The exercises are organized according to the sequence of chapters in this book. You can focus on those discussion questions and exercises that are particularly interesting or challenging to you or you can work your way, systematically, through the discussion questions and exercises as they are presented. This approach will provide you with a review of the skills and concepts presented in this book.

Chapter 1: Establishing the Foundation for Skill Development

1. Chapter 1 introduced the BETA framework. For each of the four components of that model, list relevant information about Sam:
   a. background
   b. emotions
   c. thoughts
   d. actions
2. Which of these areas is emphasized in this interview? Which are de-emphasized? Would you have changed this emphasis? If so, how?

Chapter 2: Using Technical Skills to Understand and Address Background

Open and Closed Questions
1. Identify the open questions used by the clinician in the interview with Sam. Which seem to be particularly helpful? Do any of the questions seem to be neutral or harmful? If so, write a replacement intervention that seems more helpful.
2. Identify the closed questions used by the clinician in the interview with Sam. Which seem to be particularly helpful? Do any of the questions seem to be neutral or harmful? If so, write a replacement intervention that seems more helpful.
3. Look at the first three questions asked by the clinician in this dialogue. What seemed to be the clinician's purpose in asking each of those questions?

Intake Interviews
4. Page 40 of chapter 2 list the topics usually covered in an intake interview. How well was each of these topics covered in this intake interview? Which topics, if any, warranted more attention and why?
5. What do you see as the strengths and weaknesses of this initial interview? How might it have been improved?

Specific Technical Skills Related to Background
6. Create two early memories that you think might reflect Sam's history and his orientation to life.
7. Draw a genogram of Sam Gold's family, including brief hypothetical descriptions of each family member, as was done with Eileen Carter on page 50.

8. Draw a lifeline for Sam Gold. Feel free to determine specific dates that are not provided in the interview, as long as your dates are consistent with the information provided.

Chapter 3: Using Technical Skills to Elicit, Attend to, Reflect on, Assess, and Change Emotions

Effective Listening

1. What is your assessment of the effectiveness of the clinician's listening skills in the dialogue with Sam? What techniques did the clinician use to convey effective listening?
2. What might the clinician have done to demonstrate even more effective listening?
3. Identify at least three places in the dialogue when the clinician used a verbal encourager. For each, identify what type of verbal encourager it is (accent, restatement, paraphrase, summarization).
4. How well did the clinician track or follow what Sam was saying? Can you find places in the dialogue when the clinician changed the focus of discussion or did not respond to important comments Sam made? Was each of these interventions helpful, or did it detract from the interview?

Eliciting Emotions and Communicating Empathy

5. List the emotions that Sam reported. Analyze at least one of these emotions according to the eight dimensions of emotion, listed on page 73.
6. What other emotions do you sense that Sam was experiencing?
7. Identify at least three places in the dialogue where the clinician used reflections of feeling.
8. Would you have made more or less or the same use of reflection of feeling? Explain your response.
9. The clinician paid little attention to Sam's nonverbal communications. Drawing on the picture of Sam that you have in your mind, write three reflections of nonverbal communication that the clinician might have used with Sam.

Specific Technical Skills to Promote Change in Emotions

10. Consider the use of the following strategies with Sam to help him control and modify his emotions:
    - focusing
    - recreating an emotionally charged scene in the imagination
    - introducing new perspectives
    - containment
    - distraction or thought stopping
    - reassurance and support
    - use of logic
    - guided imagery

    Which of these strategies do you think would be most effective with Sam and why? How would you go about using this strategy with Sam? Which do you think would be least effective with him and why?

Chapter 4: Using Technical Skills to Identify, Assess, and Modify Thoughts

Identifying and Disputing Distorted Cognitions

1. As you read the dialogue with Sam, you probably noticed that, at many points, Sam's thoughts seemed distorted or unrealistic. Imagine that you are going to help Sam clarify his distorted and self-critical thinking after he is unsuccessful in his efforts to obtain a job that requires an advanced degree he does not have. Add information to the case as needed, as long as it is consistent with what you already know about Sam.

   - Identify the emotions Sam is likely to experience.
   - Estimate the intensity of those emotions on a 0–100 scale.
   - Identify two to four distorted thoughts that Sam is likely to have in response to his unsuccessful job application.
   - Estimate the degree of belief he has in each of those thoughts on a 0–100 scale.
   - Identify actions Sam is likely to take in response to his distorted cognitions.

2. Describe two ways in which Sam's clinician might collaborate with him to dispute his thoughts.

3. Suggest replacements for Sam's emotions, thoughts, and actions that are more likely to be helpful to him.

Reflections of Meaning

4. Develop a reflection of meaning you might use with Sam to help him understand the significance the following experiences have had for him:
   - his diagnosis with cancer
   - Vicki's commitment to stick by him as he goes through his treatments
   - his father's disapproval of Sam's academic difficulties

Problem Solving, Information Giving, and Decision Making

5. Sam tells you he is reluctant to tell his mother he has been diagnosed with cancer; he views her as very fragile and does not want to upset her. Discuss or role-play how you might help Sam with this issue. In your dialogue or role play, be sure to make use of problem-solving and decision-making strategies presented in chapter 4. In addition, incorporate information giving into your plan, providing Sam some knowledge of the often negative impact of secrets in families.

Specific Technical Skills to Promote Change in Thoughts

6. Suggest an affirmation that might help Sam.

7. How might you use anchoring to help Sam deal with his anxiety about chemotherapy and its side effects?

8. Sam views himself as a failure because of his many unrewarding jobs and relationships. How might you use reframing to help Sam take a more positive and empowering perspective on those experiences?

9. How do you think Sam would respond to the suggestion that he use meditation to help himself relax and focus? What sort of meditation seems most likely to minimize any resistance he might have to that process?

10. Develop a mind map of how Sam feels about himself and his life. At the center, should be **Sam's Life.** Second level branches might include **My Father, My Mother,**

Relationships, My Career, Cancer, My Strengths, and My Concerns. Feel free to add other second level branches. Then extend the mind map to least one more level.

Chapter 5: Using Technical Skills to Identify, Assess, and Change Actions and Behaviors

Describing and Measuring Actions

1. Sam reported that one of the job-related problems he had was submitting work on schedule. He was critical of the reports and projects he prepared and would often spend many hours reviewing and revising them, trying to make them as perfect as possible. The result was that he missed deadlines. Develop a behavioral change plan to help Sam with this problem. Your plan should include the following elements:
   - establishing a baseline
   - formulating goals that meet the criteria listed on page 140.
   - creating a contract
   - developing skills
   - identifying obstacles and ways to overcome them
   - establishing meaningful rewards
   - planning for record keeping

2. Many of us have struggled with the challenge of meeting deadlines and judging our own work accurately and realistically. Think about such experiences you have had. You probably learned from these experiences and have some helpful advice to offer Sam. Suggest two between-session tasks that might help Sam cope with deadlines more successfully. Be sure that, although you are drawing on your own experiences with this issue, you follow the guidelines for giving clients advice and do not impose your recommendations or learning on Sam.

3. Sam has told you how much he cares about Vicki and appreciates the help she is providing at this difficult time in his life. He describes her as "the most remarkable woman I have ever met." At the same time, he creates barriers between them and resists Vicki's efforts to establish a closer relationship and discuss a future together. Write a confrontation you could use to help Sam recognize the discrepancy between his thoughts and his actions.

Specific Technical Skills to Promote Change in Actions

4. As you can tell from the dialogue, Sam tends to feel hopeless and discouraged. This gets in the way of his making good use of his considerable abilities. Identify one strategy you might use to empower Sam to take effective actions.

5. How might you use visualization to help Sam resolve his difficulties and move forward with his life?

6. How might you use behavioral rehearsal or modeling to help Sam?

7. Write a statement using possibility or presuppositional language that might be helpful to Sam.

8. Systematic desensitization can help people cope with anticipatory anxiety associated with chemotherapy. Plan how you would use this strategy to help Sam cope with his medical treatments. Your plan should include development of a hypothetical anxiety hierarchy, based on what you know about Sam.

Chapter 6: Using Conceptual Skills to Understand, Assess, and Address Background

Context of Treatment

1. Chapter 6 listed the following seven elements as important in understanding a person's initial request for clinical services:
   - demographic characteristics of the client
   - source of referral
   - choice of clinician
   - treatment facility
   - precipitant for seeking services
   - motivation
   - presenting problem(s)

   You are already familiar with Sam's demographic background. His oncologist, who perceived Sam as having considerable anxiety and depression, referred him for psychotherapy. Sam sought treatment from a woman psychologist, considerably older than he was. The psychologist was known for her work with people who had been diagnosed with cancer. Describe the seven elements listed previously as they are reflected in the case of Sam.

2. Use the steps in the modified version of Bloom's taxonomy to analyze the treatment implications of the context of Sam's treatment. (Those steps include content, comprehension, organization, analysis/synthesis, interpretation, application, and evaluation.) What does your analysis of this context for treatment suggest about Sam? How can you use that information to guide your treatment of him?

Background Information/Intake Interviews

3. You have already had the opportunity to review the intake interview that was conducted with Sam and to analyze the context of his treatment. Now analyze the intake interview according to Bloom's taxonomy. For an example of how to do this, see the analysis of Eileen Carter's intake interview beginning on page 183. Your analysis should follow the outline below:
   - Content
     - demographics
     - presenting concerns
     - prior psychological difficulties
     - current life situation
     - cultural, religious, and socioeconomic background
     - family of origin
     - current family
     - developmental history
     - career and educational history
     - medical history
     - health-related behaviors
   - Comprehension
   - Organization of concerns
   - Analysis and synthesis

- Interpretation
- Application
- Evaluation

Transference and Countertransference

4. From what you know about Sam and can infer from his selection of a therapist who is a woman, considerably older than he, what sort of transference issues are likely to emerge? What would you expect to be the first signs of the emergence of a transference reaction?
5. What steps would you take to address this transference and to use it in therapeutic ways?
6. For what types of countertransference reactions should Sam's therapist be on the alert?

Multicultural Counseling Competencies

7. What multicultural variables characterize Sam?
8. What implications have these variables had for Sam?
9. What are the central themes or topics that characterize the impact Sam's social, political, economic, religious, and cultural background has had on him?
10. What does Sam's worldview seem to be like?
11. How have the dynamics and development of Sam's difficulties been shaped by multicultural factors in his background and in his present life?
12. What are the treatment implications of this information? In other words, how will treatment be planned in light of this information, and what understanding seems important for Sam to acquire about the impact of multicultural factors on his worldview and development?
13. What issues does Sam's cultural background raise for you in light of your own cultural background? How would you address those issues so that they contribute to, rather than detract from, your treatment of Sam?

Interpretation and Insight

14. Develop clinician statements that reflect the following types of interpretations and that might be useful in treating Sam:
    - gender-based interpretation
    - developmental interpretation
    - multicultural interpretation
    - interpretation based on a particular theory of counseling and psychotherapy

Chapter 7: Using Conceptual Skills to Make Positive Use of and Modify Emotions

Building a Positive and Collaborative Therapeutic Alliance

1. Chapter 7 reviews many strategies that clinicians can use to develop a positive therapeutic alliance with their clients. Which of these strategies does the clinician use in the intake interview with Sam?
2. What strategies do you think will be particularly useful and important in developing a collaborative therapeutic alliance with Sam? What is the logic behind your choice of these particular strategies?

3. Which of Sam's characteristics and attitudes make it likely that he will benefit from treatment? Which of his characteristics and attitudes might impede the treatment process? How would you go about building up the positive characteristics and attitudes you listed and reducing the impact of those that might impede treatment?

Dealing Therapeutically with Strong Client Emotions

4. What factors, if any, in the intake interview with Sam raise the possibility that he may be considering suicide? If you have identified any factors that might predispose him toward suicide, what steps would you take in treatment to keep Sam safe?
5. The diagnosis of a life-threatening disease represents a crisis for Sam, as it would for most people. Discuss how you would use the principles of crisis intervention, presented in chapter 7, to help Sam cope effectively with this crisis?
6. During the intake interview, Sam expressed anger and frustration both toward others and toward himself. What part does anger seem to play in Sam's difficulties? What strategies would you use to help Sam understand, reduce, and redirect his anger? What led you to choose those strategies?

Clinician Self-Disclosure and Immediacy

7. What would be the pros and cons of the clinician using self-disclosure with Sam? What sorts of self-disclosures do you think would be especially helpful to Sam?
8. Give two examples of clinician self-disclosures that seem likely to enhance Sam's treatment?
9. Assume that Sam knows the clinician had been diagnosed with cancer 10 years ago. He asks her to advise him on his treatment options, based on her experience, so that he, too, can recover from his disease. How should she respond to this request? Explain your reasoning.

Client Reluctance

10. Assume that, although Sam willingly entered treatment, he often appeared resistant as treatment continued. He became argumentative in sessions, failed to complete between-session tasks he had agreed to do, and did not pay for his treatment on schedule. Think about the underlying reasons for Sam's apparent reluctance, and process these behaviors according to the modified version of Bloom's taxonomy:
    * content
    * comprehension
    * organization
    * analysis and synthesis
    * interpretation
    * application
    * evaluation

Chapter 8: Using Conceptual Skills as Frameworks for Clinicians' Thoughts

Mental Status Examination

1. Write a mental status examination describing Sam, based on the information presented in the intake interview. Your mental status exam should include the 12 categories presented on pages 266–268.

Using Tests and Inventories as Part of the Assessment Process

2. What unanswered questions do you have about Sam that might best be answered through the use of tests and inventories?
3. What types of tests and inventories are most likely to provide answers to those questions?
4. How do you think Sam would react to the use of tests and inventories as part of his treatment? What could you do to help him take a positive view of these tools?

Defining Memories

5. Although Sam's parents' marriage was unstable from its inception, a defining moment for Sam was when his father remarried. Sam knew for certain now that his parents' marriage was over. Sam, who was 8 years old at the time, served as his father's best man at the wedding. He had strong and mixed emotions at that time that he will always remember. Imagine what that experience must have been like for Sam and analyze that defining memory according to the modified version of Bloom's taxonomy. See the analysis beginning on page 276 for an example of how to do this. Your analysis should include the following categories:
   * content
   * comprehension
   * organization
   * analysis and synthesis
   * interpretation
   * application
   * evaluation

Case Conceptualization and Problem Definition

6. Using concept mapping, organize Sam's statements in the intake interview into meaningful categories.
7. Organize the information you have on Sam according to Schweitzer's inverted pyramid heuristic, described and illustrated on pages 285–286.
8. Drawing on that organizational schema and the analyses you have already done of Sam and his concerns, write a brief conceptualization of this case.

Diagnosis

9. Although you probably do not have extensive knowledge of diagnosis, review the 17 categories of diagnosis described in chapter 8. Identify one diagnosis that might reflect Sam's difficulties and provide your rationale for this diagnosis.

Treatment Planning

10. Following the DO A CLIENT MAP format, develop a plan for treating Sam. Explain your rationale for your overall treatment plan.

Chapter 9: Applying Conceptual Skills to Actions for Positive Change

Stages of Change

1. At what stage of change does Sam seem to be? What is your evidence for this conclusion?
2. What implications does this have for your initial treatment of Sam?

Referral and Collaboration

3. What referrals, if any, do you think would benefit Sam? What is your rationale for this decision?

4. How would you go about making the referral to increase the likelihood that Sam will respond well to the referral?

Structuring the Treatment Process

5. Develop a plan for your next session with Sam, following the intake interview. The 10-step format presented on page 331 gives you a prototype for that process.

6. What elements do you think will be most important in the beginning, middle, and ending phases of that next session?

Progress Notes

7. Use the STIPS or SOAP formats to guide your write-up of a brief progress note of the intake interview with Sam.

Generating Solutions

8. Vicki, who has been dating Sam for more than 2 years, has told him that they must become engaged by the end of the year or she will end their relationship. Sam cares deeply for her but does not yet feel ready to make such a commitment, especially since he will have barely completed his cancer treatments at that time. What strategies would you use to help Sam deal with this situation?

Conclusions

9. Imagine that you and Sam are ready to conclude your successful treatment. Make a list of approximately five accomplishments that Sam might have realistically achieved through his psychotherapy. In addition, list two or three goals that he still might want to work on after termination of his therapy.

Researching Your Practice

10. As you reflect on your analysis of Sam and his concerns, which sections of this exercise came easily to you? Which presented the greatest challenge? What can you learn from this about what you need to focus on in your continued reading and study?

Overview of Self-Evaluation

This section presents all the self-evaluation forms that are included throughout this book. This material can be used in the following ways:

- As you learn the material and complete the exercises in earlier chapters, you can look ahead to this section for a preview of the learning and exercises to come. This can help you put in context the information presented in earlier chapters.

- You can use these forms for a final class exercise. Divide into your usual practice groups. Ample time should be allowed for this exercise so that each person has the opportunity to role-play both client and clinician. Allow at least 30 minutes for each role play plus at least 15 minutes for processing. If necessary, the processing time can be shortened by ensuring that each session is tape-recorded for later review and analysis. If that is done, participants in the exercise can then complete their self-evaluation forms alone, with their role-played clients, or with the entire group either outside of class time or in a subsequent class session.

The role-played session should represent an initial meeting between client and clinician, with clients presenting different concerns or issues than they have addressed in earlier role-played sessions. Other than that, the focus of the session should be determined by each client. The session simulates an actual treatment session in that clinicians may have little or no information about their clients and their concerns at the initial meeting.

- A third approach to using these evaluation forms is as a stimulus for reflecting on the growth in clinical skills you achieved while you engaged in the learning provided in this book. Review your initial self-evaluations in earlier chapters and think about improvements you have made in your technical and conceptual skills. Also identify those skills that you recognize as still needing improvement. Recalling specific examples of both growth and weaknesses in your skills can help you to prepare specific and meaningful self-evaluations. Based on your reflections, complete this second set of forms, providing a written record of your progress.

Compilation of Self-Evaluation Forms to Assess Progress

The Assessment of Progress forms that follow appeared at the end of each chapter, as indicated. Complete these forms again, as described previously, based either on a final role-played exercise or on your perceptions of your overall clinical skills.

Assessment of Progress Form—Chapter 1: Establishing the Foundation for Skill Development

1. List three clinical skills that you believe are strengths for you:
   a.

   b.

   c.

2. List three clinical skills you believe you need to develop or improve:
   a.

   b.

   c.

Assessment of Progress Form—Chapter 2: Using Technical Skills to Understand and Address Background

1. Use of questions—assess your use of questions according to the following categories:
   a. balance of open and closed questions

   b. nature of questions (implicit; beginning with how, what, why, or another word)

   c. integration of questions and other interventions

   d. helpfulness of questions

2. Intake interview—assess your abilities according to the following categories:
   a. identification and exploration of presenting concerns

   b. ability to elicit relevant information on background, history, context

   c. ability to develop initial rapport

   d. strengths of intake interview

   e. omissions or areas needing improvement

3. Summary of feedback

4. Two to three goals to improve your clinical skills

Assessment of Progress Form—Chapter 3: Using Technical Skills to Elicit, Attend to, Reflect on, Assess, and Change Emotions

1. What use did you make of each of these interventions?
   a. use of accents, restatements

    b. use of paraphrases

    c. use of reflections of feeling

    d. use of questions

    e. use of summarization

2. What strengths were evident in your verbal messages? How might you have been even more successful in promoting the client's expression and understanding of emotions?

3. Tracking—How well were you able to follow the client? Did you use any strategies to redirect the discussion? How did they work? Should you have made more or less use of redirection?

4. Nonverbal messages—What impact did these have on the counseling process? How might they have been improved? Consider:
    a. eye contact

    b. posture

    c. proximity to client

    d. physical movements and gestures

    e. tone of voice and rate of speech

5. Summary of feedback

6. Progress in achieving goals from previous session

7. One or two additional goals to improve your clinical skills

Assessment of Progress Form—Chapter 4: Using Technical Skills to Identify, Assess, and Modify Thoughts

1. Building on the skills you have already learned, what use did you make of the following skills, learned in previous chapters?
    *   open and closed questions
    *   accents, restatement, and paraphrase
    *   reflection of feelings
    *   attentive body language
    *   summarization
2. Note whether and how you helped your client progress through each of the following 10 steps that are useful in helping people express, assess, and modify thoughts. Which steps felt most comfortable for you? Which were most productive? Which presented you with the greatest challenge? How might you have improved upon this process?

1. Identify key issue or event.
2. Elicit related thoughts, emotions, and actions.
3. Rate intensity of emotions and extent of belief in thoughts.
4. Assess the validity of the thoughts.
5. Categorize any unhelpful/distorted thoughts.
6. Dispute the thoughts.
7. Replace the distorted thoughts with more helpful thoughts.
8. Identify new emotions and actions.
9. Rate intensity of both initial and new emotions.
10. Rate extent of belief in both initial and revised thoughts.

3. If possible, identify two examples of your use of reflection of meaning. How successful were these interventions in helping the client clarify the meaning or importance of an experience? What contributed to, or limited, the success of these interventions?

4. Were you able to use one of the specific interventions presented in this chapter (e.g., anchoring, thought stopping, meditation, mind mapping, journal writing, affirmations, reframing) to solidify the gains your client made? If not, what got in the way of your using such an intervention? If yes, how effective was the intervention? Do you think another type of specific intervention would have been even more helpful? Use the following rating scale, introduced in previous chapters, to assess the success of your intervention:

- **Extremely helpful**—reflects accurate and insightful listening; moves counseling in a very productive direction; promotes self-awareness, new learning, or positive changes
- **Moderately helpful**—reflects generally accurate listening; moves counseling in a productive direction, but does not clearly lead to greater self-awareness, new learning, or positive changes
- **Neutral**—neither contributes to the treatment goals nor harms the therapeutic process; may not accurately reflect what the client has communicated
- **Moderately harmful**—detracts somewhat from the counseling process or alliance; reflects poor listening and perhaps disinterest
- **Extremely harmful**—damaging to the treatment process or therapeutic alliance, sounds ridiculing and critical

5. How successful was the summarization you used to wrap up the session? How might it have been improved? Did you remember to check out its accuracy with the client?

Assessment of Progress Form—Chapter 5: Using Technical Skills to Identify, Assess, and Change Actions
1. Review the skills you had targeted for improvement in this session. List them here and briefly describe what you did to improve those skills. How successful were your efforts? What do you need to continue to do or do differently?
   Skill 1:

   Skill 2:

2. What use did you make of the following skills, learned in previous chapters?
   - open and closed questions
   - accents, restatement, and paraphrase
   - reflection of emotions
   - nonverbal communication
   - summarization
   - reflection of meaning
3. As you review your session, both with your practice group and later when you listen to your tape, note whether and how you helped your client progress through each of the following 10 steps, designed to facilitate change in actions? Which steps felt most comfortable for you? Which were most productive? Which presented you with the greatest challenge? How might you have improved upon the behavioral change process?

1. Describe the undesirable actions as specifically as possible.
2. Establish a baseline, reflecting the current severity or frequency of the actions.
3. Determine realistic goals, beginning with short-term goals.
4. Develop a specific contract, specifying goals and rewards or consequences.
5. Put contract in writing and elicit client's commitment to the contract.
6. Address potential obstacles to goal achievement.
7. Provide skills and tasks that will promote goal achievement.
8. Facilitate client's efforts to track and record progress.
9. Assess progress toward goals.
10. Implement plans for rewards or consequences and, if indicated, revise contract.

4. Were you able to use one of the specific interventions presented in this chapter to facilitate your client's efforts to change behavior (e.g., empowerment, systematic desensitization, role playing, relaxation)? If not, what got in the way of your using such an intervention? If yes, how effective was the intervention? Do you think that another type of specific intervention would have been even more helpful?

5. How successful were you at coming up with a between-session task that was acceptable to your client? How successful was your summarization? Did you remember to check out both the suggested task and the summarization with the client? How might you have improved on the conclusion of your session?

6. How would you describe your overall effectiveness in this session, using this rating scale?

- **Extremely helpful**—reflects accurate and insightful listening; moves counseling in a productive direction; promotes self-awareness, new learning, or positive changes
- **Moderately helpful**—reflects generally accurate listening; moves counseling in a productive direction, but does not clearly lead to greater self-awareness, new learning, or positive changes
- **Neutral**—neither contributes to the treatment goals nor harms the therapeutic process; may not accurately reflect what the client has communicated
- **Moderately harmful**—detracts somewhat from the counseling process or alliance; reflects poor listening and perhaps disinterest
- **Extremely harmful**—damaging to the treatment process or therapeutic alliance, sounds ridiculing and critical

What might you have done differently to improve your self-ratings?

Assessment of Progress Form—Chapter 6: Using Conceptual Skills to Understand, Assess, and Address Background
   1. Describe the types of interventions you used during the intake interview.
      a. Should a particular type of intervention have been used more or used less?

      b. How effective was the balance of open and closed questions?

      c. How well were other interventions integrated with the questions?

   2. What was the flow of the interview like? What would have made it flow more smoothly?

   3. What interventions contributed to the development of rapport? What might you have done to enhance the therapeutic relationship even more?

   4. How well did you succeed at conducting a comprehensive intake interview? What topics were omitted or discussed too briefly? What issues received too much emphasis?

   5. What interventions or clinician attitudes demonstrated multicultural counseling competencies? Should you have done anything differently in dealing with multicultural issues?

   6. Summary of feedback:

Assessment of Progress Form—Chapter 7: Using Conceptual Skills to Make Positive Use of and Modify Emotions
   1. What strategies did you use to build a positive treatment alliance?
      a. Which of these seemed particularly successful? What made them effective?

      b. What else might you have done to further develop the treatment alliance?

2. Describe your use of the following skills:
    a. encouragers (restatement, summarization, paraphrase)

    b. reflection of feeling

    c. attention to nonverbal messages

3. Which of your previous interventions seemed particularly successful?

4. How might you have improved on your use of these interventions?

5. What was your strategy in dealing with the challenging situation presented by the client?
    a. What interventions were especially effective in addressing the challenging situation?

    b. How might you have dealt even more effectively with that situation?

6. Summary of feedback:

Assessment of Progress Form—Chapter 8: Using Conceptual Skills as Frameworks for Clinicians' Thoughts

1. What strategies did you use to build a positive treatment alliance?

2. Describe your use of the following skills:
    a. eliciting and exploring the critical incident

    b. reflections of meaning

    c. eliciting, analyzing, and disputing cognitive distortions

    d. use of other technical skills

3. Which interventions seemed particularly successful?

4. How might you have improved on your use of these interventions?

5. Summary of feedback:

Assessment of Progress Form—Chapter 9: Applying Conceptual Skills to Actions for Positive Change

Form 9a

1. In what ways did you adapt the treatment process to the client's stage of change? How effective was that? What would have improved upon that adaptation?

2. How well did the session follow the 10 steps in the format for structuring sessions? Which steps worked especially well? How might the process have been improved?

3. Describe the process of goal setting. Were goals clear, relevant, and specific? How might the goal setting have been improved?

4. Describe and assess your use of concreteness and specificity.

5. Assess the appropriateness of the homework task that you suggested to the client. Was the task clear, relevant to the client's problem behavior, and readily achievable? Was the client engaged in the process of formulating the homework task? How might the process of suggesting a homework task have been improved?

6. Describe the way you brought closure to the session. What were the strengths of that process? How might that process have been improved?

Form 9b

1. List the strengths and gains that you and your group observed in you over the course of the training experience.

2. List two technical or conceptual skills that warrant your continued attention.

Assessment of Progress Form—Chapter 10: Reviewing, Integrating, and Reinforcing Learning

Now that you have reviewed and revised your evaluations on the Assessment of Progress Forms in light of your overall clinical development, you should be ready to respond to the following questions to bring closure to your training with this book.

1. Pages 361–362 of this chapter presented information on qualities of the expert and empowered clinician. List three of those qualities you believe you currently possess:

   a.

   b.

   c.

   Now list three of those qualities that you have not yet fully developed and that you want to work toward developing in yourself:

   a.

   b.

   c.

2. Develop a plan to address each of the clinical skills or qualities you have identified as needing improvement, either in your assessment of progress forms or in your response to the previous question. Your plan might include, but need not be limited to, the following:
   • additional reading on particular skills
   • additional practice, with feedback and supervision
   • a conference with your professor or supervisor or with a trusted colleague
   • a specific change in your clinical work
   • discussions with colleagues and coworkers

3. Assume that you have read an advertisement for a position as a clinician that sounds exactly like what you are seeking.
   - Write the advertisement, describing the job.
   - Write your letter of application for the position, describing yourself as a clinician and highlighting your strengths.

Personal Journal Questions

1. Describe your overall reactions to the information and learning experiences provided in this book.
2. What were the most important skills this book provided to you?
3. How will you plan to use those skills in your clinical work?
4. What parts of this book were especially challenging for you? How do you explain that? How did you deal with those challenges?
5. What parts of this book were least interesting or important to you? How do you explain that?
6. How would you improve this book?
7. In three sentences or less, describe the positive changes you have made in your technical and conceptual skills as a result of your work with this book.

REQUEST FROM ONE CLINICIAN TO ANOTHER

I hope that you have learned a great deal from this book and will be able to use that learning to improve your clinical skills and your work with your clients. I also hope to learn from you. I would appreciate it if you would e-mail me your responses to the above personal journal questions at lseligma@gmu.edu. Thank you.

REFERENCES

Acosta, F. X., Yamamoto, J., Evans, L. A., & Skilbeck, W. M. (1983). Preparing low-income Hispanic, black, and white patients for psychotherapy: Evaluation of a new orientation program. *Journal of Clinical Psychology, 39,* 872–877.

Adler, A. (1931). *What life should mean to you.* Boston: Little, Brown.

Adler, A. (1963). *The practice and theory of individual psychology.* Paterson, NJ: Littlefield, Adams.

American Psychatric Association. (2000a). *Diagnostic and Statistical Manual of Mental Disorders (DSM-IV-R).* Washington, DC: American Psychiatric Press.

American Psychiatric Association. (2000b). Practice guideline for the treatment of patients with eating disorders (revision). *American Journal of Psychiatry, 151,* 1–39.

Arrendondo, P. (1999). Multicultural counseling competencies as tools to address oppression and racism. *Journal of Counseling and Development, 77,* 102–108.

Bachelor, A. (1995). Clients' perception of the therapeutic alliance: A qualitative analysis. *Journal of Counseling Psychology, 42,* 323–337.

Barett-Lennard, G. T. (1981). The empathy cycle: Refinement of a nuclear concept. *Journal of Counseling Psychology, 28,* 91–100.

Beck, A. T. (1999). *Prisoners of hate: The cognitive basis of anger, hostility and violence.* New York: Harper Collins.

Beck, A. T., & Emery, G. (1985). *Anxiety disorders and phobias.* New York: Guilford Press.

Beck, A. T., & Weishaar, M. E. (1995). In R. J. Corsini & D. Wedding (Eds.), *Current psychotherapies* (5th ed., pp. 229–261). Itasca, IL: Peacock.

Beck, J. S. (1995). *Cognitive therapy: Basics and beyond.* New York: Guilford.

Bloom, B. L. (1981). Focused single-session therapy: Initial development and evaluation. In S. H. Budman (Ed.), *Forms of brief therapy* (pp. 167–216). New York: Guilford Press.

Bloom, B. S., Engelhart, M. D., Furst, F. J., Hill, W. H., & Krathwohl, D. R. (1956). *Taxonomy of educational objectives: Cognitive domain.* New York: McKay.

Borysenko, J. (1988). *Minding the body, mending the mind.* New York: Bantam Books.

Bowen, M. (1974). Theory in the practice of psycho-therapy. In P. J. Guerin, Jr. (Ed.), *Family therapy: Theory and practice.* New York: Gardner Press.

Bowlby, J. (1978). Attachment theory and its therapeutic implications. *Adolescent Psychiatry, 6,* 5–33.

Bowlby, J. (1988). *A secure base: Parent-child attachment and healthy human development.* New York: Basic Books.

Burns, D. D. (1989). *The feeling good handbook.* New York: Penguin.

Burns, D. D. (1993). *Ten days to self-esteem.* New York: William Morrow.

Carlock, C. J. (Ed.). (1999). *Enhancing self-esteem.* Philadelphia: Accelerated Development.

Carkhuff, R. R. (1969). *Helping and human relations.* NY: Holt, Rinehart, & Winston.

Carney, J. V., & Hazler, R. J. (1998). Suicide and cognitive-behavioral counseling: Implications for mental health counselors. *Journal of Mental Health Counseling, 20*(1), 28–41.

Chambless, D. L., Baker, M. J., Baucom, D. H., Beutler, L. E., Calhoun, K. S., Crits-Cristoph, P., Daiuto, A., DeRubeis, R., Detweiler, J., Haaga, D. A. F., Bennett Johnson, S., McCurry, S., Mueser, K. T., Pope, K. S., Sanderson, W. C., Shoham, V., Stickle, T., Williams, D. S., & Woody, S. R. (1998). Update on empirically validated therapies, II. *Clinical Psychologist, 51,* 3–16.

Cochrane-Brink, K. A., Lofchy, J. S., & Sakinofsky, I. (2000). Clinical rating scales in suicide risk assessment. *General Hospital Psychiatry, 22,* 445–451.

Constantine, M. S., & Ladany, N. (2000). Self-report multicultural counseling competence scales: Their relation to social desirability attitudes and multicultural case conceptualization ability. *Journal of Counseling Psychology, 47,* 155–164.

Cottone, R. R., & Claus, R. E. (2000). Ethical decision-making models: A review of the literature. *Journal of Counseling and Development, 78,* 275–283.

Cowan, E. W., & Presbury, J. H. (2000). Meeting client resistance and reactance with reverence. *Journal of Counseling and Development, 78,* 411–419.

Cytrynbaum, S., Ginath, Y., Birdwell, J., & Brandt, L. (1979). Goal attainment scaling: A critical review. *Evaluation Quarterly, 3,* 5–40.

Davis, M., Eshelman, E. R., McKay, M. & Eshelman, E.R. (2001). *The relaxation and stress reduction workbook.* Oakland, CA: New Harbinger Publications.

Deffenbacher, J. L., & McKay, M. (2000). *Therapist protocol: Overcoming situational and general anger.* Oakland, CA: New Harbinger Publications.

de Shazer, S. (1988). *Clues: Investigating solutions in brief therapy.* New York: Norton.

de Shazer, S. (1991). *Putting difference to work.* New York: Norton.

DiGiuseppe, R. (1996). The nature of irrational and rational beliefs: Progress in rational emotive behavior therapy. *Journal of Rational-Emotive and Cognitive-Behavior Therapy, 14,* 5–28.

Division 12 Task Force. (1996). An update on empirically validated therapies. *Clinical Psychologist, 49,* 5–18.

Duys, D. K., & Hedstrom, S. M. (2000). Basic counselor skills training and counselor cognitive complexity. *Counselor Education and Supervision, 40,* 8–18.

Edwards, C. E., & Murdock, N. L. (1984). Characteristics of therapist self-disclosure in the counseling process. *Journal of Counseling and Development, 72,* 384–389.

Ellis, A. (1977). *Anger: How to live with and without it.* New York: Institute for Rational Living.

Ellis, A. E. (1995). *Better, deeper, and more enduring brief therapy.* New York: Brunner/Mazel.

Ellis, A. E., & Dryden, W. (1997). *The practice of rational emotive behavior therapy* (2nd ed.). New York: Springer.

Emmerson, G. J., & Thackwray-Emmerson, D. (1992). Clinical case conceptualizations using clinical factor analysis. *Counseling Psychology Quarterly, 5,* 403–409.

Etringer, B. D., Hillerbrand, E., & Claiborn, C. D. (1995). The transition from novice to expert counselor. *Counselor Education and Supervision, 35,* 4–17.

Fagan, J., & Shepherd, I. L. (1970). *Gestalt therapy now.* New York: Harper & Row.

Fein, M. L. (1993). *A common sense guide to coping with anger: Integrated anger management.* Westport, CT: Praeger Publishers.

Fong, M. L., Borders, L. E., Ethington, C. A., & Pitts, J. H. (1997). Becoming a counselor: A longitudinal study of student cognitive development. *Counselor Education and Supervision, 37,* 100–114.

Frankl, V. E. (1963). *Man's search for meaning.* Boston: Beacon.

Gendlin, E. T. (1996). *Focusing-oriented psychotherapy.* New York: Guilford.

Gladstein, G. A. (1983). Understanding empathy: Integrating counseling, development and social psychology perspectives. *Journal of Counseling Psychology, 30,* 467–482.

Glasser, W. (1998). *Choice theory.* New York: HarperCollins.

Granello, H. (2000). Encouraging the cognitive development of supervisees: Using Bloom's taxonomy. *Counselor Education and Supervision, 40,* 31–46.

Gustavson, C. B. (1995). *In-versing your life.* Milwaukee, WI: Families International.

Hay, C. E., & Kinnier, R. T. (1998). Homework in counseling. *Journal of Mental Health Counseling, 20,* 122–132.

Hill, C. E., & O'Brien, K. M. (1999). *Helping skills: Facilitating exploration, insight, and action.* Washington, DC: American Psychological Association.

Hill, C. E., & O'Grady, K. E. (1985). List of therapist intentions illustrated in a case study and with therapists of varying theoretical orientations. *Journal of Counseling Psychology, 32,* 3–32.

Hinkle, J. S. (1994). The *DSM-IV*: Prognosis and implications for mental health counselors. *Journal of Mental Health Counseling, 16,* 174–183.

Horvath, A. O., & Symonds, D. D. (1991). Relation between working alliance and outcome in psychotherapy: A meta-analysis. *Journal of Counseling Psychology, 38,* 139–149.

Ivey, A. (1971). *Microcounseling: Innovations in interviewing training.* Springfield, IL: Charles C. Thomas.

Ivey, A. E., Ivey, M. B., & Simek-Morgan, L. (1997). *Counseling and psychotherapy.* Boston: Allyn and Bacon.

Jennings, L., & Skovholt, T. M. (1999). The cognitive, emotional, and relational characteristics of master therapists. *Journal of Counseling Psychology, 46,* 3–11.

Juhnke, F. A. (1994). SAD PERSONS Scale review. *Measurement and Evaluation in Counseling and Development, 27,* 325–327.

Juhnke, G. A., & Hovestadt, A. J. (1995). Using the SAD PERSONS Scale to promote supervisee assessment knowledge. *The Clinical Supervisor, 13,* 31–40.

Kaslow, F. (1995). *Projective genogramming.* Sarasota, FL: Professional Resources Press.

Kivlighan, D. M., Jr., & Shaughnessy, P. (2000). Patterns of working alliance development: A typology of clients' working alliance ratings. *Journal Of Counseling Psychology, 47,* 362–371.

Knox, S., Hess, S. A., Petersen, D. A., & Hill, C. E. (1997). A qualitative analysis of client perceptions of the effects of helpful therapist self-disclosure in long-term therapy. *Journal of Counseling Psychology, 44,* 274–283.

Kohut, H. (1984). Introspection, empathy, and the semicircle of mental health. In J. Lichetenberg, M. Bornstein, & D. Silver (Eds.) *Empathy I* (pp. 81–102). Hillsdale, NJ: Erlbaum.

Kottler, J. A., & Brown, R. W. (2000). *Introduction to therapeutic counseling: Voices from the field* (4th ed.). Belmont, CA: Brooks/Cole.

Kroeger, O., & Thuesen, J. M. (1988). *Type talk.* New York: Dell Publishing.

Lambert, M. J., & Bergin, A. E. (1994). The effectiveness of psychotherapy. In A. E. Bergin & S. L. Garfield (Eds.), *Handbook of psychotherapy and behavior change* (4th ed., pp. 143–189). New York: Wiley.

Lambert, M. J., & Cattani-Thompson, K. (1996). Current findings regarding the effectiveness of counseling: Implications for practice. *Journal of Counseling and Development, 74,* 601–608.

Law, J., Morocco, J., & Wilmarth, R. R. (1981). A problem-oriented record system for counselors. *AMCA Journal, 3*(1), 7–16.

Lazarus, A. A. (1989). *The practice of multimodal therapy (update).* Baltimore: Johns Hopkins University Press.

Leach, M. M., Stoltenberg, C. D., McNeill, B. W., & Eichenfield, G. A. (1997). Self-efficacy and counselor development: Testing the integrated developmental model. *Counselor Education and Supervision, 37,* 115–124.

Lerner, H. G. (1985). *The dance of anger.* New York: Harper & Row.

Loganbill, C., & Stoltenberg, C. (1983). The case conceptualization format: A training device for practicum. *Counselor Education and Supervision, 22,* 235–241.

Mayfield, W. A., Kardash, C. M., & Kivlighan, D. M., Jr. (1999). Differences in experienced and novice counselors' knowledge structures about clients: Implications for case conceptualization. *Journal of Counseling Psychology, 46,* 504–514.

McCaulley, M. (1990). The Myers-Briggs Type Indicator: A measure for individuals and groups. *Measurement and Evaluation in Counseling and Psychotherapy, 22,* 181–195.

McGoldrick, M., & Gerson, R. (1988). Genograms and the family life cycle. In B. Carter & M. McGoldrick (Eds.), *The changing family life cycle* (pp. 164–189). New York: Gardner Press.

McLeod, J. (1994). *Doing counselling research.* London: Sage.

Meichenbaum, D. (1985). *Stress inoculation training.* Elmsford, NY: Pergamon.

Miller, D. A., Sadler, J. Z., Mohl, P. C., & Melchiode, G. A. (1991). The cognitive context of examinations in psychiatry using Bloom's taxonomy. *Medical Education, 25,* 480–484.

Miller, W. R., & Rollnick, S. (1991). *Motivational interviewing: Preparing people to change addictive behavior.* New York: Guilford Press.

Moorey, S., & Greer, S. (1989). *Psychological therapy for patients with cancer: A new approach.* Washington, DC: American Psychiatric Press.

Motto, J., Heilbron, D. C., & Juster, R. P. (1985). Development of a clinical instrument to estimate suicide risk. *American Journal of Psychiatry, 142,* 680–686.

O'Hanlon, B., & Weiner-Davis, M. (1989). *In search of solutions: A new direction in psychotherapy.* New York: Norton.

Orlinsky, D. E., Grawe, K., & Parks, B. K. (1994). Process and outcome in psychotherapy-noch einmal. In B. A. Garfield & S. L. Garfield (Eds.), *Handbook of psychotherapy and behavior change* (4th ed., pp. 270–376). New York: Wiley.

Oshinsky, J. (1994). *Discovery journal.* Odessa, FL: Psychological Assessment Resources.

Palumbo, D. (2000). *Writing from the inside out: Transforming your psychological blocks to release the writer within.* New York: John Wiley.

Patterson, W. M., Dohn, H. H., Bird, J., & Patterson, G. A. (1983). Evaluation of suicidal patients: The SAD PERSONS Scale. *Psychosomatics, 24,* 343–349.

Paulson, B. L., Truscott, D., & Stuart, J. (1999). Clients' perceptions of helpful experiences in counseling. *Journal of Counseling Psychology, 46,* 317–324.

Pavlov, I. P. (1927). *Conditioned reflexes* (G. V. Anrep, Trans.). London: Oxford University Press.

Pfeiffer, A. M., Whelan, J. P., & Martin, J. M. (2000). Decision-making bias in psychotherapy: Effects of hypothesis source and accountability. *Journal of Counseling Psychology, 47,* 429–436.

Potter-Efron, R. T. (1994). *Angry all the time: An emergency guide to anger control.* Oakland, CA: New Harbinger Publications.

Potter-Efron, R. T., & Potter-Efron, P. S. (1991). *Anger, alcoholism and addiction: Treating individuals, couples and families.* New York: W. W. Norton.

Prieto, L. R., & Scheel, K. R. (2002). Using case documentation to strengthen counselor trainees' case conceptualization skills. *Journal of Counseling and Development, 80,* 11–21.

Prochaska, J. O., & Norcross, J. C. (1999). *Systems of psychotherapy.* Belmont, CA: Brooks-Cole.

Robinson, T. L. (1997). Insurmountable opportunities. *Journal of Counseling and Development, 76*(1), 6–7.

Rogers, C. R. (1951). *Client-centered therapy: Its current practice, implications and theory.* Boston: Houghton Mifflin.

Rogers, C. R. (1967). The conditions of change from a client-centered viewpoint. In B. Berenson & R. Carkhuff (Eds.), *Sources of gain in counseling and psychotherapy.* New York: Hold, Rinehart & Winston.

Rogers, C. R. (1980). *A way of being.* Boston: Houghton Mifflin.

Sawatsky, D. D., Jevne, R. F., & Clark, G. T. (1994). Becoming empowered: A study of counselor development. *Canadian Journal of Counseling, 28,* 177–192.

Scheel, M. J., Seaman, S., Roach, K., Mullin, T., & Mahoney, K. B. (1999). Client implementation of therapist recommendations predicted by client perception of fit, difficulty of implementation, and therapist influence. *Journal of Counseling Psychology, 46,* 308–316.

Schwitzer, A. L. (1996). Using the inverted pyramid heuristic in counselor education and supervision. *Counselor Education and Supervision, 35,* 258–267.

Seligman, L. (1977). Haitians: A neglected minority. *Personnel and Guidance Journal, 55,* 409–411.

Seligman, L. (1979). Understanding the black foster child through assessment. *Journal of Non-white Concerns in Personnel and Guidance, 7,* 183–191.

Seligman, L. (1980). *Assessment in developmental career counseling.* Cranston, RI: The Carroll Press.

Seligman, L. (1986). *Diagnosis and treatment planning in counseling.* New York: Human Sciences Press.

Seligman, L. (1990). *Selecting effective treatments.* San Francisco: Jossey-Bass.

Seligman, L. (1994). *Developmental career counseling and assessment.* Thousand Oaks, CA: Sage.

Seligman, L. (1996a). *Diagnosis and treatment planning in counseling* (2nd ed.). New York: Plenum.

Seligman, L. (1996b). *Promoting a fighting spirit: Psychotherapy for cancer patients, survivors, and their families.* San Francisco: Jossey-Bass.

Seligman, L. (1998). *Selecting effective treatments: A comprehensive systematic guide to treating mental disorders* (Rev. ed.). San Francisco: Jossey-Bass.

Seligman, L. (2001). *Systems, strategies, and skills of counseling and psychotherapy.* Upper Saddle River, NJ: Merrill/Prentice Hall.

Seligman, M. E. P. (1995). The effectiveness of psychotherapy. *American Psychology, 50*(12), 965–974.

Sexton, T. L. (1995). Outcome research perspective on mental health counselor competencies. In M. K. Altekruse & T. L. Sexton (Eds.), *Mental health counseling in the 90s* (pp. 51–60). Tampa, FL: National Commission for Mental Health Counseling.

Sexton, T. L., & Whiston, S. C. (1991). A review of the empirical basis for counseling: Implications for practice and training. *Counselor Education and Supervision, 30,* 330–354.

Simone, D. H., McCarthy, P., & Skay, C. L. (1998). An investigation of client and counselor variables that influence likelihood of counselor self-disclosure. *Journal of Counseling and Development, 76,* 174–182.

Skinner, B. F. (1969). *Contingencies of reinforcement: A theoretical analysis.* New York: Appleton-Century-Crofts.

Skovholt, T. M., & Ronnestad, M. H. (1992). Themes in therapist and counselor development. *Journal of Counseling and Development, 70,* 505–515.

Smith, J. C. (1986). *Meditation.* Champaign, IL: Research Press.

Srebalus, D. J., & Brown, D. (2001). *A guide to the helping professions.* Boston: Allyn and Bacon.

Stevens, M. J., & Morris, S. J. (1995). A format for case conceptualization. *Counselor Education and Supervision, 35,* 82–94.

Stosney, S. (1995). *Treating attachment abuse.* New York: Springer Publishing.

Strean, H. S. (1994). *Essentials of psychoanalysis.* New York: Brunner/Mazel.

Sue, D. W., Arrendondo, P., & McDavis, R. J. (1992). Multicultural counseling competencies and standards: A call to the profession. *Journal of Counseling and Development, 70,* 477–486.

Tavris, C. (1989). *Anger: The misunderstood emotion.* New York: Simon & Schuster.

Teyber, E. (1997). *Interpersonal processes in psychotherapy.* Pacific Grove, CA: Brooks/Cole.

Waehler, C. A., Kalodner, C. R., Wampold, B. E., & Lichtenberg, J. W. (2000). Empirically supported treatments in perspective: Implementations for counseling psychology training. *The Counseling Psychologist, 28,* 657–671.

Walborn, F. S. (1996). *Process variables.* Pacific Grove, CA: Brooks/Cole.

Watson, J. B. (1925). *Behaviorism.* New York: Norton.

Westefeld, J. S., Range, L. M., Rogers, J. R., Maples, M. R., Bromley, J. L., & Alcorn, J. (2000). Suicide: An overview. *The Counseling Psychologist, 28,* 445–510.

Whiston, S. C., & Coker, J. K. (2000). Reconstructing clinical training: Implications from research. *Counselor Education and Supervision, 39,* 228–253.

Williams, R., & Williams, V. (1993). *Anger kills.* New York: Harper Perennial.

Wolpe, J. (1969). *The practice of behavior therapy.* New York: Pergamon.

Wubbolding, R. E. (1991). *Understanding reality therapy.* New York: Harper Collins.

Zaza, C., Stolee, P., & Prkachin, K. (1999). The application of goal attainment scaling in chronic pain settings. *Journal of Pain & Symptom Management, 17,* 55–64.

INDEX